NEUTRALITY

ITS HISTORY, ECONOMICS AND LAW

IN FOUR VOLUMES

II

THE NAPOLEONIC PERIOD

———

PREPARED UNDER THE AUSPICES OF THE
COLUMBIA UNIVERSITY COUNCIL FOR RESEARCH
IN THE SOCIAL SCIENCES

NEUTRALITY

ITS HISTORY, ECONOMICS AND LAW

VOLUME II: THE NAPOLEONIC PERIOD

BY

W. ALISON PHILLIPS, Litt. D.
MEMBER OF THE ROYAL IRISH ACADEMY
LECKY PROFESSOR OF MODERN HISTORY
UNIVERSITY OF DUBLIN

AND

ARTHUR H. REEDE
INSTRUCTOR IN ECONOMICS
PENNSYLVANIA STATE COLLEGE

NEW YORK: MORNINGSIDE HEIGHTS
COLUMBIA UNIVERSITY PRESS
1936

PREFACE

As indicated in the Preface to the first volume of this series,[1] these studies have been made with a view to analyzing the status of neutrality in its economic, historical and legal aspects. The first volume dealt with the historical origins of the subject, from the end of the fifteenth century up through the middle of the eighteenth century. That volume revealed the vicissitudes of neutrality in its formative period, noting the economic and political factors which have turned its development one way and another. It discussed examples of the rather obvious fact that the rules of neutrality have been subjected to particularly severe strains whenever a great maritime power has been a belligerent. That discussion revealed the perhaps surprising vitality of neutrality as a legal institution. When the wars of the French Revolution broke out in 1792, neutrality had a well-developed historical background of two centuries. In the years which were to follow through the Napoleonic period, it was to receive one of its most rigorous tests; no such severe trial was put upon it until another century passed and another great war broke out in 1914. It was in such periods that an effective institution of neutrality was most needed by those states which sought to hold aloof from the conflict. The same need will be felt when the world is again, if such unhappily be the case, plunged into the mad vortex of general war. Through the experiences of these titanic struggles the most valuable lessons for the future may be learned. There are those who now assert that neutrality is nothing but an historical relic of demonstrated futility; new devices, new approaches, new institutions are sought to answer the perennial cry of peoples who seek to avoid war. The volumes of this series will serve their end if they contribute, no matter how slightly, to the eventual solution of that eternal problem, whether the solution be found along old lines or new.

The researches for these studies have been conducted under the auspices of the Columbia University Council for Research in the Social Sciences and were made possible through the grant of funds

---

[1] *Neutrality, Its History, Economics and Law:* Volume I, *The Origins,* by Philip C. Jessup and Francis Deák.

to that body by the Laura Spelman Rockefeller Memorial. The whole project has been planned and directed by a committee of the Columbia University faculty composed of Professors James W. Angell, Joseph P. Chamberlain, Francis Deák, Charles Cheney Hyde, James T. Shotwell and Philip C. Jessup (chairman).

The present volume is divided into two parts. In Part One, Professor W. Alison Phillips, Lecky Professor of Modern History in the University of Dublin, has analyzed the conflict between belligerents and neutrals throughout this period of the French Revolutionary and Napoleonic Wars. Additional materials bearing upon the economic consequences of neutrality were collected and analyzed by Professor Phillips. Supplementing these data by his own researches, Mr. Arthur H. Reede, Instructor in Economics at Pennsylvania State College, has contributed in Part Two an economic analysis of the effects of this conflict upon the neutral nations. Acknowledgment is gratefully made to Professor Hans von Eckardt, formerly of Heidelberg, for his studies of early German materials; to Mr. Edmond Buron for researches in French archives; and to Professor Eli K. Heckscher of Stockholm for his generous assistance in supplying statistics of Scandinavian trade.

The third volume in this series contains an analysis of the World War period, 1914-1918, by Mr. Edgar Turlington. Volume IV is a synthesis and analysis of the preceding three volumes, together with a study of post-war developments and an examination of the present and future status of neutrality. No attempt has been made by the Committee to regiment the several portions of these four volumes. Each author has approached the general problem in his own way, thus presenting varying points of view. In Volume IV, however, the present writer has sought to draw all the threads together.

The Committee wishes to express its gratitude to the Laura Spelman Rockefeller Memorial, whose donations made possible the completion of the undertaking; to the Columbia Council for Research in the Social Sciences, which sponsored it; to the staff of the Columbia University Press for their coöperation in its publication; and to those whose researches are revealed in it.

PHILIP C. JESSUP

NEW YORK
JANUARY 1, 1936

CONTENTS

PART ONE

THE BELLIGERENTS AND NEUTRAL COMMERCE DURING THE REVOLUTIONARY AND NAPOLEONIC WARS, BY W. ALISON PHILLIPS

CONTENTS

PART TWO

THE EFFECTS OF THE WARS UPON NEUTRAL COMMERCE AND INDUSTRY, BY ARTHUR H. REEDE

TABLES

TEXT

APPENDICES

ABBREVIATIONS

A.S.P.   *American State Papers* (pub. by the United States Congress), 38 vols. (1832-1861)

Commerce and Navigation   *Commerce and Navigation*, Class IV, 2 vols.

F.R.   *Foreign Relations*, Class I, 6 vols.

Finance   *Finance*, Class III, 5 vols.

Hansard   Hansard, *Parliamentary Debates* (First Series), 41 vols. (44 Geo. III, 1803–60 Geo. III, 1820) (Vols. 1-18 have title *Cobbett's Parliamentary Debates*)

Mahan   Mahan, *The Influence of Sea Power upon the French Revolution* (1898), 2 vols.

Martens   de Martens, *Receuil des principaux traités* (2d ed., 1817), 8 vols.

Moore   Moore, *International Adjudications* (Modern Series, 1929-1933), 6 vols.

P.R.O.   British Public Record Office

Ad.   Admiralty Section

F.O.   Foreign Office

C. Robinson   Chr. Robinson, *Reports of Cases Argued and Determined in the High Court of Admiralty* (London, 1799-1808), 6 vols.

Volumes in the series edited by Samuel Flagg Bemis (1927-1929), 10 volumes, entitled "The American Secretaries of State and Their Diplomacy," are cited as follows: Anderson, *Edmund Randolph;* Ford, *Timothy Pickering;* Hill, *James Madison;* Pratt, *James Monroe;* Tansill, *Robert Smith.*

PART ONE

THE BELLIGERENTS AND NEUTRAL COMMERCE DURING THE REVOLUTIONARY AND NAPOLEONIC WARS

by

W. ALISON PHILLIPS

I
INTRODUCTION

THE CHARACTER OF THE REVOLUTIONARY WARS

In judging the manner in which belligerent rights were enforced against neutrals by the Powers at war during the Revolutionary and Napoleonic Wars, it is essential to understand the character of these wars, and in what way they differed from all those that had preceded them. There had, of course, always been wars of frank aggression, though it was usually thought expedient to veil this aggression under some legal pretext, as Frederick the Great did when he invaded Silesia. In general, however, wars were regarded by the old jurists as in the nature of trials by battle, and as quite legitimate so long as they were carried on in accordance with accepted conventions and did no violence to the public law of Europe. "Wars," wrote the French jurist Jean Domat, "are the ordinary result of the disputes between the sovereigns of two nations; who being mutually independent, and having no judges in common, do justice for themselves by force of arms, when they either cannot or will not have mediators to make peace between them. For then they accept as laws and as decisive of their differences the issue which God gives to wars." [1] These armed lawsuits were fought out by small professional armies, without hatred and in accordance with certain fixed rules, and were ended, when one side or the other found the costs excessive, by treaties in the preambles of which it was customary to proclaim oblivion for all past offenses and eternal friendship for the future. One notable exception, indeed, there was: the partition of Poland, of which Friedrich von Gentz remarked bitterly, that it had destroyed the old order of Europe, based upon the balance of power, and set an evil precedent for Revolutionary France to follow.[2]

It was not, indeed, this precedent that was consciously followed by the French at the outset. The war declared, on 20 April 1792, against "the King of Hungary and Bohemia" was ostensibly a purely

[1] Domat, *Les lois civiles dans leur ordre naturel* (ed. Paris, 1735; first pub. 1689), chap. viii, vi, i, p. x.
[2] *Fragment on the Balance of Power* (1806).

defensive one, and Vergniaud, the eloquent spokesman of the Girondin majority in the National Convention, justified it by citing the example of Frederick the Great, who had opened the Seven Years' War before the Powers whom he knew to be uniting against him had time to concert their measures. It was soon evident, however, that behind this plea of defense was the old ambition to gain for France her "natural frontiers," and beyond this again the vision of a Europe "liberated" or, in other words, forced by the arms of Revolutionary France to conform to her model and suffer her dictation. The Constituent Assembly had already shown its contempt for the old public law by abolishing the "liberties" of the princes of the Empire *enclavés* in Alsace, and still more when, by its final act, it annexed to France Avignon and the Comtat Venaissin,[3] which had belonged to the Popes since the fourteenth century. The Legislative Assembly, which was filled with young men utterly devoid of political experience, went further; it declared open war against the whole political and social order of Europe. In the face of such a threat, and of the vigorous measures taken to give it effect, it was impossible for the Powers to maintain the attitude of indifference which they had displayed towards the Revolution in its earlier phases.

As for Great Britain, the annexation of the Low Countries to France would alone have forced her into the war, since for her it was, and still is, of vital moment that no great maritime Power should hold the Netherlands, and above all Antwerp, which Napoleon was to describe as "a pistol pointed at the heart of England." It was soon clear, however, that not only were the Netherlands to be annexed, but that there was to be no limit set to the advance of the French arms. The news of Dumouriez's victory over the Austrians at Jemappes, on 6 November 1792, and of the occupation of Brussels on the 14th, completely turned the heads of the Girondin majority in the National Convention. On the 16th, without the slightest attempt at negotiation, they decreed the opening of the Scheldt, which had been closed to commerce by a series of international treaties since 1648, and three days later, urged on by the numerous foreign refugees in Paris, they passed the famous decree promising, in the name of the French nation, "fraternity and assistance to all peoples desirous of recovering their liberty."[4]

The decree of 19 November was, in effect, a declaration of war

[3] 5 Martens, p. 149.   [4] 5 Martens, p. 365.

against every sovereign in Europe, and it was clearly intended to be no empty threat. On the 26th the annexation of Savoy was decreed; and, if the absorption of Belgium and the German territories on the left bank of the Rhine into France was postponed for some years, this was due, not to any change of heart in the rulers of France, but to the temporary setbacks suffered by the French arms. As for the "liberty" which was to be bestowed upon the "liberated" peoples, the nature of this was revealed by another decree, passed by the Convention on 15 December. This measure provided that the liberty bestowed should be strictly on the French model; [5] and, above all, it laid down the principle that the peoples must pay for their own liberation. It is true that "the people" were to be relieved of all taxation, but the property belonging to the public treasury, the princes, the lay and ecclesiastical corporations, and "all partisans of tyranny" was to be confiscated and placed in reserve as a guarantee for the *assignats*,[6] which—though in France itself they were hopelessly depreciated—were to be accepted in payment at their face value. It was this legalizing of the system of rapine by which, from first to last, the wars of the Republic and of Napoleon were financed, and which supplies the best comment on the outcry raised by the French against Great Britain for refusing to respect enemy private property at sea "as we do on land."

"The foreign policy of the Gironde," says Mathiez, "was summed up in the decrees of 19 November and 15 December, which were complementary to each other. The former granted protection to the peoples, the latter laid down as a preliminary condition of this protection that the peoples should accept the revolutionary dictatorship of France." [7] The adoption of the annexationist policy of the foreign refugees, he says elsewhere, proved the decisive turning point. The war of defense was followed by a war of propaganda, and that again by a war of conquest. Thus the way was paved for the victorious general, Napoleon Bonaparte, who—to quote Napoleon III—"sprang armed from the Revolution, as Minerva from the brow

[5] Art. x of the decree runs: La nation française déclare qu'elle traitera comme ennemis les peuples qui refusant ou renonçant à la liberté, à l'égalité, voudront conserver leur prince et castes privilegiées, ou s'accommoder avec eux. . . . Martens, *loc. cit.*

[6] Bonds secured on the "national lands" (i.e., the confiscated estates of the Church), which constituted a paper currency.

[7] Mathiez, *The French Revolution* (English translation by Catherine Alison Phillips), p. 287.

of Jove." In 1812, when Napoleon's empire seemed firmly established, the crusade for the liberation of Europe had ended in the subjection of the Continent to a military despotism; and of the benefits which this despotism brought to the peoples, liberty was certainly not one.

If, for a quarter of a century, Great Britain, sometimes alone and sometimes in alliance with other Powers, waged remorseless war against Revolutionary and Napoleonic France, this was due partly to the instinct of self-preservation—on the old principle of the balance of power—but in large measure also to the conviction that it was incumbent upon her to champion established rights, guaranteed by the public law of Europe, against a Power for which neither established rights nor international law had any validity. So long as the Revolution was confined within the borders of France, Pitt—in spite of the urgency of Burke and his followers—had maintained the traditional British policy of nonintervention in the internal affairs of another State; it was not until the Revolution boiled over the frontiers of France that the British Government, reluctantly enough, began to prepare for the probability of war. Its action, however, was forestalled by the French. It was the French National Convention which, on 1 February 1793, formally declared war on Great Britain and Holland. This was of great importance, more especially in determining the attitude of the United States.

Chauvelin, the French ambassador at the court of St. James's, had done his best to avert the breach. Acting on the instructions of Lebrun, the French Minister for Foreign Affairs, he had endeavored to persuade Lord Grenville that the decree of 19 November did no more than promise assistance to peoples who, after acquiring their liberty, should invoke such assistance by an unequivocal expression of the general will, and was in no sense intended to support revolutions fomented by disgruntled minorities, while at the same time he urged that the opening of the Scheldt could not justly be considered a *casus belli*. To this attempt to tone down the significance of the decree the answer was unequivocal; for all England saw in the decree the formal declaration of a design to extend universally the new doctrines adopted by France, and to encourage revolt and disorder in all countries, even in those that were neutral.

England cannot consider such an explanation as satisfactory, but must look upon it as a fresh avowal of those dispositions which she sees with so just an uneasiness and jealousy. With regard to the Scheldt, France can have no right to annul existing stipulations, unless she also have the right to set aside equally the other treaties between all the Powers of Europe, and all the other rights of England and her allies. . . . England will never consent that France shall arrogate the power of annulling at her pleasure, and under the pretence of a pretended natural right, of which she makes herself the only judge, the political system of Europe, established by solemn treaties and guaranteed by all the Powers. This government, adhering to the maxims which it has followed for more than a century, will also never see with indifference that France shall make herself, either directly or indirectly, the sovereign of the Low Countries, or general arbiter of the rights and liberties of Europe. If France is really desirous of maintaining peace and friendship with England, she must show herself disposed to renounce her views of aggression and aggrandisement, and to confine herself within her own territory, without insulting other governments, without disturbing their tranquillity, without violating their rights.[8]

Whatever hope of peace there may have been was shattered when the news of the execution of King Louis XVI reached London. Chauvelin was now requested to leave the country, and King George, on 28 January, while announcing the ambassador's dismissal to Parliament, invited the House of Commons "to take the most effectual measures . . . for maintaining the security and rights of his dominions, for supporting his allies, and for opposing views of aggrandizement and ambition, on the part of France, which would be at all times dangerous to the general interests of Europe, but are particularly so when connected with the propagation of principles which lead to the violation of the most sacred duties, and are utterly subversive of the peace and order of all civilized society." [9]

The progress of events in France, where the Reign of Terror was presently at its height, served only to confirm this attitude, and on 29 October 1793 the Government issued to "the commanders of the forces by sea and land" a declaration the terms of which do something to explain the spirit in which the British navy and army faced the enemy and, incidentally, the neutrals who seemed to them to be the enemy's abettors. This declaration ran as follows:

In place of the old government has succeeded a system destructive of all public order—maintained by proscriptions, exiles and confiscations without number—by arbitrary imprisonments, by massacres, which cannot be remembered without horror, and at length by the execrable murder of a just and beneficent sovereign and the illustrious princess who, with unshaken firmness, has shared all the misfortunes of her royal consort. . . .

---

[8] Quoted by Browning in *Cambridge Modern History*, VIII (1904), 304.
[9] *Annual Register*, 1793, p. 128.

The Allies have had to encounter acts of aggression without pretext, open violation of all treaties, unprovoked declarations of war; in a word, whatever corruption, intrigue, or violence could effect, for the purpose, openly avowed, of subverting all the institutions of society, and extending over all the nations of Europe that confusion which has produced the misery of France. This state of things cannot exist in France without involving all the surrounding powers in one common danger; without giving them the right—without imposing upon them the duty, to stop the progress of an evil which exists only by the successive violation of all law and property, and attacks the fundamental principles by which mankind is united in the bonds of civil society.

The King will impose no other than equitable and moderate conditions; not such as the expense, the risk, and sacrifices of the war might justify, but such as His Majesty thinks himself under the indispensable necessity of requiring, with a view to these considerations, and still more to that of his own security, and of the future tranquillity of Europe.[10]

The war, in fact, was conceived at the outset as a struggle between two conceptions of right, or rather, perhaps, as a struggle of right against wrong, according to the point of view of the belligerents. The French Revolutionists, who piqued themselves on their philosophy, championed the Rights of Man, which were founded on the speculations of the philosophers; and for them—as for the Bolsheviks at the present day—no rights were to be respected which did not conform to the ideal order as they conceived it. The point of view of the English, which finds its supreme expression in the writings of Burke, was completely different. "The rights of Englishmen," Disraeli was to say later, "are five hundred years older than the Rights of Man." For them liberty was not based on a theory culled from the works of the philosophers, but had "broadened down from precedent to precedent" and was established on the firm basis of law.[11] The Revolutionary principle was, therefore, abhorrent to them, leading as it did by a logical process to the Revolutionary doctrine of conquest, which threatened to overthrow all established rights and all hard-won liberties. Great Britain, in short,

[10] Quoted in Alison, *History of Europe*, III, 184; Sir William Scott (afterwards Lord Stowell) expressed the same view in the course of his judgment on the case of the *Maria, Paulsen.* In support he cited the views of Pufendorf enunciated when, in 1689, the European coalition claimed to be defending civilization against the "insolent and exorbitant power" of Louis XIV. See *infra,* p. 96.

[11] Lord Auckland, in a note to the States General of the United Provinces, dated 25 Jan. 1793, spoke of the French Revolutionists as "those unfortunate individuals, assuming to themselves the name of philosophers," who "had the presumption to think themselves capable of establishing a new system of civil society." *Annual Register,* 1793, p. 131.

conceived herself as engaged in a life-and-death struggle against an evil power whose victory would have meant, not only her own ruin, but the destruction of the liberties of every European nation. By reason of her insular position she had long been—as Montesquieu put it—*la puissance médiatrice de l'Europe,* and she still conceived it as her duty, not only to herself but to Europe, to preserve or to restore the balance of power on the Continent; and in pursuing this policy she believed herself to be acting, not only in her own interests, but in those of all the world. In the dispatches of British Ministers, and more especially in those addressed to the Government of the United States, this claim to be acting in the interests of "civilization" is over and over again insisted on, and with obvious sincerity. It is a factor which has to be borne in mind when judging the attitude of Great Britain and her allies towards neutral States, and especially the sometimes highhanded way in which the English used their command of the seas to interfere with and regulate neutral commerce.

Since the establishment of the League of Nations it has been commonly, and somewhat arbitrarily, assumed that in the next war "there will be no neutrals." The contention of both sides during the Revolutionary and Napoleonic Wars was that there *ought to be* no neutrals and sometimes even that there were none, since to carry supplies of any kind to the enemy was in the nature of a breach of neutrality. Napoleon, "the self-styled champion of the freedom of the seas," as Friedrich von Gentz contemptuously called him, declared, in connection with his plan to stop all commercial intercourse with Great Britain, "there are no neutrals." The same idea underlay an article which appeared in the conventions and treaties signed by Great Britain with foreign Powers in the years 1793 and 1794. In a convention concluded between Great Britain and Russia, on 25 March 1793, the parties agreed, under Article III, to stop all exports of provisions and military supplies to French ports "and to take all other measures for injuring the commerce of France" and, under Article IV, "to unite all their efforts to prevent other powers not implicated in the war from giving, on this occasion of common concern to every civilized state, any protection whatever, directly or indirectly, in consequence of their neutrality, to the commerce or property of the French on the sea or in their own ports." [12] These

[12] A.S.P., F.R., I, 243.

articles were included in the treaties of alliance subsequently concluded by Great Britain with Prussia, Austria and Spain. It may be
added that the Empress Catherine of Russia, though she did not
declare war against the French Republic, not only issued an *ukaz*
forbidding her subjects to trade with France, but in the course of
the summer of 1793 notified Denmark and Sweden that she would
station a fleet in the North Sea to prevent neutrals bound for France
from proceeding.[13] Similarly, on 1 April 1793, the Spanish Council
of Finances passed an edict prohibiting all trade and intercourse
with France and her nationals, though the treaty of alliance between
Spain and Great Britain was not signed until the 25th of May.[14] The
idea underlying all these measures clearly was, that France had
placed herself by her repeated violations of the public law of Europe
outside this law, and that the best way to reduce her to order was
to apply what are now known as "economic sanctions." It was the
same method as that which has been reserved under Article XVI of
the Covenant of the League of Nations for the coercion of recalci-
trant States, and its results in the case of Revolutionary France,
therefore, convey a very useful lesson for the present generation.

The Belligerents and International Law

If International Law be rightly defined by Mahan as the common
consent of the nations,[15] it can hardly be said that it had any effective existence at the time of the outbreak of the Revolutionary
Wars. According to Sorel, indeed, it had never had any existence at
all, or if it existed, had been known only "through the declamations
of publicists and its violation by the Governments." [16] The Revolutionists, as has been already pointed out, acknowledged no law but
that of reason and the Rights of Man; and if their opponents at the
outset championed the old public law of Europe, they presently discovered that in a life-and-death struggle, such as that into which
the war developed, while the spirit of the law might give life, the
letter was apt to kill. They saw, in short, that the laws of war could
not be as the laws of the Medes and Persians which alter not, since
conditions change, and the rules and principles universally accepted

---

[13] *Annual Register*, 1793, p. 346.
[14] *London Gazette*, No. 13,537, 11-15 June 1793, p. 490. The Edict, however,
does not seem to have been published in the King's name until after 25 May.
[15] Mahan, II, 284.
[16] Sorel, *L'Europe et la révolution française* (1897), VII, 65.

in a certain set of circumstances might become wholly inapplicable in another.

The case was clearly stated by Lord Chancellor Eldon in the course of the debate in the House of Lords on the Orders in Council of November 1807. "It is vain," he said, "to refer to the law of nations for any authority on this subject, in the unprecedented circumstances in which this country is now placed. What usually passes by that name, is merely a collection of the *dicta* of wise men who have devoted themselves to this subject in different ages, applied to the circumstances of the world at the period in which they wrote, or circumstances nearly resembling them; but none having the least resemblance to the circumstances in which this country is now placed." He added, indeed, that it would be "most expedient to adhere scrupulously to the law of nations," but that if one belligerent began to violate it, the other would be justified in retaliating, the right of retaliation having been admitted by all international jurists.[17]

The expediency of adhering to the law of nations, in the matter of the exercise of belligerent rights at sea, was recognized by all the combatants; for it was clearly not to their interest to turn neutrals into enemies by violating their acknowledged rights. From the first, however, there was dissension as to the nature and extent of these rights. The rules established by "the common consent of the nations" were actually very few, and by no means covered all contingencies. It was universally acknowledged that neutrals had the right to carry on their accustomed trade with the belligerent nations, except in contraband of war; but there was no consensus of opinion as to what constituted contraband of war, or as to the right of neutrals to take advantage of channels of trade closed to them in time of peace and opened up by the war. It was generally acknowledged that a belligerent had the right to proclaim the blockade of a hostile port, and that, so long as this blockade was effective, neutral ships attempting to "run the blockade" could be made lawful prize; but there was no agreement as to what constituted effective blockade.[18] Again, while the right to seize enemy private property at sea was acknowledged, there was violent disagreement as to the right to

[17] 10 Hansard, p. 674.

[18] Russia, the principal party to the League of Armed Neutrality of 1780, described a place to be in a state of blockade, when it is dangerous to attempt to enter into it (Sir William Scott, case of the *Mercurius*, 7 Dec. 1798, in 1 C. Robinson 84). In 1780 Sir John Marriott is reported to have said that the ports of

seize it when covered by a neutral flag. The doctrine of "free ships, free goods" had been embodied in numerous treaties, even in some concluded by Great Britain, but it had never been universally accepted,[19] and in the peculiar circumstances of the opening of the Revolutionary Wars, while it was obviously expedient for the French to uphold this doctrine, it was equally obvious that it would be inexpedient for the British to do so, since its acceptance would have meant that the French, whose merchant marine was speedily swept from the seas, would have been able to carry on their export trade undisturbed in neutral bottoms.

Lord Eldon's dictum on the limitations of international law gained special force from the circumstances of the time when it was uttered; for Napoleon, now master of the Continent, was a law unto himself, and his Continental System was conceived with no regard for neutral or any other rights. It applied, however, even under less abnormal conditions. The rules laid down for the conduct of belligerents by the old jurists may have been applicable at the time they wrote, and they continued to provide convenient arguments for lawyers and diplomatists; but the measure of their application was bound to be determined, not by legal argument, but by the exigencies of warfare under changed conditions. William Pinkney, in his able legal opinion on the *Neptune* case, quoted Grotius at great length in support of his thesis that provisions could not legally be condemned as contraband.[20] In doing so he kept strictly to the text, without any reference to the conditions prevailing at the time the text was written. Now the rule laid down by Grotius, namely, that provisions should be treated as contraband only when the attempt was made to introduce them into a besieged or blockaded town *in extremis,* was reasonable enough at a time when the European countries were agricultural and thinly populated, when imported foodstuffs played only a small part in their economy, and the customary

France and Spain, then allied with the American colonists, were *ipso facto* blockaded by virtue of their geographic position (Söderquist, quoted by Heckscher, *The Continental System,* 1922, p. 31). Sir William Scott, in the case of the *Betsey,* ruled that "a declaration of a blockade by a commander without actual investment will not constitute blockade" (1 C. Robinson 92).

[19] "I believe it cannot be doubted, but that by the general law of nations, the goods of a friend found in the vessel of an enemy are free, and the goods of an enemy found in the vessel of a friend are lawful prize." Jefferson to Genêt, 24 July 1793. A.S.P., F.R., I, 166.

[20] 4 Moore, p. 384.

method of reducing them by starvation was, not blockade by sea, but systematic devastation by invading land forces. In these circumstances it was possible for belligerents to accept a rule under which neutrals could carry on their accustomed trade without giving substantial aid to the enemy. The rule was, however, by no means generally observed or universally admitted. England, more especially, from the days of Elizabeth onward treated provisions as contraband of war, save when excluded by special treaty agreements,[21] and had asserted this right whenever circumstances promised to make its exercise effective as a war measure. Thus in 1709, during the struggle against Louis XIV, when the failure of the harvest in France had produced a serious shortage of foodstuffs, the English Government pressed Denmark and Sweden to forbid the carrying of corn to France under cover of their flags and warned them "not to think it strange if their ships laden with corn for France happen to be stopp'd and brought up as they were in the last warr." [22] In 1793 the condition of France seemed even more desperate. The Revolution had disarranged the whole economy of the country; bread riots were frequent, and one of the chief preoccupations of the Government was the supply of wheat, especially to the capital. In these circumstances it was not unnatural that Great Britain should have insisted on her traditional practice of including foodstuffs among articles contraband of war.

The definition of contraband which limited it to the actual offensive and defensive weapons of war (guns, bombs, pikes, cuirasses, etc.), with the addition of saltpeter and, sometimes, horses and harness, and tacitly or explicitly excluded timber and other naval stores, was naturally upheld by those States—Denmark-Norway, Sweden and the Hanseatic cities—whose exports consisted mainly or largely

[21] England had not been very successful in gaining over other Powers to her point of view in this respect. In only four cases did she succeed in getting provisions included in the list of contraband, namely, in the treaties concluded with Spain in 1604, with Holland in 1625 and 1674, and with Sweden in 1671. Conversely, in treaties with Holland in 1667, with France in 1677, and with Spain in 1667, England agreed to include provisions in the free list. See Jessup and Deák, "The Law of Contraband of War" in *Political Science Quarterly*, XLVIII (1933), 91.

Mahan speaks of Great Britain stretching the definition of contraband in order to bring additional pressure to bear on France. He remarks, however, that it was dearth of provisions that forced the Brest fleet out to sea in 1794, and so led to the first great British naval victory of the war. See Mahan, I, 100, and compare p. 336 and note.

[22] Jessup and Deák, *op. cit.*, p. 341.

of such stores, and could be accepted by belligerents at a time when in most European countries the forests and other sources of naval supplies were still unexhausted and the additional aid given to the enemy by their importation was not sufficient to outweigh the risk of offending neutrals by attempting to stop such importation. With a change in conditions, however, this attitude also changed. Thus, in 1588, when Spain was fitting out the great Armada against England, Lord Burleigh could say that "without havyng of masts, boords, cabels, cordag, pitch, tarr and copar out of the Eastlands, all Spayn is not hable to make a navy redy to carry the meanest army that can be ymagined," and a vigorous protest was sent by the English government against the "unfriendly action" of the Hanseatic cities in assisting to equip the Spanish fleet. The protest was followed by action. In June 1589, a fleet of vessels from the Baltic was met at the mouth of the Tagus by the victorious English fleet, which captured sixty of them and took them to England as prizes, where the Privy Council justified the capture on the ground that previous warning had been given and the fact that the cargoes were composed of provisions and ship's stores.[23] There were, indeed, earlier precedents for this attitude, which was not confined to England.[24] It was, however, the England of Elizabeth which insisted most strongly on the principle during the long struggle with Spain, and though the modern law of contraband had not been formulated at this period, there is plenty of evidence to show that at the end of the sixteenth century the idea was current that a belligerent might cut off supplies going to his enemy. "When possible, the belligerent banned all trade with the enemy; when neutral pressure was too strong to permit him to do this, he confined himself to prohibiting trade in things most useful to the enemy. In all cases, munitions were obviously the most useful and the first to be banned. In the case of the English war against Spain, shipping materials and victuals were almost equally important and the ban upon them was maintained whenever practicable."[25] In effect the formulation of the "laws of war" by Grotius and his successors made little practical difference, for, after as before, when conditions changed, new rules had to be made, or old rules interpreted, to meet them.

This was what happened during the Revolutionary and Napoleonic Wars. In the case of Great Britain the rules were interpreted, amplified or laid down either by Acts of Parliament, Orders in

[23] Jessup and Deák, *op. cit.*, p. 65. [24] *Ibid.*, pp. 65 f. [25] *Ibid.*, p. 71.

Council embodying instructions to naval officers, or by the decisions in doubtful cases given by the High Court of Admiralty or the Lords Commissioners of Appeal; in the case of France, by laws or decrees issued by the central government, whether the National Convention, the Directory, the First Consul or the Emperor. The application of the rules varied with circumstances, and both sides justified more or less admitted departures from the traditional code by the right of retaliation, a plea which, in the nature of the case, was more consistently put forward by France than by Great Britain.[26]

THE WAR ON COMMERCE

Since war, in its very essence, means an attempt to settle differences by a trial of strength and endurance, it follows that belligerents will use any available means of reducing the resisting power of their enemies, subject only to the considerations which prudence may lead them to show for the rights of neutrals. Among the means of forcing an enemy to terms, economic pressure, in one form or another, has always been employed, the object being to exhaust his resources, whether in money or food, and so compel him to make peace.

Whatever form such economic pressure took—but more especially that of blockade or of commerce destruction at sea—it was bound to affect the interests of nations or states not engaged in the war; and in the interests of belligerents and neutrals alike a certain measure of agreement was reached during the seventeenth and eighteenth centuries as to the degree to which belligerents, in bringing economic pressure to bear on their enemies, would be justified in restricting the trade of neutrals with their enemies, or—to put it the

[26] Great Britain consistently maintained the right under international law to treat naval stores as contraband of war, a claim which Mahan describes as "plausible at that time" (Mahan, *loc. cit.*). This right was renounced, so far as Russia was concerned by the treaty of 1801. In the debate on this treaty in the House of Lords, on 13 November 1801, Nelson made a characteristic comment on this renunciation, which he approved. Naval stores had not been stipulated as contraband, he said, because Russia had neither produce of naval stores nor shipping enough to have freighted them for France. He almost wished she had possessed both during the latter years of the war; "because, in that case, the French would have been enabled to send their fleets out of port, which we should have fought, and the war in all probability would have been much sooner at an end." Hansard, *The Parliamentary History of England* (1806-20), XXXVI. [The early development of the international law on contraband, blockade, etc., is treated in Vol. I of this series which was not available to Professor Phillips when this manuscript was written.—Editor.]

other way round—as to how far neutrals would be justified in re-
senting belligerent interference with their freedom of trade with the
enemy. As has already been pointed out, however, the agreement
reached covered only a very narrow ground, and when the Revolutionary Wars opened there were still fundamental differences of
opinion as to the rights of belligerents and neutrals, respectively,
under the law of nations.

The questions of the rights and wrongs of the resulting controversies is complicated by the fact that Great Britain, being in command of the seas, was in general in a position to assert what she
claimed to be her belligerent rights, while France, from the first
practically powerless at sea, posed as the champion of neutral rights,
and more especially of "the freedom of the seas"; and if she violated these rights, as frequently happened, she pleaded that this was
no fault of hers, but was by way of retaliation for prior violations
by the British.

This view has met with some favor with historians in our own
day. Professor Heckscher, for instance, speaking of the "policy of
economic strangulation" pursued by both England and France, men-
tions "the blockade measures and the generally rude treatment of
maritime intercourse, in which Great Britain decidedly led the way,
but was very closely followed by France." [27] It may be admitted that
England was the first to institute blockades of enemy ports and
coasts, since she alone was in a position to do so. That she set the
example in the rude treatment of maritime intercourse is more
doubtful. The question is of secondary importance, but may perhaps deserve examination in connection with the beginnings of the
war. Before dealing with it, however, it will be advisable to examine
the conditions under which any control of the British Government
over its naval forces was exercised.

These conditions were totally different from those under which
the World War of our own times was fought, or from those that will
prevail in any future war. Communications were exceedingly slow
and very uncertain. The Order in Council of 8 June 1793, for instance, which was issued on 1 July, was not communicated to the
Danish Government till 17 July, and it was not before 24 August
that it was brought to the notice of the American Government. The
famous Order in Council of 6 November 1793, was first heard of in
Philadelphia on the 7th of the following March. In this latter case,

[27] Heckscher, *The Continental System* (1922), p. 25.

indeed, which was a temporary emergency, the whole object of the instructions would have been defeated had time been allowed for the notification to reach the United States and to be transmitted to American shipping, and this, as in other cases, led to the accusation that notice had been deliberately withheld in order that British commanders might reap a rich harvest of unwarned neutral vessels, which was certainly not the intention. It took, in fact, weeks, and sometimes months, for dispatches to reach the commanders of squadrons on distant stations or for the reports of these commanders to reach the home Government—fights between British and American frigates in remote oceans took place six months after the signature of the treaty of peace at Ghent in 1814. In these circumstances the commanders of ships of war and privateers acted perforce largely on their own responsibility, and sometimes in violation of instructions which had never reached them. If, then, maritime intercourse was sometimes rudely treated, this was often due rather to the zeal, or greed, of naval commanders than to the considered policy of the Government, which always showed itself willing to make full reparation when its agents could be proved to have exceeded their instructions or to have violated the acknowledged rules of the law of nations.

The truth is, that the laws governing the rights of neutrals and belligerents at sea were, like all laws, determined by those who had the power to enforce them. A belligerent power, conscious of its strength, might be anxious, if only from motives of expediency, to study the interests of neutrals and to avoid any injustice towards them, but, if it considered its vital [28] interests to be at stake, it would not hesitate to give its own interpretation to doubtful rules, as in the case of blockade, or to issue new laws to meet new conditions, as in the case of the Rule of 1756. It is therefore of importance, by way of preface to an account of the measures affecting neutrals adopted by the two principal belligerents during the Revolutionary and Napoleonic Wars, to give some estimate of the sea power of Great Britain and France, respectively, at the outset and in the later stages of the conflict.

---

[28] The word "vital," to use Emerson's phrase, needs "depolarizing." Its essential meaning is "involving the issue of life or death," and it is idle to imagine a strong nation, or one conscious of any power of resistance, being willing to submit a question involving issues vital in this sense to the hazards of arbitration. The word is, however, too often used loosely of interests which are really not vital.

THE BRITISH NAVY

Except in the matter of efficiency, there was at the outset no great disparity between the naval forces of Great Britain and France. A statement of the strength of the French navy presented to the National Convention on 23 March 1793, gave the number of ships of the line as eighty-one.[29] By the end of the year this number had been seriously reduced by the losses at Toulon, whereas Great Britain now had eighty-five line-of-battle ships in commission, besides numbers of frigates, corvettes and smaller craft whose functions were to act as scouts or as cruisers employed in interrupting the commerce of the enemy.

The material equipment of this great force demanded great efforts and, in the course of time, the importation of vast quantities of naval stores, which brought immense profits to the neutral countries which supplied them.[30] From first to last, however, more difficulty was experienced in manning than in equipping the fleets, and since the measures taken by the British Government to overcome this difficulty led to protracted controversy with the United States, culminating in the War of 1812, some account of them is in place, more especially as the issues involved were economic as well as political.

Two methods of recruiting the navy were employed at that time: voluntary enlistment and compulsory impressment. To encourage voluntary enlistment certain inducements were held out, namely, bounties and a proportionate share in prize money. As early as 26 December 1792, when war seemed imminent, a royal proclamation had offered a bounty of £5 to every able seaman, £2. 10s. to every ordinary seaman, and £1. 10s. to each landsman who should present himself for service before the 28th of February following,[31] the time being subsequently prolonged to the 30th of April.[32] Meanwhile, on 17 April, a royal proclamation, which was repeated on

[29] *Naval Chronicle*, Vol. 1, App. iv.

[30] In 1796, since there were not enough naval stores left to last out the war, the Government imported ship's timber from the Adriatic, masts and hemp from North America and large consignments from the Baltic. In the course of this year alone 4,000 British ships passed the Sound, laden with naval stores, corn, tallow, hides, hemp and iron. See Brenton, *Naval History*, II, 105.

[31] *London Gazette*, No. 13,528, 14-18 May 1793, p. 397.

[32] After the outbreak of war this was supplemented by private effort. Thus a subscription was opened at Dover to give an additional bounty of £2. 2s. to every able seaman and £3. 3s. to every seaman of the town who should volunteer for service. See *Naval Chronicle*, II, 491.

the 23d, declared that "the neat produce" of all prizes taken by "Our Ships and Vessels of War" was to be "for the entire benefit and encouragement" of the officers and men on board the said ships and vessels at the time of the capture.[33] Clearly, however, these inducements proved insufficient to entice seamen into the service in any numbers, and the main dependence of the Government had to be on the old law which empowered the officers of His Majesty's navy to complete the complements of their ships by impressing seamen into the service. To facilitate the process certain measures were taken. On 11 February an Order in Council laid an embargo on all British ships other than those sailing coastwise or to Ireland, "pending the completion of naval preparations," or, in other words, pending the visits of the press gangs, which embargo was extended on the 16th to all coasting craft, and so remained in force till the 26th.[34] A royal proclamation issued on the 16th offered a reward of 20 shillings for every able or ordinary seaman to any person who should discover any such seamen who might be in hiding.[35] This was extended by an Order in Council of 24 April to the following 30 June, and by another Order of the 21 June to 31 August.[36] As for the principles on which impressment was conducted, this cannot be more vividly illustrated than by quoting the answer given by the flag lieutenant of H.M.S. "Immortalité" to Jacob Faithful and his friend Tom, who objected to being impressed on the ground that, as watermen's apprentices, they were legally exempt: "Men we must have, and get them how we can. Necessity has no law; at least it obliges us to break through all laws. After all, there's no great

[33] The proportion of prize money to be distributed to the various ranks varied from ⅜ in the case of the captain to a share in ⅖ for everyone under the rank of warrant officer. See *London Gazette*, No. 13,520, 16-20 April 1793. The rules for the distribution of the produce of prizes among the officers and crews of American ships of war were laid down in the Act for the Government of the Navy of the United States of 2 March 1799, Sec. 6. Only a proportion of the produce was thus distributed (e.g., the captain receiving 3/20), the balance being paid into the fund for providing pensions and half-pay, etc., Scott, *The Controversy over Neutral Rights between the United States and France*, p. 81.

[34] P.R.O. Ad. 1. In Letters. 5179. By an Order in Council of 18 Feb. 1795, owing to the great lack of seamen to man the navy, a general embargo was laid on *all* ships in the ports of Great Britain. This was taken off piecemeal by a series of orders, but it was not till 11 March that foreign vessels belonging to friendly states were released from it. P.R.O. Ad. I. 5180. By another Order in Council, dated 8 April 1795, no foreign ship was to be allowed to sail with any of His Majesty's subjects on board, without special license.

[35] *London Gazette*, No. 13,503, 16-19 Feb. 1793.

[36] *Ibid.*, No. 13,539, 18-22 June 1793, p. 514.

hardship in serving the King for a year or two, and filling your pockets with prize money. Suppose you volunteer?" [37]

It is obvious that a fighting force recruited by such measures (and sometimes from the scourings of the gaols and debtors' prisons) could only be made and kept effective by the most rigid discipline, and that it was necessary to arm the commanders of ships of war with despotic power. This answered well enough in the case of commanders who, like Nelson or Duncan, had the interests of their men at heart and knew how to keep discipline without undue severity; it was disastrous in the case of those who enjoyed playing the tyrant or who masked cowardice under a parade of brutality. "No monarch," wrote a contemporary historian of the navy, "is more despotic, as far as respects the infliction of corporal punishment short of death, than the captain of a ship of war. If a man speaks or even looks to offend, he is ordered to the gangway; and the bloody furrows on his shoulders soon increase, beneath the vigorous arm that lays on the cat-o'-nine-tails." [38] It was a rough age, and the seamen were rough men, inured to hardship and careless of pain and danger. In battle their wrongs were forgotten; but, with the French fleets locked up in harbor, battles were few and far between, the British ships—and especially the ships of the line—were engaged for months on end in nothing but a wearisome patrol of the seas, and the men, ill-fed, crowded together in unimaginable discomfort and exposed for the slightest negligence to the boatswain's rattan or possibly even to the humiliation and torture of the triangle and the cat, had time to nurse a sense of grievance which found expression at last, in the spring of 1797, in the serious mutinies at Spithead and the Nore.[39] Such being the state of things, it is not surprising that seamen hid from the press gangs, used to

[37] Marryat, *Jacob Faithful,* chap. xxxvii. Captain Marryat's novels give invaluable contemporary impressions of the British navy at this time. A vivid account of a raid by a press gang will be found in *Peter Simple,* chap. x. British merchant ships and privateers dreaded meeting a British warship at sea almost as much as a hostile one, since they were liable to be stopped and the best members of their crews impressed. Readers of Marryat's *Mr. Midshipman Easy* will remember that it was legitimate for the men to resist impressment by force.

[38] James, *Naval History of Great Britain,* II (1837), 65. In Art. I § 4 of the Act for the Government of the Navy of the United States it is laid down, that "no commander, for any one offence, shall inflict any punishment upon a seaman or marine beyond twelve lashes upon his bare back with a cat of nine tails." See Scott, *op. cit.,* p. 73.

[39] The just grievances which led to these mutinies are discussed by Marryat in *The King's Own.*

the full their privilege of resisting force by force and ended by deserting in numbers whenever opportunity offered.

The best opportunity was presented by the greatly increased demand for seamen created by the sudden expansion of American sea-borne commerce which followed the outbreak of war and led to a rise in wages from eight to thirty dollars a month. The British Government received timely warning of this danger. Phineas Bond, who was shortly to be appointed British consul general in the Middle and Southern States and was in London at the outbreak of war, wrote to Lord Grenville, on 1 February 1793, pointing out that it would be "fatal" to refrain from impressing sailors from American ships. "The United States," he said, "have abundance of ship-building material, but they are destitute of seamen to navigate their present tonnage, even in its contracted state." They would inevitably become the carriers, in a certain degree, of the powers at war; and, if an arrangement for a fixed quota for American vessels were agreed to, British seamen would seek the security which American neutrality would grant, and "the temptation of extraordinary wages would operate as a most powerful motive." [40] From New York, some months later, Sir John Temple, British consul general in the Eastern States, wrote to the same effect. "I am apprehensive," he said, "that many, and too many, British seamen will get into employment in these States, whose navigation is rapidly increasing"; [41] and in another dispatch, dated 2 July, he added that "high wages and no danger of being impressed, will be a great inducement to them to do so." [42]

The situation was one of extreme difficulty for the British Government. On 18 February a proclamation was issued recalling all British seamen on foreign ships [43] and the right to search out all such seamen on foreign ships was claimed and exercised. But, as Richard Rush, the American minister at the Court of St. James's, was to note more than twenty years later, it was impossible to distinguish between British and American seamen, since they looked alike, wore the same clothes, spoke the same language, and used the same sea terms. Thus, as early as 1790, when war with Spain was impending, press gangs in British seaports had rounded up many American seamen; and when Gouverneur Morris, who was on a visit

---

[40] Bond to Grenville, 1 Feb. 1793. P.R.O. F.O. 5. 2.
[41] Sir John Temple to Lord Grenville, 21 April 1793. P.R.O. F.O. 5. 2.
[42] *Ibid.*, Temple to Grenville, 2 July 1793.   [43] *Naval Chronicle*, II, 491.

to London, complained of this to Pitt and the Duke of Leeds, the reply was that there was "no wish to impress American seamen, but the trouble arose from the difficulty of distinguishing British subjects from American citizens." The suggestion made by Morris that certificates of American citizenship issued by the Admiralty courts should be sufficient protection was accepted by British Ministers, but was unacceptable to President Washington, with the result that when war broke out in 1793 the matter was still unsettled.[44]

It remained unsettled to the end,[45] and was indeed incapable of settlement, owing to the fundamental conflict of both interests and legal principles involved; for, as the English law then stood, no British subject could rid himself of his allegiance by being naturalized in another country; from which it followed that all British seamen naturalized in the United States since 1783 remained British and could be legally impressed into His Majesty's service.

The practice of searching American ships for British seamen, and especially for deserters from the navy, was naturally extremely irritating to American pride and also detrimental to American interests, but it was justified from the British point of view not only by the law of necessity but by the fact that British seamen were often deliberately enticed away in American ports and provided with fraudulent certificates of United States citizenship.[46] So long, moreover, as this right of search was only exercised in the case of merchant vessels, no serious quarrel between the two countries resulted, though there were many complaints and much exchange of diplomatic correspondence on the subject. But when the news reached Philadelphia that Captain Loring of H.M.S. "Carnatic" had stopped an American warship and searched her for deserters, instructions were issued (29 December 1798) to the commanders of American men-of-war to resist all such visits by force and, if

44 MacMaster in *Cambridge Modern History*, VII (1903), 328.

45 Although this grievance was one of the principal motives for the American declaration of war against Great Britain in 1812, no mention was made of it in the Treaty of Ghent (24 Dec. 1814). With the general peace that followed it ceased to exist.

46 The British Foreign Office records contain very many reports from British consuls in the United States as to desertions of British seamen from privateers, etc., in American ports (e.g., from Edmund Thornton, in P.R.O. F.O. 5, 32, 35) and many complaints as to the ease with which fraudulent papers were supplied to British seamen in American ships (e.g., P.R.O. F.O. 5, 15, 19, 23, 49, 82).

overpowered, to surrender men and ship, but in no case the men alone.[47]

In his message to Congress of 7 January 1800, President Adams referred to this incident as the first instance of misbehaviour of any of the British officers towards American warships, adding that, according to all the evidence he had seen, the flag of the United States and the officers and men had "been treated by the civil and military authority of the British nation, in Nova Scotia, the West Indies, and on the ocean, with uniform civility, politeness, and friendship." [48] The question raised by this affair was, as the President hoped, amicably adjusted. It was not till seven years later that it was raised again, and in a far more serious form, by the famous affair of the "Chesapeake."

There can be no doubt but that, just as the greed for prize money sometimes led the British commanders to make speculative captures of neutral merchantmen, so the need for filling up their complements made them in general inclined to take the benefit of the doubt in the case of seamen on American ships who claimed to be United States citizens. From the point of view of the existing British law they seem, indeed, to have been justified in doing so. In March 1808, James Madison, the Secretary of State, reported that since the beginning of the war 4,228 American citizens had been impressed into the British navy, of whom 936 had been discharged—for what reasons is not stated. On the same day he presented to the Senate a long list of seamen from American ships who had been impressed since 5 March 1806, when the last report had been presented. This list contains 687 names, the overwhelming majority of which—though not all—are English, Scottish or Irish. Of the names on this list only 29 are acknowledged to be those of British seamen, while 129 are marked as claiming to be American citizens, but without any proof that they were so.[49] It may be suggested that, while the proofs in the majority of cases were such as satisfied the requirements of

---

[47] Clowes, *The Royal Navy: A History* (1897-1903), IV, 165.

[48] *Ibid.*, p. 166.

[49] Statement of impressments from American ships, etc., communicated to the Senate by President Jefferson on 2 March, 1808. A.S.P., F.R., III, 36. American seamen were also occasionally impressed into the French navy. See the letter of Jonathan Russell to the Duke of Bassano, 8 July 1811, demanding an enquiry with a view to the release of 23 American seamen impressed at Danzig and taken under guard to Antwerp. A.S.P., F.R., III, 504.

the United States Government, they were not such as the English courts could accept, for the reasons already stated.

It may be concluded that in this matter of impressment of American seamen both parties to the dispute were in some measure to blame. The root cause of the "misbehaviour" was on both sides the same, namely, the shortage of man power. The motives, however, were hardly comparable. For Great Britain the manning of the navy was a matter of life and death; for the merchants of the United States the manning of their vessels was only a matter of war profiteering. While, therefore, it is true enough that the action of British naval officers at sea and in foreign ports was often high-handed and hard to stomach, they had some excuse, not only in necessity, but in the knowledge that the proofs of American citizenship laid before them were often fraudulent and still more often such as were invalid in English law. The fact that British merchant ships at sea were treated with equal rigor shows that the sole object in searching American vessels for British seamen was to recruit men for the navy, not to hamper American commerce and shipping, the enormous growth of which during the war proves how little they were affected by the exercise of this and other belligerent rights claimed by the mistress of the seas.

The French Navy

Readers of "Mr. Midshipman Easy" will have been duly impressed by the fact that the doctrines of equality and the Rights of Man are incompatible with all sound ideas of naval discipline. They had certainly played havoc with the splendid French naval force which had been built up during the later years of the monarchy, had gained and held command of the Channel for three years during the American War and had made possible the independence of the thirteen colonies. As early as December 1789, there was a serious mutiny at Toulon, and this was followed a few months later by another at Brest. As the Revolution progressed the corps of officers, who were all nobles, was depleted by proscription and emigration (more than seven hundred were to perish at Quiberon) and the vacant places were filled by warrant officers and seamen who—since naval command requires more technical training than military—proved less effective than the men who rose from the ranks to high command in the army. On 11 July 1793, Cambon reported to the Convention that there were not enough cannon and men to protect the coasts, that in the ports of Brest, Rochefort and Lorient there were only six line-of-battleships fit to put to sea, and that the Mediterranean fleet was under repair in the harbor of Toulon.[50] To cap all, on the following 27 August 1793, the great naval port of Toulon joined the revolt of the southern Departments of France against the Terrorists in Paris and, with its arsenal and the finest squadron in the French navy, was handed over to the English.[51] It was retaken in December; but, before retiring, the British burned ten line-of-battleships and carried off three, together with several frigates, leaving only a shattered remnant of the squadron in the port.[52]

In these circumstances the British from the first asserted their naval superiority. Their ships were constantly at sea, blockading the enemy in his ports or scouring the ocean for prizes, and the crews, submitted to severe discipline and continually practiced in the handling of the ship, became in the highest degree efficient, while the efficiency and health of the French seamen suffered because they were practically confined to port. When, in May 1794, Admiral Villaret-Joyeuse at last sailed from Brest to cover the arrival of a convoy from America, his officers and men, inexperienced in the handling of their ships at sea, and miserably seasick, proved to be no match for the British, and the result was Howe's victory of the 1st of June. It was, however, characteristic of the uncertainties of naval warfare in the days of sailing ships that in spite of this defeat Admiral Van Stabel succeeded in reaching Brest with his convoy of 130 vessels laden with wheat.

It was not, however, until the summer of 1795 that Bridport's victory of 23 June off Belle-Île, and Hotham's indecisive success in the Mediterranean on the 12 July, decided the French Government to abandon all attempts to contest the supremacy of the British at sea. The French policy was now to keep the fleets in harbor as a threat, and to send out small squadrons, as occasion offered, to prey on enemy commerce and worry the colonies. This "squadron and division warfare," says Mahan, "backed by hosts of commerce de-

[50] Morse Stephens, *Orators of the French Revolution*, I, 511.

[51] See Declaration made to Lord Howe in the name of the Sections of Toulon ". . . the people of Toulon, and those of Marseilles, would rather have recourse to the generosity of a loyal people, who have manifested the desire of protecting true Frenchmen against the anarchists who wish to ruin them." *Naval Chronicle*, II, 102 ff.

[52] *Annual Register*, 1794, p. 63; *Naval Chronicle*, II, 302.

stroyers, was barren of results and had no influence on the issue of the war." In the course of three years the damage inflicted upon British trade was negligible, amounting only to some two to two and one-half per cent of its total volume, while at the end of this period not a single French merchant vessel ventured to sail under the French flag. The inconvenience and loss to neutrals were, however, great, and the activities of French privateers and the incompetence and corruption of the French prize courts, were not the least of the motives which drew the northern powers together in defense of neutral rights and led the United States, in 1798, to authorize reprisals which amounted to acts of war.

The French fleets were described by the Director La Revellière-Lepaux in his Memoirs as "humiliated, beaten, blockaded in the ports, stripped of resources, of provisions, of naval material, seething with insubordination, disgraced by ignorance, ruined by desertions." [53] They never recovered entirely from this revolutionary sickness, in spite of Napoleon's somewhat half-hearted efforts to revive them; but the threat of their existence was not entirely removed until October 1805, when Nelson's victory off Trafalgar made Great Britain unquestioned mistress of the seas. As for the war on commerce, by which the French Revolutionists had hoped "to force England to a shameful bankruptcy," "what they obtained was the demoralization of the navy, the loss of the control of the sea and of their own external commerce, and finally Napoleon's Continental System and the fall of the Empire." [54]

[53] Quoted by Sorel, *L'Europe et la Révolution française* (1897), V, 28.
[54] Mahan, II, 178, 202 f., 206.

II

THE OPENING MOVES OF THE ECONOMIC WAR

FRENCH DECREES AND BRITISH REPRISALS

The "policy of economic strangulation" certainly did not originate with the British, who at the outset might well have felt the force of Robespierre's scornful estimate of the chances of success which "a nation of shopkeepers" would have in carrying out such a policy against "an agricultural country" like France. It was the Girondin deputy Kersaint, an ex-noble and naval officer, who in a speech delivered in the National Convention a month before the declaration of war, outlined the plan for the economic ruin of Great Britain by the closing of her markets, a plan which was followed by successive governments of France so far as they had the power, and was ultimately adopted and elaborated by Napoleon in his Continental System.[1]

France declared war against Great Britain and the United Netherlands on 1 February 1793. The records of what immediately followed read curiously in the light of the experience of the World War. The British Government, though it laid stress on the exceptional character of this war with the revolutionists, seems to have contemplated conducting it on the lines of the old wars of the eighteenth century, when a state of war between two nations by no means involved complete interruption of social, or even commercial, relations between them.[2] The French Government, in defiance of all precedent, laid an embargo on British ships which happened to be in French ports when war was declared. On learning of this, the British Government, on 4 February, issued an Order in Council to the effect that no ships belonging to His Majesty's subjects would be permitted to enter or clear out of the ports of France, and that

---

[1] Heckscher, *The Continental System* (1922), p. 52; Sorel, *op. cit.*, III, 244 f.

[2] Sterne, when he started on his "Sentimental Journey" to France, only remembered when he got to Dover that France and Great Britain were at war. This did not interfere with his plans, however, nor did it affect the friendliness of his reception everywhere during his tour in the enemy's country. Even the fact that he had forgotten to procure a passport caused him no inconvenience until he reached Paris, where the omission was rectified without difficulty.

a general embargo would be laid on all French ships in the ports and roadsteads of Great Britain or entering them hereafter.[3] Two days later, however, this was modified by another Order in Council which directed that all packets and bye-boats, whether French or British, employed in the conveyance of letters and passengers between Great Britain and France, or countries occupied by the armies of France, were to be permitted to pass and repass as heretofore, notwithstanding His Majesty's Order in Council of 4 February.[4] On the 20th this Order was revoked by another; "except in the case of vessels employed by the Postmaster General in such numbers as may be approved by one of His Majesty's principal Secretaries of State and except such vessels as may be employed by the Directors of the Post Office in France." It was ordered, also, that passengers traveling by these boats must have passports.[5] Meanwhile an Order in Council of the 18th had so far relaxed the embargo imposed by that of the 4th as to allow 11 ships laden with goods for the Frankfurt Fair to proceed. The embargo was raised entirely on 5 July.[6]

Meanwhile, an Order in Council issued on the 11th of February announced that, whereas several unjust seizures had been made of the ships and goods of His Majesty's subjects contrary to the law of nations and the faith of treaties, His Majesty had been pleased to order that general reprisals be granted against the ships, goods and subjects of France. Four days later instructions were issued to the commanders of His Majesty's ships of war and privateers for the examination of the masters and crews of vessels visited in search of contraband or enemy property.[7]

[3] P.R.O. Ad. I. In Letters. 5179. Jan. 1793-29 Dec. 1794. "All decency and justice are outraged, if it be true, that these same Jacobins have confiscated all the British and Dutch trading Vessels that they had embargoed in the ports of France previous to their declaration of war! This is robbery and piracy with a vengeance! It is to be hoped that the British Lion will claw these fellows handsomely for their misdoing." Richard Henry Lee to Thomas Lee Shippen, 15 April 1793 (Ballagh, *Letters of Richard Henry Lee*, II, 557).

[4] *London Gazette*, No. 13,500, 5-9 Feb. 1793, p. 106.

[5] *Ibid.*, No. 13,507, p. 179.   [6] P.R.O. Ad. I. 5179.

[7] Order in Council of 15 Feb. 1793. P.R.O. Ad. I. In Letters. 5179. The interrogatories were of the most searching character. The questions to be asked were (in an abbreviated form):

1. Where were you born? Where have you lived for seven years past? Where are you living now, and how long? To what Prince or State are you subject or have ever been subject? Of what cities have you been admitted a burgher or freeman, and when and in what manner?

For some weeks neither Great Britain nor France gave any indication to neutrals of the rules they proposed to follow in dealing with neutral trade with the enemy. The first conspicuous move in the war on commerce was made by France, on 1 March 1793, when the Convention passed a decree prohibiting, on pain of confiscation, the importation of a variety of textile, metal and earthenware goods which were normally regarded as of English origin, and further providing that, after 1 April next, no foreign merchandise would be admitted into the territories of the Republic except on proof of origin in the form of certificates issued by French consuls or, in their absence, other officials. It is important to note, however, that materials for ship construction, timber, anchors, unwrought iron and salted provisions were specifically excepted from this prohibition.[8]

This decree, the first of a series of similar decrees which were to culminate in those issued by Napoleon from Berlin and Milan, proved in general ineffective.[9] The clause excepting naval stores and provisions from the boycott served to strengthen the determination of Great Britain and her allies to regard these as contraband. Article III of the Convention signed in London on 25 March between Great Britain and Russia engaged the parties "not to permit the exportation, in any case, from their ports for France, of any military or naval stores, or corn, grain, salt meat, or other provisions," and this article was repeated verbatim in the treaties of alliance

---

2. Under what colours did you sail? Are other colours on board and, if so, why? 3. What is the master's name? Have you known him long? Who appointed him? Where did he take possession? Where does he live? Has the master a fixed abode? Where did he last live? Is he married? If so, where does his wife live? Has he any interest in the cargo? What is the nature of the cargo? At what ports have you touched? Where did the last voyage begin, and where was it to have ended? . . . 13. How many bills of lading were signed? Were any of them false or colourable? 15. Was any charter-party signed for the voyage? What has become of it? When, where and by whom was it made? What were its contents? 16. What papers were on board when the ship first sailed? Have any been destroyed? . . . 30. By whom, and to whom, has the ship been sold or transferred, and how often? At what time and at what place, and for what sum or consideration was the sale or transfer made? Was the sum to be paid a fair equivalent? . . . Do you believe in your conscience that such a sale or transfer hath been truly made, and not for the purpose of covering or concealing the real property? [Cf. Vol. I of this series, pp. 218-221.—Editor.]

8 For the full text of the decree see 5 Martens, p. 192.
9 Mahan, II, 248.

subsequently by Great Britain with Prussia, Spain and Austria.[10]

On 26 March the French Convention passed another decree which, though more important in other aspects, may serve to explain the attitude of the British Government towards the disputed question as to whether provisions should be treated as contraband. Already, on 19 February, the Convention had opened the French colonial ports to American vessels on terms similar to those enjoyed by French shipping. By the decree of 26 March the vessels of the United States of sixty tons burden or under, laden only with flour and provisions, as also with the articles specified in the *arrêt* of 30 August 1784, and with bacon, butter, salt, salmon and candles, were to be admitted to the ports of the French colonies exempt from all duties, and were to be permitted to load with a certain proportion of coffee, sugar and other colonial produce on payment of the duties.[11] The object of the decree of 19 February had been to safeguard the traffic of France with her colonies by placing it under the protection of a neutral flag, and it led inevitably to the reaffirmation by Great Britain of the "Rule of 1756," which laid down that a neutral has no right to deliver a belligerent from the pressure of his enemies' hostilities by trading with his colonies in time of war in any way that was prohibited in time of peace. The decree of 26 March was clearly intended to encourage the importation of those supplies from the United States without which the French islands could not have held out against the British attacks, and it was therefore an additional inducement to the British Government not only to enforce the Rule of 1756 but also to treat provisions as contraband of war.

The Rule of 1756 was, of course, valid only so far as it could be enforced; there was no suggestion that a belligerent power was guilty of a moral lapse if it relaxed in time of war the laws made for the protection of its commerce in time of peace, or that neutrals were not morally justified in taking advantage of this relaxation; it was only that if by doing so they gave substantial aid to the enemy, they must risk the consequences, as in the case of trade in contraband or blockade running. Great Britain, whose representative at Philadelphia had been engaged for some months before

---

[10] For translations of the articles in question see A.S.P., F.R., III, 263. For the full texts of the treaties see 5 Martens, pp. 438 (Russia), 473 (Spain, 25 May 1793), 483 (Prussia, 14 July 1793).

[11] A.S.P., F.R., I, 306.

the war in a somewhat acrimonious discussion with Secretary Jefferson on the subject of the British Navigation law,[12] now found it expedient, under pressure of the sudden demand for ships and men for the purpose of war, to relax these laws in favor of American shipping. Under the Navigation Act of 1660 (12 Car. 2. cap. 18. §3) it was forbidden to carry any goods to or from the colonies in other than English-built ships, owned by Englishmen, and operated by crews three-fourths English, and no colonial produce from any part of the world was to be imported except in such ships. This act was still in force; and, though permission had been given year by year by royal proclamation to import American goods into Great Britain in American bottoms, this permission had been withdrawn in 1792, and during the early months of the war it was, as Jefferson complained in a report to Congress, only in British vessels that American produce might be imported into Great Britain. The matter had, however, already been settled in England, and on 10 April—the day following that on which Jefferson had enclosed his report to George Hammond, the British Minister in Philadelphia—an Order in Council was issued extending for another year the Act of 23 George III by which the trade relations between Great Britain and the United States were regulated and directing that certain specified articles, the produce of the United States, were to be permitted to be imported into Great Britain in either British or American vessels.[13]

This Order in Council undoubtedly gave a great impetus to the carrying trade of the United States, which was in any case bound to increase immensely as a result of the war. It is also, doubtless, true enough that British merchants and shipowners viewed with alarm a concession on the part of the Government which seemed to threaten them with serious loss. There is, however, but little warrant for the assertion which has been made [14] that it was their protests against the encouragement of this new trade rival that led to the policy proclaimed in the two later Orders in Council of 8 June and 6 November 1793. Both these Orders are susceptible of a much simpler explanation.

[12] A.S.P., F.R., I, 25 ff.
[13] P.R.O. Ad. I. 5179. The Order specified unmanufactured goods and merchandise, the importation of which is not prohibited by law (except tobacco . . . oil made from fish, etc.) and any pig iron, bar iron, pitch, tar, turpentine, rosin, potash, pearl ash, indico (sic), masts, yards and bowsprits, being the growth and production of any of the United States.
[14] Coman, Industrial History of the United States (1910), p. 176.

At this early stage of the war the British Government was far more anxious to bring it to a speedy end by using every possible means to break the resistance of France, than to safeguard British merchants from possible loss. Now, as has already been pointed out, there was at this time a serious shortage of foodstuffs in France, which not only led to internal disturbances but was one of the factors which made it impossible for the French fleets to put to sea. It was, therefore, of the utmost importance, from the point of view of Great Britain and her allies, to prevent the French from securing supplies from abroad. As early as the month of March, though Great Britain had as yet made no public declaration of the principles she intended to apply in the exercise of her belligerent rights, British cruisers and privateers were stopping and bringing in for adjudication neutral vessels laden with foodstuffs for France. Among the vessels thus captured in the following month was the American ship "Sally," laden with 2,109 barrels of flour and bound for Havre, which was brought into Guernsey by an Alderney cutter. In reporting this capture Colonel Dundas, commander of the troops in Guernsey, stated that the captain of the "Sally," when put upon his oath, had produced certain sealed papers which contained "much material of interest concerning French supplies purchased in America." [15] It had, indeed, long been known to British Ministers that the French Government had been making arrangements for the purchase of supplies on a large scale in the United States, and on 12 March Lord Grenville had written to Hammond telling him that he had received "singularly correct" information as to the instructions given by his Government to Citizen Genêt, the recently appointed envoy of the French Republic to the United States, and that, among other things, he had been instructed "to open negotiations with the American Government for liquidating the payment of their loan to France, by transmitting to the ports of that country a supply of corn and provisions equal to the amount of the outstanding debt." Hammond was to impress upon the American Government that if, as the result of such negotiation, provisions or grain were actually shipped on board American vessels on the account of the French Government, they would evidently be French property and, as such, liable to capture. As for the principle that "free ships make free goods," this had never been recognized by Great Britain, and would

[15] Thomas Dundas to the Right Hon. Henry Dundas. Fort George, Guernsey, 24 April 1793. P.R.O. F.O. 5. 1.

undoubtedly not be allowed in this case. "The affirmation of this proposition," continued Lord Grenville, "would, in its consequences, prove extremely detrimental to the interests of this country, as affording to the French those means of subsistence, and of carrying on the war, which, from the nature of their present situation, and of the forces employed against them, they must otherwise be unable to procure." He added a warning that American property carried to French ports in American bottoms would be subject to the rules as to contraband and proceeded to define contraband as all things "of such a nature as to enable the enemies of this country to carry on the war against us." [16]

By the time this dispatch reached America, Genêt's negotiations for the discharge of the remaining American war debt to France by payment in kind had proved abortive, and Hammond, therefore, did not think it expedient, in the delicate state of the relations between Great Britain and the United States, to raise the question of provisions as contraband by communicating the substance of Lord Grenville's dispatch to the American Government, and the letter was quietly buried in the archives.[17] Its abiding interest lies in the indication it gives that Great Britain intended to treat provisions as contraband, though only when the cutting off of food supplies from the enemy seemed to give a reasonable chance of reducing him to terms.[18] As for Grenville's wide definition of contra-

[16] Grenville to Hammond, 12 March 1793. P.R.O. F.O. 5. 1.
[17] Hammond showed the letter in confidence to Alexander Hamilton and reported him as saying that he agreed as to the justice of such measures, but would not be responsible for the opinion of his colleagues. Bemis, *Jay's Treaty* (1923), p. 154.
[18] As the chief legal argument in favor of this principle, British Ministers quoted what Pinkney described as a "loose passage of Vattel." This ran: "Commodities particularly used in war, and the importation of which to the enemy is prohibited, are called contraband goods. Such are arms, military and naval stores, timber, horses, and even provisions, in certain junctures, when there are hopes of reducing the enemy by famine" (*Le Droit des gens* (Leyden, 1758), Vol. I, iii, c. 7, sec. 112). It is hard to see why this passage should be described as "loose." Lord Stowell, whose knowledge of international law was unrivaled and whose impartiality was unquestioned, showed that the character of the port to which provisions were destined was the principal circumstance to be attended to in deciding whether they were to be looked upon as contraband. A cargo of provisions intended for an enemy's port, in which it was known that a warlike armament was in preparation, would be liable to arrest and confiscation; while if the same cargo were intended for a port where none but merchantmen were fitted out, the most that could be done would be to detain it, paying the neutral the same price for it he would have got from the enemy (McCulloch, *Dictionary of Com-*

band, this foreshadowed the terms of the article in the Convention between Great Britain and Russia, signed thirteen days later, which proclaimed the principle of what we should now call the "economic boycott" of France.

The British Government was not, however, the first to make public declaration of the belligerent right to seize provisions on neutral ships bound for enemy ports. On 9 May the French National Convention passed a decree authorizing the warships and privateers of the Republic to stop and bring in for adjudication neutral vessels laden, in whole or in part, either with provisions destined for the ports of the enemy or with enemy merchandise. Such merchandise was to be declared good prize and sold for the benefit of the captors, while provisions, being the property of neutrals, were to be paid for at the price they would fetch at the enemy port of destination. The ships were to be released as soon as the condemned goods had been sold, freight was to be allowed at the rate fixed by the shippers and compensation was to be paid for demurrage.

These measures were justified in the preamble to the decree on the ground that "the flag of the neutral Powers had not been respected by the enemies of France." Instances were cited by way of illustration. Two cargoes of wheat, bought before the war for the provisioning of the French navy, had been detained at Falmouth and bought by the British Government at a price below that which had been paid for them. The "Theresia" of Papenburg, laden with French property, had been seized by a British cutter and taken into Dover,[19] and the same fate had befallen a Danish ship, the "Mercure Christianlund," which was proceeding from Dunkirk to Bordeaux with a cargo of wheat, while the American ship "John," sailing from Falmouth to St. Malo with a cargo of American grain, had been captured and carried into Guernsey. "All the laws

---

merce and Commercial Navigation (1846), s.v. Contraband, p. 381). This opinion illustrates very well the impossibility of treating the old rules of international law as immutable and the necessity of interpreting them at times according to the spirit rather than the letter. In Lord Stowell's day, when internal communications were difficult, it would have sufficed for a belligerent to prevent supplies from entering the actual port where an expedition was fitting out. Under modern conditions, when internal communications are rapid and highly organized, it would matter little for the purposes of the enemy where the supplies were landed.

[19] That is, a violation of the principle "free ships, free goods," which the French championed at this time.

of nations having been thus violated," the preamble continued, it was not possible for the French Republic to behave towards all the neutral powers in the manner which it desired, that is to say, by continuing to uphold the absolute freedom of commerce.[20]

The ostensible justification of the decree was thus the right of retaliation; and the last article (v) laid down that the law would cease to have effect after the allied powers should have declared free and not liable to seizure, although destined for the ports of the Republic, provisions which might be neutral property, and merchandise loaded in neutral ships, which belonged to the French Government or to French citizens. The underlying motives were various. The decree doubtless represented an attempt to turn neutral grain ships into French ports; it was also an attempt to range the neutral powers on the side of France and to induce them to bring pressure to bear on Great Britain and her allies in order to persuade or force them to abandon their policy of the economic boycott.

In neither object did it succeed. The most important immediate effect was to strain still further the relations between the French Republic and the United States, already strained enough by the extraordinary proceedings in America of the French envoy, Citizen Genêt, who had landed at Charleston on 8 April, armed with instructions to demand a guarantee of the French West Indian Islands, in return for their opening to American trade, and generally to assume that the terms of the Treaty of Alliance of 1778 committed the United States to active participation in the war on the side of France; which instructions he had proceeded to carry out by fomenting a popular agitation in favor of war and, among other things, fitting out in American harbors privateers to prey upon British commerce and empowering French consuls in the various ports to adjudicate on the prizes they brought in.[21] At the time when the decree of 9 May was passed, the news of President Washington's declaration of neutrality, issued on 22 April, and of the untoward effects of Citizen Genêt's activities, had of course not yet reached Paris, and the hope of securing the United States as

[20] For the text of the decree see A.S.P., F.R., I, 749 (English translation) and for the French original 5 Martens, p. 381.

[21] "In very truth I think these instructions are as complete and complex an insult upon the honour and understanding of the United States as could possibly be exhibited." Richard Henry Lee to Richard Bland Lee, 5 Feb. 1794, Ballagh, *Life and Letters of Richard Henry Lee,* II, 571.

an active ally disposed the French Government to yield to the protests handed in by Gouverneur Morris, the American Minister in Paris. On the 23d, accordingly, the decree was revoked, so far as the United States were concerned, on the ground that it was incompatible with the terms of Article XXIII of the Treaty of Amity and Commerce signed by France with the United States in Paris on 6 February 1778.[22] Whatever effect this decree might have had, however, was destroyed by another decree, passed on the 28th, which so far repealed that of the 23d as to place "in a state of provisional sequestration" the vessels seized under that of the 9th.

The fact that these decrees of the 9th and 23d of May were not communicated to the American Government until the following September well illustrates the confusion of counsels caused by the extreme slowness of communications. In communicating them Genêt declared that the considerations which prompted them were, on the one hand, the desire of the French scrupulously to observe the trea- ties with the United States, and on the other hand, to show "the thorough confidence she has that the Americans will not abuse this privilege by carrying to her enemies those productions by which they ought to assist in the defence of a cause as much their own as hers." He had been informed, he said, that the British Govern- ment had declared their intention to carry into English ports all the American vessels laden with provisions for the ports of France (the reference is doubtless to the Order in Council of 8 June), and the French Republic expected that the United States would "hasten to take the most energetic measures to procure a recall of this decision." He concluded with the threat that, if these measures were "insufficient or fruitless," and the neutrality of the United States should prove, as heretofore, serviceable only to the enemies

[22] In the translation of the decree of 23 May given in A.S.P., F.R., III, 285, and quoted by Mahan, II, 242, the date of the treaty is wrongly given as 16 June 1778, and the number of the Article as XVI. 2 Martens, p. 597, also dates the treaty wrongly 6 June. The treaty was signed on 6 February 1778, ratified by the United States on 4 May and by France on 16 July, the ratifications being ex- changed in Paris on 17 July. See Miller, *Treaties and Other International Acts of the United States of America*, II (1931), 3, where the correct text of the treaty will be found.

The Article referred to is clearly XXIII, which provides that, if either of the parties are at war, the vessels of the other shall be free to trade not only from enemy ports direct to a neutral, but from one enemy port to another, and that free ships make free goods. This Article was No. XXV in the original treaty, but Articles XI and XII having been suppressed, was numbered XXIII at the time of ratification.

of France, the French Republic would exercise a very natural right in taking measures to prevent a consequence so injurious to her.[23]

It is probable that when Genêt made this communication he had been informed of a new decree (of 1 July) by which that of the 28th of May had been revoked and the terms of that of the 23d repeated; he had clearly not received the news that the decree of 1 July had in turn been revoked by another of the 27th, and still less could he suspect the terms of the new Navigation Act passed by the Convention on 21 September, which laid down, *inter alia,* that no foreign produce or manufactures were to be imported into France or her colonies except directly in ships belonging to French subjects or to inhabitants of the country of origin, on pain of confiscation of ship and cargo.[24] Of this decree Gouverneur Morris reported home, that it could do very little harm, because the fleets of France were "confined by the enemy" and the privateers by a decree of the Convention.[25] Much harm had, however, been done to American interests already. The ships seized under the decree of 9 May had not been released, and years were to pass before reparation was made for the losses sustained by the owners of these vessels and of others detained on various pretexts from time to time.[26]

The Orders in Council of 1793

It may be conjectured that the British Government waited for authoritative decisions by the High Court of Admiralty on the question of provisions destined for the enemy before notifying neutral powers of the action it proposed to take in this matter. It was at any rate in pursuance of decrees of the Admiralty Court that on 28 May instructions were sent to the commissioners for victualing His Majesty's navy "to purchase on public account all

[23] Genêt to Jefferson, 27 September 1793. A.S.P., F.R., I, 243 f.

[24] Text in 5 Martens, p. 407.

[25] To Jefferson, 22 Sept. 1793. A.S.P., F.R., I, 372.

[26] Mahan (II, 243) ascribes these repeated revocations and reissues of the exemption of the United States from the decree of 9 May to the inconsistencies of the ephemeral French parties in power. This is hardly convincing. There was no actual change of government between the beginning of May and the fall of the Girondins on 2 June, and the establishment of the Great Committee of Public Safety on 10 July provided a strong government, which survived for a whole year. The true explanation is probably to be found in a conflict of opinion as to the most effective means of enticing or forcing the United States into the war against England. Opinions as to this may well have varied according to advices received from America and elsewhere.

such parts of cargoes of neutral vessels laden with naval stores and provisions for the ports of France as may be fit for naval services in their department." [27] Ten days later, on 8 June, the Order in Council was signed which gave formal sanction of law to the principle underlying these instructions. The second and third articles are concerned with the action to be adopted towards ships attempting to enter blockaded ports. The first article, which is the only one pertinent to the question of provisions as contraband, runs as follows:

> It shall be lawful to stop and detain all vessels laden wholly or in part with corn, flour, or meal, bound to any port in France, or any port occupied by the armies of France, and to send them to such ports as may be most convenient, in order that such corn, meal, or flour, may be purchased on behalf of His Majesty's Government, and the ships be released after such purchase, and after a due allowance for freight; or that the masters of such ships, on giving due security, to be approved of by the Court of Admiralty, be permitted to proceed to dispose of their cargoes of corn, meal, or flour, in the ports of any country in amity with His Majesty.[28]

This Order was not made public until 28 June, the instructions to the commanders of warships and privateers, based upon it, being issued three days later, on 1 July. What followed well illustrates the complications caused by the extreme slowness of communications. The substance of the Order was communicated to the Danish and Swedish Governments on the 17th, and therefore, although it met with a vigorous protest,[29] as contrary to the law of nations,

---

[27] P.R.O. Ad. 2. 124. The vessels concerned were the "Jouvert," "Stapert" and "Krogeroe," laden with naval stores, and the "Neptunus," "Trendre Brodre" and "Schwalbe," laden with provisions.

[28] A.S.P., F.R., III, 264, also *ibid.*, I, 240.

[29] In the "declaratory memorial" presented to the Danish Government by the British Minister it was pointed out that the corn (grain) trade was now a Government concern in France, that it was "equally notorious" that one of the most essential expedients to compel those who had declared war against Great Britain to equitable terms of peace consisted in their being prevented to prevent, by importation, that want which was the necessary consequence of what they had done, in order to arm the whole laboring class of France against the other governments and the general tranquillity of Europe (*Annual Register*, 1793, pp. 177 f.). Count von der Goltz, the Prussian Minister, made a communication to the same effect (*ibid.*, p. 179). The reply was that, while His Danish Majesty would do all he could to prove his friendly disposition to Great Britain (e.g., by forbidding the sale of French prizes in Danish harbors and recovering British property seized in Danish ships), he would never admit that the different nature of a war could alter the nature of a mutual contract, or that mutual allowances could be considered as favors or privileges, or that any two powers should make regulations at the expense of a third power, or that belligerent States should ease the burden

there was no complaint as to any undue delay in its notification. It was otherwise in the case of the United States. It was not till 12 September that Hammond communicated the Order to the Secretary of State, which led to the suspicion that the communication had been deliberately delayed in order that Great Britain might reap a rich harvest of prizes before American ships had been warned of their danger.[30] Such a suspicion was quite unwarranted; but it is hard to see how it could have been avoided. The Orders in Council were issued to meet particular situations or emergencies, and they would have lost all effect had the instructions for their execution been delayed for months pending the receipt by distant neutrals of due notification and the despatch by them of warnings to their vessels scattered over all the seas.

The issue of the Order in Council of 8 June was notified to Hammond by Lord Grenville in a letter dated 5 July, only four days after the issue of the instructions. In this he advanced the arguments which were to be employed on the British side during all the debates that followed. "By the law of nations," he said, "as laid down by the most modern writers, particularly by Vattel, it is expressly stated that all provisions are to be considered as articles of contraband, and as such liable to confiscation, in the case where the depriving an enemy of their supplies is one of the means intended to be employed for reducing him to reasonable terms of peace." This, he said, was notoriously the case with France, where the whole laboring class had been armed against all the governments of Europe. The Order was further justified by "the circumstances of a trade which is now almost entirely carried on by the pretended Government of France itself, and which is therefore no longer to be considered as a mercantile speculation of individuals, but as an immediate operation of the very persons who have declared war, and are now carrying it on against this country." Great

---

inseparable from war by throwing it upon their innocent neighbors. The resistance of the neutral courts would be unanimous. It was impossible to combine the system of neutrality with measures which wholly destroyed it (*ibid.*, pp. 178 ff.).

[30] Secretary Randolph complained to Hammond that "the instructions of the 8th of June, operating immediately, and not handed to us until the 12th of September, were distressing our commerce for more than three months before we were apprized of our danger." P.R.O. F.O. 5. 4. Randolph to Hammond, 1 May 1794. P.R.O. F.O. 5. 4. Attached to Hammond to Grenville, 28 April. As mentioned above, the Order did not "operate immediately," and it is quite possible that dispatches sent after its publication may have taken some two months to reach Philadelphia.

Britain, he said, would have been justified in treating all provisions as contraband, whereas by the present measure France had only been prevented from being supplied with corn (wheat), omitting rice (an article so material in the scale of commerce for America), and even for the corn seized and condemned full indemnification was to be paid.[31] The substance of this dispatch was repeated almost verbatim in the letter of 12 September in which Hammond notified the Secretary of State of the proclamation of the Order in Council.[32] It is impossible to imagine that Hammond had, on his own authority, deliberately delayed the delivery of this dispatch.

Hammond reported home that the publication of the "additional instructions issued to British ships of war" had created alarm among American merchants, and that even Alexander Hamilton had denounced it to him as "a very harsh and unprecedented measure" which militated against the principal American exports.[33] Thomas Jefferson, who was still Secretary of State, at once drew up a strong protest in the name of the United States Government, copies of which were sent to both Hammond and Thomas Pinckney, the American Minister to the Court of St. James's.[34] He declared that the contention that provisions were contraband in any case but that of a place actually blockaded, was entirely new; that reason and usage alike had established that when two nations are at war those not engaged in it have the right to carry on their industries and commerce undisturbed—"in short, that the war among others shall be, for them, as though it did not exist." The only admitted exceptions to this rule, he said, were the furnishing of the belligerents with warlike weapons, which were treated as contraband, and supplying anything whatever to a place effectively blockaded. As for provisions, these had never been regarded as contraband under the

[31] Grenville to Hammond, 5 July 1793. P.R.O. F.O. 5. 1. By a supplementary Order in Council it was directed that freight and reasonable expenses were to be allowed the masters of neutral ships, if no *mala fides* or prevarication were justly presumed or suspected. Demurrage was only to be allowed, as a reasonable expense when the proceedings of the captor had been unjust, irregular, or injurious, or when the ship had been unduly detained (4 Moore, p. 17). American merchants complained that the indemnification (the invoice price plus 10 per cent profit) was quite insufficient, and this view was upheld by the Mixed Commission set up under Jay's Treaty (case of the "Neptune"). See 4 Moore, p. 372.

[32] A.S.P., F.R., I, 240.

[33] Hammond to Grenville, 17 September 1793. P.R.O. F.O. 5. 1.

[34] Jefferson to Pinckney, 7 September 1793. A.S.P., F.R., II, 239; Jefferson to Hammond, 22 September 1793. *Ibid.*, p. 240.

law of nations, and Great Britain herself had specifically excluded them in several treaties concluded by her with other powers. The state of war between Great Britain and France gave neither power the right to interrupt the agriculture of the United States, or the peaceable exchange of their produce with all nations. If the United States were to permit corn to be sent to Great Britain and to refuse it to France, this would be an act of partiality which might lead to war with the latter. If they withheld provisions from France, they would be bound to withhold them from Great Britain also and so close to themselves all the ports of Europe where corn was in demand or else make themselves a party to the war. This was a dilemma into which no pretext for forcing the United States could be found. Great Britain might desire to starve an enemy nation; "but she can have no right of doing it at our loss, nor of making us the instrument of it." [35]

Several weeks passed, of course, before Pinckney could lay this protest before the British Government, and it was not till 11 January 1794 that Lord Grenville wrote to Hammond to tell him that the principles laid down in the American note could neither be acknowledged nor acted on by His Majesty's Government. After recapitulating the arguments in favor of treating provisions as contraband under certain conditions, he went on to point out that it was "otiose" to argue that Great Britain had committed herself to the American position by expressly excepting provisions from definitions of contraband in several treaties with other nations, since "those treaties are not declaratory of the law of nations, but are restrictions and modifications of that law by special agreement between the contracting parties, and are therefore neither binding on other Powers, nor even on the parties themselves in other cases." [36] The argument of this dispatch was elaborated by Hammond in a letter dated 11 April to Edmund Randolph, who had succeeded Jefferson as Secretary of State at the end of December. Treaties arranging exceptions from international law with other powers were, he said, not binding upon Great Britain. Indeed, the American argument strengthened the British case; for of the only two existing treaties by which His Majesty's conduct was regulated toward nations neutral in the present war one (that with Sweden) expressly included provisions in the enumeration of articles *contrabande de*

[35] A somewhat fuller abstract will be found in 4 Moore, pp. 16 f.
[36] Grenville to Hammond, 11 January 1794. P.R.O. F.O. 5. 4.

guerre.[37] He also quoted Martens (II, 390) as asserting that in some treaties of commerce not only corn and other provisions, but even brandy and tobacco, are comprehended under the denomination of contraband. As to Pinckney's fear that, if the United States acquiesced in the British principle, France might regard this as a breach of neutrality, and so have a pretext for pursuing the same course, "it is notorious that the conduct of the ruling party in France with relation to provisions, the property of a neutral power, both *previously* (as it is indeed declared in the decree of the National Convention of the 9th of May) and subsequently to the instruction in question, has been such as Mr. Pinckney appears to imagine that this measure on the part of the British Government would have a tendency to produce." [38] This last sentence is interesting as suggesting the probability that the French decree of 9 May may have influenced the decision of the British Government to issue the Order in Council of 8 June, which is couched in almost identical terms. Certainly Mahan was in error in saying that the decree "seems to have escaped the notice of the British Government, which, in justifying the Order in Council of 8 June, does not mention it." [39]

The controversy over this Order in Council, which continued until it was withdrawn, so far as provisions were concerned, by that of 18 August 1794, was soon overshadowed by that arising from another Order in Council, that of 6 November 1793, which was still more damaging to American interests and offensive to American sentiment. Before dealing with this Order, it will be well to give some description of the whole situation which led up to it.

During the summer of 1793 Anglo-American relations (apart from the question of the frontier forts, with which we are not here concerned) hinged mainly on the questions of neutrality raised, for the most part, by the highly irregular activities of Citizen Genêt, which even the American declaration of neutrality did not serve to stop. Hammond's business, which he carried out with commendable zeal, was to hold the Government of the United States to the strict observance of its neutrality proclamation and of the law of nations as interpreted by itself. The attitude of the Government itself was,

[37] Art. XI. of the Treaty of Alliance of 21 October 1661, between King Charles II and His Swedish Majesty.

[38] Hammond to the Secretary of State, 11 April 1794. Enclosed in Hammond to Grenville, No. 11. P.R.O. F.O. 5. 4.

[39] Mahan, II, 234.

indeed, studiously correct; Genêt's activities were denounced as outrages on the sovereignty of the United States and his recall demanded; and finally, in his address to the Senate of 3 December, President Washington announced that the Government of the United States would compensate the British merchants and others who had suffered spoliation at the hands of the French privateers fitted in American ports or captured in American waters.[40]

But though the attitude of the Government was correct, its power of control was limited—as the long license allowed to Genêt had demonstrated. On 7 March Hammond reported to Lord Grenville that Colonel William S. Smith, a son-in-law of Mr. Adams, was collecting 40,000 stand of arms "undoubtedly for France, where he has raised a loan," [41] and later, on 3 May, he had again occasion to call Jefferson's attention to the collection of arms in New York. On 2 April he reported that Smith had used the money raised in France to purchase flour and wheat, which was to be exported to France in American bottoms, adding that "the ships papers will be so framed as to protect their cargoes under the denomination of American property." A list was enclosed of seven American ships and one French brigantine, all bound for France.[42] American merchants, indeed, were quick to awake to the fact that this traffic would bring enormous profits, and incidentally also to the fact that these profits could only be reaped in full if the American merchant marine were largely increased, which could be done most rapidly by buying up French vessels, of which large numbers were then in American harbors.[43] In spite of the vigilance of the Government to prevent "fraudulent covers," it was clear—especially in view of the wide-

[40] "The dispatches of Hammond . . . show how faithfully the United States adhered to the principles of neutrality despite the strong wave of feeling for France. They also indicate the satisfaction of the British Government with that neutrality."—Bemis, *Jay's Treaty* (1923), p. 148.

[41] Hammond to Grenville, 7 March 1793. P.R.O. F.O. 5. 1.

[42] Hammond to Grenville, No. 12, 2 April 1793. *Ibid.*

[43] "Were we to depend on home-built vessels, much of our produce would remain on our hands." Copy of a letter from Philadelphia, P.R.O. F.O. 5. 2. "I am in hopes our merchants will buy up foreign bottoms for the transportation of our produce . . . they will be entitled to passports as American property. . . . Foreign nations being bound to respect what bona fide belongs to us . . . as in this way we may suddenly enlarge our stock of shipping we shall suffer the less. The Government has accordingly entrusted the Customs House officers to furnish passports to all vessels bona fide belonging to Americans attending rigorously however to prevent fraudulent covers."—Copy of another letter from Philadelphia, of 9 June. *Ibid.*

spread sympathy with France—that there would be fraudulent transfers and, still more often, fraudulent papers guaranteeing enemy property as that of Americans. The British Government received frequent information of such frauds both from Hammond and from the consuls general,[44] and this had its effect on the character of the Orders in Council from time to time issued.[45]

The British Government, in short, had good reason to believe that, owing to the almost unrestricted opening of the French colonies to American trade, an elaborate system had been devised under which French commerce was being carried on under the "fraudulent cover" of the American flag and, incidentally, France provided with those supplies of which it was at that time imperative to deprive her. In the course of the summer of 1793 information reached the British Government which, from the British point of view, pointed to the necessity of still more drastic measures. The monstrous folly of the French National Assembly in extending the full benefit of the principles of equality and the rights of man to the slaves in the French colonies had led to the terrible insurrection

[44] "A ship called the 'Hannibal'—Captain McEvers—is now about to sail from this port. She is entirely under the direction of a French merchant residing here, and is supposed to have the greater part of the cargo of the French East Indiaman, the Argonaut, now in Delaware, on board. This valuable property, no doubt, belongs to the subjects of France; though every device will be tried to give it the appearance of American property. . . . She will, it is presumed, clear for Amsterdam, but may probably make for the first port in France that there is a prospect of her reaching in safety."—Phineas Bond to Grenville, Philadelphia, 11 August 1793. P.R.O. F.O. 5. 2.

[45] "I am glad to be able to assure, from your Lordship's dispatch, that it is not the intention of His Majesty's Government to impose unnecessary restraints on American commerce, nor indeed any others than those which the extent of the frauds practised by the American merchants in covering French property and the actual state and objects of the commerce between the French West Indian Islands and the United States have rendered indispensable."—Hammond to Grenville, No. 13, 15 April 1794. P.R.O. F.O. 5. 4.

"I have received information that many of the vessels from New York, this port, and Baltimore clear out for Falmouth, though they are actually bound for France. Exclusive however of the American ships, there are several British prizes, of which the property has never been legally transferred, and of which the cargo must be on account of the French Government."—Hammond to Sir John Temple, Philadelphia, 18 June 1794. P.R.O. F.O. 5. 5. In a subsequent dispatch to Lord Grenville (dated Philadelphia, 27 June 1794. P.R.O. F.O. 5. 5) Hammond enclosed a list of twelve vessels from Philadelphia and eight from Baltimore bound for France with cargoes of flour and other provisions. . . . Of these two were French, one a Spanish prize (the brig "Mursiano"), and seven British prizes (the ships "Flora," "Jane," "Isis," "Roehampton" and "Peacock," and the brigs "Lovely Lass" and "Prince William Henry").

of the negroes and mulattoes in San Domingo (Haiti); the whites had either been massacred or had fled, and—what was of more immediate importance—vast stores of produce, hurried down from the interior during the first alarms, had accumulated at the ports.[46] This promised a rich harvest to American speculators, who had the prospect of buying in a very cheap market and selling in France, where prices were abnormally high. They proceeded to take full advantage of the situation.[47]

It was to meet this situation that the Order in Council of 6 November 1793 was issued. Under this Order it was an instruction to commanders of ships of war and privateers "that they shall stop and detain all ships laden with goods the produce of any colony belonging to France, or carrying provisions or other supplies for the use of any such colony, and shall bring the same, with their cargoes, to legal adjudication in our Courts of Admiralty." These instructions, it seems, though issued at once to the naval commanders, were not made public till the following 23 December and not communicated to the American Minister in London until the 25th. Nor had Hammond been notified of them, or the notification had never reached him; for on 12 March 1794, he wrote to Grenville:

Packets from the West Indies announce that additional instructions have been issued (dated the 6th of November last) to take all vessels that may be either bound to the French West Indies, or that may be laden with the produce of those islands. This is regarded as peculiarly hostile to the United States and as directed against that species of commercial intercourse which at this crisis is most beneficial to their citizens as employing more than one half of their whole navigation, and consequently this city has been in a state of fermentation.

He added as further evidence of the bitter feeling in the United States, that James Madison was proposing the raising of a military force and measures "to distress the British West Indies." [48]

The state of fermentation is indeed easy to understand; for the Caribbean Sea was crowded with American vessels engaged in this trade, and upon these, without warning, the British cruisers and

[46] Grenville to Hammond, 11 Jan. 1794. P.R.O. F.O. 5. 4. Thomas Pinckney in a letter of 9 January 1794, to the Secretary of State, enclosing the new Order in Council of 8 January, reports Grenville as saying that the Order of 6 November was "intended to be temporary" and was due partly to the projected British operations against the French West Indies. A.S.P., F.R., I, 430.

[47] ". . . neutral merchants immediately rushed in, to reap the offered harvest." —Stephen, *War in Disguise* (2d ed., 1805), pp. 19 f.

[48] Hammond to Grenville, No. 7, Philadelphia, 12 March 1794. P.R.O. F.O. 5. 4.

privateers had fallen with all the zeal inspired by patriotism and the desire for prize money. The captured ships were numbered by hundreds. On 7 March Fulwar Skipwith, the American consul at St. Eustasia,[49] reported to the Secretary of State that the whole of the 220 vessels mentioned in a previous letter, together with 30 others, had been libeled in the different ports immediately on arrival, but that only those in Dominique (San Domingo), Antigua, Montserat and St. Kitt's had been so far condemned—150 in all. He added that it was the intention to stop all neutral trade with France and that "French goods will contaminate any vessel in which they are found." [50] The deep sense of grievance thus created was increased by the difficulty, if not the impossibility, of obtaining justice for the owners of the ships and cargoes thus impounded; for the vice-admiralty courts were "badly constituted," too often careless in the sifting of evidence, and usually prejudiced in favor of the captors; and, though there was a right of appeal to the courts in England, this involved delays and expenses which in many cases were prohibitive.[51] Moreover, the seizures in this case were ostensibly made under the Rule of the War of 1756, which was not generally recognized, and which, in any case, would have applied only partially to the American trade with the French islands, since this trade had been permitted before the war in vessels of sixty tons burden and

[49] He soon afterwards went, as James Monroe's secretary, to Paris where he was appointed consul general.

[50] A.S.P., F.R., I, 429.

[51] "The Vice-Admiralty Courts regarded the illegality of the trade as infallible grounds of decision and were therefore grossly remiss in taking and preserving the evidence in point of property."—Stephen, *op. cit.*, p. 22.

That the judgments of the vice-admiralty courts continued to be a legitimate source of grievance is shown by the following extracts from a letter of Thomas Barclay, the British consul general in New York, to Lord Grenville: "There are few if any of the captures in Europe, or decrees of the Courts of Admiralty in Great Britain, that are considered other than fair and equitable by the Americans; and I have never heard the Courts in England spoken of, but in terms of the greatest respect. But the cry is universal from one end of the Continent to the other, that the cruizers on these coasts and in the West Indies send every American vessel they meet into of His Majesty's ports for adjudication, and the judges of the provincial Courts of Vice-Admiralty generally condemn in cases where a decree of acquittal would be pronounced in England. To appeal, they remark, is nearly allied in its consequences to a total loss, and that it is not worth the pursuit, save in cases of immense property. . . . I am satisfied that the American merchants are in the habit of covering enemies property, and that articles contraband of war are frequently exported from these States; but I am equally certain that bona fide American Property is too often condemned in the provincial Courts of Vice-Admiralty."—N. Y. 12 March 1801. P.R.O. F.O. 5. 33.

upwards laden with certain specified articles of American origin (*arrêt* of 30 August 1784).[52]

Two months before Hammond received news of the instructions of 6 November, Lord Grenville had written to him to announce their revocation and the issue of a new Order in Council—that of 8 January 1794. The two dispatches, both dated 11 January 1794, in which Lord Grenville explains and defends the action of the Government have a special interest. In the one the writer expounds the principle of the Rule of 1756 and its particular application to the American trade with the West Indies:

A war between two nations ought, as little as possible, to prejudice the usual and accustomed commerce of a third not engaged in the quarrel. But the latter ought not, on the other hand, to desire or claim from the war new rights or pretensions, to the prejudice of either belligerent party. For this reason, when France, who monopolized in time of peace the exclusive commerce and supply of her West India Islands, attempted in time of war to open those branches of trade to neutral nations, in order to elude the naval superiority of Great Britain, the Government of this country has always resisted that measure, and has considered the neutral vessels attempting to engage in this commerce as not entitled to carry it on.

But, by the system established since the Peace of 1783, France has permitted a limited intercourse between her colonies and America, and that even in American vessels. But the articles both of importation and exportation, which this intercourse comprized, were confined; and particularly the two great articles of sugar on the one side and flour on the other were excepted from it.

In the other dispatch of the same date, in which he enclosed copies of the Instructions of 6 November and 8 January, Grenville proceeded to explain and justify the earlier Order in Council as a measure intended to meet a temporary emergency:

It is possible that, with respect to the former of these orders, a considerable degree of dissatisfaction may have arisen in America. If . . . you will confine yourself to observing that this order no longer subsists—that it was occasioned by temporary circumstances, and particularly by the notoriety that, by the extraordinary events which had taken place at St. Domingo, a large and unusual quantity of French property, the produce of that island, and destined for the European markets, had been brought to America, and that it was also known here, upon indisputable evidence, that attempts would be made to bring those goods, under those circumstances, home to Europe in American vessels. In this situation, none of the principles by which the ordinary intercourse of trade is or ought to be regulated could

---

[52] The decree of 26 March 1793 extended this privilege to smaller vessels and added flour and provisions to the articles which might be imported.

apply; and the measure of bringing in articles so circumstanced for adjudication was grounded on a just and reasonable presumption, strengthened by the knowledge that the bringing West India produce to the European market from America was a speculation, wholly out of the course of the usual trade of the latter country.

He concluded by stating that the Order of 6 November had been revoked and that new instructions had been issued "regulating the situation in which the commerce of America, in this respect, shall be allowed to stand." [53]

The Order in Council of 8 January 1794 to which Lord Grenville referred, after revoking that of 6 November directed the commanders of His Majesty's ships of war and of privateers to bring in for lawful adjudication (1) all vessels with their cargoes laden with goods the produce of the French West India islands, and coming directly from any port of the said islands to any port in Europe, (2) all ships with their cargoes laden with goods the produce of the said islands, the property of which shall belong to the subjects of France, to whatsoever port the same may be bound, (3) all ships attempting to enter any port of the said islands blockaded by His Majesty's arms, and (4) all vessels laden, wholly or in part, with naval and military stores bound for any port of the said islands.[54]

This Order, which remained in force until 25 January 1798, gave an immense impetus to American trade, since the direct voyage could be easily evaded by breaking it at some convenient American port, it being tacitly admitted that the landing of the cargo and payment of duties at such a port fulfilled the conditions of a circuitous voyage.[55] Denmark and Sweden, the only other neutral maritime States, were also benefited, since their West Indian col-

[53] Grenville to Hammond, 11 January 1794. P.R.O. F.O. 5. 4.

[54] P.R.O. Ad. 2. 125, pp. 282-284.

[55] The case of the "Polly" [2 C. Rob., p. 362] was the first in which the question of continuous colonial voyages came up for decision. Sir William Scott said that he was "strongly disposed to hold that it would be sufficient that the goods should be landed and the duties paid."

Stephen (*War in Disguise* (2d ed., 1805), p. 226, Appendix C) quotes the King's advocate as saying: "Perhaps the mere touching in the neutral country to take fresh clearances, may properly be considered as a fraudulent evasion, and is in effect the direct trade; but the high court of admiralty has expressly decided . . . that the landing the goods, and paying the duties in the neutral country, breaks the continuity of the voyage, and is such an importation as legalizes the trade, although the goods be re-shipped in the same vessel, and on account of the same neutral proprietors, and be forwarded for sale to the mother country or the colony."

onies could now serve as entrepôts.[56] It was, however, some weeks before the new Order could be brought to the attention of the United States Government, and meanwhile the situation created by the instructions of 6 November, on the one hand, and the counter measures of the French Republic on the other, threatened a serious crisis in the relations of the neutral nations, and more especially of the United States, with the belligerent powers, and more particularly with Great Britain.

FRANCE AND THE UNITED STATES

Jefferson's letter demanding the recall of Citizen Genêt was dispatched in August 1793, but it was not till early in the following year that the new French envoy, Fauchet, entered on his duties at Philadelphia. Meanwhile, the situation created by Genêt's activities was one of extreme embarrassment to the American Government. The assumption underlying them was, that the United States were bound by the terms of the treaty of defensive alliance signed by them with France in 1778 to give active assistance to the French Republic in its struggle with Great Britain, or at least, failing an immediate armed intervention, to insist on the principle of "free ships, free goods" consecrated by the treaty, and to carry out certain engagements contracted under it, namely, those committing the United States to a guarantee of the French West Indian possessions and to the granting of special privileges in American ports to French ships of war and privateers.[57] The French Government, while dis-

[56] Stephen, op. cit., p. 39.

[57] Art. XI of the Treaty of Defensive Alliance between the King of France and the United Provinces of America, signed at Paris on 6 February 1778, ran as follows: The two parties mutually guarantee each other from the present time and for ever; to wit, the United States to His Most Christian Majesty the present possessions of the Crown of France in America, as well as those which it shall be able to acquire . . . and His Most Christian Majesty guarantees . . . to the United States their soverainty, liberty and independence &c.—2 Hunter Miller, *Treaties and Other International Acts of the United States of America*, II, 3.

The Treaty of Commerce and Amity between France and the United States of America, signed in Paris on the 5 February 1778, contained the following articles:

Art. XVII. The vessels of war of His Most Christian Majesty and those of the United States as well as those which their subjects shall have fitted out for war, shall have every liberty to conduct, as shall seem best to them, the prizes which they shall have taken from the enemy, without being subject to any rights, whether of the admirals or of the admiralty or of any others whatsoever, also without the said vessels or the said prizes, entering into the harbours or ports of His Most Christian Majesty or of the United States, being subject to arrest or seizure, nor that the officers of the places shall have power to take cognizance

approving of the very undiplomatic conduct of Genêt, continued to assume the binding force of the treaty, and the exception of the United States from the decree of 9 May had been intended to prove its own meticulous fidelity to the engagements of 1778. Then the news reached Paris of the President's proclamation of neutrality (22 April 1793), and generally of the refusal of the American Government, in view of the fact that France had been the first to declare war, to implement those articles of the treaty which involved the active participation of the United States in the war on the side of France. The attempt to appeal to the American people over the heads of the American Government had failed; but the men now in power in France did not give up hope of converting the American Government itself to their views by a policy of mingled coercion and cajolery.

One of the first acts of the great Committee of Public Safety, established on 10 July 1793, was to reënact the decree of 9 May, under which no exception was made in favor of American vessels (decree of 17 July). Further unsatisfactory advices from the United States, culminating in the demand for Genêt's recall, led to further measures, intended at once to damage the British and to bring pressure to bear on the Americans: the Navigation Act of 21 September, and the decrees of 9 and 18 October. The first of these has already been referred to. The decree of 9 October (18 Vendémiaire, An II.) reënacted that of 1 March, with additional and alarming penalties for its infraction. All goods manufactured in countries subject to the British Crown were to be excluded from French territory, and everyone having such goods in his possession was to declare them. Any Customs official admitting such goods was to be sentenced to twenty years' imprisonment in irons, and the same punishment was to be inflicted on those who imported, sold or bought them, while those who wore or used them were to be "sus-

---

of the validity of the said prizes, which shall be free to leave and to sail unhindered and at complete liberty for the places stated in their commissions, which the captains of the said vessels shall be under the obligation of making known: and on the other hand there shall not be given retreat or asylum in their harbours and ports to those who shall have taken prizes from the subjects of His Majesty or of the said United States; and if they are forced to enter them by storms or peril of the sea, they shall be made to leave as soon as possible.

Art. XXII. No corsaire of a Power at war with either party is to be allowed to arm, or to sell prizes, in the harbours and ports of the other. . . .—2 Hunter Miller, *Treaties and Other International Acts of the United States of America,* II, 601.

pect." [58] Another decree, issued on 18 October, ordered that foreign vessels entering French ports were henceforth to pay dues ten times higher than those payable by French vessels.[59]

The primary objects of these measures were, doubtless, as Professor Heckscher suggests, conceived in the true mercantilist spirit and intended at once to ruin "the nation of shopkeepers" and to stimulate the production and consumption of native products.[60] They also provided, however, what may well have seemed an effective weapon for the coercion of the United States. Already, at the beginning of the war, an embargo had been laid upon American shipping in French ports, without reason given; [61] a fresh embargo was now laid on American vessels, pending adjudication under the new decrees, as many as 103 being reported as thus detained in the harbor of Bordeaux alone by the month of December.[62] The constitution and character of the French prize courts, moreover, were a crying scandal of which the Americans and other neutrals had every right to complain. By decree of the Convention, issued on 14 February 1793, all prizes were to be adjudicated on by the tribunals of commerce of the places to which they were taken or, if no such tribunal existed, by the ordinary court of the district, to whom also an appeal was to lie from the tribunals of commerce, the *juges de paix* being thus charged "provisionally" with the functions formerly exercised by the admiralty courts.[63] Since the tribunals of commerce were often composed of the merchants who owned the privateers which brought in the prizes, and the elected *juges de paix* were not necessarily even lawyers, it is easy to imagine the sort of justice meted out by them.[64] It was not till 8 November

[58] That is, liable to arrest under the terrible Law of the Suspects; Heckscher, *The Continental System* (1922), p. 26.

[59] *Ibid.*, p. 28.   [60] *Ibid.*, p. 28.   [61] Mahan, II, 246.

[62] A list of these vessels, and of others having claims against the French Government, is given in "A Statement of claims of citizens of the United States upon the French republic, presented by Mr. Skipwith, Consul-General of the United States at Paris, and also of his proceedings and remarks upon them," dated 20 November 1795.—A.S.P., F.R., I, 735-757. The Bordeaux list is on pp. 757-758.

[63] 5 Martens, p. 379.

[64] The Danish Government complained that, though their grievances were often heard in France, there was no means of getting them redressed. The municipalities, to whom application had to be made, were certainly not all alike equitable; the sentences of the tribunals of commerce were not founded upon uniform principles; the extreme means of refuge to the medium of power (a supreme court of appeal?) was totally removed; with the result that there were grievous acts of injustice. Counter Declaration of the Court of Denmark to Mr. Hailes's Memorial.— *Annual Register*, 1793, p. 181.

that the decree of 14 February was revoked by another (of 18 Brumaire, An II) which laid down that all questions as to the validity or invalidity of prizes brought in were to be determined administratively (*par voie d'administration*) by the provisional Executive Council.[65] The peculiar delays and other hardships to which this gave rise will be described in Part Two of this volume.

In these circumstances the task of Citizen Fauchet, who landed in the United States in February 1794, was no easy one, in spite of Secretary Randolph's obvious desire to "tighten the bonds" that united the two Republics.[66] Apart from other questions with which we are not here concerned, he was instructed to demand the execution of the treaties with France and, more particularly, of the articles of the treaty of commerce of 1778 concerning the admission to American ports of the prizes made by French privateers and the exclusion of those made by the privateers of their enemies. The time was past, however, for such representations to have any effect. As early as 4 August 1793, the United States Government had issued a list of the principles of international law governing neutral rights and obligations, in which the limits of the rights conceded to French privateers in American ports under the treaty of 1778 were clearly defined,[67] and in his proclamation of 3 December President Washington made the attitude of his Government in this matter perfectly plain.[68] The obligation to admit French prizes and to exclude those of the enemies of France was admitted; but nothing in the treaty committed the United States to allow the fitting out of French privateers in those ports. The President, therefore, admitted the obligation of his Government to prevent any such infractions of neutrality for the future, and to give compensation for any losses suffered in consequence.[69] In addition, shortly before

---

[65] 5 Martens, p. 384.

[66] For a succinct account of Fauchet's mission see Anderson, *Edmund Randolph*, II, 105 ff.

[67] See Bemis, *Thomas Jefferson*, II, 296. For the instructions sent in consequence to the Collectors of the Customs see A.S.P., F.R., I, 37.

[68] A.S.P., F.R., I, 21, 140.

[69] In a letter, dated 5 September 1793, to the British Minister, George Hammond, Secretary Jefferson had stated the principles on which the President intended to act in this matter. Measures were to be taken "for excluding from further asylum in our ports of vessels armed in them to cruise on nations with which we are at peace," and the British ships seized by such vessels were to be restored. In the event of the failure of such measures of restitution, the President would accept the obligation on the part of the United States to make compensation for the ves-

Fauchet presented his credentials, the Federal Supreme Court ruled that the French consular tribunals established in the United States for the condemnation of prizes were illegal, and that the American courts of admiralty were competent to take cognizance of the validity of captures asserted to have been made within the jurisdiction of the United States.[70]

Although, however, the desire of the Government of the United States to observe all the laws of neutrality had thus been made clear, the depredations by French privateers issuing from American ports continued, since there was no law under which proceedings against violators of neutrality could be taken in the courts until Congress passed the Neutrality Act on 5 June 1794.[71]

The spoliations committed by these vessels were, indeed, at this time more damaging to the trade of the United States than to that of Great Britain; for, apart from the fact that American ships were becoming increasingly the carriers of British goods, the commerce at least of the South was still conducted principally with England, and this commerce was now being seriously interrupted.[72] Even Randolph, prejudiced as he was in favor of the French Republic, could no longer disguise from himself that from the American point of view there was little to choose between the British and the French in the matter of the violation of neutral rights. On

---

sels. The President contemplated restitution or compensation in the cases before 7 August, and, after that date, restitution or compensation in similar cases, "if it can be effected by any means in our power." This letter, which was quoted in Article VII of Jay's Treaty as establishing the principle on which the British claims were based, is printed in full in 4 Moore, pp. 6 ff.

[70] Judgment in the case of the sloop "Betsey," 8 February 1794. A.S.P., F.R., I, 590. Hammond in a report home described this decision as "of considerable importance at the present conjuncture." To Grenville, No. 2, 22 February 1794. P.R.O. F.O. 5. 4.

[71] Thus, three days before the passing of the Act, Randolph wrote to Hammond in reply to a complaint of depredations of the French Privateers "Le Petit Democrate" and "Le Carmagnole" from Charleston, undertaking to ascertain their "precise state."—A.S.P., F.R., I, 464.

[72] "The commerce of these Southern States is nearly ruined by the piracies of these vessels."—Richard Henry Lee, 11 December 1793. Ballagh, Life and Letters of Richard Henry Lee, II, 562 f. On 28 September 1793, Consul John Hamilton reported to Lord Grenville "a great decrease of trade into this state since January last, both as to numbers of vessels, tonnage and men . . . in great measure due to the activities of French privateers which have infested the coast since April last." He protested against the advantage given to France by allowing her prizes, and not those of Britain, to be brought in. On 1 October he again reported that the fitting out of privateers was still connived at, in spite of the President's proclamation.— P.R.O. F.O. 5. 2.

5 March the President transmitted to Congress a report of the Secretary of State on the vexations and spoliations suffered by the commerce of the United States since the commencement of the European war. The documents, it stated, gave evidence of attacks on American commerce by the British, the French, the Spaniards and the Dutch. After a strongly worded indictment of the activities of the British cruisers and privateers, which will be dealt with elsewhere, he presented the grievances of the United States against France. French privateers, he said, had harassed American trade no less than the British; their ships of war had "committed enormities" on American vessels; their courts of admiralty were as oppressive as those of England; they had infringed the treaty with the United States by seizing American vessels trading with the enemy in merchandise declared by the treaty not to be contraband; and last, but not least, they had laid a very detrimental embargo upon large numbers of American vessels in French ports.[73]

Fauchet did his best to meet these charges. In a letter to the Secretary of State (dated 7 Germinal, An II) he pointed out that for some time past privateers had ceased to issue from French ports and that merchants who might have received injury from such could with confidence apply to the French Government for redress. In any case, it was not the fault of the French if commercial property, even that of the enemy, had not been respected amid the horrors of war. As for cases of oppression in the courts of admiralty, the possibility of these had been removed by the decree of 8 November giving the Executive Council the power of judging the validity or invalidity of prizes. As for the treating of provisions as contraband, contrary to the treaty of 1778, the horrible system of violating the law of nations in order to starve a people which could not be conquered by force of arms was not invented by France, and it would be as unjust as barbarous to require that France should allow provisions to pass to her enemies, while those destined for her were taken by them. With regard to the "detrimental embargo," it was the intention of the Committee of Public Safety to indemnify all the owners and captains who had been compelled by its operation to remain any length of time in France. The propositions to be made, he added, would be found to be advantageous to both nations.[74]

[73] See *supra*, p. 50.

[74] Randolph's Report was enclosed in Hammond to Grenville, No. 6, 10 March 1794, and Fauchet's letter in No. 12. P.R.O. F.O. 5. 4. The letter is printed in A.S.P., F.R., I, 431.

In the midst of these somewhat heated controversies a message of fraternal greeting reached Philadelphia from "the representatives of the French people, members of the Committee of Public Safety, to the citizens, members of the Congress of the United States of America." This document, which was dated 22 Pluviôse, An II (16 February 1794) and signed by all the members of the Committee, including Robespierre, after vaunting the victories of the Republic over "tyrants" everywhere, called on the Americans to draw closer the bonds which ought to unite them with their French brethren, in order to secure "that harmony which has not the cautious, selfish, mercantile policy for its principle, but the esteem, the fraternity, and all the social and beneficent virtues that flow from liberty." [75]

This effusion was hardly calculated to appeal to shrewd business men keenly conscious of the loss of expected profits. It may, however, have had its influence on the choice of the envoy whom the Government decided to send to Paris to supersede Gouverneur Morris, whose aristocratic leanings had made him a *persona non grata* to the men of the Terror, and to lay the grievances of the American nation before the French government. The choice fell upon James Monroe, a rough Virginian who shared his compatriot Jefferson's hatred of England and admiration for republican France. He received his commission on 24 May. "You will show your confidence in the French Republic," said Randolph in his instructions," without betraying the most remote remark of undue complaisance. You will let it be seen that in case of war with any nation on earth, we shall consider France as our first and natural ally." As a reply to the fraternal greeting which had been dispatched, the sending of such an envoy was naturally highly gratifying to the French. It was unfortunate that those who had signed the greeting had meanwhile fallen from power and some of them, including Robespierre, perished on the scaffold. But the new Government welcomed Monroe, literally, with open arms. On 15 August he was received at a formal session of the Convention, where he was embraced and kissed by Merlin of Douai, the president. His speech, delivered in the "American" tongue, was "a cordial declaration in the name of America in favor of France and the French Revolution." President Washington was naturally shocked when he heard of this theatrical performance, and he directed Randolph to send a rebuke. It was the first of several.

[75] A.S.P., F.R., I, 447.

III

JAY'S TREATY

The Mission of John Jay to Great Britain

If in the spring of 1794 relations of the United States with France were strained, those with Great Britain were still more so. On 5 March the President transmitted to Congress a report of the Secretary of State on British spoliations, based on numerous complaints received by the State Department. It was urged against the British, he said, that their privateers plundered American vessels, threw them out of their course by forcing them, on groundless suspicion, into ports other than those to which they were bound and continued to detain them after the hope of a regular condemnation had been abandoned. Further, that by their negligence while they held possession they exposed the cargoes to damage and the vessels to destruction, the crews also being maltreated. After mentioning the grievance of impressment, the report went on to enumerate the alleged violations of international law of which the British were accused:

By the British regulations and practice our corn and provisions are driven from the ports of France, and restricted to the ports of the British and their friends; our vessels are not allowed to clear from a British port without giving security that the cargo will be discharged in another British port; our vessels are captured for trading with the West Indies, of which extraordinary conduct no other excuse is alleged than that by some edict of a King of France this intercourse was forbidden.[1]

With the dispatch to Lord Grenville in which Randolph's report was enclosed [2] Hammond also forwarded a "Complaint of the Committee at Philadelphia," which contained yet further charges. It was the custom of many of the privateers of the belligerent powers, this ran, to send into port any American vessel bound from any port in the French West Indies to the United States. Many of these vessels had been released, but the loss by plunder, detention and incidental

---

[1] Report on the spoliations and vexations on American commerce, etc. Dated 2 March, and presented to Congress on 5 March.—A.S.P., F.R., I, 423.

[2] No. 6, 10 March 1794. P.R.O. F.O. 5. 4.

expenses had been great. In many cases, where the cargo had been valuable, the owners of privateers, after acquittal, had lodged appeals, which they never intended to prosecute, in order to get the property into their hands at an unfair valuation. There was, moreover, barefaced bribery, in order to induce seamen to give evidence in favor of the captors. As the result of all this "the commerce of the United States already begins to languish, and its products are likely to be left on the hands of those who raise them." [3]

It was in this unfavorable atmosphere that the argument as to the respective rights of neutrals and belligerents continued between Hammond and the Secretary of State. There is no need to recapitulate the arguments here; they followed the lines already indicated. The danger, as Hammond clearly perceived, was that the war of words would speedily become a war in arms. Two days after the presentation of Randolph's report news reached Philadelphia of the Order in Council of 6 November and the resultant wholesale captures of American vessels. Public excitement rose to fever heat, and there was a clamor for war. The President and his advisers were, however, determined to try all other measures before resorting to so hazardous an expedient as war, which no one in responsible quarters desired. On the 26th President Washington communicated to Congress Consul Skipwith's detailed account of the British seizures in the Caribbean, and on the same day the Senate agreed to a resolution, already passed in the House of Representatives, laying an embargo for thirty days on all vessels in United States harbors bound for foreign ports.[4]

The embargo was ostensibly directed against all the belligerent

[3] The Committee complained also of "irruptions of the Algerines from the Mediterranean in consequence of a truce concluded, it is said, by the British Minister, on behalf of Portugal and Holland." In a message to Congress, on the previous 16 December, the President had announced the arrangement of a truce, arranged by Great Britain, between Portugal and the Dey of Algiers, of which the incidental consequence was to let loose a swarm of pirates to prey on American merchant vessels venturing through the Straits of Gibraltar. The object of Great Britain in promoting this pact was to free her ally from the harassments which hampered her co-operation in the war with France; but "it was not strange that members of Congress, already in no pleasant mood, should consider only the result and not the purpose of such diplomacy." See Bemis, *Jay's Treaty* (1923), p. 186. In a conversation with the American Minister, Lord Grenville explained the affair as above, saying that Great Britain had "not the least intention of injuring the Americans." —Thomas Pinckney to the Secretary of State, 25 November 1793. A.S.P., F.R., I, 327.

[4] A.S.P., F.R., I, 428 f.

powers; but, as Randolph explained in his instructions to Monroe, it was really directed against England, and had been made general "merely because, if it had been partial against her, it would have amounted to a cause of war." [5] It was passed, as Hammond reported home, in the expectation "that a sudden and unforeseen suspension of the supply of provisions from this country would create a considerable degree of distress and embarrassment in His Majesty's settlements in the West Indies." [6] The temper of Congress was, indeed, such as to point to imminent danger of war. Resolutions had been passed in the Committee of the Whole for a large increase in the Federal army, and for the sequestration of all debts owed to British creditors, as compensation to American citizens for losses owing to the violations of international law by British commanders.[7] Moreover, while the embargo was strictly enforced against the British, it was so little enforced against the French that a large fleet of provision ships was allowed to leave Hampton Roads for France under French convoy.[8] Finally, on 25 April, in spite of the fact that news had been received of the Order in Council of 8 January revoking that of 6 November, the House of Representatives passed a Non-Intercourse Bill, which prohibited the importation of any British or Irish produce pending the settlement of outstanding disputes, and this was only thrown out in the Senate by the casting vote of Vice President Adams. On the same day, however, the embargo was extended for another month by joint resolution of the two Houses, and by the Act of 4 June it was further provided that it was to con-

[5] Anderson, *Edmund Randolph,* II, 126.
[6] Hammond to Grenville, No. 8, 28 March 1794. P.R.O. F.O. 5. 4.
[7] Bemis, *Jay's Treaty* (1923), p. 195.
[8] "It is a fact of universal notoriety, that the whole of the convoy under Rear-Admiral Vanstabel amounting to about one hundred and fifty-six vessels (including ships of war and merchant ships) did sail from Hampton Roads on the 17th of April, although the imposition of the embargo had been known there for more than a fortnight antecedently to that date and had been rigidly enforced with respect to all other merchant ships whatsoever. . . . On the 7th of April Admiral Vanstabel had ordered Mr. Cooper to seize the American brig Venus, laden with flour, on account of the French Government and detained in Norfolk harbour on account of the embargo. This he did on the 8th, and delivered the brig to the Admiral. Mr. Wilson, lieutenant-colonel commanding Norfolk County, whose duty it was to guard the law, had on the 5th given his official sanction to the propriety of the Venus joining the French fleet."—Hammond to Randolph, 7 June 1794. Enclosed in Hammond to Grenville, No. 26, 9 June 1794. P.R.O. F.O. 5. 5. This was the great corn convoy which reached Brest safely, in spite of Howe's victory of the 1st of June.

tinue in force till fifteen days after the commencement of the next
session of Congress, while the President was authorized to lay a similar embargo whenever public safety demanded it.[9]

Meanwhile, however, the moderate counsels of the Federalists had
prevailed with President Washington, and it had been decided to
send John Jay, the Chief Justice, to England in order, if possible,
to arrive at some mutual understanding on the various questions at
issue between the two countries. No further action was taken pending the outcome of this mission.[10]

Jay sailed for England on 12 May, and landed there on 12 June.
The mission came as a surprise to the British Government, which
had been totally uninformed as to what was happening in the United
States. Nothing, indeed, could better illustrate the inconveniences
and complications caused by the slowness and uncertainty of communications than this fact. Between December 1793 and June 1794
only one dispatch had reached Grenville from Hammond, and this,
which had been sent off on 22 February, took more than two months
in reaching England. The numerous dispatches written by Hammond between February and May arrived in a batch, together with
the correspondence of the Canadian governors, on 10 June, only two
days before Jay landed. As for the embargo, news of this had only
reached Grenville through an American newspaper by way of Amsterdam, and he was quite ignorant of the circumstances in which
it had been passed.[11] Nor, it seems, had he received any information
as to the way in which the instructions of 6 November had been carried out, or any complaints with regard to the decisions of the vice-
admiralty courts.[12] The sudden revelation of the untoward effects of

[9] I *Statutes at Large*, 372.

[10] Hammond, who had been obviously upset by the news of the Order in Council of 6 November and its results, was also obviously relieved by Grenville's explanations and assurances. "I am glad to be able to assure, from your Lordship's
dispatches," he wrote on 15 April, "that it is not the intention of his Majesty's
Government to impose unnecessary restraints on American commerce, nor indeed
any others than those which the extent of the frauds practised by the American
merchants in covering French property and the actual state of the commerce between the French West India Islands and the United States have rendered indispensable."—To Grenville, No. 13. P.R.O. F.O. 5. 4.

[11] Bemis, *op. cit.*, p. 218.

[12] The first information seems to have been the copy of an affidavit of forty
American sea captains captured at Martinique, which reached the Foreign Office
on 12 June. *Ibid.*, p. 235, n. 9. On 6 July Jay wrote to Randolph that he had been
surprised to hear from Lord Grenville that "not a single case, under the instructions of November, had been laid before him." On applying to Pinckney, he had

the instructions came, therefore, as an unpleasant surprise to the Foreign Secretary, who had clearly been under the impression that nothing had been done which could seriously interfere with the legitimate commerce of neutral nations. It came also at a singularly inopportune moment, from his point of view; for the alliance against France was showing the first signs of disruption, and he had enough to do to keep it together, without being troubled with what, after all, was a subordinate question, though an important one. The news of Jay's arrival must, therefore, have been welcome, as giving a better opportunity for clearing a troublesome and dangerous business out of the way than any offered by negotiations through the ordinary channels.

There is no reason to suppose that the cordial reception given to the American envoy by the British Government and in English society was dictated solely, or even mainly, by the desire to cajole him into a mood of concession.[13] John Jay's reputation had preceded him; he was known as an eminent lawyer, a man of wide culture and, above all, for his friendly sentiments toward England. In no responsible quarters in the country was there a desire for a serious quarrel, let alone a war, with the United States, which were still England's best customer and with which English people were still closely connected by social and family ties. The settlement ultimately arrived at was a compromise; and though it was widely and loudly denounced in the United States as a surrender, it was probably in all the circumstances the only possible settlement.

Jay's instructions embraced a wide variety of questions in dispute between the two countries, including the nonfulfillment on either side of certain engagements under the terms of the treaty of 1783, reciprocity of navigation to the West Indies and between the ports of the United States and Great Britain, and so on. We are concerned

---

learned that no such cases had been transmitted from America. "Mr. Crofts, a gentleman from Boston, has furnished me with the case of the Charlotte, decided in Antigua, and from which decisions an appeal was made. It unfortunately happens, that this is not among the strongest of those cases. . . ." He added that the "Charlotte," which was loaded with French produce bought by Americans in San Domingo, and bound for France, had been condemned under the Rule of 1756.—A.S.P., F.R., I, 476.

[13] "So many agreeable amenities were generally put in his way that he refrained from mentioning them in his official correspondence for fear that a false interpretation might be put upon them by the anti-British party at home."—Bemis, *op. cit.*, p. 233.

here, however, only with those arising out of the British Orders in Council and their execution. In this matter the instructions naturally put forward the American case in an uncompromising form. The principle of "free ships, free goods" was to be asserted, and proper security for neutral commerce in other respects was to be given, particularly (1) by declaring provisions never to be contraband, except in the strongest case, as in the blockade of a port; or, if attainable, by abolishing contraband altogether, (2) by defining a blockade as it was defined in the Treaty of Armed Neutrality of 1780, (3) by restricting the opportunities of vexation in visiting vessels and (4) by bringing privateers under stricter management and expediting recoveries against them for misconduct.

Thus far the instructions had been drawn up by Randolph after consultation with the rest of the Cabinet. An important addition was, however, made by the Secretary of State without any such consultation. "You will have no difficulty," he wrote, "in gaining access to the ministers of Russia, Denmark and Sweden. . . . The principles of the Armed Neutrality would abundantly cover our neutral rights, and if an entire view of all our political relations shall, in your judgment, permit the step, you will sound those ministers upon the probability of an alliance with their nations to support those principles." On the other hand, Jay was empowered to discuss the sale of prizes in American ports while the United States were neutral, though no stipulations were to interfere with the obligations of the United States to France.[14]

Although his instructions were thus sufficiently uncompromising, Jay was well aware that the Federalist majority in the American Cabinet, of whom Alexander Hamilton was the chief spokesman, were prepared to compromise in the interests of peace. Randolph's proposal to approach the northern powers with a view to an alliance was none of their doing, and was indeed inspired by a complete misunderstanding of the situation.[15] As for the vexed question of contraband, if it proved impossible to secure the acceptance of the American definition, it might be qualified, either by accepting the principle that provisions might be preëmpted, by acquiescing in the Rule of 1756, or by admitting the legality of the Order in Council of 8 June.[16] It was generally agreed, however, that the demand

[14] Instructions to Mr. Jay, Philadelphia, 6 May 1794. A.S.P., F.R., I, 472 ff.
[15] See *infra,* chap. iv, p. 94.
[16] Bemis, *op. cit.,* p. 211.

for compensation for the injuries sustained and the vessels captured under the Order in Council of 6 November was to be "strenuously pressed."

Accordingly, Jay made no protest against the seizure under the Rule of 1756 of the American ship "Charlotte," which was carrying a cargo direct from the French West Indies to France, but waited for exact information as to spoliations under the Order of 6 November. This was provided by the petition of the forty sea captains mentioned above, which he now submitted to Grenville with a request that justice might be done. Grenville met him in an accommodating spirit. The proposal, made by Jay on 6 August, that a mixed commission should be set up to afford satisfaction for vessels and property illegally captured and condemned was favorably received, and measures were at once taken to remove the very real grievance caused by the rule laid down by the vice-admiralty courts that all appeals must be lodged within a certain time.[17] An Order in Council issued on 8 August admitted "appeals on behalf of the claimants of vessels condemned by the vice-admiralty courts in the West Indies . . . who from ignorance of the rules respecting the times of appealing, and other just and reasonable causes, have been prevented from duly entering and prosecuting their appeals."[18]

Ten days later, on 18 August, a change was made in the instructions to naval commanders in the matter of the seizure of cargoes of corn, which, though interpreted as due to a desire to placate the United States,[19] was more probably dictated by the fact that an unusually good harvest in England had led to a great drop in the price of grain.[20] The Order in Council of 18 August ran as follows:

[17] Grenville had doubtless by this time read Hammond's detailed account of "a somewhat heated talk" with Alexander Hamilton on this subject. The Government of the United States, he reported, had sent a gentleman to the West Indies to look after American interests in the vice-admiralty courts and to institute appeals. If appeals were impossible, either from defect of form or the necessity of beginning them within a limited time, he said that the United States would expect ample compensation.—Hammond to Grenville, No. 15, 17 April 1794. P.R.O. F.O. 5. 4.

[18] P.R.O. Ad. I. 5179 and *Privy Council Register*, CXLI, 6., A.S.P., F.R., I, 482.

[19] "So much of the Order-in-Council of 8 June 1793 as directed the capture and preëmption of neutral grain ships bound for France was quietly set aside. By such acts the Ministry more than acceded to the conditions outlined by Hamilton as 'absolutely indispensable to an amicable adjustment.' "—Bemis, *op. cit.*, p. 235.

[20] "The quotation of the price of wheat, which on Lady-Day, 1793, had been 54s. 1d., fell at Michaelmas to 45s. The summer of 1794 was unusually hot and dry; but, owing to the harvest being unusually forward (the crops in the South

Whereas by an article of our instructions . . . given . . . on the 8th day of June 1793, we thought fit to declare, that it should be lawful to stop and detain all ships loaden . . . with corn . . . bound to any port in France . . . We not judging it expedient to continue for the present the purchase of the said cargoes on behalf of our government, are pleased to revoke the said article, until our further orders therein, and to declare that the same shall no longer remain in force . . . but all the other articles of the said instructions, and all other instructions are to be strictly observed.[21]

It will be noticed that there is nothing in the wording of these instructions to suggest that the British Government had dropped or modified its claim to regard corn and other provisions as contraband in certain circumstances. Owing to the bad harvest of 1794-1795, in fact, instructions were once more issued in the spring of the year 1795 to seize all ships laden with corn for France.

There is no need, for our present purpose, to follow any further the negotiations which led to the signature of the Treaty of Amity, Commerce and Navigation between Great Britain and the United States which is known as Jay's Treaty.[22] This treaty was signed in London on 19 November 1794, but was not ratified until 28 October 1795, and was finally proclaimed on 29 February 1796.[23] The delay in ratification was due partly to the loss of the original treaty on its way to America, partly to the strong opposition to the treaty in the United States, where Jay was accused of having allowed himself to be cajoled into the surrender of American rights and of principles of international law embodied in treaties concluded by the United States with other powers. In the end the Senate ratified the treaty, with the exception of Article XII, the operation of which was suspended by an additional article. Under Article XII it was stipulated

and Midland districts being secured by the end of July) the price did not rise enough to check the consumption, and it was not till the winter and spring following that the insufficiency of the stock on hand was discovered."—Tooke, *History of Prices*, I, 180, 181.

[21] 5 Martens, 2d ed., p. 604. He quotes the text from *The Oracle and Public Advertiser*, 1794, No. 18, 807. These instructions, of which the Admiralty draft was approved by the Privy Council on 6 August (P.R.O. *Privy Council Register*, CXLI, 6) does not appear in any of the published lists. The terms as given in Martens agree with the draft. Mahan (II, 237) is wrong in stating that the Order in Council of 8 June was revoked before Jay's mission.

[22] A full account of the negotiations, based on the unpublished records together with Jay's draft proposals and the full text of the treaty, will be found in Bemis's *Jay's Treaty* (1923).

[23] For a discussion of the text and an authoritative version, see Miller, *Treaties and Other International Acts of the United States of America* (1931), II, 245.

that American vessels under seventy tons burden were to be admitted to trade with the British West Indies on equal terms, provided they landed their cargoes in the United States only, "it being expressly agreed that, during the continuance of this article, the United States will prohibit and restrain the carrying molasses, sugar, coffee, cocoa or cotton in American vessels either from His Majesty's islands or from the United States to any part of the world except the United States, reasonable sea-stores excepted." The Senate objected to this on the ground that it would stop a profitable trade already open to American merchants, who first imported, and then reëxported to France, the produce of the French islands, this trade being legitimized, according to the decisions of the British High Court of Admiralty, by the expedient of the "broken voyage."

Of the numerous other articles of the treaty only some are germane to our subject. Under Article VII it was agreed that American merchants were to be compensated by the British Government for losses and damage sustained by reason of irregular or illegal captures or condemnations of their vessels and other property, under color of authority or commissions from His Majesty, in cases in which adequate compensation was not procurable by the ordinary course of judicial proceedings. It was to be distinctly understood, however, that this provision was not to extend to such losses and damages as had been occasioned by the manifest delay or negligence, or willful omission of the claimant. A mixed commission of five was to be set up in London to hear appeals lodged within a term of 18 months, it being further agreed that not only such cases but all that should exist at the time of the ratification of the treaty should be considered as being within the provisions, intent and meaning of this article.[24] Complaints of British subjects who had received damage by reason of the capture of their vessels or merchandise, taken within the limits and jurisdiction of the United States and brought into the ports of the same, or taken by vessels originally armed in ports of the said States, in so far as restitution had not already been made in accordance with the terms of the letter of Mr. Jefferson to Mr. Hammond, dated 5 September 1793, annexed to the treaty, were also to be referred to the Commission.

By Article XVII it was agreed that vessels captured or detained

[24] Since the treaty was not ratified till October 1795, this enabled the Commission to take cognizance of the cases arising out of the Order in Council of April 1795.—4 Moore, p. 28.

on just suspicion of having enemy property or contraband on board were to be brought into the nearest or most convenient port, that all proper measures were to be taken to prevent delay in adjudicating upon them and in the payment of any indemnification adjudged to the masters and owners, that only enemy property found on board was to be made prize, and that the vessels were to be allowed to proceed with the remainder without any impediment.[25]

Article XVIII, "in order to regulate what is in future to be esteemed contraband" defined this as comprising not only weapons and other instruments of war but timber for ship building, tar or rosin, copper in sheets, sails, hemp and cordage, and generally whatever might serve for the equipment of vessels, unwrought iron and fir planks alone excepted. As regards articles "not generally regarded as contraband," it laid down that "whenever any such articles so becoming contraband, according to the existing law of nations, shall for that reason be seized, the same shall not be confiscated, but the owners thereof shall be speedily and completely indemnified; and the captors, or, in their default, the Government under whose authority they act, shall pay to the masters or owners of such vessels the full value of all such articles, with a reasonable mercantile profit thereon, together with the freight, and also the demurrage incident to such detention."[26] It was further agreed under this article that vessels approaching a blockaded port, not having been warned of such blockade, were to be turned away; but that their cargo, unless contraband, was not to be confiscated.

In order to provide adequate security of the subjects and citizens of the contracting parties, Article XIX provided that the commanders of ships of war and privateers were to be made responsible in their persons and property for any damage inflicted by them on

[25] This article was objected to in the United States on the ground that it was incompatible with the principle of "free ships, free goods" embodied in the treaties of amity and commerce concluded with France, Prussia and the Netherlands. It was thus a concession to the British contention, in the case of provisions as contraband, that such treaty stipulations are exceptions which prove the rule.

[26] Alexander Hamilton said that the object of this provision regarding articles not generally regarded as contraband was "to leave the point unsettled, to get rid of it."—4 Moore, p. 392. The phrase "a reasonable mercantile profit" led to a difference of opinion on the Commission. In the case of the "Neptune," while the British commissioners held that a profit of 10 per cent was reasonable, the Americans, who were in the majority, decided that compensation must be paid by the Government to cover the price which the confiscated goods would have fetched in the French port to which they had been shipped. For this award see 4 Moore, p. 439.

the subjects and citizens of the other party; and for this purpose all commanders of privateers, before receiving their commissions, were to find two sureties, not interested in their venture, who together with the commander were to be jointly and severally bound in heavy sureties to cover any damages which they or their men might inflict contrary to the tenor of the treaty or to the laws and instructions for regulating their conduct.

Finally, the British grievance arising from the special privileges given to French privateers in American ports was dealt with by Article XXV, by which it was agreed that the privileges accorded to the French under the treaty of 1778 were to be extended to the British and that neither party should give shelter to prizes taken upon the subjects or citizens of the other. Nothing in this article was, however, to be construed or operate contrary to former or existing treaties with other sovereigns or States.

It was natural that the terms of this treaty should have been severely criticized in the United States. No mention was made in it of the British practice of impressing seamen from American ships; the right to make prize of enemy goods under a neutral flag was recognized and, less explicitly, the right to preëmpt cargoes of corn and provisions generally in neutral vessels bound for enemy ports. On the other hand, though the benefits promised under Article XIII were rejected as involving a more than equivalent loss, the Americans gained the recognition of the fact that they had suffered wrongs at the hands of the British Government and the setting up of machinery for their redress, together with some guarantee that the irresponsible activities of British privateers would be henceforth restrained. For the rest, the exercise of her belligerent rights at sea by Great Britain was little affected. The Order in Council of 8 January 1794, though suspended temporarily, remained in force until it was revoked by that of 25 January 1798.

THE ORDER IN COUNCIL OF APRIL 1795

The year 1795 opened under evil auspices for Great Britain and the Alliance. The French Revolutionary armies, reorganized by the genius of Carnot, were in full tide of victory. Pichegru, after conquering the Austrian Netherlands, had advanced into Holland, and on 19 January had established himself in Amsterdam, while Jourdan had overrun the territories on the left bank of the Rhine. One by one the Continental States fell away from the Alliance. Holland made terms with the French Republic on 16 May. Prussia signed the Peace of Basel on 5 April and was henceforth to remain neutral until 1806. Spain followed suit on 22 July and, after a year's neutrality, joined forces with France.

On learning that the Dutch fleet, ice-bound in the Texel, had been captured by Pichegru's cavalry, the British Government at once took action, without waiting for the formal alliance of Holland with France. Instead of issuing letters of marque and reprisal as against an avowed enemy, however, a proclamation authorized the commanders of warships and privateers to detain and bring in for adjudication all Dutch ships bound to and from the ports of Holland, as well as all vessels, of whatever country, laden with military and naval stores and bound for Dutch ports.[27]

The severe winter of 1795, which had made possible the dramatic capture of the Dutch fleet, was followed by a cold spring and the consequent fear of a failure of the harvest. The price of wheat in Great Britain, which had been 47s. 2d. in 1792, 55s. 7d. on 1 January 1795, 77s. 2d. on 1 July, rose to 108s. 4d. in August. At the same time great scarcity was looked for in other sources of supply, especially in the United States, where the Hessian fly was threatening the harvest with destruction. The British Government took special measures to meet this situation. As it was feared that merchants would not buy corn in the Baltic ports on account of the high prices, largely caused by the huge purchases on account of the French Government, agents were appointed to do so.[28] It was also decided to put the Order in Council of 8 January 1794 once more into force. Early in April, accordingly, instructions were issued to detain all ships laden with corn, flour or meal and other provisions bound for ports in France and to send them to the most convenient British port, so that the cargoes might be purchased for the British Government.[29] It was reported a couple of months later that, under this order, neutral ships were being brought in at the rate of ten or twelve a day. The cargoes were paid for with what was considered "ample profit for the proprietors." [30]

"This violent and impolitic measure," as Alexander Hamilton described it, led to a somewhat heated debate between the American representatives in England and the Government. It was defended on

[27] James, *Naval History of Great Britain*, I (1837), 277; Annual Register, 1795, p. 168. [28] Tooke, *History of Prices*, I, 181 f.
[29] 4 Moore, p. 28. [30] Tooke, *loc. cit.*

two principal grounds: it was essential owing to the serious shortage of food in Great Britain, and it was a legitimate means of bringing pressure to bear on France, where the scarcity was still greater.[31] The contention on the other side was, that there was no such scarcity or threat of scarcity in England as to justify such violent measures, and that, in accordance with Article VII of the unratified treaty of 19 November, provisions in neutral ships bound for an enemy port might only be preëmpted "in accordance with the law of nations," that is to say, when there was an immediate prospect of reducing a blockaded or invested place to surrender, and finally, that the British Government was not paying the "reasonable profit" stipulated in the treaty.[32]

In the end the matter was amicably adjusted. The instructions were presently withdrawn, not because of American protests, but because as the season advanced the fear of a shortage of corn subsided. The winter of 1795-1796 was mild, with the result that the harvest of 1796 was abundant. This, together with a large importation, brought the price down again, and though the cold and wet season of 1797 tended once more to raise prices, these declined again before the close of the year, and in 1798 wheat was quoted at 49s. 10d. the quarter, which was only 8d. more than the price in 1792, before the war.[33] It was in these circumstances that the Order in Council of 8 January 1794 was finally revoked by that of 25 January 1798. It had been held in reserve during these years, but no further instructions had been issued under it. With the French armies bestriding half Europe, it would have been folly to risk yet more serious trouble with the neutral nations by a futile attempt to starve France into submission, and Great Britain being well supplied, there was no longer any motive for preventing foodstuffs being imported into France. As for the claims of American merchants and others for damage and loss sustained under the Order in Council of April 1795, it was agreed that, failing their settlement by arbitration, they were to be referred to the mixed Commission set up under Article VII of Jay's Treaty for the examination of such claims.

---

[31] In *The Continental System* (1922), p. 44, Heckscher says that the instructions of April 1795 were intended "chiefly to force the United States to ratify Jay's Treaty." This was clearly not the case; indeed, they would have tended to have the opposite effect.

[32] See the "Opinion of Mr. Pinkney" in 4 Moore, p. 372.

[33] Tooke, *op. cit.*, I, 187 f.

The Mixed Commission on Claims

Under the terms of the Treaty of Amity and Commerce between the United States and Great Britain signed in London on 19 November 1794, two mixed commissions were set up: the one, under Article VI, at Philadelphia to settle the claims of British merchants for debts due to them in the United States, the other, under Article VII, in London, to deal with the claims of American merchants and others in respect of damage and loss sustained by reason of the action taken under the various Orders in Council, notably that of 6 November 1793, and on the other hand with the claims of British merchants and owners for damage and loss sustained at the hands of the French privateers fitted out in American ports. It is with the latter Commission that we are here alone concerned.

The Commission met on 16 August 1796. It was to consist of two American and two British representatives, together with a fifth, who was to be chosen by lot. The lot fell upon Colonel Trumbull, an American painter, which gave a decided advantage to the Americans. The question immediately arose as to the competence of the Commission to reverse judgments delivered by the British Lords Commissioners of Appeal, who in the "Betsey" case had given a decision from which the American Commissioners dissented. The latter agreed that they had no power to reverse such judgments, but argued that they were competent to award damages for such decisions if based on wrong principles. This view was contested by the British Commissioners, and when it was endorsed by the vote of the majority, they withdrew, pending a decision by the Government as to their further action. Lord Grenville referred them to the Lord Chancellor, Lord Loughborough, whose opinion proved generally favorable to the American view. At a meeting at which the American Commissioners were also present he said that, having examined all the cases but one, he thought that they might fall into three classes: (1) cases of condemnation in the high court of appeals; (2) cases in which there had been decrees of restitution, but without costs or damages, or of condemnation without freight or costs; and (3) cases in which the right of appeal had been lost. In the case of the first class he said that the decrees must stand; that they settled the property and would not be affected by any act of the Commissioners. Nevertheless, there might exist a fair and equitable claim upon the King's treasury, under the provisions of the treaty, for complete compensation for the losses sustained by such condemnation. With respect to the second class, while the property was restored, the claimant might not think this sufficient and might claim costs and damages; so that the decree of condemnation might have been legal, but the claimant expected freight. The captures under the Order of 6 November fell within this class. Again, since the captor had color of authority to seize and send in for adjudication, the court might restore the property, but would not condemn the captor in costs; yet it would be just that the claimants should receive damages and costs. With respect to the third class, he said that the court of appeals was in some instances obliged to refuse an appeal because, the limited time allowed for it having .expired, the captor had thereby acquired rights which it was not within the discretion of the high court of appeals to impair. Yet the claimant might be able to give satisfactory reasons for his not having come forward personally with the appeal. This was undoubtedly a case within the provisions of the treaty. The property could not be restored, but the full value might be awarded, and in such cases this must be paid out of His Majesty's treasury. The Commissioners were not a court of appeals above the High Court of Appeals, but they were competent to examine questions decided by the High Court of Appeals, as well as all other cases described in the treaty, and they could give redress, not by reversing the decrees already passed and restoring the identical property, but by awarding compensation.[34]

The principle having thus been decided in favor of the view of the majority of the Commission, the further question arose as to the rule of compensation to be followed in the case of preëmpted cargoes. In the case of the "Betsey" the majority decided that this should be "the net value of the cargo at its port of destination at such time as the vessel would probably have arrived there." The "Betsey" had, however, been seized under the Order in Council of 6 November 1793, and the British Commissioners held that in the cases of provisions seized and preëmpted under the Orders in Council of January and April 1794 there were distinctive circumstances which rendered the rule laid down in the case of the "Betsey" inapplicable. The question was elaborately argued and finally decided in the case of the "Neptune," a brigantine partly laden with rice which had been captured when on a voyage from Charleston to Bordeaux and brought into London, where the High Court of Ad-

[34] 4 Moore, pp. 84 ff.

miralty had ordered her cargo to be sold to the British Government
and the proceeds to be paid into court. On a claim being duly preferred, the court decreed the restitution of the cargo or its value,
and of the ship, together with freight, demurrage and expenses. The
question of the value of the cargo was then referred to the registrar
of the Admiralty Court and merchants, before whom the claimant
demanded what the cargo would probably have fetched at Bordeaux.
In accordance with the rule laid down by the Government, however,
he was only allowed the invoice price, together with a profit of 10
per cent; whereupon he applied to the Mixed Commission under
Article VII of Jay's Treaty, estimating his loss at the difference between what he was allowed and what he would probably have been
paid at Bordeaux.[35] The award, which was signed by all the Commissioners, was made on 20 June 1797. The Commissioners found
that there was a difference of £6,451 between the price paid for the
cargo by the Government (£8,293) and what the owners would have
received had they been able to sell it in Bordeaux "or even in England, if they had been allowed to dispose of their own property."
They therefore awarded the sum of £5,274 5s. 6d. as compensation
to the owners, to be paid by the Treasury on the following 1 July.[36]

The settlement of the important points raised in the cases of the
"Betsey" and the "Neptune" smoothed the way for the Commission,
whose work was conducted on both sides "with an earnest desire to
do justice to the claimants." [37] The sittings were, indeed, interrupted in June 1798 by a controversy as to the disposition to be

---

[35] 4 Moore, p. 122.   [36] *Ibid.*, pp. 439 ff.

[37] The elaborate "opinions" of the three American Commissioners will be found
in 4 Moore, pp. 372 ff. That of Pinkney, which is a monument of legal erudition,
is mainly a criticism of the Orders in Council as infringements of the law of nations. Gore's criticism was more practical. If Great Britain was threatened with a
food shortage, he argued, there were other means of averting this calamity. "Merchants do not require to be forced into a profitable commerce," and all that the
Government needed to do was to offer a price for provisions which would have
attracted them to the ports of England instead of to those of France. "After these
orders had been issued and carried into execution the British Government did
what it should have done before; it offered a bounty upon the importation of the
articles of which it was in want. The consequence was that neutrals came with
these articles until at length the market was found to be overstocked. The same
arrangement, had it been made at an earlier period, would have rendered wholly
useless the orders of 1795" (*ibid.*, p. 399). This would doubtless have been obviously true—had wireless telegraphy existed. But the fact that prices had been
raised would have taken months to communicate to foreign sources of supply, and
the instructions of April 1795 were issued to meet what was believed to be an
immediate emergency.

made of cases still pending in the courts, and they were suspended, by order of the British Government, between July 1799 and February 1802, owing to the disruption of the Commission sitting at Philadelphia under Article VI of Jay's Treaty. The proceedings of the Commission were brought to a close on 24 February 1804, its object having been fulfilled to the satisfaction of everybody. The magnitude of the business transacted may be judged by the number of claims entered and awards made. When the sittings were suspended, on 16 November 1799, 476 American claims had been entered, of which 37 had been dismissed, seven withdrawn, and 393 were still pending, while of 58 British claims ten had been dismissed and 43 were still pending. When the Commission met again, in February 1802, the number of American claims entered had greatly increased, and by the time the Commission closed 512 awards had been made against Great Britain. The total amount awarded to Great Britain as compensation for the spoliations committed by French privateers fitted out in American ports was $143,428.14.[38] The total amount awarded by the Commission to American claimants and paid by the British Government, or recovered from captors and otherwise, was £2,330,000.[39] It is not surprising that the merchants of Boston entertained Mr. Gore, one of the American commissioners, on his return home at "a very sumptuous and elegant public dinner," at which thirty-eight toasts were drunk, and many speeches made, with commendatory references to the Jay Treaty as having been "dictated by enlightened policy, and executed with good faith." [40]

The Rupture of Relations between the United States and France

The signature of Jay's Treaty placed the relations between Great Britain and the United States on a fairly settled basis, and they so continued till the Peace of Amiens and, after the renewal of the war, till the famous decision of the High Court of Admiralty in the

[38] For an account of the activities of the French privateers operating from American ports, and the consequent neutrality claims against the United States, together with the decisions of the Mixed Commission thereon, see 4 Moore, pp. 130 ff.

[39] According to Trumbull (Autobiography (1841), p. 237) this was the figure given by Samuel Cabot, one of the assessors of the Board, who was esteemed peculiarly trustworthy.—4 Moore, p. 161.

[40] Ibid., p. 163.

"Essex" case. Complaints there were, of course, for British cruisers still at times seized American trading vessels on slight suspicion, and the delays of the admiralty courts were very vexatious. But captures were not numerous,[41] and whatever losses were suffered by American and other neutral merchants were more than compensated for by the enormous increase in their overseas trade, especially with Great Britain.

Very different was the effect of the treaty on the relations between the United States and France. Monroe had been instructed to press the claims of American merchants and shipowners against the French Government for damage and losses suffered owing to wrongful detention and condemnation of their vessels, and his secretary, Fulwar Skipwith (who was presently appointed consul general in Paris) was busy preparing the comprehensive report on these claims which he forwarded to Philadelphia in November 1795. The French Government, on the other hand, insisted on the principle that neutral rights were also belligerent rights, in other words, that it was the duty of the United States to assert their rights against Great Britain, and that their failure to do so constituted a practical alliance with the enemy and so justified a retaliatory disregard of neutral rights by France. By way of asserting this principle the Executive Committee, on 15 November 1794, the day before the signature of Jay's Treaty in London, issued a decree in which it reiterated that enemy goods under a neutral flag were liable to seizure, until the powers, enemies of France, should declare French property to be free on board neutral ships. The treatment of the cargoes of American vessels, that is to say, was to depend, not upon the treaty engagements of France with the United States, but upon the conduct of Great Britain.[42]

The news of Jay's mission did not cause much alarm in Paris. Monroe's sympathies were wholly French, he was not kept informed of the nature or progress of the negotiations in London, and his assurances led the French Government to believe that the mission would fail and that war between the United States and Great Brit-

[41] In June 1797 Timothy Pickering, the Secretary of State, in a report to Congress, said: "captures and losses by British cruisers, it is presumed, have not been numerous; for the citizens of the United States having, these three years past, been accustomed to look to the Government for aid in prosecuting these claims, it is not to be doubted that, generally, these cases have been reported to the Department." —Mahan, II, 241.

[42] Decree of 25 Brumaire, An III, A.S.P., F.R., III, 285.

ain would be its probable outcome.[43] Even when the news of the signature of the treaty arrived, he still felt justified in assuring the French Government that it contained nothing inconsistent with the treaty engagements of the United States with France, and the shock was all the greater when at last he learned its terms. For him it was "the most shameful transaction of the kind" he had ever known, and when the news of the exchange of ratifications in London on 28 October 1795 reached him, he was at a loss how to meet the angry protests of the French Government, and the only reply he could find it in his heart to make to the reproach that the terms of Jay's Treaty sacrificed the treaties with France in the interests of Great Britain and thus constituted a breach of neutrality, was that the United States, having no fleet, had no choice in the matter.[44]

Whether Monroe's attitude deceived the French Government or not, it certainly did not represent that of the Government in the United States, where on 20 August 1795 Randolph had been succeeded as Secretary of State by Timothy Pickering, a New England Puritan with little sympathy for the atheistic radicalism of republican France and a keen appreciation of the fact that 90 per cent of American trade was with Great Britain. Shortly after taking office, on 12 September, he had addressed to Monroe a long dispatch, in which he defended the terms of Jay's Treaty, pointing out, *inter alia*, that the provisions of Article XVIII would actually encourage the export of food to France, since they assured shippers of a profitable market in any event.[45] This dispatch Monroe had thought fit not to communicate to the French Government, which he continued to attempt to placate by language which was far from representing the mind of those in authority in Philadelphia. On 16 February 1796 he had written to Pickering informing him that the Directory had decided that the alliance with the United States would be at an end from the moment Jay's Treaty was ratified, and that it would appoint an envoy extraordinary to notify this to the American Government. Four days later he reported a conversation with the French Minister for Foreign Affairs, in which he had said that the intention to appoint an envoy had filled him with deepest concern, that the

[43] On 21 July 1795 Randolph, still Secretary of State, wrote to Monroe that the outcome would probably be the return of the treaty for amendment and that that would be the last of it.—Ford, *Timothy Pickering*, II, 175.

[44] A.S.P., F.R., I, 733. For the complaints of the French Government against the United States see 5 Moore, pp. 188 ff.

[45] Ford, *Timothy Pickering*, II, 187.

issue of war and peace would be suspended on that mission, and that he himself was satisfied that France had no real friend except America. This timorous and apologetic attitude was too much for the feelings of President Washington and Secretary Pickering, and on 22 August the latter sent Monroe a letter announcing his recall, and the appointment in his place of General Charles Cotesworth Pinckney.[46] It was not, however, till the following December that the arrival of Pinckney put an end to Monroe's mission.

Meanwhile the French Government had begun the series of those "wild measures"—to quote Mahan—intended to coerce neutrals into resisting British restrictions on trade, which was to culminate in the decree of 18 January 1798. A decree of the Executive Committee, dated 14 Nivôse, An III (3 January 1795), had revoked Article V of that of 25 Brumaire, An III (15 November 1794), which directed the seizure of enemy goods on neutral vessels, and reaffirmed the principle that free ships make free goods.[47] This was now in turn revoked by a decree of the Executive Directory dated 14 Messidor, An IV (2 July 1796) which, since the preamble sets forth the principles on which it was based, may be quoted in full:

The Executive Directory, considering that, if it belongs to French loyalty to respect the treaties or conventions which assure to neutral or friendly Powers the commercial advantages of which the result ought to be common to the

---

[46] Pickering's language was characteristically strong. As for the President, "it is impossible," he wrote, "to conceal his sensations on receipt of your letters of February 16 and 20 and March 10 and 5." A.S.P., F.R., I, 741. It seems, however, that Monroe had in the meanwhile made some effort to justify Jay's Treaty. In a letter of 14 July to the French Minister of Foreign Affairs, who had taken exception to Article XVII as a violation of the principle of "free ships, free goods" embodied in the treaty of 1778, he argued that this article had not violated any existing obligation or the law of nations. He presumed that it would not be denied that, in time of war, belligerents had the right to take the goods of their enemies in a neutral ship. "This doctrine," he said, "is established by the most eminent writers, and admitted in practice by all nations, between whom particular treaties have not stipulated the contrary. . . . If the law of nations was not so, why were special treaties entered into by particular nations to stipulate the contrary? . . . Or was it thought, when our treaty of 1778 was made, that, in this respect, it made no change, or, in other words, stipulated nothing? But you say that the law of nations has changed, and that the principles of that treaty have become since, in that respect, the general law of all civilized nations. . . . It cannot be said that the assent of a particular number of nations to a rule which ought to operate between themselves only, is to become a rule for other nations, who have never assented to it."—A.S.P., F.R., I, 740. It will be noticed that this was precisely the argument used by the British Government in the controversy with the United States on the question of provisions as contraband.

[47] A.S.P., F.R., III, 284.

contracting Powers, these same advantages, if they are turned to the benefit of our enemies, either through the feebleness of our allies or of neutrals, through fear, from views of interest, or from any other motive would provoke, indeed, the inexecution of the articles by which they should be stipulated, decrees as follows:

It shall be notified, without delay, to all neutral or allied Powers that the flag of the French Republic shall be used against neutral vessels, be it for the purpose of confiscation, search, or detention, in the same manner that they suffer the English to use theirs in regard thereto.[48]

The existence of this measure was reported by Monroe to Pickering, though in a somewhat inaccurate form, in August; but it was not formally notified to the American Government by Adet, the French representative in Philadelphia, until 27 October.[49] Meanwhile, on 7 October, Monroe had been officially informed in Paris that the French Minister to the United States had been recalled.

The Directory now took up the policy which had been outlined by Kersaint in 1792 and which was to culminate in Napoleon's Continental System—that of breaking England's resistance by excluding her from all commerce with the Continent of Europe. Already, in August 1795, a minute of the Committee of Public Safety, drafted by Sieyès and addressed to Barthélémi, the Minister of Foreign Affairs, had outlined the plan.

The alliance with Holland [it said] offers perhaps the most interesting results of all, that of excluding the English from the Continent and closing it to them in time of war from Bayonne to beyond Friesland, together with access to the North Sea and the Baltic. The trade of Germany will then return into its natural channels. . . . Deprived of these immense outlets . . . England will become extremely embarrassed with its Indian and colonial wares and will perish of abundance, just as she wished to vanquish us by shortage. We greatly desire that M. Yriarte (the Spanish Minister) shall be as sensible as we are of the importance of a treaty which, followed shortly by the accession of Portugal, would make it possible to close the gates of the Continent to our common enemy from Gibraltar to the Texel.[50]

Instructions in this sense were forwarded to the French representative at The Hague (Fructidor 6 and 7, An III, 23-24 August 1795). The plan was, however, useless unless the command of the Baltic could be secured, and an endeavor was made to persuade or bribe

---

[48] A.S.P., F.R., III, 287. The decree is given by Moore (*op. cit.*, V, 194) with slightly different wording and references to A.S.P., F.R., I, 577 and Davis, *Notes, Treaties and Conventions between the United States and Other Powers*, p. 1300. For the French text see 5 Martens, p. 388.

[49] His letter notifying it embodied the words of the preamble.

[50] Sorel, *L'Europe et la Révolution française* (1897), IV, 389.

Sweden and Denmark into combining against Russia. The attempt broke down; for the northern neutral powers, whose position in regard to the belligerents on both sides was much the same as that of the United States, had learned by their experience in the previous year the futility of a league of armed neutrality to which Russia was not a party.[51]

Nevertheless, as the year advanced the victorious progress of the French arms seemed to justify a fresh attempt to force England to terms by the ruin of her continental trade. Spain and Holland were French vassal states, Belgium had been annexed, Italy had been overrun; Lord Malmesbury's peace mission to Paris looked like a sign of weakening, and the situation in the Mediterranean had become such that in November the British fleet withdrew from that sea. "Let us concentrate our activities on the naval side (*du côté de la marine*)," wrote Bonaparte to Talleyrand on 18 October, "and we shall destroy England. That done, Europe is at our feet." [52]

The law of 10 Brumaire, An V (31 October 1796) was primarily intended for this purpose, but it also seriously affected the interests of neutrals. It totally forbade the importation and sale of any English goods, and any ships entering laden with such goods were to be confiscated. In order to prevent all evasion, a full list was given of goods which were to be "reputed English, whatever their origin," this list including woolen and cotton materials, cutlery, watches, ironmongery, glass, sugar (powdered or loaf) and pottery. Goods already in stock were to be notified to the authorities, sealed by them, and then reëxported. Articles not included in the above list were only to be admitted if duly certified as not of enemy origin. Indian goods were only to be admitted if certified by French consuls to be "objects of trade" of the Dutch or Danish East Indian colonies.[53]

Meanwhile, on the other side of the Atlantic, the French envoy, unconscious as yet of his recall, was doing his best to persuade the Americans, and more particularly the unsympathetic Secretary of State, that the measures adopted by his Government in restraint of neutral trade were both just and reasonable. When, in reply to his note announcing the issue of the decree of 2 July, Pickering asked him whether orders had been given to capture American merchantmen and, if so, what were the precise terms of these orders, he gave

---

[51] *Ibid.*, p. 392. See *infra*, chap. iv.   [52] Sorel, *op. cit.*, V, 192.

[53] 5 Martens, 2d ed., p. 389.

no direct answer, but merely recapitulated the grievances of the
French Government against the United States and apostrophized
the American people, "covered with noble scars" in the fight for
freedom, with an exuberant eloquence which might have appealed
to the sensibility of Paris, but had little effect in the sober atmosphere of Philadelphia.[54]

No direct answer was, in fact, possible; for the orders were anything but precise. The decree, in effect, authorized the seizure of
neutral vessels by French commanders whenever, in their judgment,
the conduct of the British justified it, and left the decision as to the
fate of prizes thus taken to a tribunal whose judgments were gov-
erned only by its own opinion on the same subject. As for the instructions to the captains of privateers, these were drawn up by the
owners, who indicated to them what they might seize and what they
were to release.[55] The result was to expose the commerce of the
United States to the attacks of what were to all intents and purposes
pirates.

The decree of 2 July was followed a month later (1 August) by
one issued by the Executive Directory of the Windward Islands
which, in flagrant violation of the law of nations, ordered the seizure
and condemnation of all vessels carrying contraband of war. The
question involved had been raised by Adet as early as the previous
January, when he had protested to Pickering against the export of
horses from Virginia to England and claimed that no contraband of
war could be furnished to a belligerent without the other belligerent
having the right to oppose it *in any manner whatever*. Pickering had
objected to the phrase in italic, maintaining that the belligerent
had a perfect right to seize contraband goods at sea, but not to con-
fiscate or otherwise penalize the vessel carrying it.[56] A month or two
later (11 March) Adet had again approached Pickering on the
subject, arguing that the United States Government ought, at the request of the French Government, to forbid the export of horses
to Great Britain as contraband.[57] Needless to say, he received no
satisfaction, and it was the continuance of this trade that led to the
issue of the decree above mentioned.[58] A further decree, issued by

---

[54] Ford, *Timothy Pickering*, II, 200 ff.   [55] Mahan, II, 244 f.
[56] A.S.P., F.R., I, 645.   [57] *Ibid.*, p. 646.
[58] *Ibid.*, p. 759. Affidavit of Josiah Hempstead, master of the brigantine "Patty,"
from New London to St. Bartholomew's, captured on 2 September and taken to
Guadeloupe. On the 5th the vessel was condemned at Bassetierre without trial.

the French authorities in the West Indies on 27 November 1796, ordered the capture of American vessels bound for, or coming from, British ports.

That these decrees, though issued without the express orders of the French Government, fairly interpreted its purpose, may be inferred from the numerous captures of American ships in European waters by French cruisers and privateers at this time, and from the further fact that the French consuls in Malaga and Cadiz interpreted the decree of 2 July as authorizing the capture and condemnation of such ships for no better reason than that they were bound for a British port.[59] Over three hundred vessels were thus seized, and most of them were condemned. Before the full measure of these losses was known in the United States, however, events had occurred in Paris which completed the breach between the two governments.

In his instructions to Pinckney, the new American envoy to the French Republic, Pickering dealt with the charge of ingratitude brought by the French against the Americans, citing certain diplomatic incidents during the war of independence to show that the benefits derived by the United States from France had "resulted from her exertions to advance *her own interest* and secure *her own safety.*" The object of the treaties of 1778, he said, was to keep the United States in dependence on France. For the rest, he rebutted the charges made against the American Government of unneutral conduct and violation of treaties and instructed Pinckney to press for the repeal of the obnoxious decrees.[60] Pinckney, however, was to have no chance of acting on these instructions. He had hardly arrived in Paris when he was informed (11 December) that the French Government would not recognize or receive a minister plenipotentiary from the United States until the reparation which the French Government had the right to expect had been made for the violations of neutrality and of treaty obligations of which the Americans had been guilty.[61] On the following 25 January Pinckney was ordered to leave the country, as an unauthorized alien. Monroe had

[59] Report of the Secretary of State, 21 June 1797. A.S.P., F.R., II, 28; Mahan, II, 245-246.
[60] Ford, *Timothy Pickering*, II, 205. Further instructions from Pickering, dated 16 January 1797, and containing an elaborate exposition of the American case, are in A.S.P., F.R., I, 559 f.
[61] Ford, *op. cit.*, p. 212.

meanwhile been entertained at an official farewell banquet and had left on 30 December in the packet for Ireland.[62]

Obnoxious as the decree of 2 July was, it was made more so by a further order issued on 2 March 1797 (dated 12 Ventôse, An V). After a long preamble, in the course of which it was asserted, among much else, that Jay's Treaty was a violation of Article II of the treaty of 6 February 1778 between the United States and France and certain articles containing instructions as to the principles and procedure to be followed by the prize courts in the case of neutral vessels claiming exemption from the execution of the decree of 9 May 1793, the decree went on to abrogate the stipulations of the treaty of 1778 as regards neutral rights and to substitute the provisions of Jay's Treaty. Thus enemy goods under a neutral flag were to be confiscated, as in Article XVII of the treaty of 19 November 1794; the definition of contraband was extended as in Article XVIII; "following Article XXI of the Treaty of London" any American citizen holding a commission from the enemies of France, as well as every American seaman serving on board their vessels, was *ipso facto* declared a pirate and punishable as such,[63] while every American ship was declared good prize which should not have on board an accurate crew list in the form prescribed by the model annexed to the Treaty of Commerce and Amity of 1778, the observance of which was required by Articles XXV and XXVII of that treaty.[64]

When the news of Pinckney's dismissal reached Philadelphia, President Adams called a special session of Congress to consider the situation. In his address, presented on 16 May 1797, he drew at-

[62] It is interesting to note that the state of war does not seem to have interrupted the service of the packet boats, carrying passengers and mails, between the hostile countries. See *supra*, p. 28.

[63] This goes far beyond Article XXI of Jay's Treaty, which ran: "If any subject or citizen of the said parties respectively shall accept any foreign commission or letters of marque for arming any vessel to act as a privateer against the other party, it is hereby declared lawful for the said party to treat and punish the said subject or citizen having such commission or letters of marque as a pirate."—See Bemis, *Jay's Treaty* (1923), p. 338.

[64] Neither in the Articles cited nor in the annexed model of a passport was there any reference to such a list. "It is probable, therefore, that . . . there was not an American ship afloat with the required document; and it is equally probable that the French Government . . . knew that to be the fact. The decree was, therefore, equivalent in its operation to a declaration of maritime war against American commerce."—Scott, *The Controversy over Neutral Rights between the United States and France,* p. 15. For the text of the decree see 5 Martens, 396 ff. and A.S.P., F.R., III, 287.

tention to the recent decrees of the French Directory and the spoliations on American commerce which had been their result, mentioning incidentally that the greater part of the cruisers engaged in these spoliations had been built, and some of them equipped, in the United States. "Some of our citizens resident abroad," he said, "have fitted out privateers, and others have voluntarily taken the command, or entered on board of them, and committed spoliations on the commerce of the United States." To meet this situation he recommended an increase in the naval establishment.[65] The situation was, indeed, serious enough to warrant even stronger measures. Privateering, hardly distinguishable from piracy, had become a very lucrative and fairly safe investment, especially in the Caribbean, the prizes being carried into the French West Indian ports, where they were liable to be condemned without too meticulous an inquest. On 22 June 1797 Pickering reported to Congress that 316 American vessels had been captured by French cruisers since the previous July, in addition to numerous captures by those of Spain.[66] In a report of the previous 27 February he had pointed out that not only enemy property but the whole cargoes had in many cases been confiscated, contrary to the law of nations, that compensation was hard to secure, and that more often than not it was paid in *assignats* at their face value and, later, in *mandats* which had greatly depreciated even before they were put in circulation.[67]

[65] Text in Scott, *op. cit.*, p. 25.

[66] A.S.P., F.R., II, 28. In a note of 6 May Martinez de Casa Yrujo, the Spanish Minister, had protested against Jay's Treaty as a violation of the treaty of 27 October 1795 with Spain.—Ford, *Timothy Pickering*, II, 221.

[67] Of 170 claims listed in Fulwar Skipwith's report of 20 Nov. 1795 compensation had been awarded in 39 cases, sometimes in specie, sometimes in *assignats*, and sometimes in both. As an illustration of the difficulty of obtaining adequate compensation, the case of the ship "George" of Boston may be cited. This had been carried into Morlaix, and the claim was for compensation for detention. The arbitrators made an award for demurrage in *assignats*, but Skipwith, "after repeated applications to the committee of government," obtained a payment of £1,355 sterling in silver. In the case of the "Alexander" he reports that the award was made in specie, but the payment made in *assignats*. In this case he had himself paid the captain in specie. In several cases, though compensation had been awarded, no payment had as yet been made.—A.S.P., F.R., I, 753-757. The truth seems to be, that the French machinery for adjudicating on prizes was no exception to the general corruption of the government under the Directory. Merlin of Douai, Minister of Justice and later a Director—who, as President of the Convention, had kissed Monroe so fraternally—"gained immense sums from the sale of prizes taken in complete violation of the existing treaty."—Sears, *History of American Foreign Relations* (1927), p. 80.

The decree of 2 March 1797 made the situation even worse, and
in his message of 23 November, President Adams pointed out to
Congress that the numerous captures of American vessels by French
and Spanish cruisers had occasioned considerable expenses in making and supporting the claims of American citizens before their tribunals, while great numbers of American seamen had been thrown
ashore in foreign countries, destitute of all means of subsistence, the
sick, in particular, being exposed to grievous sufferings.[68] Long before this Pickering, with the support of the majority of the Cabinet,
had been urging that strong measures should be taken. President
Adams, however, was averse from extreme action so long as a chance
survived of a peaceful solution, and in this attitude he was supported even by Alexander Hamilton, who feared that in the then not
improbable event of the collapse of the British resistance,[69] the
whole weight of the French arms might be turned against the United
States, while in any case to have declared war against France at that
moment would have been to have risked a serious conflict of opinion
within the United States, where the mass of the people, totally ignorant of the true issues involved in the European struggle, was
acclaiming the victories of Bonaparte with enthusiasm. It was, therefore, decided to send a special mission to Paris, to attempt to arrive
at some accommodation with the French Government.

The envoys selected were General Pinckney, Elbridge Gerry and
John Marshall, their instructions being to suggest a modification of
the Treaty of Amity and Commerce of 1778 on the lines of Jay's
Treaty, the United States being willing, for their part, to renounce
the reciprocal guarantee under Article XI of the treaty of alliance
of that year. Marshall and Gerry arrived in Paris at the end of September and were joined by Pinckney on 4 October. On 27 January
1798 Marshall drew up a long statement of the American proposals,
which was presented to the French Minister of Foreign Affairs. It
was waste of time and energy. On their arrival the envoys had been
informed that their case would only receive consideration if they
opened it by paying a *douceur* of £50,000 to Talleyrand and other

---

[68] A.S.P., F.R., I, 44 ff. For spoliations by Spanish privateers holding French
commissions, see Montague, *John Marshall*, II, 274 ff.

[69] The year 1797 saw not only the withdrawal of the British fleet from the
Mediterranean and the alarming mutinies of the Nore and Spithead, but also an
unusually large loss of British merchant vessels captured by enemy cruisers and
privateers (949, as compared with 489 in 1796). This year also saw the lowest
degree of depression in British trade.

persons in authority. This having been refused, Talleyrand replied to Marshall's note by curtly informing him that the United States were pursuing a "system of exasperation and alienation" and that he was not disposed to treat except with the one of the three whose opinions, "presumed to be impartial, promise more of that reciprocal confidence which is indispensable." It is unnecessary to follow the story of this luckless mission further, except to say that, Marshall and Pinckney having been eliminated, Gerry remained to play the same sorry part as that of his predecessor Monroe.[70]

Some days before Marshall's note was presented, indeed, the French Government had taken a further step, which rendered any hope of accommodation otiose. This was the issue of the decree of 18 January 1798, which opened a new phase in the economic war. On 4 January the Directory had addressed a message to the Council of Five Hundred stating that it was taking measures to seize all British goods which, in violation of the law of 10 Brumaire (31 October 1796), had found their way into France.

> Such is the first act [it said] by which, now that peace is given to the Continent, the war declared long since against England is about to assume the real character that belongs to it. . . . The French will not suffer a Power which seeks to found its prosperity upon the misfortunes of other states, to raise its commerce upon the ruin of that of other states, and wishes to introduce everywhere the articles of its own manufacture and to receive nothing from foreign industry, any longer to enjoy the fruits of its guilty speculations. . . . But [the message continued] neutral vessels enter British ports, carry British goods, and even manage to introduce them into France, and by so doing they aid Great Britain and actually take part in the war.

In other words, every neutral ship engaged in the British carrying trade was a help to England and therefore an enemy to France and liable to capture.[71] The decree of 29 Nivôse, An VI (18 January 1798) therefore directed that (1) the character of vessels in what

---

[70] For an account of the mission, see Scott, *op. cit.,* pp. 17 ff., and 5 Moore, *op. cit.,* pp. 197 ff. On 3 April Talleyrand wrote to Gerry "on the supposition that Messrs. Pinckney and Marshall have thought it useful and proper to quit the territory of the Republic." This was a hint that could not be mistaken, and the two envoys left. Gerry remained, protesting that he would "do everything in his power to restore harmony and a cordial friendship between the two Republics." Meanwhile Pickering had written to him telling him that, if on receipt of these instructions he was not in treaty with persons duly authorized by the Directors, he was to demand his passports. Gerry remained, however, till near the end of July, Pickering having meanwhile sent him a peremptory recall on 25 June.—Ford, *Timothy Pickering,* II, 218-220.

[71] Mahan, II, 230 n., 231.

concerns their quality as neutral or enemy, shall be decided by their cargo; in consequence, every vessel found at sea laden in whole or in part with merchandise coming (*provenant*) from England or her possessions shall be declared good prize, whoever may be the proprietors of these productions or merchandise, (2) every foreign vessel which shall, during her voyage, have entered a port of England shall not be admitted into a port of the French Republic, save only when there is a necessity for her entering (*de relâche*), in which case she shall be bound to leave the said port so soon as the cause of her entering (*de sa relâche*) shall have ceased.[72]

This decree was aimed against the great system of trade which had grown up as the result of the British Order in Council of 8 January 1794, with the possibility this gave of using the expedient of the "broken voyage." Its results were, however, more disastrous to France than to England. The immediate effect was a relaxation by Great Britain of the rules for the regulation of neutral trade. An Order in Council, dated 25 January 1798, "in consideration of the present state of the commerce of this country, as well as of that of neutral countries," revoked the instructions of 8 January 1794 and instructed commanders of ships of war and privateers to bring in for adjudication (1) all vessels laden with goods of any islands or settlements belonging to France, Spain or the United Provinces, and coming directly from the said islands . . . to any port in Europe not a port of this kingdom nor a port of that country to which such ships, being neutral ships, shall belong, and (2) all ships laden with produce belonging to subjects of France, Spain and the United Provinces and coming directly from the ports of the said islands to whatsoever port the same may be bound.[73]

Just as a whole series of decrees, issued by the Committee of Public Safety and by the Directory, foreshadowed Napoleon's Continental System, so this Order in Council foreshadowed the policy, which developed in opposition to the Continental System, of forcing neutrals to make England the storehouse and tollgate of the world's commerce.[74] By allowing direct trade by neutrals between the enemy colonies and their own countries in Europe it tended to deflect their shipping from French ports, and this tendency was increased by the French decree of 18 January and the methods by which it was enforced. No warning was given to neutral ships, which were seized in

[72] A.S.P., F.R., III, 288. French text in 5 Martens, 2d ed., p. 398.
[73] A.S.P., F.R., III, 264.   [74] Mahan, II, 263.

large numbers as they approached the French coast; and, once seized, they had very little chance of not being condemned. In view of the importance of British industry at this time, it was all but impossible for a vessel to sail without having on board some article of British origin, and the discovery of the most insignificant object of British manufacture on board was enough to ensure the confiscation of vessel and cargo. Add to this the utter corruption of the French prize courts, the members of which were, as often as not, commercially interested in the captures, and it is easy to understand that neutral ships now preferred to give the French coast a wide berth.[75] The result was revealed in a message of the Directory to the Council of Five Hundred on 13 January 1799, which reported an immense diminution in the entries of neutral tonnage into French ports, a decrease of importations, and therefore a smaller sale of French goods, while the decrease in neutral carriers impeded the export of agricultural produce and manufactures, as well as the importation of essential raw materials. In the Council of Ancients, on 17 January, a deputy painted the resulting situation in the gloomiest colors:

Neutrals repelled from our ports; our agricultural produce without any outlet abroad; our industry and commerce annihilated; our colonies helpless; our shipping routes deserted; a balance of 20,000 sailors in English prisons; our ships of war without seamen—such are the political effects of the law which is ruining, crushing us.[76]

The decree of the 18 January, perhaps precisely because of these effects on the commerce of France, marked the close of the period of severe depression through which that of Great Britain had been passing. With the law of 18 January, says Mahan, began a development of British trade, at first gradual, but soon becoming rapid, in which the neutrals driven from France bore an increasing part.[77]

Meanwhile, it was not till 4 March 1798 that any account of the American mission reached Philadelphia. A few days before, on 28 February, Secretary Pickering had presented to Congress, on the

---

[75] See Heckscher, *The Continental System* (1922), pp. 48 f. Professor Heckscher points out that the policy of the Directory had the effect of a self-blockade. As Mahan pointed out, the power which was excluded from the sea was the one which really had need of the neutrals for the procurement of supplies, and therefore had most to lose by a policy of violence against them.

[76] Speech of Couzard, in the debate beginning 17 January 1799. *Moniteur*, An IX, p. 502, quoted by Mahan, II, 255.

[77] *Ibid.*, II, 265.

petition of citizens of Philadelphia, a long statement of the losses sustained by them through the capture of their property by French armed vessels at sea, by the long-continued and distressing embargo on American ships at Bordeaux in 1793-1794, by the nonpayment of their bills, and by the forced sales of the cargoes of their vessels and the appropriation of them to public use without paying for them, or paying for them inadequately, or delaying payment for a great length of time.[78] The news from Paris, though it was to be yet several weeks before the full story of the mission was known, gave additional point to these complaints, and on 19 March President Adams advised Congress, in view of the prospective failure of the mission to France, to take measures for the protection of American commerce. Then came the news of the decree of 18 January. Congress was still in session, and from the beginning of May onward the whole story of the insults to which the American envoys had been exposed in Paris was gradually unfolded to it.[79] This revelation ensured a backing of public opinion for whatever strong measures might be taken. Accordingly, on 28 May, an Act of Congress was approved authorizing the capture of any French armed vessel committing depredations on American commerce on the coasts of the United States;[80] on 7 July another Act abrogated all existing treaties with France;[81] and two days later a decree was issued directing the seizure of French armed ships anywhere on the high seas, not only by public armed vessels but by privateers, which the President was authorized to commission. All commerce with the French colonies was likewise forbidden.[82]

Quite apart from the immediate subjects of quarrel with the French Republic, there were reasons enough for vigorous action. The remoteness of the French and Spanish colonies from the mother countries, together with the difficulty of communication due to the British command of the seas, had withdrawn them from all control, and the privateers which issued from their ports were no better than pirates. In these circumstances the small but highly efficient American naval force, which had been organized as a defense for American commerce against the Barbary corsairs, proved of great service. The

[78] A.S.P., F.R., I, 748.
[79] Through the presentation of the "X.Y.Z. dispatches," so called because the names of the French ministers who had demanded bribes were suppressed and these three letters substituted.
[80] Scott, *op. cit.*, p. 56.   [81] *Ibid.*, p. 65.   [82] See 5 Moore, pp. 201 ff.

public warships of the United States scoured the seas, and a number of naval engagements were fought with French and Spanish armed ships in which the Americans, whose frigates were built on a new and improved model, gained notable successes. The French Directory, conscious of its impotence at sea, first retaliated by laying an embargo on American ships lying in French harbors and then, when this failed to have the due effect, tried an appeal to the better feelings of the United States Government. By a decree dated 29 Thermidor, An VI (16 August 1798) the embargo was raised, in consideration of the belief that "notwithstanding the hostile manifestations of the United States, which had occasioned a momentary embargo upon their vessels, that government would take measures conformable to the pacific disposition of the French Republic." [83] This appeal had no effect, however, since the French depredations continued as before. The Directory relieved its feelings by issuing the decree of 8 Brumaire, An VII (29 October 1798), which extended the ban as pirates on American seamen serving in enemy ships to all natives of allied or neutral countries,[84] and the further decree of 24 Brumaire (14 November) inviting all allied and neutral Powers to recall their nationals serving in British ships.[85]

Though war had not been formally declared, the Americans and French were now actually in a state of war,[86] and so continued for more than two years. Formal war would, indeed, have resulted but for the pacific temper of President Adams and a change in the government of France which gave an opportunity for reopening negotiations. Bonaparte, whom the *coup d'état* of 18 Brumaire (9 November 1799) had made supreme in France, had been taught by the issue of the battle of the Nile the meaning of British sea power; he had no mind to risk an increase of this power by an Anglo-American alliance; and he was therefore in a mood to listen to the commissioners whom, after summarily dismissing Pickering from the Secretaryship of State, President Adams dispatched to Paris for the purpose of making a fresh attempt at an accommodation.[87] The outcome was the treaty of 30 September 1800.

The terms of this treaty, or convention, which was negotiated and

[83] A.S.P., F.R., II, 229.   [84] 5 Martens, p. 399.   [85] *Ibid.*, p. 400.

[86] On 27 February 1800 an Act of Congress suspending all commercial intercourse between the United States and France was approved.—Scott, *op. cit.*, p. 85.

[87] For their instructions and the negotiations and the resulting treaty see 5 Moore, pp. 203 ff.

concluded by the American commissioners without consulting the home Government, were as follows: By Article II it was agreed that, since it had been found impossible to come to an agreement as to the obligations imposed by the treaty of alliance of 6 February 1778 and the treaty of commerce and amity of the same date, or as to the indemnities mutually due and claimed, negotiations on these points should be postponed to a later and more convenient time, and that, until the parties should have come to such an agreement, the said treaties and conventions were to be of no effect, the relations between the two countries being meanwhile regulated as follows: public ships captured were to be restored (Art. III); captured property, not yet definitely condemned or captured before the ratification of the treaty, was to be mutually restored, with the exception of contraband, on certain specified proofs of ownership (Art. IV); private debts were to be settled, but this was not to apply to indemnifications claimed for capture and condemnation (Art. V); in the matter of privateers and prizes there was to be mutual most favored nation treatment (Art. VI); citizens of the two nations were to be free to navigate and carry their merchandise from any port to any other port belonging to the enemy of the other nation, and to navigate and trade freely in the countries, ports and places of the enemies of both countries, not only to neutral ports, but to any enemy port not actually blockaded (Art. XII); contraband was defined as warlike material only (Art. XIII); the principle "free ships, free goods" was reaffirmed (Art. XIV); goods found in enemy ships were to be esteemed enemy goods (Art. XV); captors of ships were to give receipts for papers and were not to open cargoes except in the presence of officials, while goods were not to be sold till legally condemned (Art. XX); vessels were to be condemned only by competent prize courts (Art. XXII); commanders of privateers were to deposit caution money, as compensation for any wrongs inflicted by them (Art. XXIII); ships of war, privateers and their prizes were not to be required to pay dues on entering the ports of either party, the said prizes were not to be seized or detained, nor were the officials of the ports to have power to take cognizance of their validity, it being understood, however, that the provisions of this article were not to go beyond the privileges of the most favored nations (Art. XXIV); privateers of an enemy of one of the parties were not to be permitted to arm in the ports of the other, nor to sell or exchange prizes, nor to take in more provisions than might be necessary to carry them to the nearest port of the Prince or State from which they held their commission.

The treaty was submitted to the Senate on 16 December and was ratified by the United States on 18 February, but subject to the proviso that Article II was to be eliminated and an agreement substituted by which the convention was to remain in force for eight years from the time of the exchange of ratifications. To this the French Government in turn objected, and though it ratified the treaty on 31 July 1801, it agreed to do so only on condition that a clause should be written in by which both sides renounced "the respective pretensions which are the object of Article II." Thus amended, the treaty was resubmitted to the Senate on 11 December, was ratified unconditionally on the 19th, and proclaimed by the President on the 21st.[88]

The treaty represented a compromise. France undertook, in somewhat general terms, to correct the abuses connected with her captures of neutral vessels, and in return the United States once more endorsed the principle that the neutral flag covers enemy property, and ensured to France most-favored-nation treatment of her privateers in American ports. The most important outcome, however, was the settlement foreshadowed in Article II and the added clause, viz., the arrangement by which the United States were relieved of the "entangling alliance" of 1778 in exchange for taking over from France the claims of American citizens against the French Republic for indemnification and damages. This settlement was ultimately arranged during the negotiations which led up to the purchase of Louisiana from Napoleon, and was embodied in a Convention signed on 30 April 1803, the treaty completing the sale of Louisiana being of the same date. According to the terms of the new Convention, the claims of citizens of the United States against France were not to exceed 20,000,000 francs (Art. II), were to include only debts due for supplies, reparations for embargoes and captures at sea, in those cases in which appeals had been properly lodged within the limit of time prescribed in the previous Convention of 8 Vendémiaire, An VIII (Art. IV), were to apply only to captures for which the Council of Prizes had offered reparation, and not to extend to American citizens who had established houses elsewhere than in the United States (Arts. V). The principal and interest of these debts

[88] For the French and amended English texts of the treaty see Miller, *Treaties and Other International Acts of the United States of America,* II (1931), 456 ff.

were to be discharged by the United States when Louisiana had been formally handed over (Art. III), the rate of interest being fixed at 6 per cent.[89]

From the American point of view this settlement was far from satisfactory. The sum of 20,000,000 francs ($3,750,000), which was fixed as the limit of the obligation of the United States, was found to cover only a fraction of the claims; [90] there was nothing in the agreement about claims for spoliation, the only claims considered being those which had arisen, before 30 September 1800, out of capture and detention of ships for which the Council of Prizes had decreed reparation and claims of American citizens for supplies furnished, the decision as to the justice of these claims being left wholly to the decision of the venal French courts.[91] But, such as it was, the settlement ended the period of acute tension with France and enabled the United States, whose trade had prospered exceedingly during the two years of quasi-alliance with Great Britain,[92] to resume once more the controversy with the British Government on the subject of alleged British violations of the law of nations.

[89] French text in Martens, *Supplément au Recueil de traités,* III (1802-1808), 476 ff.

[90] "The obligations thus assumed," wrote Professor Louis Martin Sears in 1927 (*History of American Foreign Relations* (1927), p. 88), "have been met most tardily. Even a preliminary payment was deferred till 1891. By 1915 the Court of Claims had cleared its docket, but no payment has been authorized by Congress since 1915."

[91] See Hill, *James Madison,* III, 32 f.

[92] The hostilities between the United States and France influenced the decisions of the English High Court of Admiralty. Thus, in the course of his judgment on the "Santa Cruz" case, Sir William Scott said: "In the present state of hostility (if so it may be called) between America and France, the practice of this Court restores American property on its own rule, without enquiring into the practice of America."—1 C. Robinson, p. 64, 7 December 1798.

Just as, during the Seven Years' War, American merchants carried on what Pitt described as an "iniquitous traffic" with the enemy, so now the embargo on trade with France and the French colonies was evaded wholesale. "Great numbers of these smugglers," wrote James Stephen (*War in Disguise* (2d ed., 1805), p. 248), "were captured by our ships of war, from an opinion that, on account of the inchoate hostilities between the United States and France, they were lawful prize, as being engaged in a trade with a common enemy."

IV

THE NEUTRAL NORTHERN POWERS AND THE BELLIGERENTS

The conclusion of Jay's Treaty, while it embroiled the United States with France, established American relations with England for some years to come on a fairly satisfactory basis. Meanwhile, however, trouble had been brewing in another direction. The two neutral powers of the North, Denmark-Norway and Sweden, had a long tradition of friendship with Great Britain, which had been, and continued increasingly to be, the best market for their produce.[1] Their sovereigns, in a series of ordinances, had laid down in accordance with "the accepted principles of international law" rules for the conduct of their subjects trading with belligerents during the war; they claimed to have made it a point of honor to see that these rules were strictly observed; and they therefore declared it to be, not only an injury, but an insult when their merchant ships were seized on the high seas by the belligerents in obedience to French decrees or British instructions of which they did not acknowledge the legality.

In the case of Great Britain the trouble arose, partly from a serious difference of opinion as to what constituted the accepted principles of international law, partly from the fact that, in spite of the ordinances, enemy ships and property were being protected by fictitious transfers to Danish subjects, while Danish vessels, sailing from one French port to another, made it possible for France to carry on her coastwise trade under cover of a neutral flag. As to the principles of international law, Denmark and Sweden maintained the rights of neutrals as laid down in the Convention of Armed Neutrality of 1780, namely, that free ships make free goods,

---

[1] Oddy, writing after the Convention of Armed Neutrality of 1800, says: "they have looked upon us as rivals, when they should have considered us as their best friends and customers. They are countries rich in natural produce; Great Britain buys, manufactures, and consumes more than other nations ever did. It buys largely and pays liberally. Who purchases most of their produce, pays with ready money, and gives their merchants credit, thereby enriching all classes in those countries?" —Oddy, *European Commerce* (1805), p. 3.

and that provisions and ordinary naval stores cannot lawfully be treated as contraband of war. These were principles which Great Britain had never acknowledged as of general application.[2]

THE CONVENTION OF 27 MARCH 1794

The French Committee of Public Safety saw in this conflict of principles a chance of uniting the neutral maritime powers—Sweden, Denmark, Turkey, Poland, Genoa and the United States—in a league for the purpose of enforcing "justice to the neutral flag," and used all the arts of diplomacy, not only to detach from the European Alliance those powers which were now showing signs of weakening, but to incite the neutral States to combine in resisting the "tyranny" of Great Britain on the seas.[3] From the point of view of Denmark and Sweden, however, there was little to choose between France and Great Britain in this respect. The French decree of 9 May 1793, indeed, ordering the capture of ships laden with provisions for the enemy or with enemy property, had preceded the Order in Council of 8 June; the Navigation Act, passed by the Convention on 21 September, which forbade foreign vessels to import into France products other than those of their own country or to engage in the coasting trade of France, had dealt a shrewd blow at the carrying trade of neutrals;[4] the decree of 18 Vendémiaire, An II (9 October 1793) prohibiting the importation of any articles manufactured in the British dominions had been yet another blow.[5] In these circumstances, before the French project could be submitted to them, Denmark and Sweden concluded, on 27 March 1794, a Convention "for the common defense of the Liberty and Safety of Danish and Swedish Commerce and Navigation" of which the point was directed equally against Great Britain and against France.

In this Convention no appeal was made to the principles laid

[2] Their occasional inclusion in treaties between England and individual powers was regarded as the exception which proves the rule. Thus the principle of "free ships, free goods" was included in the treaty of 1674 between England and Holland, and Denmark now claimed the right to the application of the same principle in her own case on the ground that under paragraph 40 of the treaty of 11 July 1670, with England she was to obtain "equality of favours with Holland."— Ewald Bosse, *Norwegens Volkswirtschaft vom Ausgang der Hansaperiode bis zur Gegenwart* (Jena, 1916), I, 446.

[3] Bemis, *Jay's Treaty* (1923), p. 221.   [4] Text in 5 Martens, p. 407.

[5] Heckscher, *The Continental System* (1922), p. 26.

down in the Armed Neutrality treaty of 1780, though this had proclaimed these principles as "a natural system founded on justice which would serve as a rule for the ages to come." [6] The Signatory Powers now claimed "no privileges not clearly founded on their respective treaties with the powers at war" (Art. II) and "no advantage not founded on the universal law of nations hitherto acknowledged and respected by all the powers of Europe" (Art. III). They announced that they would protect "the innocent navigation of their subjects" (Art. IV) and that to this end each of them would equip eight line-of-battle ships, with a proportionate number of frigates (Art. V). The protection thus afforded was to be mutual (Art. VII). The Baltic, as always, was to be closed to the warships of distant powers at war (Art. X). In the event of a belligerent power molesting the innocent navigation of the subjects of their Danish and Swedish Majesties, and of just claims made not being satisfied within four months, their Majesties would make use of reprisals wherever it should be thought proper, the Baltic always excepted.[7]

As already mentioned, Secretary Edmund Randolph had instructed Jay to sound the Ministers of Russia, Sweden and Denmark in London "upon the probability of an alliance with their nations to support those principles," that is to say, the principles of the Armed Neutrality. After the signature of the Convention of 27 March the United States were, in fact, invited to accede to it. In a dispatch to Hammond, the British Minister in Philadelphia, Lord Grenville commented on this in language which is worth quoting, since it vividly illustrates the point of view of the British Government.

The Conduct of American Ministers [he wrote] appears to have been hitherto uninfluenced by that scandalous partiality toward the Criminal System now prevailing in France [8] which has disgraced the Councils of Denmark and Sweden; and the Navigation and Commerce of the United States have in return been very favourably considered by this Country. . . . The United States should know the risks they would run if they acquiesced in the proposal now made by Denmark, to be drawn into an eventual Contest with this Country, in support of the collusive and fraudulent commerce which has been so openly carried on from the Ports of the Baltic. . . .

---

[6] Martens, *Supplément au Recueil de traités,* II (1802-1808), 344 f.

[7] Text in 5 Martens, p. 606; English translation in Scott, *The Armed Neutralities of 1780 and 1800* (1918), p. 440.

[8] The Reign of Terror was now at its height.

Of what avail, he asked, would such a league be against the united strength of Great Britain, Holland, Spain and Russia.[9]

The question was a pertinent one, and the dominant opinion in the American Government was against following a policy which Randolph, indeed, had suggested in the instructions to Jay without having consulted the Cabinet. The formidable coalition of maritime powers mentioned by Grenville, it is true, was soon to break up; in December Pichegru's cavalry captured the ice-bound Dutch fleet, Holland was in the grasp of the French Republic, and on the following 9 February a British Order in Council gave instructions for all Dutch vessels bound to or from the ports of Holland to be brought in; on 22 July, Spain made peace with France. But so long as the British and Russian fleets commanded the Baltic and the high seas there could be no question of effective resistance to the exercise of belligerent rights which they were agreed in enforcing. The Convention of 27 March was, in fact, stillborn. An Armed Neutrality of the North could only hope to be effective if and when Russia should be a party to it. It was not till 1800 that, under the auspices of the mad Tsar Paul, another league of Armed Neutrality came into existence which seemed to give substance to this hope.

Privileges for Convoyed Ships

Meanwhile, in order to protect their commerce from molestation by the cruisers of either combatant, the Danish and Swedish governments decided to provide convoy for their merchant ships, at the same time asserting the principle that merchantmen under convoy were not subject to the belligerent right of visitation and search, and that the assurance of the commanders of the convoys that they carried nothing contraband should be sufficient proof of their "innocence." If the belligerents should attempt to enforce the right of search, the commanders of the convoys were instructed that "violence must be opposed by violence." These were claims which it was impossible for Great Britain to admit; for, apart from fundamental differences of opinion as to what constituted contraband, there could be no certainty that the utmost vigilance of a neutral government, acting in perfect good faith, would be able to ensure the innocence of all cargoes shipped under its flag; as Lord Grenville put it, "neither the neutral Government nor its officer can have sufficient means to

[9] Grenville to Hammond, No. 12, 10 May 1794. P.R.O. F.O. 5. 4.

examine into the truth, nor is it likely that they should feel a sufficient interest in detecting the fraud." "From the moment that examination cannot take place," said Lord Whitworth, "fraud no longer fears discovery." [10] The right of visitation and search was, indeed, regarded by Great Britain as of vital moment.

All other questions of maritime law would at once be superseded by this new principle [wrote Lord Grenville] nor can any question of prize ever again be raised, respecting merchant vessels, or a single capture be made by the British navy, since all that will be required is that in the whole circle of the civilized world one neutral State shall be found (however small) sufficiently well disposed to our enemies to lend its flag to cover their commerce, without risk to itself, and with the certainty of a large pecuniary recompense.[11]

"The question is," said Pitt in the House of Commons on 2 February 1801, "whether we are to permit the navy of our enemy to be recruited and supplied, whether we are to suffer blockaded ports to be furnished with warlike stores and provisions, whether we are to suffer neutral nations, by hoisting a flag upon a sloop or a fishing boat, to convey the treasures of South America to the harbours of Spain, or the naval stores of the Baltic to Brest or Toulon." [12] Resistance to search, in short, was regarded as a hostile act, and any vessel thus resisting might legally be condemned for this alone.

The legal issue involved in this was first raised in the case of the *Maria, Paulsen*.[13] This was the leading case of a fleet of Swedish merchantmen, laden with naval stores and other Swedish products, and bound for various French, Portuguese and Mediterranean ports, under convoy of a Swedish frigate, whose commander had instructions to resist visitation and search by force. In January 1798, this convoy was intercepted in the Channel by a British squadron and, after some show of resistance, was brought in for adjudication. The case was brought up for trial before the High Court of Admiralty in December 1798 and, after an adjournment pending the receipt of further evidence, was concluded on 11 June 1799. In giving judgment for the captors Sir William Scott laid stress on the "incontestible right" of the lawfully commissioned cruisers of a

---

[10] To Bernstorff, 21 August 1800. 7 Martens, p. 143, English translation, Scott, *op. cit.*, p. 485.

[11] Grenville to Whitworth, 2 August 1800. P.R.O. F.O. 22. 39; quoted in Piggott and Omond, *Documentary History of the Armed Neutralities 1780 and 1800* (London, 1919), pp. 403 f.

[12] Quoted in Mahan, II, 261.

[13] 1 C. Robinson, p. 340; and Scott, *op. cit.*, p. 446.

belligerent nation to visit and search neutral merchantmen, a right so clear in principle, that no man could deny it who admitted the legality of maritime capture; because "if you are not at liberty to ascertain by sufficient inquiry whether there is property that can legally be captured, it is impossible to capture." "Even those who contend for the inadmissible rule, that free ships make free goods, must admit the exercise of this right at least for the purpose of ascertaining whether the ships are free ships or not." He further laid down, that "the authority of the sovereign of the neutral country being interposed in any manner of mere force cannot legally vary the rights of a lawfully commissioned belligerent cruiser, a principle which would be equally applicable if Sweden were the belligerent and England the neutral." Were such action to be taken, "it would very much resemble an opposition of illegal violence to legal right."

In the introduction to his judgment Sir William Scott laid down the principles which should guide the decisions of the Court. "The seat of judicial authority," he said in a famous passage, "is indeed locally here, in the belligerent country, according to the known law and practise of belligerent nations; but the law itself has no locality. It is the duty of the person who sits here to determine this question exactly as he would determine the same question if sitting at Stockholm. . . ." The succeeding paragraphs have a special interest, as illustrating what may be called the moral claim of Great Britain to the full exercise of her belligerent rights. "The only special consideration," he said, "which I shall notice in favour of Great Britain (and which I am entirely desirous of allowing to Sweden in the same or similar circumstances) is, that the nature of the present war does give this country the rights of war, relatively to neutral States, in as large a measure as they have been regularly and legally exercised, at any period of modern and civilized times. Whether I estimate the nature of this war justly, I leave to the judgment of Europe, when I declare that I consider this as a war in which neutral States themselves have an interest much more direct and substantial than they have in the ordinary, limited, and private quarrels (if I may so call them) of Great Britain and its great public enemy." If authority for this statement was needed, he would quote the answer given by the great Swedish jurist Pufendorf, at the time of the European coalition against Louis XIV, to a lawyer named Groningius, who wanted to support the claims of neutral commerce in a treatise he was projecting, and had consulted him on the subject:

I am not surprised that the northern powers should consult the general interest of all Europe, without regard to the complaints of some greedy merchants, who care not how things go, provided they can but satisfy their thirst of gain. These princes wisely judge that it would not become them to take precipitate measures, whilst other nations are combining their whole force to reduce within bounds an insolent and exorbitant power which threatens Europe with slavery, and the Protestant religion with destruction. This being the interest of the northern Crowns themselves, it is neither just nor necessary that, for the present advantage, they should interrupt so salutary a design, especially as they are at no expense in the affair, and run no hazard.[14]

Counsel for the claimants, in the course of his argument, pointed out that "at the time of the passing of the French decree against British merchandise" Swedish merchants applied to their Government for the protection of convoy, and that therefore the probability was "at least as great" that the convoy was intended as a protection against French cruisers as against British. The reference is apparently to "the unjust decree" (to which the King's Advocate also referred) of 18 January 1798, which declared all vessels laden wholly or in part with British goods to be lawful prize.[15] In view of the fact, however, that this particular convoy was captured in this same month of January, it is hard to believe that a decree passed on the 18th of the month had anything to do with it, though it is conceivable that counsel, arguing the case in the following December, may have thought that it had.[16] However this may be, the decree certainly had a great effect in extending the practice of convoy. It was, for instance, in consequence of this decree that the British Government commissioned a line-of-battle ship and two frigates to convoy a fleet of American vessels to their own coasts.[17] Together with the decree of 8 Brumaire, An VII (29 October 1798),[18] more-

[14] 1 C. Robinson, p. 352.

[15] See *supra*, chap. iii, p. 83.

[16] The "unjust decree" is nowhere specified in the course of the proceedings in the Court of Admiralty. A reference by the King's Advocate to "a certificate of the French consul" seems to point to the decree of 10 Brumaire, An V (31 October 1796), for which see p. 77 above. Mr. James Brown Scott (*op. cit.*, p. 447, n. 1) refers it to the decree of 18 January 1797, but the date 1797 is clearly an error or misprint.

[17] Macpherson, *Annals of Commerce*, IV (1805), 440.

[18] See *supra*, p. 87.

over, it served as an excuse for the Danish and Swedish governments to increase their convoys, even where there was clearly less
to fear from the French than from the British.[19] Thus it came that,
while the neutral United States were carrying on a desultory naval
war with French cruisers in American waters, the neutral powers
of northern Europe challenged Great Britain to unequal combat by
armed resistance to the right of visitation and search.

It was some months after the judgment in the "Maria" case was
pronounced that the first of the incidents occurred which were to
lead to the crisis in the relations between Great Britain and the
northern powers. In December 1799, a convoy under the Danish
frigate "Haufruen" was encountered near Gibraltar by some British
frigates. The Danish commander, Captain von Dockum, questioned
as to his destination, gave unsatisfactory answers and announced
his intention of resisting any attempt at search. The British commander thereupon signaled to make the examination. The boat
launched for this purpose by the frigate "Emerald" was fired upon
by the Dane, and a sailor was badly wounded, while another boat,
the "Flora," was seized, and not released until the British commander threatened to open hostilities. The convoy was then escorted
to Gibraltar. This incident was the subject of an exchange of notes
between Mr. Merry, the British chargé d'affaires in Copenhagen,
and Count Bernstorff, the Danish Minister for Foreign Affairs, the
former demanding formal disavowal of Captain von Dockum's
action, together with an apology and reparation for "an act of hostility" which he was persuaded "could not have been enjoined on
the commanders of Danish ships of war in their instructions," the
latter replying by a repudiation of the "hitherto unknown doctrine"
that ships under convoy were subject to visitation, the assertion that
"in resisting an act of violence" Captain von Dockum was only
doing his duty, and a counter claim for reparation.[20]

For some months no further incident occurred to increase the
gravity of the situation. On 25 July 1800, however, a British squadron cruising in the Channel encountered the Danish frigate "Freja"

[19] Martens, *Supplément au Recueil de traités*, II (1802-1808), 346. He speaks of
these proceedings as "legitimate in themselves, but which experience has shown to
be always looked upon with disfavour by belligerents." In illustration he quotes
the objection raised by Sweden in 1741 to Dutch convoys.

[20] Text in 7 Martens, p. 130; Scott, *op. cit.*, pp. 471 ff.; Piggott and Omond,
Documentary History of the Armed Neutralities 1780 and 1800 (London, 1919),
pp. 393 ff.

convoying a number of merchantmen. The British commander, Captain Thomas Baker, hailed the "Freja" to say that he was sending a boat to visit the convoy. Captain Krabbe, of the "Freja," replied that he would resist any such action; and this he proceeded to do. A battle ensued, with some loss on both sides, and ended in the yielding of the Danes to superior force. The "Freja," with her convoy, was now escorted to the Downs, where by order of the admiral commanding the station she was allowed to keep the Danish ensign and pendant flying.[21]

The news of this affair quickly reached London, and on the 29th Count von Wedel-Jarlsberg, the Danish Minister, sent a strong note of protest to Lord Grenville against this "unheard-of act of provocation," which he denounced as "a direct attack on the independence of Denmark." Lord Grenville, in reply, found it hard to believe that "it was on the instructions of his Danish Majesty that a Danish officer opened hostilities by firing on a British ship of war."[22] The matter was considered so serious, that it was decided to send Lord Whitworth on a special mission to Copenhagen, in the hope of arriving at an amicable settlement. "To give additional weight to his lordship's arguments, he was accompanied by a squadron of four sail of the line (to which six more were afterwards added), three fifty-gun ships, and several frigates and smaller vessels, under Vice-Admiral Dickson, in the 74-gun ship Monarch."[23]

The presence of this formidable force before Copenhagen certainly helped to moderate the Danish attitude. There was an interchange of notes between Whitworth and Bernstorff, in which the usual arguments on both sides were once more brought forward and enlarged upon.[24] On 26 August Bernstorff, finding that his arguments produced no impression, proposed that the mediation of the Emperor of Russia should be invited; to which Whitworth replied that, though there was no one whom His Britannic Majesty would more trust than the Russian Emperor, it was "useless to recur to that intervention," and that the questions at issue could be settled between Denmark and Great Britain alone. The result was a com-

[21] James, *Naval History of Great Britain*, III (1837), p. 64.
[22] 7 Martens, pp. 133 ff.; Scott, *op. cit.*, pp. 476 ff.; Piggott and Omond, *op. cit.*, pp. 398 ff. (B. Correspondence relating to the case of the Danish frigate "Freya.")
[23] James, *op. cit.*, III, 64.
[24] Texts in Piggott and Omond, *op. cit.*, pp. 403 ff. (C. Lord Whitworth's Mission to Copenhagen).

promise, which was embodied in a Convention signed on the 29th. The question of the right of visitation of vessels under convoy was reserved for future discussion (Art. I). The frigate "Freja" was to be immediately released, and to be supplied with all the materials necessary for her repair (Art. II). For the avoidance of similar encounters, His Danish Majesty would suspend his convoys, until such time as ulterior explanations as to this same object should have succeeded in effecting a definitive convention (Art. III).[25] This agreement, of course, merely "papered over the cracks." The questions at issue were soon raised in a far more serious form, precisely owing to the action of the imperial madman whose mediation Count Bernstorff had wished to invoke.

Intervention of Russia and Prussia

Russia was still in alliance with Great Britain, but the Emperor Paul, who esteemed himself the divinely appointed arbiter of the North, was deeply offended by the attack on the "Freja" and still more so by the news that a British squadron had passed the Sound, thus violating the neutrality of the Baltic, which he regarded as a *mare clausum,* if not as a Russian preserve. No sooner did the news of the capture of the "Freja" and her convoy reach St. Petersburg than he issued an invitation to Sweden, Denmark and Prussia to join with Russia in concluding a Convention of Armed Neutrality, on the old principles, his object being "to avoid similar outrages to his own subjects." [26] Then he heard the news of the British passage of the Sound, and on 29 August—the very day on which the preliminary Convention between Great Britain and Denmark was signed—he issued an *ukaz* sequestrating all British property in Russia, "as security against any injury which might arise therefrom to the trade of Russia." [27] This was an act of war; and, coinciding as it did with the Tsar's invitation to join in a new league of Armed Neutrality, it created something like consternation in the Courts of Denmark and Sweden, which had no desire to become involved in a war with Great Britain. They might resent the manner in which the mistress of the seas used, or misused, her power; but,

---

[25] 7 Martens, p. 149; Scott, *op. cit.,* p. 492.

[26] The text of the *Declaration,* which is dated 16/27 August 1800, is in 7 Martens, p. 150, and Piggott and Omond, *op. cit.,* p. 417; English translation in Scott, *op. cit.,* p. 489.

[27] 7 Martens, p. 153; Piggott and Omond, *op. cit.,* p. 419.

after all, England was their best customer; it was to her that the bulk of their exports (especially naval stores) were sent; if this source of supply were to be cut off, it would be easy for Great Britain to obtain all she wanted from the United States or from her own overseas dominions; and, finally, if she were defeated and her sea power overthrown, she would no longer want naval stores in any quantity. All efforts were therefore used to induce the Tsar to moderate his counsels. These efforts were so far successful that, on 22 September, the Emperor Paul withdrew the offensive *ukaz*.

Meanwhile, however, an event had occurred which was destined to bring matters to a crisis. On 5 September the British took Malta from the French. Now the Emperor Paul, though a heretic and a schismatic, had been elected by the Knights of Malta as their Grand Master, in the hope that under his powerful patronage they might recover their lost inheritance, and it happened that the Tsar was prouder and more enamored of this new dignity than of the fact that he was Autocrat of all the Russias. It was the refusal of the French to restore the island to the Knights that had been a chief inspiration of his hostility to France. He now demanded its return from the British and, on their refusing the demand, turned his wrath against them. On 18 November 1800, an imperial *ukaz* laid a fresh embargo upon all British vessels in Russian ports.[28]

Meanwhile Prussia had also been drawn into the quarrel. The "Triton," sailing under the Prussian flag and loaded with a cargo of timber from Emden to Amsterdam, had been captured by the British in the Texel. The prize, having been driven by stress of weather into Cuxhaven, was claimed by the Prussian Government on the ground of unlawful seizure; whereupon, in the hope of settling a troublesome controversy, the Hamburg authorities bought it and restored it to its owners. On 23 November, however, the Prussians occupied the district of Ritzebüttel, with the port of Cuxhaven, on the pretext of safeguarding the mouths of the Elbe from acts of hostility in violation of the neutrality of North Germany.[29] To the British Government, which had just received news that the Swedish Minister in St. Petersburg had received full powers to sign a Convention of Armed Neutrality on the model of that of 1780,

[28] For documents see Piggott and Omond, *op. cit.*, pp. 420 ff. (C. The Czar's claim to Malta.)

[29] Proclamation of the King of Prussia, 23 November 1800: 7 Martens, p. 165; Scott, *op. cit.*, p. 518; Piggott and Omond, *op. cit.*, p. 435.

and that similar powers were expected to be given to the Ministers
of Prussia and Denmark, this proceeding seemed of ominous import.
"The period of the occupation of Cuxhaven," wrote Lord Grenville
to Lord Carysfort, the British ambassador in Berlin, "coincides so
perfectly with the date assigned by this intelligence for the signature of this Convention, that it is impossible not to believe the two
circumstances to be connected with each other," and he instructed
him to ask if it was the intention of Prussia still to maintain
friendly relations with Great Britain.[30] Carysfort duly protested
against the Prussian action. The "Triton," he pointed out, was laden
with contraband and caught in the act of entering an enemy port,
and he insisted on respect being paid to British rights secured by
old treaties with Hamburg. As for the occupation of Cuxhaven, this
was calculated to arouse "the most lively alarms to commercial
nations." To this Count Haugwitz, the Prussian Minister of Foreign
Affairs, replied, that the capture and the restoration of the "Triton"
had both been irregular, that the Prussian troops were already in
occupation of Cuxhaven and intended to remain there, but that this
need give no cause for alarm, since every facility would be given
for trade and for the communication of the British Government with
Hanover.[31] Events were soon to prove that the British Government
had good reason to distrust these assurances.

THE LEAGUE OF ARMED NEUTRALITY

Russia and Great Britain were now in a state of war with each
other, though war had not been declared, and the resulting situation
was exceedingly awkward for the Scandinavian States. Neither
Sweden nor Denmark wanted war with Great Britain, which would
have meant the ruin of their overseas trade; but both feared the
possible action of the irresponsible Autocrat of the Russias. Denmark especially, apart from the fact that she was more dependent
on Russia owing to treaties concluded from 1773 onward, remembered too well the consequences to herself when, in September 1799,
the Emperor Paul had closed Russian harbors to Danish ships.
Placed thus between the devil and the deep sea, the Scandinavian
States elected to face the remoter peril. On 4/16 December they
signed at St. Petersburg Conventions with Russia which embodied

[30] Grenville to Carysfort, 9 December 1800. P.R.O. F.O. 64. 59. Piggott and
Omond, *op. cit.*, p. 438.
[31] 7 Martens, pp. 166, 168, 169.

the principles of the Armed Neutrality of 1780 and provided for mutual assistance in the task of enforcing these principles. Prussia, moved partly by resentment at the British treatment of her sea-borne commerce, but more particularly by fear of a possible rapprochement between France and Russia, signed a similar Convention two days later.[32]

Prussia's fear of a rapprochement between France and Russia was by no means an idle one. In the archives of the French Directory there are two projects for a Franco-Russian Alliance, drawn up in October and November 1799, the underlying idea being the formation of a great continental confederation which—to quote an addition in Napoleon's own hand—"would end forever the English command of the seas."[33] The Emperor Paul's new-born hatred of Great Britain and the renascent Armed Neutrality of the North seemed to the First Consul a good opportunity for realizing this idea; for, with Russia favorable, it would be no difficult task to make the other northern powers sharers in the enterprise, since both Denmark and Prussia were open to invasion. On 20 January 1801, as a first advance, he issued a decree forbidding the seizure of Russian ships, on the ground that France and Russia were now at peace.[34]

The British Government was, of course, fully alive to the possibility of such a development, and it took measures to meet the danger. In a note to Count Bernstorff, on 27 December, Mr. Drummond, the British Minister in Copenhagen, mentioned the "common talk" of a confederacy between Denmark and other powers, and that Denmark was carrying on negotiations very hostile to the interests of Great Britain.[35] In reply to his request for a *démenti* of these rumours Count Bernstorff denied that there was any hostile intent and stated that it was merely a question of renewing the engagements of 1780 and 1781, the principles of which Denmark had always maintained.[36] This was taken as revealing an alliance

[32] The French texts are in 7 Martens, p. 172 (Sweden), p. 181 (Denmark), p. 188 (Prussia), also in Piggott and Omond, *op. cit.*, pp. 439 ff.; English versions in Scott, *The Armed Neutralities of 1780 and 1800* (1918), pp. 672 ff.

[33] Sorel, *L'Europe et la Révolution française,* VI (1897), 29 f.

[34] The treaty of peace between France and Russia was not concluded until 6 October.

[35] Piggott and Omond, *op. cit.*, p. 465.

[36] 7 Martens, pp. 198 ff.; Scott, *op. cit.*, pp. 552 ff.; Piggott and Omond, *op. cit.*, p. 466.

between Denmark and Russia, which was no longer neutral, and on 14 January 1801, the British Government issued a proclamation laying an embargo on all Swedish, Danish and Russian vessels in British ports, giving as the reason the seizure of British ships in Russian ports and the alliance "of a hostile character formed in opposition to the interests of His Britannic Majesty." [37]

Lord Grenville further justified this action in a note addressed on the 15th to the Swedish and Danish representatives in London:

He had seen, he said, with veritable pain that, at the very moment when the Court of St. Petersburg was taking the most hostile measures against the persons and property of His Majesty's subjects, the two Courts concluded with this Power a Convention for the formation of an armed martial alliance of the North of Europe. Whatever doubts might have existed as to the objects of this alliance had been dissipated by the Declaration and conduct of the Court of St. Petersburg, and above all by the last declaration of the Cabinet of Copenhagen. It was well known with what hostile intentions the attempt was made in 1780 to establish a new code of maritime rights, and to support by force a system of innovations prejudicial to the most cherished interests of the British Empire. . . . This attitude had been completely abandoned, and at the beginning of the war the Court of Russia had formed ties with Great Britain which not only were inconsistent with the Convention of 1780, but entirely contrary to it.

The attitude of Great Britain and of her prize courts towards the other Baltic Powers had been perfectly consistent, and had been determined by the principles on which, before 1780, the procedure of the prize courts of all other nations had been based.

He added, that since the powers were arming in order to enforce the new rules, His Majesty had been forced to take "preliminary measures to resist this aggression." The embargo was such a measure.[38]

The proclamation of 14 January had not laid an embargo on Prussian ships, for British Ministers hoped that Prussia might be detached from the "confederacy" if she could be made to realize its probable ulterior consequences. Prussia, however, had ulterior designs of her own, which were to appear when she occupied

---

[37] Text in 7 Martens, p. 202, and Piggott and Omond, *op. cit.*, p. 468.

[38] 7 Martens, p. 203. In his reply of the same date Count Wedel-Jarlsberg protested against this "hostile act" and urged that Sweden and Denmark were merely acting on principles which they had always asserted and had solemnly notified to the British Government in 1794. "Russia, when at war, had merely deferred the application" of these principles. He might have added "according to the usual practice of nations at war." For the texts see also Piggott and Omond, *op. cit.*, pp. 469 ff.

Hanover and Bremen in the following month on the pretext that Great Britain had declared herself an enemy.[39] When, therefore, Lord Carysfort sought to justify the embargo and pointed out that Great Britain had broken off diplomatic relations with the Court of St. Petersburg, Haugwitz replied by denying that the League of Armed Neutrality was "hostile," while at the same time he denounced the "arbitrary acts" of Great Britain, and ended by saying that, in view of all the vexations Prussia had suffered, His Prussian Majesty had no difficulty in informing His Britannic Majesty that "in the maritime association of 16 December he had recognized his own principles, and that he had formally acceded to it." [40] It was characteristic of the Emperor Paul's mad humor that he chose this moment to issue an *ukaz* forbidding his subjects to export wares through Prussia, as he had been informed that Russian produce and merchandise were passing by this route to England.[41]

Matters were now rapidly coming to a head. On 4 March Baron d'Ehrenswärd announced the adhesion of Sweden to the Convention in language which was not calculated to turn away wrath. "The Government which has so often tried to convince Europe of its pacific intentions," he wrote, "now wants to begin a war for the enslavement of the seas, after having so often boasted that it was fighting for the liberty of Europe." He went on to complain of the offensive conduct of British naval officers in the very ports of Sweden, conduct which had never been punished; of the inquisitorial interrogations of the captains and crews of the ships detained in the West Indies and in England; and of the detention of the convoys in 1798, "accompanied by the mendacious chicanery of the courts, equivalent to an absolute denial of justice." [42] In his reply Hawkesbury stated calmly "the unalterable determination of Great Britain

---

[39] A declaration of the King of Prussia as to the occupation of Hanover, dated 30 March 1801, stated that England, by an unexpected step (the embargo) had disconcerted the amicable design of the northern powers to communicate the Convention to the belligerents, that she had declared herself an enemy, and that therefore Prussia proposed to take possession of the mouths of the Elbe, Weser, and Ems and of the States of His Britannic Majesty in Germany.—Text in Piggott and Omond, *op. cit.*, p. 491.

[40] 7 Martens, pp. 212 ff.; Piggott and Omond, *op. cit.*, pp. 478 ff.; Scott, *op. cit.*, pp. 513 ff.

[41] *Ukaz* of 12/23 February 1801. 7 Martens, pp. 219 ff.; Scott, *op. cit.*, p. 582; Piggott and Omond, *op. cit.*, p. 485.

[42] 7 Martens, pp. 221, 224; Scott, *op. cit.*, pp. 585, 588; Piggott and Omond, *op. cit.*, p. 476 (summary).

to uphold the accepted principles of maritime law, established by the experience of centuries, and perfectly adapted to secure the rights of neutrals and belligerents alike." He added that, while the Convention of 1780 was general in character, the present one could be aimed at Great Britain alone.[43]

THE BATTLE OF COPENHAGEN

Clearly, it was necessary to reinforce the arguments of British diplomatists by something more convincing than words. On 12 March, accordingly, a fleet of fifteen line-of-battle ships, with a number of frigates and smaller craft, sailed from England for the north under the command of Admiral Sir Hyde Parker, with Nelson as his second in command. The fleet reached the Naze of Norway on the 18th, and here on the 23d it was joined by the Hon. Nicholas Vansittart, who had been sent a fortnight earlier to negotiate with the Danish Government and now brought the news that it was obdurate. On the 29th there was published a Danish ordinance placing an embargo on all British shipping, and on the following day the Swedish government interdicted all trade with England. The hostilities were not, however, to be of long duration. On the 30th, the British fleet, which had been reinforced by three more battleships, entered the Sound, passing the Swedish and Danish batteries without sustaining any damage. The fleets of the northern powers, though collectively far superior to the British, were scattered and unready, and Admiral Parker hoped that his show of force would bring the Danes to terms without bloodshed. On 2 April, however, on their refusal to enter into a defensive alliance with Great Britain or, alternatively, to disarm and leave the League of Armed Neutrality, the battle was opened, and ended, after a brave resistance, in a crushing British victory. On the 9th an armistice of fourteen weeks was concluded, under the terms of which the engagements of Denmark with the other northern powers were suspended pending further negotiations. On the 19th Admiral Parker appeared before Carlskrona with his fleet, and summoned Sweden to abandon the Russian alliance, whereupon the Swedes agreed to open negotiations.[44]

The battle of Copenhagen might not have been decisive of the

[43] P.R.O. F.O. 73. 29; Piggott and Omond, *op. cit.*, p. 477.
[44] 7 Martens, pp. 236 ff.; for the text of the notes see Piggott and Omond, *op. cit.*, p. 493.

questions at issue but for an event which happened a few days before it was fought. This was the assassination of the Emperor Paul on 24 March. His successor, the young Tsar Alexander I, at once reversed a policy which had been inspired mainly by insensate personal vanity and had proved ruinous to Russian trade. He first turned his attention to the situation of Hamburg, which was of supreme importance to Russia both as a financial center and as an entrepôt for her transit trade.[45] The Prussians still held Hanover and Ritzebüttel, at the mouth of the Elbe, and the blockade of the great waterway was a nuisance to everyone concerned. The Tsar accordingly requested the King of Prussia, in the interests of peace, to withdraw his troops from Hanover and the mouth of the Elbe. Meanwhile, however, on 29 March the Danes had occupied Hamburg itself, and the King of Prussia now pressed them to terminate this occupation, as a condition essential to his own acceptance of the Russian proposal. The matter was amicably adjusted, on 7 May, by an exchange of notes between Sir James Crawford, the British Minister in Hamburg, and Prince Charles of Hesse, the commander of the Danish occupying force. The terms agreed upon were, that the Elbe was to be neutral, that British merchandise was to be exempt from sequestration and from every sort of inquisition, and that Great Britain would supply Danish vessels plying between the Elbe and Greenland or Norway with passports exempting them from visitation.[46]

THE CONVENTION OF ST. PETERSBURG, 17 JUNE 1801

Negotiations for the settlement of the questions arising out of the Armed Neutrality now proceeded with reasonable celerity. On 18 May an imperial *ukaz* raised the embargo on British ships in Russian ports, and on the following day a Swedish ordinance raised that on British vessels in the ports of Sweden. On 4 June an Order in Council raised the embargo on Swedish and Danish ships in British ports. On 5/17 June Great Britain and Russia concluded at St. Petersburg a convention relative to neutral trade, to which Denmark acceded on the following 23 October and Sweden on 30 March 1802.

The terms of this convention represented a compromise. It was agreed that the ships of the neutral powers might navigate freely

---

[45] See *infra*, Pt. II, Appendix III.   [46] 7 Martens, pp. 246 f.

to the ports, and upon the coasts of the nations at war (Art. III, 1)
and that a blockaded port was to be defined as one where, by the
dispositions of the power which attacked it with ships, stationary
or sufficiently near, there was evident danger in entering (Art. III,
4).[47] Conformably to Article XI of the Treaty of Commerce concluded between Great Britain and Russia on 10/21 February 1797,
provisions and ordinary naval stores were not to be regarded as
contraband of war and were only to be seized when proved to be
enemy property (Art. III, 3). Effects embarked on board neutral
ships were to be free, with the exception of contraband of war and
enemy's property; and it was agreed "not to comprise under the
denomination of the latter merchandise of the produce, growth or
manufacture of the countries at war which should have been acquired by the subjects of the neutral power, and should be transported for their account, which merchandise cannot be excepted in
any case from the freedom granted to the flag of the said power"
(Art. III, 2). The right of the belligerent power to search merchant
ships under neutral convoy was conceded, but this right was to be
exercised only by ships of war and was not to extend to privateers
(Art. IV, 1). The convoying ship was not to be permitted, under
any pretext whatsoever, to resist by force the detention of merchant
ships by a belligerent ship of war, but was not to be bound to
observe this obligation in the case of letters of marque and privateers (Art. V). The right of search was only to be exercised if,
after examination of the ship's papers and certificates, there was
found just cause of suspicion, and elaborate provisions were made
to guard against abuse of the right, to ensure that vessels detained
should be tried without delay, and to secure full compensation in
case of wrongful detention. An attempt was also made to guard
against the abuse of the neutral flag by establishing "an invariable
rule, that any vessel whatever, in order to be considered as the
property of the country whose flag it carries, must have on board
the captain of the ship, and one-half of the crew of the people of

[47] In the course of an elaborate attack on the treaty in the House of Lords, on
13 November 1801, Lord Grenville commented severely on this article. "All naval
operations," he said, "depend on the variations of the weather; a squadron blockading a hostile port, and fully equal to that service, may occasionally be unable to
remain either stationary before the port, or even near enough to create at all
times an evident danger of entering, and the article must therefore wholly destroy
the system of blockade by cruizing squadrons."—Hansard, *The Parliamentary History of England* (1806-1820), XXXVI, 241.

that country, and the papers and passports in due and perfect form." [48]

In Article VI of the convention it was stipulated that the High Contracting Parties would mutually agree on some additional articles, which should fix the regulations to be observed, accelerate judicial proceedings upon captures made at sea, and so on. These articles were signed at Moscow on 8/20 October, together with a Declaration intended to clear up any doubt or misunderstanding as to the terms of Article III, section 2. This Declaration, which was signed separately, was of first-rate importance. "The High Contracting Parties," it ran, "have agreed to declare that the liberty of commerce and navigation accorded by the said article to the subjects of the neutral power shall never authorize them to transport, in time of war, merchandises and provisions of the colonies of the belligerent power direct into its continental possessions nor, vice versa, those of the mother country into enemy colonies, but that the said subjects shall nevertheless enjoy for this commerce the same advantages and facilities as those enjoyed by the most favored nations, especially the United States of America." [49] Whereas, that is to say, under the original terms of the convention the principle was admitted that the property of a belligerent, after bona fide sale to a neutral, becomes neutral in character and therefore not liable to seizure, an exception was now made in the case of the produce of the enemy colonies, which could not be carried direct to the mother country even if it were genuinely neutral property, while the right of neutrals to carry on a direct trade between an enemy country and its colonies was equally renounced. "Great Britain," comments Mahan, "thus obtained an explicit acknowledgment of the Rule of 1756 from the most formidable of the maritime Powers, and so strengthened her hands for the approaching dispute with the United States." [50]

[48] French text in 7 Martens, p. 260; Piggott and Omond, *op. cit.*, pp. 504 ff.; and Scott, *op. cit.*, p. 688; English translation in Scott, p. 595.

[49] French text in 7 Martens, p. 271, and Scott, *op. cit.*, p. 695. Denmark acceded to the additional articles in March 1802 (7 Martens, p. 273) and Sweden on 31 March 1802 (*ibid.*, p. 276).

[50] Mahan, II, 262. Curiously enough, Lord Grenville, in attacking the treaty in the House of Lords on 13 November 1801, stated the very reverse of this. He pointed out that, while the instructions of 8 January 1794 had mitigated those of 6 November 1793 so far as to allow the produce of the French colonies to be carried to the United States in neutral vessels, the earlier instructions had in other respects remained in force, and that from that moment till the close of the pre-

Though the stipulations of the Convention of 17 June were to be "regarded as permanent" and to "serve for a constant rule to the Contracting Parties in matters of commerce and navigation," there was from the first no great belief that they had removed all causes of friction or obviated all danger of a revival of the Armed Neutrality in some form or other. J. Jepson Oddy, when a year or two later he was engaged in writing his *European Commerce,* saw the possibility of such a revival and was at pains to point out the inevitable effects on the northern powers were they to be so rash as to take up arms against the British power. He pointed out that, since 1785, the value of imports from Russia into Great Britain had risen from £450,000 to £2,300,000, while that of the imports from Denmark and Sweden had doubled, and that this profitable market would be destroyed were the northern powers to be so ill advised as to revert to an attitude which had "originated rather in private motives than in justice." To this warning to neutrals, however, he added some wise words of advice to his own government. "The British Government," he said, "should consider that its great commerce and naval power do certainly excite envy and tend to the humiliation of other nations; and, therefore, every harsh or vexatious proceeding should be studiously avoided on its part. It is only by such conduct . . . that we can expect to avoid discontents at some future period; for, as the convention grants to the northern powers more than we wished to give, though something less than they wished to have, it is vain for us to deceive ourselves in thinking that either party is fully satisfied." [51]

Opinions certainly differed as to the effects of the convention, and this difference is reflected in the judgments of historians. Sorel, who was wholly French in his outlook, said bluntly that "it had served

---

ceding year, "amidst the numerous and often groundless complaints of neutrals," he did not recollect a single voice having been heard "either to question the justice of our principle, which confined their commerce with the enemy to those branches only which they had carried on before the war; or to dispute the correct application of that principle, as detailed in the instructions under which the British navy has uniformly been acting." The indulgence to the United States, he added, had been given because of the peculiarity of their geographical position, whereas now there was to be "unlimited trade with the enemy colonies."—Hansard, *The Parliamentary History of England* (1806-1820), XXXVI, pp. 218 ff. He seems to have overlooked the terms of the Order in Council of 25 January 1798 (see *supra,* p. 84).

[51] Oddy, *European Commerce* (1805), pp. 52 f.

no purpose." [52] A Swedish historian, on the other hand, has hailed it as "the first real mitigation of England's tyrannical sea power." [53] British merchants at the time, however, who had seen their carrying trade ruined by the drain of seamen for the navy, were indignant at the comparative immunity secured under the convention for the illicit trade of their foreign rivals. The practice of covering enemy property by fraudulent certificates of origin or fictitious sales to neutrals continued as before, and was indeed encouraged by the provisions of Article III, section 2, of the convention. The Declaration of October was, doubtless, intended to allay these discontents. But the prohibition of a direct carrying trade by neutrals between enemy colonies and their mother countries was easily evaded by the simple device of "a colorable importation into some port with which trade was not prohibited, and thence carrying the cargo to some prohibited port." [54] This practice had, in fact, been facilitated, if not legalized, by the judgment of Sir William Scott in the *Polly, Lasky* case, which was the first in which the question of continuous colonial voyages came up for decision. "I am strongly of opinion," he said, "that it would be sufficient that the goods should be landed and the duties paid." [55] It was not till some years later, when experience had shown how easily the expedient of the broken voyage could be abused, that the decision of the Lords Commissioners of Appeal in the *Essex, Orne* case, by making the question of the "broken" or "continuous" voyage depend, not on the landing of the cargo and the payment of duties, but on proof produced of the original purpose and intention of the voyage, exposed large numbers of American vessels to the risk of condemnation and so once more strained the relations between Great Britain and the United States.

[52] Sorel, *L'Europe et la Révolution française,* VI (1897), 148.
[53] Hildebrand, *Sveriges Historia intill tjugonde seklet,* VIII, 239.
[54] Stephen, *War in Disguise* (2d ed., 1805), Appendix C.
[55] 2 C. Robinson 361 (1800).

V

RENEWED TENSION BETWEEN THE UNITED STATES AND GREAT BRITAIN

In December 1800, Bonaparte wrote to Roederer a very clear exposition of his views regarding England. "England," he said, "cannot desire peace, since we are masters of the world. It is essential, then, to make the sea useless and disastrous for the English, to blockade them in their island, to exhaust them, ruin them, invade them, fetter them; to turn to their confusion, their subjection and their isolation from the world that insular position which is the cause of their insolence, their wealth and their supremacy." [1] The signature by the northern maritime powers of the Convention of Armed Neutrality seemed to him a glorious opportunity for realizing these aims. "Your sovereign and I," he said to the Russian ambassador, "are called to change the face of the world." There floated before his eyes the same vision as that which, later, he sought to realize at Tilsit—the vision of a lasting alliance with Russia, based on a fundamental antagonism to Great Britain, of an extended league of the maritime powers, which should wrest from England the mastery of the seas, of France advanced securely to her natural frontiers and mistress of the Mediterranean, of an Asiatic empire, raised on the ruins of the British power in India, which should revive and outshine the glories of Alexander the Great. [2]

The British guns at Copenhagen dissipated this vision for the time being. But Bonaparte had foreseen this possibility, and was prepared with another plan for bringing the proud islanders to their knees. "We must win fresh victories on the Continent," he had written in March 1800. "It is by dominating all the coasts of Europe that we shall succeed in bringing Pitt to an honorable peace . . . if the seas escape us, there is not a port, not the mouth of a river, that is not within reach of our sword." [3] The seas had once more escaped him; but, while maturing his plans for ruining British trade by its exclusion from the Continent, he looked beyond

[1] Sorel, *op. cit.*, VI, 22.   [2] *Ibid.*, p. 88.
[3] *Ibid.* Quoted from *Mémoires de Lucien*, I, 377.

the ocean to the growing power of the United States, which sooner or later would successfully challenge the supremacy of Great Britain at sea. It was thus that he justified, as a stroke of policy, the sale of Louisiana. There were, of course, other motives: the disastrous failure of the French expedition to San Domingo, the impossibility of establishing a French dominion in America so long as the British held command of the sea, and perhaps also the pressing need for money to finance his insatiable ambition. But the avowed political motive was, to give the United States a vast accession of strength with a view to that armed contest with Great Britain which it was one of his objects to bring about.

The peace which was signed at Amiens on 27 March 1802, and which lasted little more than a year, only served to show how impossible it was for Great Britain to come to terms with Napoleon; and when, in May 1803, hostilities were resumed, it was clear that the war could only end with the complete overthrow of one or other of the chief combatants. The British command of the sea, confirmed by the battle of Trafalgar in 1805 and finally secured by the destruction of the Danish fleet in 1807, deprived Napoleon of any hope of a successful invasion of England and forced him to attempt to deprive Great Britain of the sinews of war by closing the Continent to her trade and so bringing about her financial ruin. Already the ports of Spain and of Italy were thus closed; a few fresh victories and all continental Europe would be within reach of his sword, and his Continental System would be complete.

CRIMINATIONS AND RECRIMINATIONS

The British Government was fully alive to the danger, and so were British traders. "At the present time," wrote Oddy, "the prosperity of the Empire is attacked altogether in a new way. Our enemy, the most bitter one we ever had, aims at increasing our expenses and diminishing our means of supporting them, as the surest way of bringing on our ruin; and it is a fact, that, with regard to the whole of the South of Europe our commerce is at a stand. It is totally interrupted." [4] It is, then, hardly surprising to find evidence of an increasing volume of complaints from English traders and others, not only of the way in which neutrals were taking advantage of the war to supply markets from which the British had been ousted, but more especially of the fraudulent devices by which

[4] Oddy, *op. cit.*, p. 2.

they sought to protect their illicit commerce with the enemy. It is not surprising that these frauds increased the tendency of the commanders of British cruisers and privateers to detain vessels on mere suspicion, while the loose methods and unjudicial bias of the vice-admiralty courts undoubtedly led to many condemnations which could not be justified even by the most rigorous interpretation of British prize law.

John Marshall, during his short tenure of office as Secretary of State, had instructed Rufus King, the American Minister in London, to present to the British Government a reasoned indictment of the conduct of Great Britain towards neutral commerce. His action, he said, was not due to the negotiations opened with France, with which the United States had been "at open war." The United States had avoided, and would continue to avoid, any political connections which might engage them further than was compatible with neutrality, while they had repelled, and would continue to repel, "injuries not doubtful in their nature and hostilities not to be misunderstood." England was playing havoc with American commerce, almost all cargoes being treated by her as contraband, regardless of their character or port of destination. He instanced, more particularly, the interpretation put by the British courts of admiralty on the words in Jay's Treaty "and generally whatever may serve directly to the equipment of vessels" as including whatever might by any possibility be applied to the equipment of vessels, although the articles might be unsuitable for that purpose and not usually so applied. This interpretation he stigmatized as "unfriendly and unjust" and urged that the word "directly" had no meaning except as limiting the description to materials which in their ordinary application are in considerable quantities proper for and "serve *directly* to the equipment of vessels."

He proceeded to protest against "declaratory blockades" as giving undue power to the belligerent and working wrong to the neutral, and he laid down that blockade requires the port to be invested both by land and sea. It is to be remarked that in both these contentions he was subsequently supported by judgments of the High Court of Admiralty. In the case of the *Betsey, Murphy* Sir William Scott ruled that "a declaration of blockade by a commander without actual investment does not constitute a blockade." [5] In the case of

[5] 1 C. Robinson 93.

the *Jonge Pieter* his judgment contained the following passage:

> If the cargo is American property, I am inclined to think it would not be
> affected by the blockade on the present voyage. The blockade of Amster-
> dam is, from the nature of things, a partial blockade—a blockade by sea;
> and, if the goods are going to Emden, with an ulterior destination by land
> to Amsterdam, or by an internal canal navigation, it is not, according to my
> conception, a breach of the blockade.[6]

These cases may, indeed, be taken as well illustrating both the way
in which British commmanders sometimes exceeded their powers in
perfect good faith and the impartiality of the High Court of Admiralty in remedying the wrongs thus inflicted.

Marshall did not, indeed, question the impartiality of the judgments of the High Court of Admiralty. His complaint was, that the
authority of this court had not as yet sufficed to curb the activities
of British cruisers and privateers. "The temptation a rich commerce
offers to unprincipled avarice," he wrote, "at all times powerful,
becomes irresistible, unless strong and efficient restraints are imposed by the Government which employs it," and he added that it
was only by infusing a spirit of justice and law into the courts of
vice-admiralty that these excessive and irritating vexations could
be restrained.[7]

THE QUESTION OF IMPRESSMENTS

The British Government, which had been informed by its own
agents of the unsatisfactory constitution of some of these courts and
the mischief caused by their activities, had tried to meet the
grievance by facilitating appeals and the prompt payment of the
reparations decreed as the result of such appeals when successful.[8]
For the rest, however, it might well have replied to Marshall's
strictures by a *tu quoque;* for it was certainly not only the British
who yielded to the temptation a rich commerce offers to unprincipled avarice. Great Britain could view the transference of the
bulk of her carrying trade to American bottoms with comparative
equanimity, since this served her purpose in time of war. It was
otherwise in the case of the drain of British seamen enticed into the
American merchant service by the high rates of pay, for this seriously impaired the manning of the navy and thus, in view of the

---

[6] 4 C. Robinson 79 (1801). See also the "Stert" case, *ibid.*, 65.
[7] Instructions to Rufus King, 20 September 1800. A.S.P., F.R., II, 486, 490.
[8] See *supra*, p. 62.

great wastage of war, threatened the very existence of the nation. The right to impress British sailors from American ships was therefore one which, in the circumstances of the time, Great Britain could not surrender; and since it often happened that, for reasons already stated, American citizens were also thus impressed, there resulted a standing cause of dissension between the United States and Great Britain which it was found impossible to adjust.

Marshall, whose sentiments were in general friendly to England, had put forth the American view in his instructions to King in a manner sufficiently uncompromising; it was pressed with even more energy when, on 4 March 1801, Thomas Jefferson became President of the United States, with James Madison as his Secretary of State. The situation become ever more serious after the renewal of war in 1803. American overseas trade, which had shrunk during the year of peace, now increased by leaps and bounds. The tonnage of the American merchant marine expanded at the rate of about 70,000 tons annually, which involved an annual demand for some 4,200 additional seamen; and of these, according to Albert Gallatin, as many as 2,500 were British.[9] The transfer of these latter was facilitated by the scandalous ease with which American consuls all over the world granted certificates of American citizenship for a nominal fee.[10] To Lord Grenville's request that the American consuls should be instructed to refrain from these practices, Rufus King replied by proposing that the consuls should issue certificates only to those entitled to them and that the British Government should instruct its officers to respect the certificates thus issued. This was not a proposal likely to commend itself, since there could be no guarantee that the consuls would obey these instructions, and in any case British and American ideas differed fundamentally as to the qualifications which would entitle applicants to receive such certificates. Impressments of real or pretended American citizens therefore con-

[9] Hill, *James Madison*, III, 81.

[10] Lord St. Vincent, the First Lord of the Admiralty, commenting on the protests presented by Rufus King, said: "Mr. King is probably not aware of the abuses which are committed by the American consuls in France, Spain and Portugal, from the generality of whom every Englishman, knowing him to be such, may be made an American for a dollar. I have known more than one American master to carry off soldiers, in their regimentals, arms and accoutrements, from the garrison at Gibraltar; and there cannot be any doubt but the American trade is navigated by a majority of British subjects; and a very considerable one too."—Quoted in Mahan, *Sea Power in Its Relation to the War of 1812*, I, 124.

tinued, which led Madison to instruct King to inform the British Government that, if these outrages did not cease, the policy of the United States could "scarcely fail to take some shape more remedial than that hitherto given to it." There was, however, no immediate danger of this threat being put into execution, since the United States were involved in the controversy with Spain about the cession of the Floridas, and Spain was the ally of France.[11]

Meanwhile, the British, fighting for their lives and liberties, nursed a grievance against the Americans which outweighed even that caused by the drain of seamen. The principle of the Rule of 1756 had been admitted by Jay's Treaty;[12] but, under the Order in Council of 25 January 1798, British commanders were limited by their instructions to the detention of neutral ships carrying the produce of enemy colonies direct to any country but Great Britain and their own. It was thus left open to American vessels engaged in carrying such produce to European ports, whether enemy or neutral, to secure immunity from capture and condemnation by touching at some port in the United States, landing their cargo there, paying the duties on it, and then reshipping it for its original destination. The decision of the High Court of Admiralty in the *Polly, Lasky* case justified this procedure.[13] From the British point of view, indeed, there was at first no strong reason for objecting to it, since it was an effective check on enemy commerce so long as, under the law of the United States, the goods landed had to be weighed, measured and gauged, the duties had to be paid before the drawbacks on reëxportation could be obtained, and the process of obtaining them was "attended with difficulty, casualty and trouble."[14] In March 1799, however, Congress enacted a measure of which the object was "to make the most of the large concessions contained in the Royal Instructions of 1798, by giving every legal facility to the indirect trade in question, that consisted with the

---

[11] That American seamen were also sometimes impressed by the French is shown by a letter of Jonathan Russell to the Duke of Bassano, dated 8 July 1811, in which he demands the release of 23 American seamen impressed at Danzig and taken under guard to Antwerp. A.S.P., F.R., III, 504.

[12] "The neutral Powers have all assented to the rule of 1756, in point of principle, by submitting to its partial application."—Stephen, *War in Disguise* (2d ed., 1805), p. 146.

[13] See *supra*, p. 48.

[14] Operation of the Act laying duties upon imports. Report of the Secretary of the Treasury, 22 April 1790. A.S.P., *Finance*, I, 46.

security of the duties on imports consumed in America." [15] Under
this act certain goods could at once be reshipped, the duties on them
being secured by bond and drawn back with a deduction of only
3½ per cent. It was noticed that scarcely any articles were specified
in the act save those which were "the ordinary and peculiar objects
of trade between Europe and the West Indies." [16]

Under these new conditions American overseas trade prospered
exceedingly. It was no hardship for vessels bound from the West
Indies to Europe to break the voyage, for the trade winds forced
them in any case to run northwards until they met the westerly
winds prevailing in higher latitudes, and there was therefore no
great delay involved in making for an American port and there
transshipping a cargo destined for Europe.[17] Often enough, doubtless, the ceremony of landing and reloading was dispensed with,
with the connivance of the local authorities. A flagrant instance of
this fraud was exposed in the case of the *Maria, Roberts,* which
was adjudicated on by the High Court of Admiralty in January
1802. "By all the documents found on board," said Sir William
Scott in his judgment, "the cargo appeared to have been laden at
Charlestown [*sic*] ; among them being an attestation sworn at the
customhouse, that all the parts of the cargo which were of foreign
growth or manufacture, had been legally imported, and the duties
thereon paid or secured. . . . It came out, however, that the cargo
had been laden at the Havannah, and that it had never been
landed at Charlestown, the place of the alledged shipment." It being
evident that the touching at Charleston was "for the mere purpose
of giving the voyage the colour and appearance of having begun
there," judgment was given for the captors.[18] Less flagrant, but
probably more characteristic, was the case of the *William, Trefry,*
on which judgment was delivered by the Lords Commissioners of
Appeal on 11 March 1806. Vessel and cargo had been condemned
by the vice-admiralty court at Halifax on 17 July 1800, and an
appeal had been lodged by the owners, W. and N. Hooper of Marblehead, Mass. In giving judgment against the claimant Sir William
Grant said: "The cargo was taken on board at Leguira. It was at
the time of capture proceeding to Spain; but had touched at an
American port. The cargo was landed and entered at the custom-

---

15 Stephen, *op. cit.*, Appendix B.   16 *Ibid.*
17 Mahan, II, 269.   18 5 C. Robinson 400.

house, and a bond was given for duties to the amount of 1,239 dollars. The cargo was reshipped, and a debenture for 1,211 dollars by way of drawback was obtained. All this passed in the course of a few days. The vessel arrived at Marblehead on the 29th of May; on that day the bond for security and duties was given. On the 30th and 31st the goods were landed, and weighed and packed. The permit to ship them is dated the 1st of June, and on the 3rd the vessel is cleared out as laden, and ready to proceed to sea." The landing, he concluded, had "little appearance of having been made with a view to actual importation." [19]

The Frauds of the Neutral Flags

The effect of these ingenious devices was to make the Rule of 1756 of no effect, and in England a great cry arose that British merchants and shippers were being robbed of their profits by the frauds of the neutral traders. Authoritative utterance was given to these complaints by James Stephen, whose long practice in the Prize Appeal Court of the Privy Council gave him a unique knowledge of what was happening, while his reputation for probity lent additional weight to his evidence.[20] "We are still the unrestricted masters of every sea," he wrote, "and the open intercourse of our enemies with their colonies was never so completely precluded; yet we do not hear that the merchants of France, Holland and Spain are ruined, or that their colonies are distressed. . . . They have, in effect, merely changed their flags and chartered many vessels that are really neutral." [21] As for the coasting trade, hostile property in this trade, as in the rest, was "covered by such abundant and accurate perjury" that cargoes could rarely be condemned.[22] Neutrals, he maintained, had benefited from the war quite apart from the acceptance of "a bribe from the weaker party to protect him from the arms of the stronger"; for, owing to the comparative cheapness of their navigation, they had supplanted the belligerents in the commerce with other neutrals, while belligerents naturally gave them the carriage of the commodities which they had in time of peace carried to such neutral countries in their own ships.[23] This pref-

[19] 5 C. Robinson 385.
[20] His *War in Disguise, or the Frauds of the Neutral Flags* was first published on 21 October 1805, the day of Trafalgar, a second edition appearing in the same year.
[21] Stephen, *op. cit.*, p. 9.   [22] *Ibid.*, p. 166 n.   [23] *Ibid.*, p. 155.

erence for neutral carriers he ascribed partly to the fact that the rates of insurance worked out at less for neutral ships carrying enemy produce than for British ships under convoy.[24] "We traverse the ocean," he wrote, "at greater charge, even for security on the passage, than those who have no share in the domain." [25] As for the trade of enemy countries, that had scarce been interrupted; for France and Holland had simply assigned the whole of this trade to neutral merchants, while Spain had made an almost entire transfer of her trade with her colonies in America, importing even her bullion from Vera Cruz, Cartagena and La Plata in neutral bottoms.[26] American ships, entering French ports, returned by way of the United States with supplies for the French West Indian colonies, Antwerp being "a favourite haunt of the American West India- men." [27] "The looms and forges of Germany," he complains, "are put in action by the colonial produce of our enemies, and are rival- ling us, by the supplies sent under neutral flags, to every part of the New World." [28] This last statement is exaggerated; for, as will be shown later, German industries were actually suffering severely from British competition. There was no exaggeration, however, in the account Stephen gave of the prosperity of neutral traders under war conditions. "Merchants," he wrote, "who, immediately prior to the last war, were scarcely known, even in the obscure sea-ports in which they resided, have suddenly started up as sole owners of hundreds of ships, and sole proprietors of rich cargoes, which it would have alarmed the wealthiest merchants of Europe, to hazard at once on the chance of a market, even in peaceable times. A man who, when the war broke out, was a petty shoemaker in a small town in East Friesland, had at one time 150 vessels under the Prussian flag." [29]

This immense increase in the carrying trade of neutrals, especially of the United States, was accompanied by a serious decrease in that of Great Britain, which was affected by the drain of seamen for the navy, the risks of capture and the delays due to the legal obligation to sail under convoy.[30] At the same time British manufactures, as

[24] Stephen, *op. cit.*, p. 85. "For one per cent. Lloyd's gives an honorary guaran- tee against perils of capture and discovery." The rates for British ships under convoy did not exceed 12 per cent after 1802 and in 1810 were 6 per cent.

[25] *Ibid.*, p. 151.   [26] *Ibid.*, p. 70.   [27] *Ibid.*, pp. 73, 74.

[28] *Ibid.*, p. 73.   [29] *Ibid.*, p. 96.

[30] As from 20 June 1803 (Act of 43 Geo. III, cap. 57). The first Convoy Act was passed in January 1798, and was reënacted in 1803.

a result of the industrial revolution, were growing apace, and both on the Continent of Europe and in America there was an immense demand for them, because of their cheapness and superior quality. As a result of these conditions the British Government had found it necessary repeatedly to relax the Navigation Acts, so that by the year 1800 more than half the carrying trade of Great Britain was carried on in foreign bottoms.[31] In a large measure this served British purposes for the time being, but was none the less resented by British merchants, and this resentment was increased by the activities of neutrals, especially of Americans, in the then all-important West Indian trade. On 24 June 1803, shortly after the beginning of the "second war," instructions were issued to the commanders of British warships and privateers not to seize any neutral vessels found carrying on trade directly between the colonies of the enemy and the country to which the vessel belonged, and laden with the property of the inhabitants of such neutral country, the usual reservation being added as to contraband and attempts to run the blockade.[32] These instructions, which embodied in a different form the relaxation of the Rule of 1756 contained in those of 25 January 1798, gave an equal opportunity for covering the trade of the enemy with "the frauds of the neutral flags," while at first nothing was done to check the abuse of the liberty accorded to neutrals to carry on an indirect trade between the enemy colonies and Europe.

When Pitt returned to power, in 1804, an attempt was made to encourage British trade in the Caribbean by extending the system of free ports in the various colonies, and for a time with some success.[33] In the long run, however, this expedient broke down owing to the prosperous trade conducted by the Americans between the enemy colonies and Europe under cover of the "broken voyage." This reduced the price of coffee on the European Continent and so diminished the amount reëxported from England, with serious results for the British revenue and the profits of the planters, whose stocks accumulated at the free ports while the British ships chartered to carry them lay idle.[34] James Stephen was but voicing the

---

[31] In 1792 the tonnage of British vessels engaged in the carrying trade of Great Britain was 3,151,389, that of foreign vessels 479,630; in 1800 it was 2,825,078 and 1,448,287, respectively. Quoted from Macpherson's *Annals of Commerce* in Mahan, II, 229.   [32] Stephen, *op. cit.*, p. 36.   [33] Mahan, II, p. 267.
[34] See the petition of the West Indian planters, *infra*, pp. 143-144.

opinion of all classes in England when he exposed and denounced
the tricks by which the American traders evaded belligerent rights,
and criticized the weak and accommodating policy of the Government which had made such evasion not only possible but easy.

For Stephen the root of all the trouble lay in the relaxation of the
Rule of 1756 under the instructions mentioned above. He was, indeed, too sound a lawyer to assert that all relaxations had been
illegitimate. "At certain free ports of the French West Indies," he
wrote, "importation and exportation of certain specified commodities
under a foreign flag were allowed before the last war. Certain provisions, lumber, etc., were admitted in American bottoms, in return
for rum, taffia and molasses. So far, therefore, a relaxation of the
Rule of 1756 is demanded by the principles of that rule, in favor of
the free ports; and it seems due also in respect of all the ports of
the hostile West Indies on another score; for we have relaxed our
own colonial monopoly, in an irregular manner,[35] during the last and
present war, so as to admit American provisions and lumber, and
export rum and molasses in American bottoms." He therefore concluded that, on the principle of reciprocity, the trade thus limited
could not legitimately be interfered with, quoting the maxim: *In
jure belli, quod quis sibi sumit, hostibus tribuendum est.*[36] But
though, in his view, certain relaxations of the Rule were thus obliga-
tory, he insisted that the vital interests of Great Britain demanded
that the equally valid obligations of neutrals under the Rule should
be enforced.

[35] From 1793 to 1801 the governors of the British West India islands exercised
the power of granting, as necessity required, permission to import provisions and
timber from the United States, and every year a bill was passed by Parliament indemnifying those concerned in this "irregular" traffic. In 1801, owing to the confusion caused by the change of Ministry, the customary bill was not introduced.
The practice, however, continued, and on 31 March 1805, Lord Auckland introduced a bill to indemnify those engaged in it (6 Hansard, p. 594). This became an
Act of Parliament (46 Geo. III, cap. 53) on 23 May.

By the Acts of 45 Geo. III, caps. 34 and 57, and 46 Geo. III, cap. 111 (American Intercourse Act), liberty to trade with the British West Indies was greatly
extended, sixteen free ports being established there to which small vessels of any
nationality, including those of the enemy, were to be allowed to import cargoes.

This whole policy was shaply criticized in Parliament. George Rose, who was to
be President of the Board of Trade in the Tory Government, pointed out that,
whereas before 1793 there had been a great increase of British shipping engaged
in the colonial trade, the number of ships thus engaged had sunk, since the relaxation of the Navigation Acts, from 937 to 167 (Debate of 21 April 1805, 6 Hansard,
p. 835).

[36] Stephen, *op. cit.*, p. 200.

THE ESSEX, ORNE DECISION

Stephen's book made a great sensation, for it was written not only with vigor but with authority, and it undoubtedly helped to stiffen the attitude of the British Government toward the "frauds of the neutral flag." Some months before the book appeared, indeed, a more rigorous application of the Rule of 1756 had been initiated by the famous judgment of the Lords Commissioners of Appeal in the *Essex, Orne* case, which established the principle that the question of a "broken" or "continuous" voyage must be determined by proof of the original intention. While, however, this was the leading case establishing the principle, the principle itself was no new one. It had been asserted in the course of the judgment of the Lords Commissioners of Appeal in the case of the *Eagle,* in May 1803.[37] The case of the *Essex* had come on for hearing in the High Court of Admiralty in the following August, though the judgment was not confirmed until May 1805, and on the same day the schooner *Freeport,* which had carried a cargo from Cadiz to Boston and was captured on the way to one of the Spanish colonies, was condemned on the confession of the master that it had been his intention to sell the goods in these colonies.[38]

It seems, indeed, that the prominence given henceforth to the principle of intention in the judgments of the Courts of Admiralty was due, as Mahan suggests, to the fact that the change in the law of the United States had only recently been forced on the attention of the judges. The exact significance of the decision in the *Essex, Orne* case was pointed out by Sir William Scott in the course of his judgment in the case of the *Maria, Jackson* on 18 September 1805. So far as the principle of law in the question of continuous voyage was concerned, he said, this had been decided by the Court of Appeal in the case of the *Essex.* It was there laid down that "the mere touching at any port without importing the cargo into the common

---

[37] After stating that the cargo had been landed at Philadelphia and the duties paid there, the judgment continued: "But we did not so limit our enquiry. To discover the real purpose and intention of the owner, we called for the orders he had given concerning purchase and shipment at Balboa, and also for the insurances made from thence. . . . Could it be supposed that we would pay no regard to that result of the enquiry which we had directed, but would ascribe to the payment of duties such conclusive effect, as would have rendered every other part of the enquiry perfectly nugatory."—5 C. Robinson 401.

[38] 5 C. Robinson 402.

stock of the country, will not alter the nature of the voyage, which continues the same in all respects, and must be considered as a voyage to the country to which the vessel is actually going for the purpose of delivering her cargo at the ultimate port." This principle, he pointed out, was not a novel one: "the *Essex, Orne* was in fact the first case which called for the direct decision of the Superior Court; but the same doctrine would have been held in any other case; if such a case had occurred at an earlier period; and cases had occurred before, very sufficient to convey a full admonition on the subject." As the *Essex*, however, happened to be the leading case on the subject, he thought that it would not be improper for him to state what he considered to be the substance of it. The *Essex*, he said, which was an American vessel owned by William Orne of Salem, Mass., had cleared from America for Lisbon and, finding the market there bad, had proceeded to Barcelona, where it had loaded a cargo of Spanish produce for Havannah under direction from the agent in Europe "that she go to the Havannah, first *touching* at Salem, where the owner resided, who adopted the plan and sent the vessel on." It was clearly the intention, originating in the mind of the authorized agent and adopted by the owner, that this vessel should go to the Havannah. It was, he concluded, "a case of a trade from the mother country to the colony, with the full knowledge of the circumstances, and a distinct adoption of the purpose on the part of the owner." [39]

As a result of the decision in the *Essex* case, and of others that followed, great numbers of American vessels were seized and brought in for adjudication. By no means all were condemned; in the case of two of those mentioned above, for instance, the *Eagle* and the *Maria,* restitution was ordered on proof being given that the cargoes were really intended for the American market. But the long process of trial, even if the release of ship and cargo with due compensation followed, was a serious interruption to trade, and honest American merchants had some reason to complain. It was natural enough, too, that those who had used the expedient of a fictitious broken voyage to cover their actual intention, should feel a sense of grievance when, after a long period of immunity, their vessels were seized and condemned when in the opinion of the British courts the duties had only nominally been paid. "It is hard to see the objection to these

[39] 5 C. Robinson 365, 369.

decisions," says Mahan, "based on the validity of payments, but the British Government must be censured for not having given notice of its decision no longer to accept, as proof of importation, the payment of duties by bond, on which drawback was given." It ought, he says, to have known the American law.[40] The decision, however, lay not with the British Government but with the British courts, and it was impossible in the nature of things to arrive at such a decision at once. The new American law was enacted in 1799; the case of the *William* referred to above was first decided in the Vice-admiralty Court in Halifax in July 1800, but was not finally decided on appeal until 11 March 1806. Apart from the slow procedure in prize cases in general, such delays were inevitable when intention had to be proved, for the matter of intention could only be judged by the circumstances and these could only be determined by the production of papers and other evidence which it sometimes took months to procure. That there were grounds for complaint on both sides may be admitted, but it is hard to apportion the blame. The unfortunate fact remains that the difference of opinion between the Americans as neutrals and the British as belligerents thus early produced a tension between the two kindred countries which, during the titanic struggle between the mistress of the seas and the master of the Continent in the years that followed, was to reach the breaking point.

[40] Mahan, II, 269.

VI

THE CONTINENTAL SYSTEM

The year of peace that followed the Treaty of Amiens was but a period of deceptive calm before a renewed outbreak of the storm with even greater violence. So far as trade relations between the two great antagonists were concerned, indeed, there was no peace; for Napoleon was determined to lose no opportunity for stimulating French commerce at the expense of the "nation of shopkeepers." By a decree of 9 Thermidor, An X (22 July 1802), accordingly, he fixed a customs tariff from 50 to 100 per cent higher on goods imported from foreign colonies than on those imported from the colonies of France, an arrangement that was practically unchanged in the new customs statute of 8 Floréal, An XI (22 April 1803), under which the high duty of 8 francs per kilogram was also imposed upon cotton goods, with the obvious intention of damaging the British textile industry.[1] The British Government, on the other hand, while not retaliating in kind, took certain precautionary measures. For the encouragement of trade an Act was passed permitting certain goods imported into Great Britain to be secured in warehouses without payment of duty while, for revenue purposes, another Act imposed duties "on goods imported into, and exported from, Great Britain, and on the tonnage of ships and vessels entering outwards or inwards, in any port of Great Britain, to or from, for foreign ports." Above all, it was noted that no undue haste was made in paying off ships of war, and that an unusually large number of seamen remained on the peace establishment.[2]

The "second war" broke out in May 1803, and at once brought with a resumption of the commercial war. At first this was conducted, generally speaking, on the old lines. On 17 May an Order in Council directed the seizure of all French and Dutch ships lying in British harbors. Napoleon, on the other hand, created a new and un-

[1] Heckscher, *The Continental System* (1922), p. 83.

[2] In spite of this, neutral shipping employed fell from 28 per cent in 1801 to 18½ per cent in 1802. Mahan, II, 265. The number of foreign ships entering the ports of Great Britain from the United States fell from 728 in 1801 to 375 in 1802.

happy precedent by ordering the arrest of the thousands of Englishmen who had taken advantage of the peace to travel in France and were surprised by the declaration of war. On 20 June (1 Messidor, An XI) he issued a decree directing the confiscation of any produce of British colonies and any British manufactures introduced into France, and laying on neutral vessels entering French ports the obligation to present papers, signed by the French consul at the port of embarkation, certifying that no part of the cargo was of British origin.[3] Holland, though still nominally independent, was forced to adopt the same measure. On the 24th a British Order in Council was issued which regulated neutral trade with enemy colonies on lines somewhat more favorable to this trade than those laid down in the instructions of September 1798.[4]

THE CONTINENTAL SYSTEM AND BRITISH COUNTER MEASURES

Meanwhile Napoleon, elaborating the old plan of excluding British trade altogether from the Continent, had occupied Hanover and taken military measures to sever all intercourse of Great Britain with Hamburg and Bremen, the two most important centers of seaborne commerce, measures which promised to be successful after the district of Ritzebüttel, with Cuxhaven, at the mouth of the Elbe, had been occupied by a French force. The reply of the British Government was to proclaim a blockade of the Elbe (28 June) and Weser (26 July), the immediate effect of which was to ruin the trade of the two great Hanse cities, which had hitherto gained enormous profits from the war.[5] As for the trade of Great Britain, that was simply diverted into other channels, the Prussian ports—notably Emden in East Friesland and Stettin at the mouth of the Oder—gaining much of the commerce which the Hanse cities had lost.[6]

The year 1804 produced no sensational developments. The British relied on a system of blockades, which had the advantage of being easy to modify according to circumstance, but also the disadvantage of being difficult to make effective.[7] Thus in January a blockade was

---

[3] Heckscher, op. cit., p. 84.   [4] See supra, p. 117.
[5] See infra, p. 276.   [6] See infra, pp. 289 and 297.
[7] Mahan points out that a blockade of the French coast similar to that of the Confederate States during the American Civil War was impossible. The weather in the Southern States is more moderate and the gales blow along shore, while in the Bay of Biscay they blow dead on shore, and there is an absence of similar sheltered anchorages. Steamers favour blockade, while sailing ships have to gain an offing before the gale, and drift helpless while it lasts.—Mahan, I, 99.

proclaimed of the French colonies of Guadeloupe and Martinique, and this was extended in April to Curaçoa; on 8 August an Order in Council declared all the French ports on the coasts of the Channel and North Sea to be blockaded. Napoleon, for his part, elaborated his policy of prohibition. The customs statute of 22 Ventôse, An XII (13 March 1804), indeed, so far modified the provisions of the decree of Messidor as to allow goods from ports where there was no French consul to be imported without certificates; but, on the other hand, it made them more strict by prohibiting the admission into any French port of vessels which had cleared from, or unnecessarily put into, any British port.[8] This last regulation anticipated the Berlin Decree, which was to be the foundation charter of what Napoleon himself named "the Continental System."

Trade is like water: if its course is obstructed, it seeks another channel; if the obstruction is not impervious, it creeps through every crevice. Thus Napoleon once more discovered that, in spite of all his prohibitions, British goods and vessels cleared from British ports were still finding their way into the ports of his Empire. To stop this infiltration, which threatened to swamp all his plans, he decided to settle the difficulty of distinguishing what goods were of British origin by setting up a prohibitive tariff barrier against all foreign goods alíke. The foundation of this barrier was laid by the Customs Tariff of 17 Pluviôse, An XIII (6 February 1805), which greatly increased the duties on colonial and cotton goods, but it was not completed until the spring of the following year. Two decrees, issued on 22 February and 4 March 1806 and embodied in the customs code of the Empire in the following April, laid enormous extra duties on colonial goods and, in doing so, made little or no distinction between those of French and those of foreign origin. For the battle of Trafalgar had made Great Britain more than ever the mistress of the seas, and it was more than probable that the French colonial trade of the French colonies would fall into the hands of the English in one way or another.

If Nelson's victory of 21 October 1805 had given Great Britain the unchallenged command of the sea, Napoleon's crushing victory at Austerlitz in December of the same year gave him unchallenged command of the greater part of western Europe, and thus enabled him to extend his system of prohibitions and high tariffs over the

[8] Heckscher, *op. cit.*, p. 84.

wide area covered by his own Empire and its satellite States. The object of this system, as Professor Heckscher has made clear, was twofold: on the one hand, to cut off British trade with the Continent, and on the other hand to protect the industries and trade of France.[9] The first object seemed to be within sight of attainment when, on 15 February 1806, Prussia sacrificed her neutrality to the temptation of acquiring Hanover, and signed a treaty with Napoleon under the terms of which she closed her ports to Great Britain. But the ring-fence was even now not complete. Apart from the Baltic ports of Russia, whence British goods could be carried by river or road into central Europe, there were still gateways left open for British trade to enter on the south coast of the Baltic. These were Bremen, Lübeck and Stralsund, the port and capital of Swedish Pomerania, which stands on the west bank of the Oder opposite the island of Rügen.

The possibilities presented by this latter port had been recognized by the British Government; for, though Stettin was the natural route to the interior of Germany, Prussia at the best of times was "not accommodating," and, in the event of communications with the Continent being only possible by way of Gothenburg, the route by way of Stralsund and the Oder "would be a safe channel." [10] As early as 3 December 1804, accordingly, Great Britain had signed a preliminary and secret convention with Sweden, under which a subsidy was granted for the specific purpose of putting the port in a state of defense.[11] It was not, indeed, until 3 October 1805 that King Gustavus IV, moved by indignation at the murder of the Duc d'Enghien, formally joined the Coalition; but in the previous May he had granted to British subjects "during the continuance of the war between Great Britain and France, the right of warehousing at

[9] The way in which Napoleon sacrificed the interests of the vassal and allied States of his Empire to the interests of France is well illustrated by the case of his own Kingdom of Italy. Here, in 1806, a number of articles, especially textile goods, were declared, in accordance with earlier examples, to be *eo ipso* British, and were consequently prohibited when they did not come from France—a declaration which was in reality directed principally against the continental rivals of France (Heckscher, *op. cit.*, p. 86). In reality, says Professor Heckscher, "those measures which affected industrial products were felt most severely, not by Great Britain, but by her continental competitors, especially those in the then Duchy of Berg, or what is now the Ruhr district east of the Rhine" (*ibid.*, p. 84).

[10] Oddy, *European Commerce* (1805), p. 319.

[11] Martens, *Supplément au Recueil de traités,* IV (1802-1808), 158.

Stralsund all goods and merchandise, the produce of Great Britain or of its colonies, conveyed in English or Swedish vessels." [12]

Prussia was destined to pay dear for what was an act of shameless aggression. Hanover was occupied on 28 March, and on 1 April a royal patent proclaimed its annexation. The reply of the British Government was prompt. On 23 April an embargo was laid on all Prussian ships lying in British harbors, and a blockade of all Prussian ports was proclaimed. This was followed by an Order in Council authorizing the seizure of all ships sailing under the Prussian flag, of which as many as four hundred were presently captured.[13] The Prussian maritime cities, more especially Stettin, suffered severely, not only from the interruption of their trade, but from the havoc wrought among their shipping.[14]

Meanwhile, the death of Pitt, on 23 January 1806, had seemed to promise some relaxation of the severity of the British measures in restraint of neutral commerce with the enemy; for under the new prime minister, Lord Grenville, Charles James Fox was charged with the conduct of the Foreign Office, and his attitude while in opposition had been consistently favorable to an accommodation with the Revolution and with France. Once in office, however, he was brought face to face with the realities of the situation and discovered that no drastic change of policy was possible. He had objected to the application of the Rule of 1756 while he was in opposition; he found it impossible to reverse it when he was in office.[15] Its application was, however, modified by an Order in Council of 16 May, which placed the coast of the Continent from Brest to the Elbe in a state of blockade. This blockade was to be absolute against all commerce only between the Seine and Ostend. Outside these limits, on the coast of France west of the Seine, and the coasts of France, Holland and Germany east of Ostend, the rights of capture attaching to blockades would be forborne in favor of neutral vessels, provided they had not cleared from, and were not bound for, one of the enemy's ports, and carried none of his goods or contraband.[16] This meant that the admission of neutral ships to ports thus partially blockaded, or to enemy ports not subject to blockade, was

[12] Oddy, *loc. cit.*
[13] *Annual Register*, 1806, pp. 159, 161; 6 Hansard, pp. 882, 886.
[14] See *infra*, p. 298.
[15] Mahan, *Sea Power in Its Relation to the War of 1812*, II, 269.
[16] Mahan, *op. cit.*, I, 104 ff.

to be determined, not by the origin of the cargo, but by the port of lading; thus the trade between enemy colonies and the mother country by way of American ports was tacitly admitted, while the question of principle in dispute with the United States was tacitly waived. The order, in fact, represented a compromise. The object of relieving the strict blockade of the Elbe and Weser, already established, was doubtless partly to encourage neutrals to carry British goods to the northern ports, which was also the object of the further Order in Council of 21 May directing that neutral ships were not to be stopped in the Baltic. Like all half-measures, however, this modified system proved ineffective, since it satisfied neither the demands of British traders nor the claims of neutrals. "It was at least doubtful," comments Mahan, "whether the British would be able to secure an effective blockade from Brest to the Elbe. But the United States and Napoleon had no doubts about it. Therefore, by a singular irony of fate, it fell to Fox, as almost the last act of his life, to fire the train which led to the Berlin and Milan Decrees, the Orders in Council of 1807, and war with the United States." [17]

The Berlin Decree

The reaction of the United States to the developments of the economic war in Europe will be more conveniently dealt with in a separate section. So far as the situation in Europe is concerned, the British blockade served indeed as the pretext for the Berlin Decree, but the train leading up to this decree had long been laid, and its promulgation was due to Napoleon's confident belief that he was at last in a position to be able to ruin Great Britain by entirely cutting off her commerce with the Continent. His confidence, indeed, seemed to be justified. Prussia, which had been the unwilling executor of his economic policy, had been goaded into war with him, and on 12 October had suffered ruinous defeat at the battle of Jena. On the 26th, Napoleon was in Berlin and in a position to perfect his plans for closing the hitherto neutral ports of northwestern Germany to British trade. The great Hanse seaports were still neutral, and had become independent states with the ending of the Holy Roman Empire in the previous August; but these were details which Napoleon could afford to ignore. Lübeck was occupied by his troops on 4 November, Hamburg on the 19th of the same month, and Bremen,

[17] Mahan, *op. cit.*, II, 270. Fox died on 25 September 1806, and was succeeded at the Foreign Office by Lord Howick (better known later as Earl Grey).

with the line of the Weser, on the 21st. Meanwhile, the British Government, by an Order in Council of 25 September, had removed the partial blockade of the coast between the Ems and the Elbe, and many neutral ships clearing from British ports had taken advantage of this relaxation. The reply of Napoleon was the decree of 13 November ordering the seizure on this coast of any vessel which had touched at a British port. Finally, on the 21st he published from Berlin the famous decree which was, in effect, a declaration of war *à outrance* not only against British commerce, but against that of all those who should dare to trade with her or carry on her trade.

The preamble to the Berlin Decree justified the severity of the measures proposed in it by pleading the right of retaliation. In its treatment of neutrals, it was urged, the British Government had violated all the rules of international law; it regarded as an enemy every individual belonging to a hostile State and so had made prisoners, not only the crews of privateers, but also those of innocent merchantmen; it had extended to ships and objects of trade that right of conquest which could only be properly asserted in the case of public property; it had included commercial cities and harbors, and the mouths of rivers in the hardships of blockade, which, on the best interpretation of the law of nations, could only be applied to fortified places, and it had declared blockades of entire coasts and a whole Empire where it had not a single ship of war. It had been guilty of all these monstrous violations of the law of nations with the sole object of obstructing the communications of other people and of elevating the industry and commerce of England upon the ruins of those of the Continent. This being the evident design of England, whoever dealt on the Continent in British merchandise favored this design and became a sharer in it. Therefore, since every belligerent had the right to combat the enemy with his own weapons, it was decreed: (1) that the British Islands were placed in a state of blockade, (2) that communication of any kind with them was forbidden, (3) that every British subject found in the territories occupied by the troops of France or her allies was to be made a prisoner of war, (4) that all merchandise belonging to British subjects, or coming from British colonies, was to be lawful prize, (5) that all trade in English goods was to be prohibited, (6) that half the proceeds from the sale of such goods confiscated was to go toward the indemnification of merchants whose vessels had been seized by the British, (7) that no vessels coming from Great Britain and the British colonies, or which should have touched at a British port, were to be allowed to enter the harbors of the French Empire and (8) that vessels entering by means of false declarations were to be confiscated.[18]

News of the Berlin Decree was received in England at the beginning of December and produced something like a panic in the mercantile world. The rates of insurance on goods shipped from Great Britain to the Continent rose sharply [19] and, according to the evidence of merchants given before a parliamentary committee, exports to the Continent practically ceased during the months of December 1806 and of January and February 1807.[20] It soon became clear, however, that no attempt was being made to enforce the decree at sea and that the attempts to enforce it on land were, to say the least, very ineffective. By decrees issued on 2 and 3 December, Napoleon had established a customs cordon along the northwest coast of Germany and ordered his generals to guard the great waterways and to seize any vessels attempting to enter laden with British goods, while all such goods already landed were to be confiscated. The generals and customs officials, however, saw in these measures only a glorious opportunity for enriching themselves,[21] and since the profits of trade with the Continent amply covered the necessary bribes and any probable losses by confiscation, British shipments to the Continental ports were resumed in March 1807 and by August were "on a greater scale than at any former period." [22] Nothing, indeed, could better illustrate the weakness of the barriers thus far erected against British trade by the decree than the fact that, during the winter of 1806-1807, the French army was clothed and shod with British goods, imported by the French Minister in Hamburg.[23]

---

[18] French text in 1 Martens, p. 437; English text in *Annual Register*, 1806, p. 201 and A.S.P., F.R., III, 262.

[19] For example, insurances on goods shipped to Holland rose from 6 guineas to 10 guineas per cent. Evidence of Mr. Dewar, an underwriter. 13 Hansard, App. II, xxxvi.

[20] *Ibid.*, xxxiii. Evidence of William Hall.

[21] For the activities of Marshal Brune at Hamburg, and the behavior of the customs officials generally, see Heckscher, *op. cit.*, p. 165.

[22] 13 Hansard, App. II, xxxiii.

[23] Bourrienne, *Mémoires*, VII, 292; Mahan, *Sea Power in Its Relation to the War of 1812*, II, 273.

The Order in Council of 7 January 1807

At the close of the year 1806, however, these developments could not be foreseen and, in view of the critical situation in which British trade seemed to be placed by the decree, Lord Grenville's Government decided that it was necessary to take counter measures. On 7 January 1807, accordingly, an Order in Council was issued forbidding vessels to trade between ports belonging to or in the possession of France or her allies, or so far under her control as to prevent British vessels freely trading thereat, while naval commanders were instructed to warn ships bound for such ports and if the warning were disregarded to bring them in for adjudication as lawful prize. These instructions were justified in a long preamble, which pointed out that the French Government had issued certain orders, in violation of the usages of war, purporting to prohibit the commerce of neutral nations with His Majesty's dominions and to prevent such nations from trading with other nations in any articles of British origin, and had further declared His Majesty's dominions to be in a state of blockade "at a time when the fleets of France and her allies are confined within their own ports by the superior valour and discipline of the British navy." Such attempts on the part of the enemy would have given His Majesty "an unquestionable right of retaliation" and have warranted him in enforcing a similar prohibition of all commerce with France, "a prohibition which the superiority of His Majesty's naval forces might enable him to support, by actually investing the ports and coasts of the enemy with numerous cruisers and squadrons, so as to make the entrance or approach thereto manifestly dangerous." If this had not been done, it was because His Majesty was "unwilling to follow the example of his enemies, by proceeding to an extremity so distressing to all nations not engaged in the war, and carrying on their accustomed trade." [24]

This "very mild and lenient measure of retaliation," as the historian Sir Archibald Alison described it,[25] was attacked by Spencer Perceval in the House of Commons as too mild to serve any effective purpose. With the principle of retaliation enunciated in the order he had no quarrel, for "it was the maddest proposition that ever was laid down, that any belligerent power should be restrained by laws which its enemy had renounced." But the two main objects

---

[24] 10 Hansard, p. 127; *Annual Register*, 1807, p. 671; Heckscher, *op. cit.*, App. I, p. 389.   [25] Alison, *History of Europe*, XI, 156.

of retaliation were to counteract the evil effects on Great Britain of the measures of her enemies, and to make them feel the ill effects of their own injustice; and the provisions of the Order in Council would attain neither of these objects. As for the evil effects of the Berlin Decree on British trade, he hoped that these would be counteracted "by the elastic principle of trade itself" and that, in spite of all prohibitions, British commodities would continue to find their way to the Continent. But that some harm would be done was certain, if only because the risks of capture and condemnation would send up the rates of insurance, which would force the seller to enhance his price, and so enable others to compete with him and even to undersell him. To attack the enemy's coasting trade would do nothing to remedy this, quite apart from the fact that this trade was the most difficult to attack effectively, since the vessels carrying it on could take refuge in inlets and shallows or under the guns of shore batteries. It would be better, he considered, to prohibit altogether the importation into France of the produce of the French and Spanish colonies; for, even if this could not be done completely, the cost of such importation would be increased, the prices of the articles imported would be raised, and so enable British commodities "to meet them with advantage." Finally, he threw out a suggestion which was embodied, under the new Tory Government, in the famous Orders in Council issued in November of the same year.

You might [he said] turn the provisions of the French decree against themselves, and as they have said that no British goods shall sail freely on the seas, you might say that no goods should be carried to France, except they first touched at a British port. They might be forced to be first entered at the customs-house, and a certain entry imposed, which would contribute to enhance the price, and give a better sale in the foreign market to your own commodities.[26]

Perceval was supported in a vigorous speech by Lord Castlereagh. It had been suggested in the course of the debate that the mild character of the Order in Council had been due to fear of offending the Americans, and so of imperilling the ratification of the treaty of commerce and amity which had been concluded with the United States on 31 December.[27] With reference to this, Castlereagh contended that the Government should not be deterred from taking vigorous measures by "considerations of forbearance towards Amer-

[26] Speech in the debate of 4 February 1807, 8 Hansard, pp. 620 ff.
[27] Speech of Sir Thomas Turton, 8 Hansard, p. 647.

ica," which, instead of taking action as in 1798, had wasted its time in futile negotiations with the French Government. "If they were to wait till the American Government should insist upon those principles by which the law of nations is upheld," he said, "they might wait till doomsday, as, whatever might be their feelings, the commercial people would attend to their commercial interests." The situation of France, he urged, was wholly different from what it had been in 1798, when she had not identified herself with the whole of Europe, as she now did, and unless more vigorous measures of retaliation were adopted, she would have a larger share of the trade with her own and the Spanish colonies than heretofore, and would not only be able to supply herself with colonial produce but would have a monopoly of all the continental markets. As for America, "it was an aggravation that she had, by a secret understanding with the French Government, contrived to take her shipping out of the operation of the decree, which was at first general and so placed herself in a situation of connivance with the French Government." [28]

[28] 8 Hansard, pp. 640 ff. The reference to a "secret understanding" is to an exchange of notes between General Armstrong, the American Minister in Paris, and Admiral Decrès, the Minister of Marine and the Colonies, when the latter gave "such a construction of the decree of November 1806, as would substantially exempt the United States from its operation." Decrès's letter, which is dated 24 December 1806, runs as follows:

"I consider the Imperial decree of the 21st of November last as, thus far, conveying no modification of the regulations at present observed in France, with regard to neutral navigators, nor consequently of the Convention of the 30th of September 1800 (8th Vendémiaire, 9th year) with the United States.

"But although, by this answer, the four questions upon which your excellency has desired to know my opinion have been implicitly resolved, I think I can add

1st. That the declaration expressed by the first article of the decree of the 21st of November, not at all changing the present French laws regarding marine captures, there is no reason for inquiring what interpretation, or restriction, or extension, may be given to this article.

2nd. That seizures, contrary to the present regulations concerning cruising, shall not be allowed to the captors.

3rd. That an American vessel cannot be taken at sea, for the mere reason that she is going to a port in England, or is returning from one; because, conformably with the 7th article of the said decree, we are limited in France not to admit vessels coming from England or the English colonies.

4th. That the provisions of articles 2nd and 5th of the said decree, naturally apply to foreign citizens domiciliated in France, or in the countries occupied by the troops of His Majesty the Emperor and King, inasmuch as they have the character of a general law; but that it will be proper that your excellency should communicate with the Minister of External Relations as to what concerns the correspondence of the citizens of the United States with England." This is the official translation given in A.S.P., *Commerce and Navigation*, I, 805.

In reply to these criticisms, Lord Howick asked if Ministers were to be condemned for not going the full length of imitating the wildness and extravagance of the enemy,[29] while Sir John Nicholls, the attorney general, pointed out that to shut the door on neutral commerce would mean shutting the door also, in a great degree, on that of England, and he argued that the restriction of trade from one enemy port to another, a trade which was mainly carried on in neutralized vessels, would hit the enemy hard and with the least possible harm to neutrals.[30]

PROTEST OF DENMARK-NORWAY

This view was not, however, shared by the neutrals concerned. The reaction to the Order in Council in the United States will be discussed later. In Europe, where neutrals were now few, the power most interested was Denmark-Norway, whose merchants had taken advantage of the war to build up a flourishing carrying trade between the ports of France and her allies on the Atlantic coasts and, more especially, those of the Mediterranean. J. G. Rist, the Danish chargé d'affaires in London, was therefore instructed by his Government to present a protest against the Order. In doing so he pointed out that the Berlin Decree was "limited in its application," since it did not pretend to interrupt direct trade between Denmark and Great Britain; that it so evidently obliged France herself and her allies to share in the evils and annoyances directed against the commerce of neutrals as "to carry with it the guarantee of its lenient execution, and probably of its short duration"; and that it was to be feared that the effect of the Order in Council would be to drive Napoleon to further extremes.

Lord Howick replied in unequivocal terms. The decree of 21 November, he said,

is a manifest act of hostile aggression (though immediately directed against Great Britain) against the rights of every state not engaged in the war, which, if not resisted on their part, must unavoidably deprive them of the privileges of a fair neutrality, and must suspend the operation of treaties formed for the protection of neutral rights, thus fundamentally violated in their first and most essential principles.

Neutrality [he pointed out], properly considered, does not consist in taking advantage of every situation between belligerent states by which emolument may accrue to the neutral, whatever may be the consequences to either belligerent party; but in observing a strict and honest impartiality, so as not

---

[29] 8 Hansard, p. 651.   [30] 8 Hansard, p. 636.

to afford an advantage in the war to either; and, particularly, in so far restraining its trade to the accustomed course which it held in time of peace, so as not to render assistance to one belligerent in escaping the effects of the other's hostilities.

In this respect the conduct of Denmark had been far from neutral. "It is notorious," he said, "that the trade thus carried on is supported by the shameful misconduct of neutral merchants, who lend their names for a small percentage, not only to cover the goods, but in numberless instances to mask the ships of the enemy." He went on to suggest that the trade was illegitimate even when carried on in vessels sailing honestly under their own neutral flag.

The coasting trade of the enemy in time of peace [he said] is carried on by his own navigation. Even the other branches of trade referred to, namely from Holland to France, to Spain, and to the hostile ports of the Mediterranean, in time of peace, chiefly pass by the navigation of those countries respectively. . . . It is principally from the success of the British maritime force, which has almost annihilated the navigation of the enemy, that the ships of Denmark and other neutral states are employed as carriers from hostile port to hostile port, in order to relieve the enemy from his distress. Whenever it can be shown [he added] that a Danish or other neutral vessel, after having delivered her outward cargo, or any part of it, at one of the ports in the possession of France or her allies, or occupied by that power, shall bona fide propose to proceed to another, solely for the purpose of shipping a cargo, consisting of such articles as she may require for the homeward voyage, it is clear that such vessel would not be considered in our courts of prize as liable to the penal consequences of the Order. In framing the Order in Council of the 7th of January, his majesty's government has indeed studiously endeavoured to avoid distressing nations not engaged in the war. Neutrals are still free to trade with hostile countries. . . . The object of the Order in Council is to prevent the enemy carrying on his coasting trade through the means of neutral bottoms, at a time when the naval superiority of Great Britain precludes him from effecting it in vessels navigating under his own flag.

The Order, in short, was intended to damage the trade of the enemy with as little harm as possible to the legitimate trade of neutrals.[31]

Rist pointed out that Danish subjects would be the principal sufferers.

They are menaced [he said] with the deprivation of a branch of their navigation, which has occupied until the present time hundreds of vessels,

---

[31] In the debate in the House of Lords, on 15 February 1808, Lord Hawkesbury (afterwards Earl of Liverpool) described the Order in Council in question as "only a trifling enlargement of the principle of the war of 1756."—10 Hansard, p. 484.

thousands of sailors and industrious workmen, and considerable capitals. Henceforth the Mediterranean will, for the most part, be shut against their enterprises: a voyage from Holland to France, from Italy to Spain, from the Hanse towns to the ports of the Mediterranean, will render their vessels and their cargoes subject to confiscation . . . it is wished that they shall renounce, not only the considerable advantages which the neutrality of their flag insures them in carrying on the coasting trade, but also the continuance of an essential part of their direct and legitimate commerce with the ports above-mentioned. After having sold their planks, fish and corn in the northern ports of Holland, they will have to return in ballast because unable to obtain in Italian and Spanish ports such merchandise as the countries of the north have occasion for. To fetch oil, wine, brandy &c. they will have to sail in ballast to the Mediterranean ports.[32]

The reply of Howick was, that "if third parties suffer from these measures, their demand of reparation must be made to that country which first violates the established usages of war, and the rights of neutral states." [33] British Ministers, indeed, scented in the Danish protest a revival of the spirit of the Armed Neutrality, and in this they were right. The Order, in all the circumstances, was certainly not without justification; but it was among the contributary causes which, later in the year, ranged Denmark-Norway as a belligerent on the side of France.

Rist's suggestion that the Order in Council would drive Napoleon into greater extremes seemed to receive speedy confirmation. The Emperor was at Warsaw when the news of the issue of the new Order reached him, and he promptly decreed the confiscation of all British goods and all colonial produce accumulated in the Hanse Towns. Meanwhile the British Government, well knowing that the states of northern Germany were but unwilling partners in Napoleon's schemes, decided to relax the instructions under the Orders in Council in their favor. On 28 January a treaty of peace was signed with Prussia, by the terms of which Prussia renounced all claim to Hanover and opened her ports to British navigation and commerce. On 4 February an Order in Council instructed naval commanders not to interrupt neutral vessels coming from any port not strictly blockaded and laden with certain specified articles, the most important of which were grain (subject to the provisions of the corn laws) and naval stores.[34] On 18 February yet another Order ap-

[32] See *infra*, p. 250.

[33] For the Howick-Rist correspondence see Papers relating to Denmark and the Order in Council of 7 January 1807, presented to Parliament 15 February 1808. 10 Hansard, p. 397.

[34] Text in Heckscher, App. I, No. II, p. 390, and 10 Hansard, 128.

proved the draft of instructions directing that ships and goods belonging to the cities of Hamburg, Bremen and other places and countries in the North of Germany, engaged in the trade to or from the ports of the United Kingdom, were to be suffered, until further order, to pass free and unmolested, notwithstanding that the said countries were or might be in the possession or under the control of France and her allies.[35] These Orders were clearly inspired by the desire to encourage the British trade with the Continent, which, as already mentioned, had revived when it was observed that the Berlin Decree was not being enforced with any rigor, reaching its highest point at the beginning of August. Yet it was not any desire not to proceed to extremes which inspired Napoleon's delay in enforcing the provisions of the Decree, but his preoccupation with the war on land and the fact that his Continental System could only be perfected if Russia could be forced or persuaded to become a party to it.

This latter object was accomplished before long. The battle of Friedland was fought and won by Napoleon on 14 June, and a few days later he had his famous interview with the Tsar Alexander I on the barge moored in the middle of the river Niemen, in the course of which he dazzled the eyes of the young autocrat by the vision of sharing with him the empire of the world. The outcome was the Treaty of Tilsit, signed on 8 July, under the terms of which Russia undertook to close her ports to British trade and to join Napoleon in summoning the remaining neutral powers—Sweden, Denmark, Portugal and Austria—to do the same. The hopes of Prussia, based on the alliance with Russia and Sweden under the Convention of Bartenstein, concluded in April and adhered to by Great Britain in June, were now dashed, and on 19 July she was forced to sign a humiliating treaty with France. Under Article XVIII of this treaty all countries under the rule of Prussia were to be shut against British trade and navigation, and no shipments were to be made to or from Great Britain or her colonies. The order closing the Prussian ports was issued on 2 September, and Austria had no choice but to follow suit.[36]

[35] Text in Heckscher, *ibid.*, App. I, No. II, p. 391, and 10 Hansard, 129.

[36] Austria acceded to the Continental System on 28 February 1808. "In Austria, and especially in Bohemia, the industrialists welcomed the Berlin Decree, as freeing them from British competition. They remembered how, in 1805, the British had smuggled a million guldens' worth of cotton goods and thread into Austria and sold it 30 per cent under value, in order to crush Austrian industry."—Her-

British Seizure of the Danish Fleet

Dispatches had meanwhile been received by George Canning, the British Minister of Foreign Affairs, informing him that the two Emperors had agreed at Tilsit to summon the Courts of Copenhagen, Stockholm and Lisbon to close their ports to British commerce and declare war on Great Britain. The information was not altogether trustworthy; but there was plenty of reason to believe that Napoleon intended to force Denmark into his System and to add her fleet to the already formidable force with which he hoped successfully to challenge Great Britain's supremacy at sea. He denounced Denmark for allowing the British fleet, which had sailed to the relief of Stralsund, to pass the narrows; he insisted on the cessation of all correspondence between the Courts of Copenhagen and St. James's; Denmark, he said, "must either make war with England or with me." Finally, on 16 August, he ordered a demand to be sent to the Danish Government for the exclusion of British ships and wares from the ports of Denmark-Norway and for the coöperation of the Danish fleet with that of France.

This action had, however, been forestalled by the British Government. On 26 July a fleet of seventeen ships of the line, under Admiral Gambier, sailed from Yarmouth for Elsinore, where it arrived on 5 August. A special envoy had meanwhile been sent to the Danish crown prince regent at Kiel, to demand an explicit declaration of his policy, and to propose to Denmark a secret defensive alliance with Great Britain, of which the principal terms were the handing over of the Danish fleet, to be kept as a "sacred pledge" by the British until the peace, the payment of a subsidy of £100,000 to Denmark by way of compensation and an offer of armed assist-

---

mann Hallvich, *Firma Franz Leitenberger* (Prag, 1893), quoted in Tarle, *Deutsch-französische Wirtschaftsbeziehungen zur napoleonischen Zeit*, p. 177. The cheapness of British cotton goods was, of course, due to the new mechanical processes of manufacture. Under the Continental System there was a considerable development of industries in Austria, in spite of a certain shortage of raw materials, but after Napoleon's fall "innumerable undertakings" collapsed, since British wares had now only to reckon with the Austrian tariff and not with Napoleon's series of barriers (Tarle, *loc. cit.*). There was no lack of colonial wares during this period; for, although Austria was cut off from the sea, she continued to import these wares from the neighboring lands, Poland, Moravia and the Turkish provinces, the Danube taking the place of the Rhine.—Tarle, *op. cit.*, p. 175; Heckscher, *op. cit.*, p. 232.

ance in the event of Denmark being attacked by France. The position of the crown prince was a painful one. Napoleon's troops, under Bernadotte, were in occupation of Hamburg and ready at a moment's notice to invade Holstein, while from the sea Denmark was threatened by the British fleet at Elsinore and by that which was returning from Stralsund. The regent had long been suspected of French leanings, and it is probable that the somewhat humiliating terms proposed to him put an end to his hesitations. He refused the British terms, whereupon the British fleets converged upon Zealand, where an army some fifteen thousand strong was landed and proceeded to lay siege to Copenhagen. The bombardment began on 2 September and, after a gallant defense, the defenders capitulated on the 7th. The surrender of the fleet was now agreed to, and hostilities ceased. During their progress the British had occupied Heligoland, then a Danish possession, which was soon to become the great entrepôt for the smuggling trade on the northwest coast of Germany. It is perhaps not surprising that Denmark rejected the renewed offers of friendship and alliance made by Great Britain or that, when the stipulated six weeks' British occupation of Zealand was over, she formally joined the ranks of England's enemies. Canning's high-handed action had preserved England from a great danger, but at a great cost.[37]

Strict Enforcement of the Berlin Decree

Meanwhile, on 6 August, Napoleon had issued commands for the strict enforcement of the Berlin Decree. The ban on all trade with Great Britain was now made absolute, and "inspectors and customhouse officers in all the lands occupied by the French made search for English goods the excuse for innumerable frauds, vexations and

[37] For a discussion of the moral and other issues involved see Rose, *Life of Napoleon I*, II, 140 ff., and Rose in *The Cambridge Modern History*, IX (1906), 295 ff. Mr. H. W. Wilson (*ibid.*, p. 236) says: "That the attack was necessary no one will now deny. England was fighting for her existence; and, however disagreeable was the task of striking a weak neutral, she risked her own safety if she left in Napoleon's hands a fleet of such proportions." Dr. Holland Rose says that "Canning's policy . . . rested on an induction the premises of which were insecure, but which was based on a sound estimate of Napoleon's character and of his probable action." Canning, he says, was deeply chagrined by the tragic outcome of his policy. He had hoped that Denmark, having the excuse of British pressure, would have agreed to join Great Britain and Sweden in a coalition against Napoleon. Perhaps the best justification for the *coup* was that, when Napoleon heard of its success "his rage knew no bounds."

iniquities." [38] On 18 September, in order to avoid all doubt as to the scope of the Decree, instructions were issued to French armed vessels to seize all ships having on board British goods, even if these were the property of neutrals. The immediate effect of these measures on British trade with the Continent was disastrous. When the news of the seizures in Holland reached London, the rates of insurance on ships and their cargoes bound for Continental ports rose from 4 per cent (early in August) to 15, 20 and 30 per cent; indeed, "it was with the greatest difficulty that insurance could be effected; it could not be done at any price to a considerable extent." [39] The export trade to the Continent, in fact, was stopped, this being done "by all merchants habitually supplying the Continent," [40] and during the months of September and October there were sixty-five applications to the Commissioners of Customs to allow the relanding of cargoes which had been shipped for Continental ports.[41] The direct trade with America also suffered; for, though the French fleets were locked up in harbor, French privateers and cruisers were very active in the narrow seas, so that the rate of insurance on direct voyages from the United States to Great Britain rose from an average of 2½ per cent in 1806 to 3½ per cent in 1807. The comparative ease with which Napoleon's measures were to be circumvented by means of the organized smuggling trade, and their inevitable relaxation owing to the needs of Napoleon himself, had not as yet been foreseen. To the British Government it seemed clear that, if Napoleon was not to achieve his purpose of ruining British trade and so forcing Great Britain to conclude a disastrous peace, vigorous counter measures must be taken.

PLIGHT OF THE BRITISH WEST INDIES

The Grenville Ministry had resigned on the 18th of March, and had been succeeded by a Tory Government, under the Duke of Portland, in which Spencer Perceval held office as Chancellor of the Exchequer and Castlereagh as Secretary for War and the Colonies. It was therefore to be expected that the more vigorous policy advocated by these Ministers when in opposition would be adopted now that they were in office. The immediate occasion for fresh action was a petition from the West Indies, which had been presented to

---

[38] Alison, *History of Europe*, XI, p. 154.
[39] Evidence of Mr. Dewar, the underwriter, 13 Hansard, App. II, xxxvi.
[40] Evidence of William Hall, *ibid.*, xxxiii.   [41] *Ibid.*, xliv.

the House of Commons on 27 February and referred to a select committee. The petitioners complained that, since the tragedy of San Domingo (which had given a "temporary and accidental" advantage to the British colonies) the colonial system of the Empire had been varied and departed from to the disadvantage of the colonies, whose situation was now desperate, since it was only on the largest plantations that it was still possible to cultivate sugar and coffee without actual loss.

The case is desperate [ran the petition] because the superiority of the British navy has not been used to impede the transit of the colonial produce of the enemy to its European market, whereby the inducement, which the enemy might have, to except colonial produce from the rigour of our general exclusion from the continental trade is taken away, and the British colonist, under all the increased and increasing expenditure of war, is subjected to contend, now and henceforward, with rivals, exempted from those charges, and enjoying the most advantageous markets, without the impediment of British competition.

In urging their claim to protection, the petitioners pointed out that nearly one-third of British imports and exports were "involved in the West Indian trade." [42] The report of the select committee, which was printed in August, emphasized the truth of these grievances, and Perceval, during the debate that followed, declared that "Ministers would not lose any time that could profitably be applied to this subject." [43]

The time and occasion seemed, in fact, to have come for carrying out the plan suggested by Perceval during the debate of 4 Febru-

---

[42] For the text see 10 Hansard, p. 85. In the course of the debate on the petition, George Hibbert, member for Seaford, pointed out (*ibid.*, 96) that the drawbacks on reëxported sugar had been reduced, and the bounties withdrawn, on the ground that the British monopolized the continental market. In 1799, however, of the ships laden chiefly with sugar and coffee entering the port of Hamburg, 146 were from America, 3 from Havana, 7 from the East Indies (with sugar), 56 from Lisbon and Oporto, or 230 in all, while from all British ports there had entered only 211 ships, of small tonnage and not entirely laden with colonial produce. The drawbacks had then been restored, but with how little effect was shown by the prices obtained by the West Indian planters. These were, for sugar:

1786-1787 ....19s. 6d. per cwt. free
1799-1800 ....10s. 9d. "   "   "
1803 { before the new tax ....18s. 6d. "   "   "
{ after the tax ....12s. 6d. "   "   "
1805 ....12s.   "   "   "
1806 ....,......nothing

[43] 9 Hansard, p. 1153.

ary,[44] and the first step was taken on 19 August by the issue of an Order in Council directing that all vessels under the flags of Mecklenburg, Oldenburg, Papenburg and Kniphausen were to be warned not to trade in future at any hostile port, unless they were sailing to or from a port of the United Kingdom, and that if, after the expiration of six weeks, any such vessels were to be found trading with a hostile port without having come from, or being bound for, a port of the United Kingdom, they were to be seized and condemned as lawful prize.[45]

[44] See *supra*, pp. 134-135.

[45] 10 Hansard, p. 130; Heckscher, *op. cit.*, App. I, No. IV, p. 392. The colors of Mecklenburg, Oldenburg, Papenburg and Kniphausen had been much in request to cover the more dubious and risky "neutral" commerce at sea. Oldenburg and Mecklenburg were restored to their dukes by Napoleon, after Tilsit, on condition that they should close their ports to British trade. Papenburg, now a flourishing town in the Prussian province of Hanover, on the bank of the Ems, was at that time an insignificant little port, whose sole importance was derived from the misuse of its flag and certain facilities it provided for smuggling. The flag of Kniphausen has a more remarkable history. The free barony of Kniphausen, situated on the river Jade and with a coast line of some ten kilometers long northward of Rüstringen, was an immediate fief of the Empire and had come into the possession of the Bentinck family by marriage in 1757. In 1672 its neutrality had been formally recognized by Louis XIV of France, and Count Wilhelm von Bentinck, who had succeeded to the title in 1787, pleaded this fact when the barony was occupied by the French during their advance into North Germany. The plea seems to have been accepted, for the French evacuated the barony after only a few days' occupation. Kniphausen thus became, with the exception of Sweden, the only European State whose neutral flag was specially favored.

The question of the Kniphausen flag provided a famous precedent in international law owing to the decision of the British High Court of Admiralty in the case of the *Minerva, Knuttell*. This vessel was a Dutch armed East Indiaman which, at the beginning of the war in 1803, had been chased into Bergen by a British frigate, had there been bought by private individuals and again sold by them to Count Bentinck, ostensibly to be employed in the trade of Kniphausen with the island of St. Thomas. She was taken, however, by a British frigate when obviously making for the Texel, and was found to be commanded by a native Dutchman and manned by a crew mainly recruited in Holland. In giving judgment for the captors Sir William Scott said that "such a sale could only be allowed under all circumstances of communicated preventive caution, that might secure the belligerent from the just apprehension of abuse," and that in this case the sale had been conducted in a manner which could not be considered legal (6 C. Robinson, p. 396 ff.).

No record remains of the number of ships which sailed under the neutral flag of Kniphausen. On 11 November 1807, the barony was incorporated in Holland, and its neutrality came to an end. At the Congress of Vienna it was decided that Kniphausen was an immediate fief of the Empire "with exceptional liberties" and it became the smallest of the constituent States of the German Confederation. In the thirties of the nineteenth century it once more played a part as provider of a neutral flag for those in need of one.

THE ORDERS IN COUNCIL OF NOVEMBER 1807

Napoleon's decree of 18 September was doubtless a reply to this Order, and the decree in its turn strengthened the determination of the British Government to develop the policy which took shape in the famous Orders in Council of November 1807.[46] Three were issued on the 11th. Of these the first, after stating that the Order of 7 January had not answered the desired purpose, either of compelling the enemy to recall the decrees aimed at the resources of Great Britain, or of inducing neutrals to interpose, with effect, to obtain their revocation, ordered that all enemy ports and those from which, though not actually at war with Great Britain, the British flag was excluded, were to be subject to the same restrictions as regards trade and navigation as if actually blockaded by a naval force. In order "not to subject neutrals to any greater inconvenience than is absolutely inseparable from the carrying into effect of his majesty's just determination to counteract the designs of his enemies," however, it was further ordered that these instructions should not extend to the capture and condemnation of any vessel or cargo, belonging to any country not declared by this Order to be "subjected to the restrictions incident to a state of blockade," which should have cleared out of the country to which it belonged, either in Europe or America, or from some free port in the British colonies, direct to some port or place in the colonies of His Majesty's enemies, or from such colonies direct to the countries to which such vessels belonged, or to some free port in His Majesty's colonies with such articles as it might be lawful to import into such free port—nor to any vessel, or the cargo of any vessel, belonging to a country not at war with His Majesty, cleared from a port of the United Kingdom, or from Gibraltar or Malta, or from a port belonging to His Majesty's allies, and proceeding direct to the port specified in her clearance—nor to any vessel or the cargo of any vessel, belonging to a country not at war with His Majesty, coming from any port in Europe declared by this Order to be subject to the restrictions incident to a state of blockade direct to a port or place in Europe belonging to His Majesty. These exceptions were, however, not to be understood as exempting from capture any vessels or their cargoes which were liable thereto owing to their having entered or cleared from

[46] The full texts of the Orders issued in 1807 will be found in 10 Hansard, p. 126 ff., and Heckscher, *op. cit.*, App. I, pp. 389 ff.

a port actually blockaded, or because they were enemy property, or for any other cause than the contravention of this Order. Any vessel which after having received due notice of this Order was found in the prosecution of any voyage contrary to the restrictions contained in it was to be captured and, with her cargo, condemned as lawful prize.

The Order further laid down that, since neutral countries had acquiesced in the French decrees prohibiting all trade in the British produce and manufactures and had given countenance and effect to those prohibitions by accepting from "persons styling themselves commercial agents of the enemy" certain documents termed "Certificates of Origin" declaring the articles of the cargo not to be of British origin, any vessel found carrying such a certificate was to be adjudged lawful prize to the captor, together with the goods laden therein.

The second Order in Council of 11 November was supplementary to the first. Under the law as it stood, the diversion of neutral ships and their cargoes to the ports of the United Kingdom would have served no purpose, since the products of foreign countries could only be imported in British ships or in those of the country of origin when specially authorized by Order in Council. Therefore, in view of the Order of the same date, respecting the trade to be carried to and from the ports of the enemy, and of the expediency of allowing the importation into Great Britain of articles produced in enemy countries, it was ordered that all goods, etc., specified in the schedule of the Act 43 George III (1803), entitled "an act to repeal the duties payable in Great Britain, and to grant other duties in lieu thereof," might be imported from any port or place not at amity with His Majesty, in ships belonging to any state at amity with His Majesty, subject to the payment of such duties, and liable to such drawbacks, as were imposed by law upon the importation of the said goods, etc., in ships navigating according to law; and it was further ordered that, in respect of such of the said goods, etc., as were authorized to be warehoused under the Act 43 George III, entitled "an act for permitting certain goods imported into Great Britain to be secured in warehouses without payment of duty," [47] and of all articles of which the importation into Great Britain was prohibited, were to be reported for exportation to any country at amity with

[47] See *supra,* p. 126.

His Majesty. Vessels loaded before receiving the warning under the earlier Order, and putting into Gibraltar, Malta or a port of the United Kingdom in consequence of such warning, were to receive a certificate from the collectors or comptroller of customs, and to be then permitted to sail for their original destination or any port of a country at amity with Great Britain; or, in case any vessel so arriving should prefer to import her cargo, she was to be allowed to enter and import the same, upon the same terms and conditions as those which would have been imposed had she sailed after having received notice of the said Order, and in conformity thereto. Finally, it was ordered that "all vessels which shall arrive at any port of the United Kingdom, or at Gibraltar or Malta, in conformity and obedience to the said Order, shall be allowed, in respect of all articles which may be on board the same, except sugar, coffee, wine, brandy, snuff, and tobacco, to clear out to any port whatever, to be specified in such clearance; and with respect to the last-mentioned articles, to export the same to such ports and under such conditions and regulations only as his majesty, by any licence to be granted for that purpose, may direct."

The third Order in Council of 11 November was directed against the abuse of the neutral flag. It declared that, whereas the sale of ships by a belligerent to a neutral was considered by France to be illegal, while a great part of the shipping of France had been saved from capture by transfers, or pretended transfers, to neutrals, such sales or transfers would not in future be deemed to be legal, or in any manner to transfer the property or alter the character of the vessel, and that, after a reasonable time for receiving notice of this Order, vessels thus transferred would be captured and brought in for adjudication as lawful prize.

An Order in Council, issued on 18 November, approving the draft of instructions to the commanders of warships and privateers to act in conformity with the Orders of 11 November, contained certain modifications or explanations of these Orders which are of interest. "Nothing in the said Order," it was stated, "shall extend or be construed to extend to prevent any vessel, not belonging to any country declared to be under the restrictions of blockade as aforesaid, from carrying from any port or place of the country to which such vessel belongs, any articles of produce or manufacture whatever, not being enemies property, to any port or place in this kingdom." Articles of British manufacture (not naval stores) were to be restored by the

Courts of Admiralty or Vice-admiralty, on whatever voyage they might have been captured, to whomsoever they might appear to belong. It was further directed, that nothing in this Order should be construed to extend to repeal or nullify the additional instructions of 4 February, under which neutral vessels laden with the articles therein enumerated and coming to any port of the United Kingdom, were not to be interrupted, provided they had not cleared from a port in a state of rigorous blockade. In order to lessen the inconvenience to neutrals, the masters of neutral ships, when warned to proceed to a British port, were to be allowed to choose the port most convenient to them and were then to be supplied with a certificate stating that they were bound for such port.

No less than five further Orders in Council were issued on 25 November. The first of these was in elaboration of the clause in the Order of 11 November exempting from the restrictions of the Order "all vessels which shall have cleared out of any port or place in this kingdom under such regulations as His Majesty may think fit to prescribe." It was now ordered that all neutral vessels were to be allowed to lade at any port of the United Kingdom any goods produced or manufactured in His Majesty's dominions and, on payment of the lawful duties, freely to convey them to the enemy colonies in the West Indies and America, and likewise to lade and convey, in the same way, any articles of foreign produce and manufacture lawfully imported into the United Kingdom, "provided His Majesty's licence shall have been previously obtained for so conveying such foreign produce or manufactures." Neutral vessels were also to be allowed, under the same conditions, to lade British goods and foreign goods lawfully imported (except sugar, coffee, wine, brandy, snuff and cotton) and to clear with them for any port, not strictly blockaded, though such port was "under the restrictions of the said Order," and "to lade, clear out, and convey foreign sugar, coffee, wine, brandy, snuff, and cotton, which shall have been lawfully imported, provided His Majesty's licence shall have been previously obtained for the exportation and conveyance thereof." But no vessel laden with goods imported into the United Kingdom was to be allowed to clear for any country subjected to the restrictions of the Order in Council without having first entered and landed the goods in some port of the United Kingdom, "except the cargo shall consist wholly of flour, meal, grain, or any article or articles the produce of the soil of any country which is not subjected to the restrictions of the said Order," or of cotton, imported in an unmanufactured state from the producing country, not being subject to the restrictions imposed by the Order and in ships belonging to such country.

The second Order of 25 November approved the draft of instructions directing that any vessel laden in a port of the United Kingdom was not to be interrupted or molested in proceeding to any port in Europe not strictly blockaded, and that any vessel coming from any such port direct to a port in the United Kingdom, with goods for importation, was likewise not to be interfered with.

The third Order modified the provision of the first Order of 11 November which declared that all trade in articles produced or manufactured in enemy countries or colonies was to be deemed unlawful, by directing that "nothing in the said Order contained shall extend to subject to capture and confiscation any articles of the produce and manufacture of the said countries and colonies, laden on board British ships, which would not have been subject to capture and confiscation if such Order had not been made."

The fourth Order merely specified the dates at which it was assumed that due notice of the Orders would have been received in different parts of the world.

The fifth Order, after stating that it was expedient to encourage the trade of Malta and Gibraltar to the countries under the restrictions imposed by the Order of 11 November, directed "that all sorts of flour and meal, and all sorts of grain, tobacco, and any other article in an unmanufactured state, being the growth and produce of any country not being subjected by the said Order to the restrictions incident to a state of blockade (except cotton, and naval and military stores) which shall have been imported into Gibraltar or Malta, direct from the country where the same were grown and produced, shall, without any licence, be permitted to be cleared out to any port or place, not being in a state of blockade, without being compelled to land." This applied, apparently, only to vessels laden and sailing before they had had time to receive news of the Order in Council of the 11th, for the instructions next direct that

neither the said article of cotton, however imported, nor any article which is not the growth, produce or manufacture of this kingdom, or which has not been imported in a British ship, or from this kingdom direct, (except fish), and which shall have been laden at the original port of shipment after the period directed by an Order of this date to be taken as the time at which notice of the said Order of the 11th Nov. shall be considered as having been received at such port of shipment, shall be permitted to be exported from Gibraltar or Malta, except to some port or place in this kingdom: and all other articles of the growth, produce and manufacture of this kingdom, or which shall have been imported into Gibraltar or Malta in a British ship, or from some port or place in this kingdom, together with the article of fish, however imported, may be exported to any ports or places in the Mediterranean or Portugal, under such licence only as is hereinafter directed to be granted by the governors of Gibraltar and Malta respectively.

The provisions as to these licenses were fairly liberal. The governors were empowered to grant licenses in the King's name to export from Gibraltar direct to any Mediterranean or Portuguese port, or to any Spanish port outside the Mediterranean as far north as Cape Finisterre, and from Malta to any Mediterranean port, any articles produced in His Majesty's dominions, any articles imported from the United Kingdom (not being naval stores) in any neutral vessel or in any unarmed vessel of less than one hundred tons' burden belonging to the country to which she was bound, and to import in any such vessels from any Mediterranean, Portuguese or Spanish port (south of Finisterre) "any article of merchandize whatsoever and to whomsoever the same may appear to belong," subject to such regulations as might be inserted in the licenses. Vessels of the Barbary States were to be allowed to sail for any Mediterranean or Portuguese port without being obliged to touch at Gibraltar or Malta.

Finally, on 18 December, an Order was issued, the terms of which were obviously intended to help remove the grievances of which the West Indian planters had complained in the petition to Parliament. This Order directed "that nothing in His Majesty's Order in Council of the 11th of Nov. last, shall extend or be construed to extend, to permit any vessel to import any articles of the produce or manufacture of the enemy's colonies in the West Indies, direct from such colonies to any port of this kingdom." All vessels arriving direct from such colonies were, however, to be released on proof that the charter party or other agreement for the voyage had been entered into before notice of this Order had been received.[48]

[48] Six Acts of Parliament supplementary to the Orders in Council were passed in the spring of 1808. Of these the most important were "An Act for granting to His Majesty, until the end of the next Session of Parliament, Duties of Customs on the Goods, Wares, and Merchandize herein enumerated, in furtherance of the Provisions of certain Orders in Council" (48 George III, cap. 26) and "An Act for making valid certain Orders in Council, and Warrants of the Commissioners of the Treasury, for the Entry and Warehousing of certain Goods imported in Neutral Vessels, and for indemnifying all Persons concerned therein; for remitting

If the impression made by the above abstracts of the Orders in Council of November 1807 is somewhat confused, it may be pleaded that in this respect they accurately reflect the character of the originals. Professor Heckscher describes the Orders as "marvels of obscurity and rambling"; Lord Grenville, attacking them in the House of Lords, said that "they were clothed in a number of words which even those who framed them did not understand, and were very difficult to understand by others." [49] In the various Orders, following closely on one another, there are repetitions and seeming contradictions,[50] and the legal phraseology of the documents is so involved and long-winded that it is not difficult to imagine the feelings of the naval commanders whose duty it was to carry out the instructions contained in them and, more particularly, the feelings of the neutrals whose fortunes they affected.

---

of Forfeitures in certain Cases; and for enabling His Majesty to allow, during the Continuance of Hostilities, and until Two Months after the Commencement of the next Session of Parliament, the Importation of Goods from Countries from which the British Flag is excluded, in any Vessels whatever" (48 George III, cap. 37). By the latter statute (sec. iii) it was enacted: "That it shall be lawful for His Majesty, by Order in Council or Licence, and in Ireland for the Lord Lieutenant or other Chief Governor or Governors, and the Privy Council of Ireland, by Order in Council or Licence, when and as often as the same shall be judged expedient, to permit during the continuance of hostilities . . . any such Goods, wares or merchandize as shall be specified in such Order or Licence, to be imported into any port of Great Britain or Ireland respectively, from any port or place from which the British flag is excluded, in any vessel belonging to any country, whether in amity with His Majesty or not; any Law in force in the United Kingdom, or in Great Britain or Ireland respectively, to the contrary in anywise notwithstanding." It may be noted that this particular relaxation of the Navigation Laws was anticipated in 1803. By the Act of 43 George III, cap. 153, par. xv, it was enacted that, "whereas Orders in Council have been issued permitting the importation of certain goods . . . being British or neutral property, contrary to the Law now in force, and it is expedient to permit, during the continuance of hostilities, . . . the importation in any neutral ship of any goods . . . from any port or place belonging to any kingdom or state not in amity with His Majesty, every importation of goods . . . made by virtue of such Order or Licence heretofore shall be deemed to be good in law" notwithstanding anything in the Act of 12 Charles II.

The provisions of two of the remaining Acts (48 George III, caps. 29 and 33) were little creditable to the British Government. These forbade the exportation of Jesuits' bark (quinine) from Ireland and Great Britain, except to Great Britain and Ireland, respectively. This prohibition was justly denounced in Parliament as needless and inhumane. For the texts of the Acts see *Collection of Public Statutes*, 1808, pp. 199 ff.

[49] 12 Hansard, p. 775.

[50] Lord Grenville said that "he would take upon himself to prove that in four clauses of the same paragraph they contained four direct contradictions" (Debate of 15 Feb. 1808, 10 Hansard, p. 480).

It is then perhaps not surprising that opinion is still divided as to the meaning and, above all, the intention of the Orders. Professor Heckscher, as a result of his analysis of their provisions, distinguishes their real from their pretended object. The intention officially proclaimed was to retaliate for the Berlin Decree, and thus to compel the enemy to revoke this measure or to induce neutrals to bring pressure to bear on him to do so; the real object, inspired by the current mercantilist ideas, was to encourage British trade by making it more difficult for neutrals to compete with it in the Continental markets. "The fundamental principle," he says, "is to be found practically in the germ as early as Perceval's speech in February." [51] Hence the practical nullification of the blockade restrictions by a series of exceptions which made neutral trade possible with the countries subject to these restrictions, on condition that the vessels which conducted this trade should break their voyage at a British port. According to Mahan, too,[52] the object of the Orders was "to make the United Kingdom the centre and warehouse of the world's trade," and he explains the relaxations of the rigors of the blockade, not as the result of any consideration for neutrals, but as due to the perception of British Ministers that "the greater the commerce of the outside world, the greater the advantage, or toll, resulting to Great Britain." He acquits them, however, of meanly mercantile motives in adopting this policy, which was dictated solely by the exigencies of the war. "The object which could not be obtained by any means acknowledged as lawful," he says, "the British Ministry determined to compass by sheer force, by that maritime supremacy which they unquestionably wielded, and which they could make effective for the ends they had in view: to maintain the commerce and shipping of Great Britain on which her naval strength depended, to force the enemy's trade to pass through her ports, and thus to raise her revenue to the point necessary to her salvation in the life and death struggle in which she was embarked." [53]

THE SECOND MILAN DECREE

This was precisely the object which Napoleon was determined to frustrate, and his reply to the Orders in Council was the second Milan Decree, issued on 17 December. Every neutral ship submitting to search by the British or to an enforced voyage to a British

[51] Heckscher, *The Continental System* (1922), pp. 114 ff.
[52] Mahan, II, 286.   [53] *Ibid.*, II, 284.

port was to be considered as denationalized and as lawful prize, if captured by the vessels of France or her allies, and any ship sailing from a British port or country occupied by British troops was to be lawful prize if taken by a French war vessel or privateer. These measures, it was astutely added, would not be enforced against the neutral State which should compel Great Britain to respect its flag.[54] The obvious intention was to bring pressure to bear upon the United States, in order to force them to take action against Great Britain. The process had, indeed, begun before the Orders in Council were issued. The decree of 18 September, which ordered the seizure of ships having British goods on board, had already given the lie to Decrès's assurances to General Armstrong that American ships were excepted from the provisions of the Berlin Decree.[55] On 7 October Champagny, who had succeeded Talleyrand as French Minister for Foreign Affairs, told the American Minister explicitly that no such exception would henceforth be made; and, when Armstrong protested, Napoleon himself dictated a reply in which he said that, since American vessels allowed themselves to be visited and searched, suffered impressment, and submitted to being turned from their course into British ports, they must conform to the rules of the Berlin Decree or take the consequences.[56] On 23 November, before the news of the British Orders in Council had reached the Emperor, he issued the first Milan Decree, which extended to his whole Empire the rules as to the treatment of British ships and goods which had been applied to the coast of northern Germany, and ordered the confiscation of any vessels, together with their cargoes, which should have touched at a British port.[57]

PARLIAMENT AND THE ORDERS IN COUNCIL

In the British Parliament, on the other hand, where the Opposition denounced the Orders in Council as violations of international law and as ruinous to the trade of neutrals and Great Britain alike, Ministers laid stress on the temporary character of the Orders, which were only intended to meet the critical situation created by the Berlin Decree. In the course of the debate in the House of Lords, on 15 February 1808, Earl Bathurst pointed out that the

[54] Heckscher, op. cit., pp. 123 f.
[55] A.S.P., F.R., II, 805; 10 Hansard, pp. 557 f.
[56] Champagny to Armstrong, 24 November 1807. A.S.P., F.R., III, 247.
[57] Heckscher, op. cit., p. 123.

Order of 7 January, issued when the Grenville Ministry was in power, "asserted a permanent right of preventing, during war, all trade between one port of the enemy and another, whilst the Order of 11 November arose out of the violence of the ruler of France, and with that would cease." Moreover, he added, the Order of 7 January had been evaded and turned to the advantage of the enemy "in carrying on a circuitous route" through British ports. Thus, while the rate of insurance on a cargo of wine shipped direct from Bordeaux to Amsterdam was 30 per cent, it was only 5 per cent when shipped through Great Britain. This and similar transactions might, he said, be prevented by forbidding reëxportation; but in that case the merchant would suffer if he found the British market overstocked, and it had been therefore considered expedient to regulate a trade which could not be prohibited, and it was with this object that the Government had issued the Orders in Council, which represented "a compromise between belligerent rights and commercial interests." He added, that it was the intention to allow all American domestic produce to pass through Great Britain without payment of duty; and moreover, since the surplus of the produce of the British colonies, above the needs of Great Britain, did not amount to one-third of the Continental demand, that it was judged expedient to permit trade with the enemy's colonies, "with the intention, however, that the produce of such colonies should, in the circuitous trade through this country, be subjected to a duty sufficiently high to prevent its having the advantage over our own colonial produce." [58] The object of the Orders in Council, in short, was not to damage the trade of neutrals or to secure new markets at their expense, but to safeguard British trade against the effects of the increased risks and charges with which it was threatened under the Berlin Decree. "It is intolerable," said Lord Hawkesbury in the course of the same debate, "that England has enjoyed little advantage from her maritime superiority; and that France, who does not dare show a flag on the ocean, has carried on such a trade by neutral bottoms that the people of that country consume colonial produce at a much less rate than the English." [59] It was to remedy this that customs duties of from 20 to 30 per cent were imposed on enemy produce in neutral ships reloaded in British ports,[60] the assumption being that the ad-

[58] 10 Hansard, p. 471.   [59] *Ibid.*, p. 485.
[60] The rates were 28s. per cwt. on coffee, 10s. on brown sugar, and 14s. on white sugar.—Tooke, *History of Prices*, II, 398, 414.

ditional burden would fall, not on the neutral trader, but on the Continental consumer, which would incidentally have the effect of increasing the economic pressure on France and her allies. It seems clear, however, from the provision of the Act of 48 George III, cap. 26, sec. 16, which allowed owners to destroy cargoes in port without payment of duty, that the Government from the first recognized that the duties might prove burdensome, and even in certain cases prohibitive, to neutral trade.

It was to this latter point, indeed, that the criticisms of the Opposition were mainly directed. In the House of Commons, on 18 February 1808, Lord William Petty attacked the Orders as violations of international law and as calculated to lead to war with the United States. A war between France and the United States, he added, would be almost as injurious to British interests as one between the United States and Great Britain, since the neutrality of America was the means of diffusing British manufactures.[61] On 8 March Lord Erskine took up the parable in the House of Lords. The Orders in Council, he argued, were a violation not only of international law but also of the law of the land; and, representing as they did "a distinct assumption of the dispensing power of the Crown," they were in flat contradiction to the principles of the Revolution settlement on which the throne itself was established. They had been issued when Parliament was not sitting, when the opinions of merchants and other experts could not be heard, and Acts of Parliament were to be introduced to give them legal force. It was owing to the pressure brought to bear by London merchants, he said, that the original Order of 11 November had been followed by a series of "supplemental" Orders, which were not supplemental but "manifestly repugnant and inconsistent." The right of retaliation he admitted, but this retaliation must be exercised upon the enemy and his allies, not upon neutrals. Retaliation upon neutrals would only be legitimate in the event that British trade suffered as a result of neutral acquiescence in the unjust measures of the enemy; and there had been no such suffering. A whole year had passed between the issue of the Berlin Decree and that of the Orders in Council, and what had happened? America, the only great maritime power that remained neutral, was virtually excluded from the operation of the Decree; "the air was white with her sails, and the sea

61 10 Hansard, p. 682.

pressed down with her shipping, nearly half as numerous as our own, bringing her produce into every port of England and carrying our commodities and manufactures into every corner of Europe." The Decree had, in fact, become a dead letter, since France had no ships with which to make it effective, and what with the connivance of French officials and the licenses for contraband trade issued by the French Government, America was able to smuggle British goods into France for her own interest, and France bought them for hers. In these circumstances there was no justification for a policy which risked an alliance between the United States and France and the consequent combination of the whole world against Great Britain.[62]

British Ministers were by no means blind to this danger, which loomed all the larger in view of the conditions on the Continent of Europe at the close of the year 1807. Russia and Denmark were now the allies of Napoleon, and Portugal, the traditional ally of Great Britain, had fallen to his arms. Of the remaining States of Europe those which were not merely subsidiary to his Empire had been so recently vanquished that they were not in a position to resist his demand that they should adopt the Continental System, to which even Turkey was forced to accede. Sweden alone, Great Britain's last ally, remained outside; and against her, at Napoleon's instigation, Russia now launched the attack which was to end in the annexation of Finland to the Empire of the Tsars. The vision of bringing the "nation of shopkeepers" to their knees by ruining their trade, a vision which had floated before the eyes of the Convention and the Directory, seemed about to be realized on a scale and with a completeness of which its earlier seers had never dreamed. Great Britain, fighting for her very existence, was faced with a choice of evils: either—as the Opposition suggested—to trust to the "elastic principle of trade itself" to sap and ruin the formidable barriers erected by Napoleon, or to take vigorous counter measures, with little regard for the rules of international law, and so to risk adding the United States to the ranks of her enemies.

The Government chose the latter alternative, but at the same time made it clear that the legitimate interests of neutrals would be safeguarded, subject only to the paramount necessity of taking any such measures as might be necessary in order to achieve the overthrow of Napoleon's tyranny. This may help to explain the apparent

[62] 10 Hansard, pp. 930 ff.

inconsistencies of the Orders in Council. The extreme provisions of the Order of 11 November were, doubtless, partly intended as a mere retaliation for the Berlin Decree, the terms of which they echoed, but they were also conceived as powers held in reserve, to be applied or relaxed as circumstances dictated.

THE SYSTEM OF LICENSES

The means for such relaxation were provided by the system of licenses, which had grown up under the mercantilist régime, not in Great Britain only, as a method of circumventing the ordinary law whenever the exigencies of trade or the need of the Government for money seemed to make it expedient to do so. So it was now. While the Orders in Council and the Acts of Parliament which confirmed them remained the law of the land, licenses dispensing the holders from the restrictions imposed by the law were issued by the Privy Council in the name of the Crown. This system enabled the Board of Trade to maintain a certain control over the course of traffic, to counter the unfair competition of neutrals under the Berlin Decree and, whenever it seemed possible and expedient to do so, to remove the restrictions on the trade of neutrals and even of the enemy.[63]

During the war the system was at first developed only tentatively and with reluctance by the British Government. Thus, on 11 March 1806, Lord Auckland, the President of the Board of Trade, informed Lord Grenville that an application had been made for a license to send a very large cargo of British cottons in a neutral ship to Mar-

---

[63] "An examination of the text of these Orders in Council, which differ widely from the travesties of fact too often presented in histories, suffices to show that Great Britain, while pressing severely on all States which freely placed their resources at the disposal of Napoleon, yet sought to lessen the hardships of those on which the Continental System was imposed by force. The facilities granted to neutrals were clearly of such a kind as to dispose of the charge that George III's Government deliberately sought to ruin neutral commerce."—Rose in *Cambridge Modern History*, IX (1906), 367.

In the debate on the Orders in Council in the House of Commons on 18 February 1808, the attorney general characterized as nonsense the contention of the Opposition that the strict enforcement of the Berlin Decree was due to the issue of the Orders in Council, pointing out that as early as October it was reported in the newspapers that Napoleon had restored their territories to the dukes of Oldenburg and Mecklenburg on condition of their excluding British goods. There was no difference in principle, he said, between the Orders in Council of November and that of the 7th of January, which had been issued by the late Government. This principle had been completely set forth in Lord Howick's note to Rist.—10 Hansard, p. 673.

tinique. The license had been refused; but Lord Auckland suggested that the whole subject seemed to call for consideration.

We refused the license [he said], and yet under a full sense that there is both an inconsistency and detriment resulting from the King's instructions respecting the point to which the case relates. This same neutral ship (if German) may go with the cargo first to Embden or Hamburgh, and then proceed to Martinique; or (if American) she may go first to a port in the United States and thence to Martinique. Either of these obvious operations will gratuitously throw the whole commission profit of six or eight percent to the neutrals; besides other evident ill effects.[64]

The decision of Sir William Scott in the *Essex, Orne* case did not seem to him to mend matters.

It is understood [he said] that in all cases where *continuous voyage* is proved, forfeiture follows. But are we to admit that cargoes of colony produce *bona fide* landed and warehoused from French and Spanish possessions, and even *become bona fide* the property of subjects of the United States, may afterwards be exported from the United States to France or Spain? It appears to me that such an admission would soon become the means of an undisturbed transfer of the produce of hostile colonies to the mother country.[65]

In these circumstances, he remarked, Great Britain seemed to be placed in a "dilemma."

Grant licenses [he said] and enemy colonies have the benefits of peace, refuse them and the United States benefits at our expense. Might we not at least offer licenses to neutral vessels to carry our manufactures to the French and Spanish islands, but not to bring back produce? It is a great and difficult question.[66]

Whatever the initial doubts as to the soundness of the system of licenses, however, this soon attained proportions which seemed to nullify the provisions of the Orders in Council. As early as January 1808, complaint was made in the House of Commons that the granting of licenses by the Privy Council had never been carried to so serious an extent.[67] The number issued in 1807, however, which was 1,600, was soon greatly exceeded, rising to over 15,000 in 1809 and 18,000 in 1810.[68] This was the highwater mark of the system; for the seizure in the Baltic ports by Napoleon's orders, in the late summer of 1810, of some 600 neutral vessels provided with British licenses, and laden with 40,000,000 dollars' worth of British prop-

---

[64] *Dropmore Papers*, VII, 53.   [65] To Grenville, 20 August 1806. *Ibid.*, p. 288.
[66] To Grenville, 25 November 1806. *Ibid.*, p. 441.   [67] 10 Hansard, p. 185.
[68] 18 Hansard, p. 1105.

erty, discouraged applications for licenses, of which only 7,500 were issued in 1811.[69]

Under the terms of the license the vessel holding it was to be allowed to proceed "notwithstanding all the documents which accompany the ship and cargo may represent the same to be destined to any neutral or hostile port, or to whomsoever such property may appear to belong." [70] This, according to Lord Brougham, was to give up to the enemy all that remained of the principle of the Orders in Council. "If anyone can get a license," he asked, "what becomes of the blockade?" [71] He pointed out that the ships of Kniphausen, Papenburg and Emden, provided with British licenses, were plying direct to enemy ports, with the result that, during the year 1810, there had been an increase of 1,100,000 tons of foreign shipping engaged in British trade, while in the course of four years the number of seamen thus engaged had risen from 29,000 to 60,000, and "all this at the expense of the Americans." It was a trade, he complained, which was open to the enemy, but which was shut to all neutrals except those who chose to be partakers of the licensing system.

As a matter of fact, neutrals were only too ready to avail themselves of this system, which enabled them to carry on a highly lucrative trade in British wares and colonial goods with the Continent; for a British license admitted them to any port from which a British blockade excluded them, and since such a license could only be obtained in a British port, they naturally loaded their ships with the most paying goods they found there, whatever their origin.[72] A large share in this trade was, moreover, taken by the Americans, who were the principal carriers of British goods conveyed to the Baltic or distributed by organized smuggling from the entrepôt established on Heligoland, and those of their ships which were not tied up in home ports continued to carry on this traffic even after President Jefferson's proclamation of the embargo. The development of the system also made possible the withdrawal or modification of the Order in Council of 11 November by an Order of 26 April 1809, which raised the blockade on the whole coast of the Continent north of the Ems; for, whatever concessions might be made under this Order, the old regulations could still be maintained

[69] Mahan, II, 323.
[71] Ibid., p. 1105.
[70] 18 Hansard, p. 1110.
[72] Mahan, II, 299 ff.

by making the granting of licenses conditional on their being obeyed.[73]

The immediate effect of the system seemed wholly favorable to Great Britain, whose object—as Lord Wellesley, the Foreign Secretary, put it—was "not to crush the trade with the Continent, but to counteract an attempt to crush the British trade," and to encourage that of neutrals through Great Britain.[74] In 1808 Napoleon was occupied in Spain, and in the following year with the Austrian war; his unwilling vassals could venture to disregard his decrees, and a brisk trade developed once more between Great Britain and, more especially, the Hanse Towns and Holland, where King Louis incurred his formidable brother's wrath by conniving at the illicit traffic. In 1809 the whole trade of the world seemed to be under the control of Great Britain. "Never before was the shipping of this country employed at higher freights; and scarcely a ship belonging to any other nation could sail without a licence from the government of this country. The whole of the exportable produce of the East and West Indies, and of a great part of South America, came to our ports; and no part of the Continent of Europe could obtain a supply of coffee, sugar, and other colonial articles, or of the raw materials of some of their manufactures, except from this country." [75] Gothenburg now became the chief entrepôt for the trade of Great Britain with the Baltic, which was carried on by ships flying various neutral flags and provided with British licenses. These sailed under convoy through the narrows to Hanö Bay, on the southeast coast of Sweden, whence they scattered to the various Baltic ports, including St. Petersburg. After discharging their cargoes of British manufactures and colonial goods, they loaded up with Russian and Prussian timber, tallow, hemp, etc., and so returned to the rendezvous. "As soon as they had accumulated about 500, and the wind came fair, they sailed from Hano under convoy to the Belt, where a strong force was always kept to protect them from the attacks of the Danish gunboats. The tyrannical decrees of Buonaparte were thus rendered null and void on this part of the Continent." [76] As already mentioned, the confiscation by Napoleon's

---

[73] Heckscher, *The Continental System* (1922), p. 208.
[74] Heckscher, *loc. cit.*
[75] Tooke, *History of Prices,* I, 105.
[76] *Memoirs and Correspondence of Admiral Lord de Saumarez* (ed. Ross), II, 196.

orders of several hundred neutral vessels in the Baltic ports put a sudden stop to this trade in the late summer of 1810, and it seemed to be altogether doomed when, in the following November, Napoleon forced Sweden to declare war on Great Britain. This state of war was, however, regarded on both sides as a fiction, and British trade with, and through, Sweden continued with the connivance, and even the assistance, of the Swedish Government until, in 1813, it reached its highest level with the collapse of the Continental System.[77]

Meanwhile, it had become increasingly clear to Napoleon that his Continental System was failing to achieve its main object, which was the ruin of Great Britain. The obstacles to British trade with the Continent, though they added to the distress in England caused by the interruption of commerce with the United States, were being rapidly overcome owing to the general passive resistance of the peoples to the French regulations, the great development of organized smuggling, and, to quote a contemporary writer, "the corruption that ever hangs about custom-houses and increases with the duties." In these circumstances Napoleon was glad to avail himself of the opportunity afforded by the example of Great Britain to alter the system established under the Berlin Decree, without any formal repeal of what had been proclaimed as "a fundamental law of the Empire." He, too, would regulate and profit by the illicit traffic which it had been found impossible to suppress, and by a system of licenses, combined with high tariffs, encourage the industries and commerce of France at the expense both of Great Britain and his own allies. Above all, he saw in this system a ready expedient for drawing into his treasury the vast sums of money needed for the financing of his limitless schemes of ambition.

As early as April 1808, in a letter to King Louis of Holland, with instructions for the smuggling of gin into Great Britain, he enjoined him to issue licenses for voyages to England, but with strict injunctions that the cargoes thus transported were to be paid for only in gold or silver specie and bullion.[78] The system, however, did not receive any great development until more than two years later,

---

[77] See *infra*, p. 265.
[78] Heckscher, *op. cit.*, p. 71. On 25 Nov. 1811, Gaudin, the French Minister in Holland, mentioned the object of the licensing system in a report to the Emperor, as being "the extraction of metallic money from England, the exportation of French goods, and activity in our ports."—*Ibid*.

when it was elaborated in connection with the policy of largely increased tariffs. Since colonial goods were pouring into the Continent in spite of the System, it seemed expedient to Napoleon to relax this System in the interests of his revenue. On 12 January 1810, accordingly, he issued a decree authorizing the importation of forbidden goods (except certain cotton fabrics and hosiery, assumed to be of British manufacture) on payment of a duty of 40 per cent when they came from prizes captured from the enemy. The latter restriction was purely formal, and in practice all colonial goods were admitted; [79] but under the Trianon Tariff, issued on 5 August, enormously increased duties were imposed upon them.[80] A characteristic Napoleonic touch was an apparent concession made to the United States under this tariff. Three-quarters of the duties were to be remitted in the case of the cargoes of American vessels imported direct; which was in fact no concession at all, since the British command of the sea made such a direct voyage practically impossible.

On 25 July 1810, some ten days before the promulgation of the Trianon Tariff and in close association with it, the so-called "Licence Decree" was issued, which laid down that, from 1 August onward, no vessel bound for a foreign port would be allowed to leave a French port without a license signed by Napoleon himself. If the vessel was bound for a port of the Empire, or engaged in the Mediterranean coasting trade, it was to provide itself with a more general permit (*acquit-à-caution*) and with a written bond which was only to be annulled on proof given that the vessel had actually arrived at a French port.[81] Henceforth all ships engaged in overseas trade were obliged to have a license, the reason given being that, since no such traffic was possible without calling at a British port or at least suffering visitation and search by the British, the vessels engaged in it were *ipso facto* "denationalized" and liable to be confiscated under the Milan Decree. In instructions supplementary to the decree, indeed, Napoleon clearly indicated his intention of using the licensing system to create a complete monopoly for the French

---

[79] *Bulletin des lois,* 4 ser., Bull. 260, No. 5122, cited in Heckscher, *op. cit.,* pp. 199 f.

[80] Specific duties by weight were imposed on certain kinds of colonial goods. The rate in 1804 had been 1 franc per 100 kilogrammes, which had been raised to 60 francs in 1806. Under the Trianon Tariff, e.g., the duty on South American and long-stapled Georgia cotton was raised to 800 francs per 100 kilogrammes.

[81] Text in Martens, *Nouveau recueil de traités,* I (1817), 512.

mercantile marine. Thus, in a letter to Lebrun, his lieutenant in recently annexed Holland, dated 20 August 1810, he asserted that he granted licenses only to French vessels. "I will not hear of a neutral vessel," he said, "and as a matter of fact there is in reality no such thing; for they are all vessels which violate the blockade and pay tribute to England." [82] Foreign vessels were, therefore, not to be allowed to trade with France or to leave French ports. An embargo was consequently laid on all foreign ships, whether neutral or allied, which happened to be lying in French harbors, including a large number belonging to Napoleon's long-suffering ally Denmark.

The French Emperor's pressing need for money, however, soon led to a relaxation of this rule. Thus on 15 September an order was issued allowing licensed vessels to clear from Hamburg, Bremen and Lübeck for French ports. The license, which had to be paid for at the high rate of a dollar per ton, only covered the return voyage; but the vessel carrying such a license, though not allowed to import British goods, was exempted on her arrival in France from all question as to search by British cruisers and might even land her cargo at a British port. She was, in fact, exempted from the operation of the Berlin and Milan Decrees.[83]

With the general effect of these decrees on the Continent of Europe we are not here concerned. During the year 1810 Napoleon made vigorous efforts to enforce them: the Hanse cities and the duchy of Oldenburg were annexed to France and a military cordon was established along the northwest coast of Germany, while on 18 October the Fontainebleau Decree prescribed severe penalties for organized smuggling, ordered all smuggled colonial goods to be confiscated and all wares of British origin to be publicly burnt, and established special customs courts (*cours prévôtales des douanes*) to see to the execution of these orders.[84] But this Draconian legislation was of no avail in view of the rapid extension of the licensing system by which Napoleon himself sapped, and ultimately destroyed, the protective barriers which he had erected against the flood of British goods. The epitaph of the Continental System, as

---

[82] Heckscher, *op. cit.*, p. 219.

[83] Napoleon defined a license as follows: "A license is a permission, accorded to a vessel that fulfills the conditions demanded by the said license, to import or export a certain kind of merchandise specified in that license. For these vessels the Berlin and Milan Decrees are null and void."—To Eugene, Viceroy of Italy, 19 Sept. 1810, quoted in Heckscher, *op. cit.*, p. 215.

[84] *Ibid.*, p. 203 n. 2.

Professor Heckscher points out, was contained in a memorandum of Napoleon, dated 22 December 1812, in which he stated his need for 150,000,000 francs from the ordinary and extraordinary customs revenues. "Undoubtedly it is necessary to harm our foes," he wrote, "but above all we must live." [85]

The system thus adopted by both belligerents placed the owners and masters of neutral and neutralized vessels in an awkward predicament. To make for a port "subject to the restrictions incident to a state of blockade" without a British license was to risk almost certain capture and condemnation; to arrive without the French papers certifying the "innocence" of ship and cargo meant the confiscation of both. In these circumstances it became customary for trading ships to carry a double set of papers, one or both of these being so skillfully forged that they could "scarcely fail to deceive the cruizers of either belligerent with respect to the real destination of the cargo." [86] The facility with which the Privy Council granted licenses, indeed, made the forgery of them comparatively unprofitable; for they were easy to transfer and were articles of sale on the Continent. The forgery of French licenses and consular certificates, on the other hand, was presently organized on a commercial scale,[87] the intention being "to deceive the customs officer, if zealous, or give him a fair excuse for admitting the goods, if lukewarm . . . paper, wax, seals and signature being carefully imitated." [88] As a further precaution these papers had to be certified as

---

[85] *Ibid.*, p. 253.

[86] *Quarterly Review*, May 1811, p. 461.

[87] The following circular was quoted by Lord Brougham in the course of his attack on the Orders in Council in the House of Lords, on 3 March 1812 (18 Hansard, p. 1113): "Gentlemen, We take the liberty to inform you, that we have established ourselves in this town for the sole purpose of making simulated papers, which we are enabled to do in a way which will give ample satisfaction to our employers, not only being in possession of foreign documents of the ships' papers, and clearances to various ports, a list of which we annex, but our Mr. G—— B—— having worked with his brother, Mr. J—— B——, in the same line for the last two years, and understanding all the languages.

"Of any changes that may occur in the different places on the Continent, in the various customs houses, and other offices, which may render a change of signatures necessary, we are careful to have the earliest information, not only from our own connections, but from Mr. J—— B——, who has proffered his assistance in every way, and who has for some time past made simulated papers for Messrs. B—— and P——, of this town, to whom we beg leave to refer you for further information."

[88] A.S.P., F.R., III, 341.

genuine by the master of the vessel on oath, which led—as such precautions are apt to do—to a vast amount of perjury. It is not surprising that there was widespread agreement with Lord Brougham when he lamented "the labyrinth of mystery and fraud" by which the mercantile transactions of the day were enveloped and obscured, and when he expressed misgivings as to the effects likely to be produced by a system which involved the careful training of young clerks in the art of forgery.

Opposition to the Orders in Council in Great Britain

As time went on, indeed, the opposition in Great Britain to the Orders in Council and the licensing system which had grown out of them increased in volume and intensity. One effect of the enforced passage of all Continental trade through British ports had been to flood the British market with foreign goods and to produce a vast accumulation in the warehouses of those for which no market could be found. A writer in the *Quarterly Review* for May 1811, pointed out that, during the two years succeeding 1808, Great Britain had been "inundated by an excess of imports"; [89] that there had been much speculation in the export of British and colonial produce; that the fleets thus laden had been successively confiscated; and that, as the result, in spite of swollen customs receipts, the situation of the mercantile world was "calamitous beyond all former example." [90] The immense importation of colonial and American produce, at a time when intercourse with the Continent was becoming increasingly precarious, had led to many bankruptcies.[91] First the

[89] Tooke (*History of Prices*, II, 300 ff.) speaks of the imports as "of overwhelming magnitude." Thus the imports of cotton, which in 1808 amounted to 43,605,982 lbs., rose in 1810 to 136,488,935 lbs., and those of sugar from 417,642 cwts. in 1807 to 4,808,663 in 1810.

[90] *Quarterly Review*, May 1811, p. 465.

[91] The imperative necessity for disposing of these accumulated goods led to the adoption of new devices. The Trianon Tariff and the Fontainebleau decree led to the shifting of the trade in colonial goods and British manufactures from the regions of the Rhine, Weser, Elbe and Oder to eastern Europe and the Danube basin. Thus ships laden with sugar, coffee, tobacco, cotton-twist, etc., were sent from Great Britain at very high rates for freight and insurance to Salonica, where the goods were landed and thence carried on mules and horses through Serbia and Hungary to Vienna, and so to Germany at large and possibly even to France.—Tooke, *History of Prices*, I, 310 n. In spite of the opening of this new route, however, the glut continued. "Between 1807 and 1814 there was no corresponding export of the colonial produce brought here; as it was only in 1814 that an adequate vent could be found, on the opening of the continental ports, for the accumulation of sugar, coffee, etc., during the preceding five years."—*Ibid.*, p. 108.

Embargo, and then the Non-intercourse Act, had stopped all regular trade with the United States; and though a new outlet for British exports had been found in the young Latin American republics, this market was soon glutted, and it was the news of the failure of the speculations in South America which, together with the confiscations in the Baltic, was the immediate cause of the financial crisis of 1811.[92]

This crisis, indeed, was not confined to Great Britain, but extended also to the European Continent and to the United States,[93] and Great Britain was the first to recover. This recovery was due partly to the change in the political situation in Europe—the expulsion of the French from Portugal, the opening up of Spain and the relaxation of the Continental System by the Emperor Alexander of Russia,[94] partly to the end of the glut in South America and the West Indies, where early in 1811 a brisk demand for British manufactured goods arose.[95] But the crisis gave a great impetus to the agitation in Great Britain against the Orders in Council and the whole system of licenses. Petitions against them poured into Parliament, and but few in their favor,[96] while the spokesmen of the Opposition redoubled their attacks. In reply to the contention that

[92] *Ibid.*, p. 303.

[93] "Such times for money were never known . . . all confidence between merchants is totally destroyed. Since the middle of December there have been between 60 and 70 failures in this city, and many more are expected." Letter from New York, dated 11 February 1811.—*Ibid.*, p. 307.

[94] Under the Tilsit agreement Russia had at first rigorously excluded British goods (decrees of 1 April 1808 and 7 May 1809); but it was soon found out that there would be no too meticulous enquiries into the genuineness of ships' papers, and Alexander had never undertaken to exclude neutrals. He soon wearied of his engagements with Napoleon, and trade with Great Britain revived under cover of neutral flags. On 4 November 1810, Napoleon wrote to Alexander pointing out that not a single ship entered Russia with so-called American papers but came really from England. He summoned the Tsar to join with France in demanding of Sweden the seizure of the vast stores of merchandise landed by the British, under various flags, at Gothenburg. "But Russia," he complained, "has followed opposite principles, and of this but one proof need be given: namely, that the colonial merchandise which appeared at the last Leipzig fair was carried there by 700 wagons coming from Russia; finally, that the 1,200 ships which the English have convoyed by 20 ships of war, disguised under Swedish, Portuguese, Spanish and American flags, have in part landed their cargoes in Russia" (*Corr. de Napoléon,* xxi, p. 296). The effective reply of Alexander was the *ukaz* of 31 December 1810, which virtually allowed the importation of colonial goods.

[95] Tooke, *op. cit.,* I, 317.

[96] For the petitions to Parliament see 23 Hansard, pp. 164, 181, 202, 219, 232, 247, 289, 351, 392.

the Orders in Council were responsible for the decline in British trade, Ministers brought evidence to prove the contrary,[97] and pointed out that, even without the Orders in Council, licenses would have been necessary as dispensations from the prohibition of trade with the enemy which, under certain restrictions, it was to the interest of Great Britain to allow. The question, Lord Eldon argued, was not whether or no there had been a decline in British trade after the issue of the Orders in Council, but what that decline would have been had they not been issued.[98]

The case against the system established by the Orders in Council was summed up with great vigor in the *Quarterly* article for May 1811, to which reference has already been made. The licensing system, the writer urged, had not only been disastrous to British trade and shipping, but had directly fostered those of the enemy. "Whilst we," he wrote, "issue licences which expressly protect against the vigilance of our cruizers vessels bearing any flag except the French . . . it would be strange indeed if the enemy should find any difficulty in availing himself of an expedient by which he is relieved of the expense of insurance." Under this protection, even French vessels, sailing under neutral flags, had undisturbed access to the coasts of Great Britain, thus incidentally training seamen for Napoleon's navy. There were even examples of vessels, licensed to import commodities from France, being employed in the French coasting trade, and "during the summer of 1810 whole fleets, privileged to bring cargoes from Russia and Denmark to Great Britain, were actually employed in importing naval stores and other Baltic produce into those parts of Prussia and Swedish Pomerania occupied by French troops," while in the same year thirty-seven ships, provided with British licenses, arrived from Archangel in the ports of

---

[97] George Rose, the President of the Board of Trade, pointed out that the value of British exports had risen from £34,566,572 in 1807 to £45,869,860 in 1810, and that in the same period, in spite of "partial prohibition" (i.e., the Non-importation Act), exports to America and the West Indies had risen in value from £14,800,000 to £20,418,000. He also gave figures to show that the tonnage of British shipping and the number of British seamen employed had also increased (18 Hansard, pp. 1116 ff.). It may be noted that, in the course of the same debate, George Canning gave it as his opinion, that the principles on which he had always thought the Orders in Council to rest had been shaken by the speech of the President of the Board of Trade, "which seemed calculated to show how these Orders had succeeded as a measure of commercial rivalry, rather than as a dignified retaliation of one belligerent upon another" (*ibid.*, p. 1140).

[98] In the debate of 30 May 1808. 11 Hansard, 709.

Holland with naval stores. Of the last two hundred vessels sent in for adjudication, the writer added, at least three-quarters were proceeded against for carrying on trade with the enemy under British licenses.

In the opinion of the critics of the Orders in Council, however, the widespread distress in Great Britain was above all due to the interruption of trade with the United States, which, after as well as before their independence, had been the principal market for British manufactured goods. The causes of this interruption, the reaction generally of the United States to the policy of the belligerents as formulated in the Berlin Decree on the one side and the Orders in Council on the other, and the circumstances in which the strained relations between the United States and Great Britain issued in the unhappy War of 1812, will be examined in the following chapter.

VII

THE UNITED STATES AND THE BELLIGERENTS,
1805-1812

The year 1805 witnessed a decided turn for the worse in the relations of the United States with both France and Great Britain. As far as France was concerned, American trade was hard hit by Napoleon's new tariff policy, which aimed at a general prohibition of all foreign goods (decree of 17 Pluviôse, 6 February), and by the continued activities of the French cruisers and privateers, which in the Caribbean especially often amounted to sheer piracy.[1] These grievances, however, seemed small as compared with those against Great Britain: more particularly, the continued impressment of seamen from American ships and the fresh blow to American commerce dealt by the decision of the High Court of Admiralty in the *Essex, Orne* case,[2] with the consequent seizure of a large number of American merchantmen on the high seas.[3]

The news of the *Essex* decision reached Washington in September, and was soon followed by that of the consequent captures. James

[1] On 1 July 1805, Josiah Blakely, the American consul at San Iago, Cuba, wrote to the Secretary of State: "the scene of robbery, destruction, evasion, perjury, cruelty and insult, to which the Americans captured by French pirates, and brought into this and the adjacent ports, have been subjected, perhaps has not been equalled in a century past."—A.S.P., F.R., II, 670. In December of the same year the Rhode Island Insurance Company submitted a formal complaint, recounting the losses sustained owing to captures by French privateers.—*Ibid.*, pp. 770-772.

[2] See *supra*, p. 123.

[3] In July 1806, James Monroe complained to Fox, the British Prime Minister, that "about one hundred and twenty vessels had been seized, several condemned, all taken from their course, detained, and otherwise subjected to heavy losses and damages."—A.S.P., F.R., III, 115. In a letter to Lord Auckland, dated 18 February 1806, Lord Grenville made the following comments on the protests of President Jefferson against the restrictions on American trade: "You will observe the stress which Jefferson lays on the supposed unreasonableness of our claim to deprive other nations of a trade which we carry on ourselves. But this is a sophism. We have a right to prevent that which is injurious to us, and may, if we think right, in cases where we think the advantage to ourselves compensates or overbalances the injury; a principle manifest in the case of a siege, where we exclude all the world from intercourse with the town besieged, but carry it on ourselves, whenever we think it beneficial to our interests to do so."—*Dropmore Papers*, VII, 36.

Madison, the Secretary of State, sent instructions to James Monroe, who had returned to London from his mission in Spain in July, to protest against these seizures and once more to raise the question of impressment. Then, in April 1806, occurred an episode which made the situation even worse. Only a few miles from New York harbor, just outside territorial waters, the British frigate "Leander," asserting the right of search, fired across the bows of an American merchantman, and the ill-directed shot killed the master's brother. By way of retaliation for this outrage, and for the new English doctrine of "continuous voyage," Congress now hurriedly passed the first Non-importation Act (18 April 1806), which excluded various classes of British goods from importation. The Act was, however, suspended pending the outcome of the negotiations which had meanwhile been opened in London.

MISSION OF WILLIAM PINKNEY TO LONDON

These negotiations were of special importance owing to the impending lapse of the commercial articles of Jay's Treaty (XI to XXVI), which were valid only for twelve years from the date of ratification, and Madison sent William Pinkney, an astute Baltimore lawyer, to join Monroe in a mission extraordinary charged "to settle all matters of difference" with Great Britain, the question of impressments being once more put in the forefront.[4]

Before the negotiations were opened in London Anthony Merry had been replaced as British Minister in Washington by the Hon. David Erskine, whose wife was an American and who was otherwise inclined to do more than justice to the American case.[5] He at once reported home on the dangerous state of tension in the United States, pointing out that more ill will was caused by the few illegal captures immediately off the coast of the United States, and by the insulting behavior of British commanders in American harbors and waters, than by the most rigid enforcement of maritime rights on the other side of the Atlantic. The enforcement of these rights, he

[4] Madison himself drafted the clause dealing with impressments to be inserted in the expected treaty. For his instructions to Monroe and Pinkney, dated 17 May 1806, see A.S.P., F.R., III, 119 ff.

[5] The appointment had been made at the suggestion of Lord Erskine who, in pressing the claims of his eldest son on Lord Grenville, pointed out that he had been four years in the United States, where he would be most popular, and that he was less stubborn than Phineas Bond, who was anxious to retire. Lord Erskine to Lord Grenville, 22 May 1806.—*Dropmore Papers*, VII, 152.

urged, bore heavily on American commerce, and he expressed the fear that, if nothing were done to remove American grievances, especially in the matter of impressment, restrictions would be laid on British trade with the United States. In England, too, there was every disposition to meet the views of the Washington Government, as far as this could be done without imperiling the vital interests of Great Britain,[6] and the task of conducting the negotiations with the American commissioners was entrusted to Lords Holland and Auckland, whose friendly attitude towards the United States was to be proved later by their strenuous opposition to the Orders in Council.

It was soon clear, however, that these Whig lords were as little inclined as the Tory opposition to yield in the matter of the "ancient right" of impressment, on which the manning of the navy at that time depended; and when, on 31 December, a new treaty of amity and commerce between the United States and Great Britain was signed the subject of impressment was not mentioned in it. The most that the British commissioners would consent to do was to deliver to their American colleagues a formal note, approved by the Cabinet, pledging the British Government to see to it that in future there would be no abuse of the practice. For the rest, the treaty embodied notable concessions to the Americans, particularly in the matters of colonial trade,[7] the exercise of the right of visitation and search, the extension of neutral rights five miles out to sea, and

[6] The attitude of the British Government was doubtless affected by the results of Napoleon's crushing victory at Austerlitz. "The American question is certainly the most important of the moment," wrote Auckland to Grenville on 7 April 1806 (*Dropmore Papers*, VII, 85), and two days later, after pointing out that "the effects of the Austro-Russian campaign extend their mischiefs to our most distant interests," he added: "if it be expedient to make concessions to the United States would it not be desirable to bring the considerations forwards as soon as possible, in the form of an avowed suspension of the general system, and as a measure complying with the novel circumstances of the world, but not abandoning the ancient principles and usages of the laws of war and of nations."—*Dropmore Papers*, VII, 87.

[7] Article XI provided, in substance, that during the existing war European products might be carried to any port of any colony belonging to the enemy of Great Britain, provided they were entered and landed in the United Kingdom, and paid the ordinary duties; and on reëxportation should, after the drawback, have been subject to a duty equivalent to not less than one per cent, ad valorem, and were bona fide the property of American citizens. The produce of enemy colonies might also be brought to the United States, and there entered, landed and having paid duties be exported to any part of Europe, subject to a duty, after the drawback, of not less than two per cent, ad valorem.

most-favored-nation treatment for American commerce.[8] The treaty was, however, stillborn; for President Jefferson refused to submit it to the Senate, on the ground that it contained no mention of impressments.

THE BERLIN DECREE

A fresh disturbing factor had, moreover, been introduced into the situation. This was the Berlin Decree, news of which reached London during the late stage of the negotiations leading up to the treaty. The result of this was that the British commissioners, after signing the treaty, presented a note to Messrs. Monroe and Pinkney intimating that its ratification would depend on the attitude adopted by the United States towards the Berlin Decree. Unless the ruler of France abandoned his policy or

the United States by its conduct or assurances will have given security to his Majesty that it will not submit to such innovations on the established system of maritime law, . . . his Majesty will not consider himself bound by the present signature of his commissioners to ratify the treaty, or precluded from adopting such measures as may seem necessary for counteracting the designs of his enemy.

The commissioners of the United States [they added] will therefore feel that at a moment when his Majesty and all neutral nations are threatened with such an extension of the belligerent pretensions of his enemies, he cannot enter into the stipulations of the present treaty without an explanation from the United States of their intentions, or a reservation on the part of his Majesty in the case above mentioned.[9]

The American commissioners forwarded this note to Washington, with the assurance that they had not given it "in any slightest degree their sanction." [10] British Ministers, on the other hand, could not wait for an answer from the other side of the Atlantic before taking measures to counter the blow aimed at England by Napoleon, and a week later came the issue of the Order in Council of 7 January, one effect of which was the ruin of the lucrative coasting trade carried on by American ships, notably in the Mediterranean. In vain British Ministers pointed out, in reply to the strong protests of Secretary Madison, that the blame for this must be laid at the door of the author of the Berlin Decree; for the American Government had been completely taken in by Decrès' assurance to General Arm-

[8] A.S.P., F.R., III, 147 ff.; 10 Hansard, pp. 570 ff.

[9] Lords Holland and Auckland to the American commissioners, 10 Hansard, p. 560; A.S.P., F.R., III, 152.

[10] A.S.P., F.R., III, 147.

strong, the United States Minister in Paris, that the decree did not apply to American ships.[11] The negotiations, however, continued, though the chance of an amicable settlement was not improved by the fall of Lord Grenville's Government (18 March) and the consequent replacement of the conciliatory Lord Howick at the Foreign Office by the masterful George Canning. President Jefferson, on the other hand, was extremely anxious to avoid war with either of the belligerents, and in response to the representations of the British Government he twice postponed the date for carrying the Non-importation Act into effect, in the hope that a treaty satisfactory to the United States might yet be concluded. Such was the situation when an event occurred which fanned the flames of American resentment against Great Britain into a blaze, and made all hope of a speedy accommodation impossible.

THE "CHESAPEAKE" INCIDENT

In February 1807, five seamen of the British frigate "Melampus," which was at anchor in Hampton Roads, deserted and rowed ashore to Norfolk, where three of them were enlisted in the crew of the American frigate "Chesapeake," which was about to sail for the Mediterranean. Their example was speedily followed by five of the crew of the British frigate "Halifax," who were likewise taken on board the "Chesapeake." A demand for their return was refused by the American authorities, whereupon Vice-Admiral Berkeley, commanding the North American station, gave orders for the "Chesapeake" to be intercepted when she put to sea and searched for deserters. In obedience to this order the commander of H.M.S. "Leander," on 22 June, intercepted the "Chesapeake" after she had left Hampton Roads and summoned her to heave to and submit to search. The demand was very naturally refused, whereupon the "Leander" opened fire, with the result that the "Chesapeake," which was entirely unprepared for battle, was forced to yield. Only one of the deserters was found on board, but three other seamen were impressed as British subjects.[12] It is not hard to imagine the effect on public opinion in the United States when the crippled frigate, with its tale of dead and wounded, limped back into port.

[11] See *supra,* p. 136.

[12] For the British point of view see the account given by the Earl of Selkirk in the House of Lords (14 Hansard, pp. 344 ff.). "Nothing can be more absurd," he said, "than to talk of the attack on the *Chesapeake* as an unprovoked outrage."

This unhappy affair, in which both sides must take their share of blame, concerns us here only in so far as it affected the relations of the two countries concerned. Its immediate effect was the putting into force, in July, of the Non-importation Act. Long-drawn-out negotiations followed, George Rose being sent by the British Government on a special mission to Washington, which effected nothing. If for the time being an outbreak of war between the United States and Great Britain was avoided, this was due partly to the pacific temper of Jefferson, partly to the fact that the Emperor Napoleon chose this time to take measures equally offensive to American sentiment and damaging to American interests, so that, if war were declared, it looked as though it would have to be declared against both France and Great Britain, which would have placed the United States in an exceedingly perilous position in the event of a complete victory of one or other of the great antagonists. From Paris General Armstrong reported home that Napoleon, in spite of Decrès's assurances, was assuming a more and more free hand in dealing with neutral commerce. The instructions, issued on 18 September, to seize all vessels laden with British goods dealt a shrewd blow at American trade. Then, on 7 October, Champagny (Duke of Cadore), who had succeeded Talleyrand as French Minister of Foreign Affairs in August, announced formally to Armstrong that the Berlin Decree henceforward held out no exceptions to American vessels; and, when the American Minister protested, Napoleon dictated a reply in which he said that, since American vessels allowed themselves to be visited and searched, permitted impressments, and submitted to being turned from their course into British ports, they must conform to the Berlin Decree or take the consequences.[13]

In taking this attitude Napoleon's intention was to force the United States into a declaration of war against Great Britain. But as General Turreau, the French Minister in Washington, had reported to Talleyrand earlier in the year, the Americans, in spite of the "Chesapeake" incident, still remained in subjection to Great Britain both in their affections and their habits,[14] and Champagny's

---

[13] Champagny to Armstrong, 24 November 1807. A.S.P., F.R., III, 247. This letter came from Milan, where the news of the Orders in Council of 11 November had not yet reached Napoleon. Its terms, however, foreshadowed the famous Milan Decree of 17 December, which was his reply to the Orders in Council.

[14] This state of feeling and the slight effect which war between two nations had in interrupting social relations between them are vividly illustrated in the letters of Samuel Morse. When the Anglo-American war broke out in 1812 Morse

communication might have had the reverse of the effect intended, if a satisfactory understanding could have been reached between the American and British Governments. Unfortunately this proved to be impossible. In December, almost simultaneously with General Armstrong's report, news reached Washington that the British Government, in order to meet the urgent need of men for the navy, had issued a proclamation recalling British seamen in foreign service and renewed instructions for the impressment of British subjects from neutral merchantmen. On 13 December, too, James Monroe, full of wrath against Jefferson for rejecting the treaty which he had negotiated, landed at Norfolk, and his reports, together with those received from Pinkney in London, made it clear that, for the time being, all hope of concluding a commercial treaty with Great Britain was at an end.

JEFFERSON'S EMBARGO

In these circumstances, since the United States had at that time neither military nor naval forces such as would have justified an appeal to arms, President Jefferson decided to show Europe "that there are peaceable means of repressing injustice by making it the interest of the aggressor to do what is just and abstain from future wrong." [15] A precedent was ready to hand in the embargo which,

---

was a student at the Royal Academy in London, of which an American, Sir Benjamin West, was president. It was during the war that he gained the gold medal for sculpture. In his letters home he denounces the pride and insolence of the British, which needed chastising. Yet he rejoices at the news of every British victory over the French. "The Marquis Wellesley," he writes, "has achieved a great victory in Spain, and bids fair to drive the French out very soon. At this I rejoice as ought every man who abhors tyranny and loves liberty. I wish the British success against everything but my country. I often say with Cowper: 'England with all thy faults I love thee still.' " Asked if the ruling party in America was not very much under French influence, he replied that this was not so; that, on the contrary, he believed that nine-tenths of the American people were prepossessed strongly in favor of England, urging as proof the universal prevalence of English fashions, manners and customs, the general rejoicings at the success of the English over the French, etc. "On the other hand," he added, "the French are a people most universally despised in America, and by at least one-half hated. As in England, they are esteemed the common enemies of mankind; French fashions are discountenanced and loathed; a Frenchman is considered as a man always to be suspected; young men are forbidden by their parents, in many instances, to associate with them, they considering their company and habits as tending to subvert their morals, and to render them frivolous and insincere."—Edward Lind Morse, *Life of Samuel Morse*, I, 90.

[15] Jefferson to W. H. Cabell, Governor of Virginia, 29 June 1807. Quoted in Hirst, *Life and Letters of Thomas Jefferson*, I, 422.

under Madison's leadership, had been passed by Congress in 1794, when for thirty days no vessel had been allowed to clear from an American for a foreign port. On 18 December 1807 the President laid before Congress a proposal for a similar embargo, to which however no limit of time was to be set, and four days later the bill embodying this proposal had become law. Under this statute departure was forbidden to "all ships and vessels in the ports and places within the limits or jurisdiction of the United States, cleared or not cleared, bound to any foreign port or place." The only exceptions were American Government vessels, foreign vessels in ballast or with a cargo on board when notified of the Act, and armed vessels possessing public commissions from a foreign power. Vessels engaged in the coasting trade had to furnish bonds, double the value of ship and cargo, that the goods carried would not be landed save in a port of the United States.[16]

Jefferson's policy of the embargo has been hailed by an English writer as "a shining example of Christian and democratic statesmanship," which will appeal to all those "who accept the Sermon on the Mount as applicable to the moral conduct of nations." [17] Apart from the fact that the "economic boycott" is nowhere suggested in the Sermon on the Mount, the results of Jefferson's embargo were hardly such as to commend it as a substitute for war, but rather tended to prove the futility of economic boycotts as instruments of coercion. In spite of increasingly severe penalties, the law was constantly evaded or defied; for men will take great risks in the hope of great rewards. American ships which were in foreign waters when the law was passed steered clear of American ports; others, caught in American harbors, slipped out without waiting for their papers; others again, ostensibly engaged in the coasting trade, were "driven by stress of weather" into foreign ports. Sometimes governors of maritime States made fortunes by granting licenses to break the law, while on the Canadian border there developed, as under the later régime of prohibition, a vast smuggling trade with which the authorities were quite unable to grapple.

In spite of these evasions and breaches of the law, however, the suffering caused in the United States by the embargo was great. The fact that a few industries were able to establish a precarious existence in the absence of foreign imports was small compensation

[16] 2 *Statutes at Large* 451.   [17] Hirst, *op. cit.*, I, 423.

for the ruin which fell on the shipping and agricultural interests. Thousands of sailors were thrown out of work, and many ship-owners went bankrupt. Agricultural produce, deprived of its over-seas markets, sank to half the price it had previously fetched, while the cost of clothing and all manufactured articles hitherto imported increased, so that the expenses of the farmers grew while their power to purchase diminished.[18]

In spite of all this self-inflicted suffering, the embargo failed in its object. It might perhaps have succeeded, but for the happy chance which, in 1808, opened up Spain and the Latin American colonies as new markets for British manufactures;[19] for at first it hit the English manufacturing interests hard and greatly increased the already severe privations of the British working classes, thus helping to swell the chorus of protest which rose, in ever increasing volume, against the Orders in Council.[20]

The Orders in Council, as James Stephen pointed out in the House of Commons,[21] were not in fact the cause of the embargo. It is,

[18] For a very full account of the embargo and its effects see Sears, *Jefferson and the Embargo* (1927). See also Heckscher, *The Continental System* (1922), pp. 130 ff., and Coman, *Industrial History of the United States* (1910). Mr. Hirst, in the work cited, displays a wholehearted admiration for Jefferson and his great experiment in making war without weapons. Professor Sears sums up the abiding interest of Jefferson's experiment more convincingly as "a study of a humanitarian autocrat administering a panacea for the woes of mankind" (Sears, *op. cit.*, p. 73). Such a study is certainly of special interest at the present time, when humanitarian autocrats are tending to increase in numbers.

[19] Speaking in the House of Commons, on 6 March 1809, George Rose, the President of the Board of Trade, said: "Instead of impending ruin from the Em-bargo, our trade has suffered very little diminution." He pointed out that, while exports to the American States had sunk from £11,774,000 in 1806-1807 to £5,784,000 in 1808, those to all parts of America, exclusive of the United States, had risen from £8,629,000 in 1806-1807 to £12,859,000 in 1808 (12 Hansard, p. 1196). This new avenue of escape from the consequences of the embargo, and the resulting change of public opinion in England, caused Jefferson "profound disap-pointment."—Sears, *op. cit.*, p. 113.

[20] See *supra*, p. 166.

[21] James Stephen, speaking in the debate on Whitbread's motion in the House of Commons, 6 March 1809, said: "It is true that our American trade is at a stand: but by what means? By the American Non-Importation Act, passed long anterior to any of the British Orders in question; and by the Embargo, which was imposed by the legislature of the United States before our Orders of November were known to their Government" (13 Hansard, App. II, li). George Rose, during the same debate, made a similar statement (12 Hansard, p. 1196). Stephen's speech on this occasion may be taken as representative of the dominant British sentiment at this time. "If there are men among us," he said, "so insensible to all the sympathies arising from a common extraction, from unity of language, manners and religion,

indeed, just possible that news of the issue of the Orders in Council of November reached Jefferson before he laid his proposal for the embargo before Congress on 18 December; for Monroe, who left London on 14 November, the day the Orders were published, arrived at Norfolk on 13 December. But, though the President communicated them to Congress on 2 February, three weeks before Erskine formally communicated their terms, with the reasons for their issue, to Secretary Madison,[22] it is clear that the embargo policy had been decided on long before the Orders in Council were known to him. This point, however, was of importance only in the debates in Parliament, where the opposition maintained that the embargo would be lifted but for the Orders in Council; the fact remained, that what with the Embargo on one side and the Orders on the other, the relations between the United States and Great Britain were strained almost to the breaking point. That the breach was not completed at this time was largely due to the tactless attempts of Napoleon to force the United States into the war on his side.

As the result of the issue of the second Milan Decree [23] numerous American vessels had been captured by French cruisers and taken into the ports of France and her allies. In reply to General Armstrong's protests, Champagny enlarged on the outrages committed by the British on American commerce, declared that the United States and Great Britain were already *de facto* at war, and that the Emperor was confident that a formal declaration of war on the part of the United States would follow. Meanwhile, no definitive measures would be taken against American vessels brought into French ports, but they would remain sequestered until the disposition of the American Government had been expressed.[24] This was clearly a threat of consequences if the Americans failed to fall in with the views of Napoleon, and in the actual temper of the American people it was scarcely calculated to have the effect intended.

---

and from a common attachment to the principles of civil liberty, as to desire a quarrel with our brethren of the United States of America, I trust they are but few; and I beg the honourable gentleman at least to believe that I am not one of their number. . . . To avoid a war with the United States I would sacrifice much, but not rescind our Orders in Council on the terms proposed by America, for that would be in effect to submit to the utter ruin of our commerce and, by a necessary consequence, to the loss of our naval ascendancy—our grand security . . . against the arms of France."

[22] Erskine to Madison, 23 February 1808. A.S.P., F.R., III, 209.

[23] See *supra*, p. 153.

[24] Champagny to Armstrong, 15 January 1808. A.S.P., F.R., III, 247 f.

Opinion in the United States was, indeed, divided, the Republicans being disposed to throw the whole blame on Great Britain, since the Milan Decree was in retaliation for the Orders in Council, while the Federalists denounced Napoleon and all his works, and condemned Jefferson as his tool.

The position of the American Government was one of singular difficulty, especially since it was increasingly clear that the embargo, the only available weapon of offense, was becoming unpopular. Madison, whose bias was in favor of France, left Erskine's note of 23 February for a whole month without an answer and, when at last the answer was delivered, it was a vigorous denunciation of the Orders in Council as intended to promote the commercial and fiscal policy of Great Britain by "ruinous depredations" upon the lawful commerce of the United States.[25] The tension was increased when, in order to relieve the distress in the British West Indies caused by the embargo, the British Government, on 11 April, issued a supplementary Order in Council directing naval commanders to permit neutral vessels laden with provisions and lumber to sail freely, with or without papers, to the West Indies and South America, and to allow them to proceed, after obtaining a passport, to any unblockaded port.[26] This order, which was taken as a direct incitement to American shipowners and mariners to break the law, was denounced by Madison as "a disorganizing and dishonorable experiment."

While, however, the tension between the United States and Great Britain was thus increasing, American relations with France were becoming equally strained. On 17 April Napoleon issued the Bayonne Decree, which referred to the embargo and ordered the sequestration of American ships entering French harbors, on the ground that, since American ships could not legally leave their own ports, all vessels claiming to be American were really British and lawful prize.[27] Even before the news of this reached Washington, Congress

[25] Madison to Erskine, 25 March 1808. *Ibid.*, p. 210; 12 Hansard, pp. 246 ff.
[26] A.S.P., F.R., III, 281.
[27] "It was pretended, in vindication of this measure, that, as under our Embargo law no American vessel could navigate the ocean, all those which were found on it were trading on British account, and lawful prize. The fact, however, was otherwise. At the time the embargo was laid, a great number of our vessels were at sea, engaged in their usual commerce, many of them on distant voyages. Their absence, especially as no previous notice could be given them, was strictly justifiable under the law."—Monroe to Joel Barlow, 26 July 1811. A.S.P., F.R., III, 511.

had been forced to recognize the fact that diplomatic arguments carry little weight unless backed by a sufficient show of force, and before it adjourned on 25 April it had taken measures to strengthen the army and navy. It had also taken what proved to be a fateful step by authorizing the President to suspend the embargo, in whole or in part, in the event of the belligerents changing their attitude.

Madison at once used the diplomatic weapon thus placed in his hands. At the beginning of May he instructed Armstrong and Pinkney to inform the French and British Governments, respectively, of the power conferred on the President to suspend the embargo, in whole or in part, whenever the safety of American commerce should have been secured. He pointed out to Armstrong that, if Napoleon were to be the first to cancel his decrees, Great Britain would be forced to yield or, if she refused, would make a collision between herself and the United States inevitable, since the latter in that event intended to reopen trade with France. On the other hand, if Great Britain were to take the initiative by canceling the Orders in Council, the position of France would be doubly embarrassing.[28]

Napoleon, who had previously attempted to bribe the United States by hints of French aid in securing the Floridas, was however now in no accommodating temper, since he had just established his brother Joseph on the Spanish throne and so denied that he had ever suggested an American occupation of the Floridas, which could only be done with the consent of his friend and ally the King of Spain. His only effective reply to the advances of Washington was to order a rigorous enforcement of the Bayonne Decree, several American vessels being captured at sea by French cruisers and burnt as British. But, even before receiving the dispatches which announced these things, Madison had contemplated the possibility of war with France. In a letter to Armstrong of 22 July 1808, which was to be communicated to Champagny, he wrote: "If France does not wish to throw the United States into a war against her . . . she ought not to hesitate a moment in revoking at least so much of her decrees as violate the rights of the sea, and furnish to her adversaries the pretext of his retaliating measures." [29] This dispatch was, however, never communicated to Champagny. In explaining his reasons for suppressing it General Armstrong remarked that the embargo, as a "means of coercing the two great belligerents to a course of

[28] Madison to Armstrong, 2 May 1808. A.S.P., F.R., III, 252.
[29] To Armstrong, 22 July 1808. A.S.P., F.R., III, 254.

justice," had been somewhat overrated. "The embargo," he said, "is a measure calculated, above all other, to keep us whole and to keep us in peace; but, beyond this, you must not count upon it. Here it is not felt, and in England . . . it is forgotten." [30] This latter statement was justified at the time by the change of feeling in England owing to Wellesley's victories in Spain and the opening up of new markets in the Iberian Peninsula and Latin America; and these altered circumstances had their effect on the attitude of the British Government towards the proposals which Pinkney was instructed to lay before it.

In presenting Madison's protest against the Orders in Council to Canning, on 23 August, Pinkney expressed his conviction that, if the Orders were repealed, the President would raise the embargo as far as Great Britain was concerned. An interchange of notes followed, in the course of which Pinkney argued that, if the British Orders and the American embargo were rescinded in the manner suggested, commercial intercourse between the two countries would be immediately revived; that, if the French followed the British example and retracted their decrees, the avowed purpose of the Orders would be accomplished; and that, if France refused to retract, and the American embargo continued as against her alone, this would occupy the place of the British Orders and would perform their office better than they could perform it themselves.[31] Canning, for his part, noted that all this seemed to represent only Pinkney's own opinion. Seizing on an expression quoted by Pinkney from Madison's instructions, he expressed his gratification at learning that the embargo—so often represented as a result of the Orders in Council—was really "a measure of precaution against reasonably anticipated peril"; for the rest, he refused to admit that the Orders were violations of international law, once more asserting "the unquestionable right of his Majesty to resort to the fullest measures of retaliation in consequence of the unparalleled aggressions of the enemy," and insisting that, if third parties suffered, they must seek redress from the power which was the first to violate the established usages of war and the rights of neutral States.[32]

[30] To Madison, 30 August 1808. *Ibid.,* p. 256.

[31] Pinkney to Canning, 10 October 1808. 13 Hansard, App. I, viii.

[32] Canning to Pinkney, 23 September 1808. 13 Hansard, App. I, iii, iv. For the whole interchange of notes see "Papers relating to the Correspondence with America" presented to Parliament on 1 February 1809. 12 Hansard, pp. 241-262, and "Papers . . ." ordered to be printed on 22 February 1809, 13 *ibid.,* App. I.

In the United States, meanwhile, feeling against the embargo had been rapidly gaining ground, and when Congress reassembled, on 5 November, it was made the subject of angry debates, in the course of which the Federalists accused Jefferson of undue subservience to France. The Administration, however, strong in the support of the majority of the representatives, succeeded in maintaining an unyielding attitude for more than four months. At the very outset Erskine reported to Canning that Madison was in favor of recalling both Pinkney and Armstrong, and of making preparations for war; and a month later that the Government and the party in power had stated their intention not to remove the embargo, except by substituting war measures against both belligerents, in the event of either or both of them not relaxing their restrictions upon neutral commerce. Thus inspired, Congress passed three resolutions: that the United States could not submit to the edicts of France and Great Britain; that the vessels and the products of these two powers should be denied the right of entry; and that preparations should be made for defense. With the turn of the year, however, it became clear that the repeal of the embargo was only a question of time. The Federalists had always been against it, and now, under pressure from their constituents, the Republican representatives were also becoming restive. In these circumstances the Government took the initiative, and on 30 January, William Cary Nicholas, a friend of Madison's, moved the repeal of the embargo as from 1 June 1809 and the authorization of the issue of letters of marque and reprisal against both France and Great Britain. But when, on 27 February, the repeal was carried, the Federalists had proved strong enough to substitute the 4th of March for the 1st of June as the date of its application and to strike out the authorization of armed reprisals.[33] Instead, Congress passed a Non-intercourse Act, under the terms of which American vessels were forbidden under bond to enter any French or British ports, or to engage in trade with them either directly or indirectly, while the public vessels of France and Great Britain were excluded from American waters and any French or British ships entering the ports of the United States were to be confiscated. This Act, which was to remain in force till the end of the

[33] Jefferson ascribed this to "a sudden and unaccountable revolution of opinion . . . chiefly among the New England and New York members," who voted for the earlier date "in a kind of panic."—To Thomas Mann Randolph, 7 February 1809, quoted in Sears, *op. cit.*, p. 140.

next Congress, and so remained law until May 1810, was approved by Jefferson on 1 March. Four days later his term as President came to an end, and James Madison ruled in his stead.

The Erskine Incident

Meanwhile, on 23 January 1809, Canning had written to Erskine instructing him to lay before the Secretary of State the conditions on which Great Britain would be prepared to withdraw the Orders in Council. The terms were sufficiently explicit. The American Government was to withdraw the interdiction of its harbors to ships of war and all non-importation and non-intercourse acts so far as respected Great Britain, but to leave them in force with respect to France and the powers which adopted or acted under her decrees; the United States were to renounce during the present war the pretension of carrying on in time of war all trade with the enemy colonies from which she was excluded in time of peace—in other words, to recognize the validity of the Rule of 1756; and, lastly, Great Britain was to be considered at liberty to capture all American vessels attempting to trade with the ports of France or those of States acting under her decrees.

I flatter myself [Canning wrote] that there will be no difficulty in obtaining a distinct and official recognition of these conditions from the American Government. For this purpose you are at liberty to communicate this dispatch *in extenso* to the American Secretary of State. Upon receiving from you, on the part of the American Government, a distinct and official recognition of the three above-mentioned conditions, his Majesty will lose no time in sending to America a minister fully empowered to consign them to a regular and formal treaty. As, however, it is possible that the delay which must intervene before the actual conclusion of the treaty may appear to the American Government to deprive this arrangement of part of its benefits, I am to authorize you, if the American Government should be desirous of acting upon the agreement before it is reduced into regular form, either by the immediate repeal of the Embargo, and the other acts in question, or by engaging to repeal them on a particular day, to assure the American Government of his Majesty's readiness to meet such a disposition in the manner best calculated to give it effect. Upon the receipt here of an official Note, containing an engagement for the adoption by the American Government of the three conditions above specified, his Majesty will be prepared, on the faith of such engagement, either immediately (if the repeal shall have been immediate in America) or on any day specified by the American Government for the repeal, reciprocally to recall the Orders in Council, without waiting for the conclusion of the treaty.[34]

---

[34] Canning to Erskine, 23 January 1809. 14 Hansard, pp. 881 ff.

What followed forms a singular and very unfortunate chapter in the history of diplomacy. Erskine, who was anxious to establish good relations between the two countries, shrank from putting forward proposals which he felt would only widen the breach between them, and he kept Canning's instructions to himself. But this was not all. On 17 April, acting on instructions from his Government, he presented to the new Secretary of State, Robert Smith, an apology and offer of reparation for the attack on the "Chesapeake," which was acknowledged in a polite note of the same date. In these notes reference had naturally been made to the desirability of establishing and maintaining good relations between the two kindred nations, and on the following day Erskine wrote to Smith telling him that, "with a view to contribute to so desirable an object, His Majesty would be willing to withdraw his Orders in Council of January and November 1807, so far as respects the United States, in the persuasion that the President would issue a proclamation for the renewal of the intercourse with Great Britain." Since there was no word in this of the conditions laid down in Canning's instructions, the Secretary of State was able at once to announce the President's acceptance of the proposal; whereupon, without referring the matter home, Erskine informed him that he was authorized to declare that His Majesty's Orders in Council of January and November 1807 would have been withdrawn, so far as the United States were concerned, on the 10th day of June next.[35]

More than a month passed before Erskine's dispatches announcing the arrangement he had made reached Canning's hands. His dismay and anger knew no bounds; he at once addressed sharp notes to Erskine, pointing out the obvious discrepancy between the instructions he had received and the agreement made; and before Erskine could reply, another note, dated 30 May, announced to him his recall. Once more the extreme slowness of communications was to be the cause of a serious trouble which in these days would have been avoided. Believing that the agreement concluded with Erskine represented the views of the British Government, President Madison raised the embargo as from the 10th of June, and it was not till more than a month later that it was known in Washington that Canning had rejected the agreement as unauthorized by the British

[35] A.S.P., F.R., III, 296. For the notes interchanged between Smith and Erskine see also 17 Hansard, cli, and for the subsequent Erskine-Canning correspondence, *ibid.*, cxix ff.

Minister's instructions. Meanwhile, the embargo having been raised, large numbers of American merchantmen had put to sea in ignorance of the fact that they were still liable to capture under the Orders in Council.

The critical situation thus created was not improved by the diplomatic methods of Erskine's successor, Francis James Jackson, who reached Washington on 8 September 1809.[36] His instructions were uncompromising: no further agreement was to be negotiated except on the basis of the conditions laid down in the original instructions to Erskine, and any proposals the American Government might make were to be referred to London for consideration.[37] Any chance of an agreement on these conditions was remote, and it was made still more remote by the somewhat hectoring tone adopted by Jackson in his negotiations with the Secretary of State, who in November refused to receive any further communications from him.[38] It

[36] "He had but recently been among the scenes at Copenhagen, which had illustrated Nelson's maxim that a fleet of ships of the line were the best negotiators in Europe."—Mahan, I, 223.

[37] Canning to Jackson, Nos. 1-5, 1 July 1809. P.R.O. F.O. 5. 68. For the interchange of notes between Canning and Pinkney on the subject of the Erskine agreement see F.O. 5. 67.

[38] William Pinkney, the American Minister in London, justified this action of his Government in a long letter, dated 2 January 1810, to the Marquess Wellesley, who had meanwhile succeeded Canning at the Foreign Office. The Government of the United States, he said, had expected from Mr. Jackson some explanation of the grounds on which the British Government had refused to abide by the agreement made with Mr. Erskine. Since Mr. Jackson had no powers to make such an explanation or, in the matter of the Orders in Council, to propose any substitute for the agreement made, or to agree to any counter proposals which the American Government might be disposed to put forward, it had seemed useless to continue "loose conversations, having in view no definite result, or none that was attainable." As for Jackson's behavior, "it was not to have been expected that he would seek to irritate where he could not arrange, and sharpen disappointment by studied and unprovoked indignity." What rankled most, it seems, was his accusation that the American Government had made the agreement with Erskine well knowing that its terms were in violation of his instructions. This was "to fasten upon the Government of the United States an imputation most injurious to its honour and veracity." Had it known that Erskine was disregarding his instructions, it would never have acted as it had done. *Papers Presented to Parliament in 1813*. Papers relating to America. A. No. 1. After communicating with Jackson, Wellesley informed the American Minister, on 14 March, that His Majesty, being sincerely anxious to cultivate the intercourse of the two Governments on the most friendly terms, had recalled Mr. Jackson, though he did not appear to have committed any intentional offense against the Government of the United States. "His Majesty," he added, "has not marked with any expression of his displeasure the conduct of Mr. Jackson, whose integrity, zeal, and ability have long been distinguished in His Majesty's service."—*Ibid.*, No. 5. For the correspondence between Jackson and the Secretary of State see A.S.P., F.R., III, 308 ff.

was a fateful moment. Both the President and the Secretary of State believed that it was impossible for the United States to continue in a state of strained relations with both France and Great Britain. Therefore, since it seemed impossible to arrive at an accommodation with the British Government, they turned to France.

THE UNITED STATES AND NAPOLEON

In this direction, it is true, the auspices were also by no means propitious. The conduct of the French Emperor towards American trade was certainly, within the limits of his power, far more arbitrary than any that could be charged against the British Government, a fact which was soon to find ample confirmation. The American Non-intercourse Act had merely warned French ships that, if they entered an American harbor after 20 May 1809, they would be confiscated. Napoleon's reply was the Rambouillet Decree, signed on 23 March but not published until the middle of May, which ordered the seizure of all American vessels which had entered French ports since the coming into force of the American Act of 20 May 1809, and their sale for the benefit of the imperial *Caisse d'amortissement*. As a result, some hundred American ships, with cargoes valued at $10,000,000, which had been lying under sequestration in French ports since the issue of the Bayonne Decree, were finally confiscated.[39] Nor was this all. The annexation of Holland to the French Empire, on 9 July, was followed by the sequestration of all American vessels found in Dutch harbors, and a still larger number were among the six hundred ships under neutral flags which, later in the year, were seized in the Baltic ports by Napoleon's order.

The news of these happenings might have been expected to arouse in the United States a feeling against France at least as strong as that against Great Britain. But, as an American historian has pointed out, "for some unexplained reason, Americans seemed never to resent Napoleonic rapacity as one would expect," [40] and Napoleon himself, an adept in the art of diplomatic cajolery, was swift to avail himself of this accommodating temper. His chance came

[39] Mahan, *Influence of Sea Power*, II, 292; Heckscher, *Continental System*, pp. 135 f.

[40] Tansill, *Robert Smith*, III, 177. J. P. Morier, the British chargé d'affaires at Washington, in a letter to Wellesley, dated 29 December 1810, comments on "the indifference with which the object of the restitution of their property is abandoned" in the correspondence with the French Government. *Parl. Papers*, 1813. America. B. No. 8.

when the news reached him of the lapse of the Non-intercourse Act and the substitution for it, on 1 May 1810, of an Act of Congress which provided, *inter alia,* that in case either Great Britain or France should, before the third day of March next, revoke her edicts or modify them in such a way that they would no longer violate the neutral commerce of the United States, the President was to proclaim the fact, and that if the other nation did not, within three months of the proclamation, take similar action, the Non-intercourse Act was to be revived against that nation.[41] It seems clear that, from the first, the American Government conceived this as a measure for bringing pressure to bear upon Great Britain, rather than upon France, and that as such it would be welcomed by the French Government. On 5 June Secretary Smith wrote to General Armstrong, the American Minister in Paris, instructing him, in the event that the French Government acceded to "the overture contained in the Act of Congress, by repealing or so modifying its Decrees, as that they will cease to violate neutral rights," at once to inform Pinkney, to charter a special vessel to convey the news to America and to send several copies of the agreement to Pinkney, to be forwarded from British ports.[42] A month later, in a dispatch to Pinkney in London, he instructed him to urge the British Government to repeal not only the Orders in Council but also the "spurious blockade of May 1806."

Without this enlightened precaution [he wrote] it is probable, and may indeed be inferred from the letter of the Duke of Cadore to General Armstrong (of 14 February), that the French Government will draw Great Britain and the United States to issue on the legality of such blockades, by acceding to the Act of Congress, with a condition, that a repeal of the Blockades shall accompany a repeal of the Orders in Council, alleging, that the Orders and Blockades, differing little, if at all, otherwise than in name, a repeal of the former, leaving in operation the latter, would be a mere illusion.

If the British Government asked for explanations as to the extent of the repeal of the French Decrees which would be required, it was to be informed that the repeal "must embrace every part of the French decrees which violate the neutral rights guaranteed to us by the law of nations." He added that the United States, as a neutral nation, had no right to demand a repeal of such parts of the decrees

---

[41] 2 *Statutes at Large* 605-606; *Parl. Papers,* 1813. America. A. Inclosure 3 in No. 11.

[42] *Ibid.,* B. Inclosure 3 in No. 8.

as did not affect them, and that Great Britain, as a belligerent nation, could have no pretext for urging the demand.[43]

In a dispatch of the same date to General Armstrong he said that, since he had not obtained from the British Government an acceptance of the condition on which the French Government was willing to concur in putting an end to all the edicts of both against American commerce, this was a good opportunity for the French Emperor to make good the declaration, made in the Duke of Cadore's letter of 14 February, that he would do justice to the United States in the case of a pledge on their part not to submit to the British edicts. "Instead of submission," he said, "the President is ready, by renewing the Non-Intercourse Act against Great Britain, to oppose to her Orders in Council a measure which is of a character which ought to satisfy every reasonable expectation." If necessary, the General was to assure the French Government that a repeal of the "illegal blockades" of a date prior to the Berlin Decree, namely, that of May 1806, would be included in the conditions required of Great Britain. At the same time he was to protest against the enormity of the outrage committed by the French Government in selling the confiscated American ships, of which news had just been received in Armstrong's dispatch of 16 April. "A satisfactory provision for restoring the property lately surprized and seized by the Order, or at the instance of, the French Government," he said, "must be combined with a repeal of the French edicts." [44]

Napoleon at once saw the opportunity presented to him of embroiling Great Britain with the United States. He had no intention of revoking the Berlin and Milan decrees, which—as he told Champagny—"would cause disturbance and not fulfil my object," but if he could persuade the American Government that he intended to withdraw them, the Non-intercourse Act would be revived against Great Britain alone, and war between her and the United States would almost certainly follow. He accordingly instructed Champagny to inform the American Minister in a diplomatic note that he might rest assured that the decrees would not be enforced after 1 November, and that he could regard them as revoked. This note—the so-called "letter of the Duke of Cadore"—was drafted by Napoleon himself and was delivered, with but slight alterations, to General Armstrong by Champagny on 5 August. "I am authorized to

[43] *Ibid.*, A. Inclosure 2 in No. 8.   [44] *Ibid.*, A. Inclosure 4 in No. 8.

declare to you," it ran, "that the decrees of Berlin and Milan are revoked, and that after 1 November they will cease to have effect; it being understood that, in consequence of this declaration, the English shall revoke their Orders in Council, and renounce the new principle of blockade which they have wished to establish; or that the United States, conformably to the Act which you have just communicated to me, shall make their rights respected by the English." The note ended with more than a touch of cajolery, which should have warned the Americans of its insincerity: Napoleon, it seems, loved the Americans, and their prosperity and commerce were "within the scope of his policy." [45]

Though the note was published in the *Moniteur* on 9 August, it was soon clear that, in the absence of any more formal revocation, the decrees were still in force, even against American ships. During the autumn of 1810, indeed, a few concessions were made to the United States, such as the lowering of the Trianon Tariff on goods (other than British) imported direct in American bottoms, and the issue of licenses to American vessels wishing to import certain classes of American colonial produce, with French consular certificates in cipher as a precaution against their being British masquerading as American. The sequestered American ships, however, were not released, or—what was particularly significant—there were released only those which had conformed to the conditions laid down in the Berlin Decree.

But though Napoleon had not withdrawn the decrees, he had by a trick induced "an over-eager President of the United States" to believe that he had done so.[46] Acting on this belief, President Madison, on 2 November 1810, proclaimed the revival of the Non-intercourse Act against Great Britain alone, the Act to take effect on the 2d of February following. It was soon clear, however, that this belief had little or no foundation, and the revelation placed American statesmen in an exceedingly awkward position in their negotiations with Great Britain; for, while they were maintaining in London that the French decrees had been revoked, in Paris they were pressing the French Government to make this revocation a reality.[47] So

[45] A.S.P., F.R., III, 386 f.: *Parl. Papers*, 1813. America. A. No. 15. Pinkney to Wellesley, 25 August, enclosing the full text of the letter, with a translation.

[46] Mahan, II, 291.

[47] In reference to the revocation of the decrees, published in the *Moniteur* of 9 August, Pinkney, in the letter to Wellesley of 25 August cited above, said: "That it has taken effect cannot be doubted" and later he used even stronger lan-

far from this pressure having any effect, however, the French Government proceeded to take measures which threatened the trade of the United States with the European Continent with total extinction. Hitherto consular certificates of origin had been issued to American vessels not only to the ports of France, under the decree of 1 Messidor, An XI (20 June 1803), but also to neutral and allied ports, by a circular of the Minister for Foreign Relations of 20 April 1808. This latter privilege was now withdrawn by a decree of 15 July, the terms of which were embodied in a circular issued by the Duke of Cadore on 30 August 1810, which prohibited the delivery of certificates for merchandise of any kind, or under any pretext whatever, if the vessels were not destined for France. But this was not all. The circular also laid severe restrictions upon imports from America into France, "the importation of cotton and tobacco being, at this moment, especially prohibited." It was not till 10 December that General Turreau, the French Minister in Washington, informed the Secretary of State of this new move, and the terms in which he did so betrayed its underlying political motive. He had reason to believe, he said, that some modifications would be made to this absolute exclusion, but these would depend upon "other measures . . . which the two Governments will continue to adopt, to withdraw from the monopoly and the vexations of the common enemy a commerce necessary to France as well as to the United States." [48] The reply of Secretary Robert Smith was, in effect, an endorsement of the British contention that the decrees had not been "effectively" revoked.

> From the Decree of the 15th July [he said] it moreover appears, that there can be no importation into France, but upon terms and conditions utterly inadmissible, and that, therefore, there can be no importation at all of the following articles, the produce of the United States, namely fish-oil, dye-wood, salt-fish, cod-fish, hides and peltry. As these enumerated articles constitute the great mass of the exports from the United States to France, the mind is naturally awakened . . . to the consideration that no

---

guage. "The French revocation," he wrote to Wellesley on 10 December, "turns on no condition precedent, is absolute, precise and unequivocal." But in a letter to Jonathan Russell, the American chargé d'affaires in London, dated 15 November 1811, Madison spoke "of the delicacy of our situation, having in view, on the one hand, the importance of obtaining from the French Government confirmation of the repeal of the decrees, and on the other that of not weakening the ground on which the British repeal was urged."—U. S. State Department MSS, quoted by Mahan, *Sea Power in Its Relation to the War of 1812*, I, 266.

[48] *Parl. Papers*, 1813. America. B. Inclosure 1 in No. 9.

practical good, worthy of notice, has resulted to the United States from the revocation of the Berlin and Milan Decrees, combined, as it unexpectedly has been, with a change in the commercial system of France, so momentous to the United States.

If France, by her own acts, has blocked up her ports against the introduction of the products of the United States, what motive has this Government, in a discussion with a third power, to insist on the privilege of going to France? Whence the inducement to urge the annulment of a blockade of France, when, if annulled, no American cargoes could obtain a market in any of her ports? [49]

At this very time, indeed, what British Ministers regarded as "incontestible proof" that the Decrees had not been revoked was being provided on the other side of the Atlantic. On 11 December Jonathan Russell, American chargé d'affaires in Paris, reported home that the New Orleans Packet had been seized under the Berlin and Milan decrees, and enclosed a letter of protest which he had addressed to the Duke of Cadore on the previous day. "The case of the New Orleans Packet," he told the Duke, "is the first that has occurred since the 1st of November, to which the Berlin and Milan decrees could be applied, and if they be applied to this case, it will be difficult for France to show one solitary instance of their having been practically revoked." [50] The vessel was restored, after enquiry by the Council of Prizes, by special decree of the Emperor; but that this was done, in this and other cases, in order to disarm American resentment, was not taken by the British Government as proof that the decrees had been repealed, but rather the reverse.

It was soon, indeed, clear to all the world that Napoleon had no intention of altering his system. In two speeches, delivered in March 1811 to the representatives of the Hanse Towns and the French

[49] *Ibid.*, Hon. Robert Smith to General Turreau, 18 December 1810. B. Inclosure 2 in No. 9. J. P. Morier, the British chargé d'affaires in Washington, protested against the phrase "the common enemy" in General Turreau's letter and the failure of the Secretary of State to repudiate it in his reply. It seemed to him "a pretty plain declaration that the French Government and that of the United States, regarding Great Britain as their common enemy, are united in pursuing certain common measures against her." Mr. Smith was "evidently much embarrassed" by this protest, describing the phrase as "a mere flourish" of the French Minister, a circumstance so trivial that he had not noticed it until his attention had been drawn to it by Mr. Morier. On the latter pressing for an assurance that the language of Turreau had "nothing equivocal about it," he said he had intended to reply to this part of the General's letter but "from the pressure of business, it had slipped his memory."—*Ibid.*, No. 10. Morier to Wellesley, 24 January 1811.

[50] *Ibid.*, B. Inclosures 1 and 2 in No. 11.

Chamber of Commerce, respectively, he repeated that the Berlin and Milan decrees were fundamental laws of his Empire, adding that he was prepared to admit American ships to his harbors if they respected the same principles. If the United States could not by other means force England to respect them, they should declare war on her.[51]

THE NON-INTERCOURSE ACT PUT INTO FORCE AGAINST GREAT BRITAIN

This attitude of Napoleon, and the continued ill treatment by the French Government of American traders produced a certain effect in the United States, and led to a widespread opinion that the President had exceeded his powers in issuing the proclamation of 2 November, since under the terms of the Act of 1 May he was to assure himself that one of the belligerents had withdrawn the offensive edicts before reviving the Non-intercourse Act against the other. There was, however, no question of retreating from the attitude taken up; for, in addition to the determination to secure the withdrawal of the British Orders in Council, there were other factors which made the prospect of a war with Great Britain not unwelcome: notably the determination to annex the Floridas, which belonged to Spain, now England's ally, and the eagerness of the "new West" to expand at the expense of Canada. In order to avoid all doubt as to the interpretation of the earlier Act, therefore, Congress on 2 March 1811 passed a new measure putting the Non-intercourse Act into force against Great Britain alone.[52]

This measure had its effect; the bales of cotton accumulated on the quays of Charleston, while in Lancashire mills closed down and operatives starved. Petitions for the repeal of the Orders in Council poured into Parliament, where the Opposition renewed its attacks upon them in debate after debate. The British Government, however, stood firm. In a note to Pinkney, dated 29 December 1810, the Marquess Wellesley, Canning's successor at the Foreign Office, had pointed out the ambiguous and equivocal character of Champagny's note to Armstrong of the previous August. The repeal of the French decrees, he said, was to be dependent, not only on the revocation

[51] *Ibid.*, C. Inclosure in No. 1 (text); see also Heckscher, *op. cit.*, 143, where further authorities are cited.
[52] *Ibid.*, A. Inclosure in No. 29.

of the Orders in Council, but on the renunciation by England of "the new principles of blockade which they have attempted to establish," which principles were not new and were in complete harmony with the established rules of international law.[53] If the revocation of the Orders alone would have secured the continuance of the repeal of the French decrees, he would not have hesitated to declare the perfect readiness of the British Government to fulfill that condition, but Great Britain, both in her own interests and those of other nations, could not renounce belligerent rights as to the legality of which there could in reality be no dispute. The British Government, he affirmed, retained "an anxious solicitude" to revoke the Orders in Council as soon as the Berlin and Milan decrees should have been effectually repealed.[54]

Since the British Government thus refused to make any concessions acceptable to the United States, the proclamation of nonintercourse with Great Britain alone took effect from 2 February 1811. During the months that followed, however, it became increasingly clear that this produced little or no effect upon the highhanded treatment of American commerce by the French. Napoleon, indeed, asserted that, in spite of the continued confiscation and sequestration of American ships, the decrees had been revoked, at least in so far as the United States were concerned, since under the Act of Congress of 1 May American ships were forbidden to go to England, and that those disobeying this law were really British.[55] This was an attitude which could hardly be regarded with satisfaction in Washington, where doubts increased as to whether the de-

[53] For a discussion of the conflicting British and American views as to what constituted a legitimate blockade see Mahan, *See Power in Its Relation to the War of 1812*, I, 110 ff. Mahan supports the British contention. The fact that Madison endorsed the French view, he says, laid him open to the charge of being a partisan of Napoleon. "The United States," he adds, "have received their lesson in history. If the principle contended for by their representatives, Marshall and Pinkney, had been established as international law before 1861, there could have been no blockade of the Southern coast in the Civil War. The cotton of the Confederacy, innocent 'private property' could have gone freely; the returns from it would have entered unimpeded . . . supplies, except contraband, would have flowed unmolested; and all this at the price merely of killing some hundred thousands more men . . . in the effort to maintain the Union, which would probably have failed."

[54] *Parl. Papers*, 1813. America. A. No. 16; A.S.P., F.R., III, 408.

[55] Unpublished message to the Conseil d'administration du commerce (29 April 1811), quoted in Heckscher, *op. cit.*, 144.

crees had been repealed, or even modified, in regard to the United States. Even Joel Barlow, an ardent partisan of France, who had succeeded Armstrong in Paris at the end of September 1811, began to suspect the sincerity of the French Government when he found that his friendly advances were met with coldness and his protests against the continued violations of the neutral rights of Americans treated with contempt.[56]

It is a moot question whether, in these circumstances, a frank withdrawal of the British Orders in Council would or would not have best served the vital interests of Great Britain. The spokesmen of the Opposition in Parliament enlarged on the importance of the American market for British commerce, on the effects of the financial crisis which was at its height during the year 1811, and on the disastrous possibilities of another war with the United States, which seemed increasingly inevitable if the Orders were not withdrawn. The spokesmen of the Government replied that so long as the French decrees remained in force it would be impossible to withdraw the Orders, and that there was no evidence that the decrees had been formally repealed, even as regards America. "If the Orders in Council had not been issued," said Spencer Perceval, the Prime Minister, "France would have been free to trade with her colonies by means of neutrals, and we should have been shut out from the Continent. . . . The object of the Orders in Council is, not to destroy the trade of the Continent, but to force the Continent to trade with us." [57]

BRITISH EFFORTS AT AN ACCOMMODATION

The Government, none the less, fully appreciated the importance of restoring friendly relations with the United States, and to this end, while stigmatizing the non-intercourse proclamation as "an un-

[56] "True, the blockade of the British Isles has been literally revoked and no United States vessels are now taken. But what advantage to American commerce has resulted? Municipal orders and regulations in France still performed the work of the Imperial Decrees.

"It is now a year since the Maritime Decrees were declared to be repealed and there are at this day no American ships in the ports of France except those that are detained by force and a few others under special licenses."—Barlow to the Duke of Bassano, 10 November 1811, quoted in Beckles Willson, *America's Ambassadors to France*, p. 108.

[57] Debate of 3 March 1812. 21 Hansard, 1152.

friendly act," made every effort to come to an accommodation with the American Government. The auspices were hardly favorable. In February 1811 William Pinkney "took leave" of the Prince Regent, ostensibly on the ground of the delay in appointing a British envoy to succeed Jackson at Washington. The delay was explained as due to the confusion caused by a temporary crisis in the Government, but it was not till 2 July that A. J. Foster presented his credentials to President Madison as British Minister Plenipotentiary. He brought with him proposals for the settlement of the "Chesapeake" question which proved acceptable to the American Government and finally closed a very unfortunate incident.[58] In the matter of the Orders in Council, however, his mission was less fortunate. At the outset there seemed some promise of an accommodation being possible; for James Monroe, who had succeeded Robert Smith as Secretary of State *ad interim* on 3 April, was favorable to a good understanding with England. In the long interchange of notes that followed, however, it was found impossible to find a basis of agreement. The British Government justified the Orders in Council on the principle of "defensive retaliation," refused to withdraw them without specific proof that the Berlin and Milan decrees had been repealed, and equally refused to accept Champagny's note of 5 August as such proof. It further repudiated the American contention that the French decrees were in retaliation for the blockade of May 1806 and that this blockade was a violation of international law. Finally it demanded that the United States should insist that the French Government respect not only American rights but neutral rights generally, which were being violated by the destruction of British goods belonging to neutral owners.[59]

The replies of the Secretary of State revealed no disposition to yield anything on the part of the American Government. "Propositions tending to degrade a nation," he said, "can never be brought into discussion by a Government not prepared to submit to the deg-

[58] For the interchange of notes on this subject between Foster and the Secretary of State see *Parl. Papers*, 1813. America. C. No. 19 and inclosures.

[59] "The Orders in Council were founded on a distinct principle—that of defensive retaliation; France had declared a blockade of all the ports and coasts of Great Britain and her dependencies; without assigning, or being able to assign, any force to support that blockade: such an act of the enemy would have justified a declaration of the blockade of the whole coast of France, even without the application of any particular force to that service. Since the promulgation of the Orders in Council, the blockade of May 1806 has been sustained and extended by

radation." He asserted that the Berlin and Milan decrees, in so far as they concerned the United States, had been absolutely revoked by the letter of the Duke of Cadore, and he gave as proof the restoration of the ships seized under the decrees since 1 November.[60] The complaint that the United States had not resisted the regulations of the decrees and had not insisted that France revert to the practice which had been established by the usage of civilized nations, he interpreted as a demand that they should force her to admit British goods, whereas the exclusion and confiscation of such goods were, he maintained, matters of "municipal regulation" with which no neutral nation had a right to interfere. The American Government, he said, could demand the repeal of the decrees only in so far as they affected American ships, and this demand had already been granted. The Non-intercourse Act might be "an unfriendly act," nevertheless,

---

the more comprehensive principle of defensive retaliation, on which those regulations are founded; but if the Orders in Council should be abrogated, the blockade of May 1806 could not continue, under our construction of the Law of Nations, unless the blockade should be maintained by a due application of an adequate naval force. The American Government seems to think that the blockade of 1806 was an act of aggression which led to the retaliation of the Berlin Decree. . . . The blockade of 1806 cannot be considered contrary to the Law of Nations . . . because it was maintained by an adequate force . . . the Decree of Berlin was not therefore justified, either under the pretexts alledged by France, or under those supported by America. . . .

"The American Government has viewed the letter (of the French Minister for Foreign Affairs, of 5 August 1810) as such an unconditional and unqualified revocation of the Decrees of Berlin and Milan, as required us, under our uniform declarations, to revoke our Orders in Council; and has added a demand for the annulment of the blockade of 1806. But the French letter of 5 August announced, not an immediate or absolute, but a prospective and conditional repeal of the Decrees. . . . This construction of the letter . . . has been confirmed in the most unequivocal manner, not only by the subsequent conduct of France towards America, but by the formal and personal declaration of Buonaparte himself, in his speech addressed to the Deputies of the Hanse towns, on the 20th of March 1811, of which a copy is annexed to this dispatch."—Wellesley to Foster, 10 April 1811. *Ibid.*, C. No. 1.

"If the Decrees are revoked, bona fide, and are really no longer in existence, some instrument must exist by which that revocation was effected. If the production of such an instrument be pertinaciously refused, or studiously evaded, the inducements for requiring this satisfaction, on our part, are greatly strengthened by the suspicions which must arise from the colour of the whole transaction."— Wellesley to Foster, 22 October 1811. *Ibid.*, C. No. 8.

[60] In a letter to Monroe, dated 3 March 1812, Foster gave further recent instances of American ships seized and condemned under the Berlin Decree. Has Great Britain, he asked, "no reason to suspect Champagny's note of August 1810?" —*Ibid.*, D. Inclosure in No. 12.

if England refused to make similar concessions it would remain in force.[61]

In view of the unsatisfactory results of the negotiations with Foster, President Madison summoned Congress to meet on 4 November, a month before the usual time. In his message, communicated on the following day, he enlarged on the accumulated grievances of the United States against Great Britain. It had been hoped, he said, that the confirmation of the repeal of the French decrees would have induced the British Government to revoke the Orders in Council, but they had been enforced more rigorously than ever, and all redress for American wrongs had been refused. The conduct of France, it was true, was also far from satisfactory; for, though the French Government had revoked its decrees, it had so far failed to restore American property unjustly seized and had imposed upon American trade "rigorous and unexpected restrictions" which would lead to retaliation. It was, however, the practices of Great Britain which had "the character of war as well as the effect of war" upon the lawful commerce of the United States, and it was to resist her "hostile inflexibility in trampling on rights which no independent nation can relinquish" that he called on Congress to put the United States "into an armor and an attitude demanded by the crisis, and corresponding with the national spirit and expectations." In spite of the somewhat feeble response to this clarion call, it was clear that war could now only be avoided by timely concessions on the part of Great Britain.

The British Government, however, while expressing the utmost anxiety to conciliate the American Government, did not give up hope of converting it on the main issue. An excellent opportunity for doing so seemed to be presented by the report presented, on 10 March 1812, to the Conservative Senate by the Duke of Bassano (Maret), who had succeeded Champagny as Minister for Foreign Affairs, and the *senatus-consulte* based upon it. This document, addressed to the "omnipotent" Emperor in terms of fulsome flattery,

[61] Monroe's attitude at this time is in striking contrast to that revealed in his letter to Jefferson of 28 February 1808, when he was smarting under the rejection of the treaty he had signed in London. "When I took into view the prosperous and happy condition of the United States, compared with that of other nations," he then wrote, "that as a neutral power, they were almost the exclusive carriers for the whole world; and that, in commerce, they flourished beyond example, notwithstanding the losses which they occasionally suffered, I was strongly in the opinion that these blessings ought not to be hazarded in such a question."—Callender, *Economic History of the United States*, p. 251.

after commending him for the incorporation of his latest conquests in the French Empire, declared that "the Decrees of Berlin and Milan ought to remain in force in respect of those powers which shall allow their flags to be denationalized," and that "the ports of the Continent ought not to be opened to denationalized flags and English merchandise." "Peace will come," it said, "when England recognizes the law of nations as consecrated by the Treaty of Utrecht." [62]

LORD CASTLEREAGH'S PROPOSALS

Lord Castlereagh, who had succeeded Wellesley at the Foreign Office in March, forwarded this report to Foster, together with a long dispatch in which he pointed its moral.

It will be at once acknowledged [he wrote] that this paper is a republication of the Berlin and Milan Decrees, if possible, in a more aggravated form, accompanied as it is with an extension of all the obnoxious doctrines which attended those Decrees; inflamed by a declaration, that Buonaparte has annexed to France every independent state in his power, which had eluded them; and that he was proceeding against all other maritime parts of Europe, on the pretence that his system could not be permanent and complete, so long as they retained their liberty regarding it. The outrageous principle here avowed connects itself obviously with the proposition too much countenanced by America, that the continental system of Buonaparte, as far as it operates to the confiscation of neutral property on shore, on the ground of such property being British produce or manufacture, is a mere municipal regulation, which neutral or belligerent nations have no right to resent, because it does not violate any principle of the Law of Nations.

Buonaparte, he continued, was intent on destroying whatever independence still existed, in order to guarantee his system, and if the United States had not been invaded by his armies, their immunity was due the superiority of Great Britain at sea. But as he could not hope to shut the American ports against Great Britain by occupancy and invasion, he hoped "to effect his purpose by management and fraud, and to accomplish that by insidious relaxation, which he could not accomplish by power." It was clear from the Duke of Bassano's report that America had been too credulous and Great Britain justified in the suspicion she had entertained of the enemy's bad faith. It was impossible that America should not now see that France had deliberately attached conditions to the repeal of the decrees

[62] Text in *Parl. Papers*, 1813. America. D. Inclosure in No. 3. The Report was published in the *Moniteur* of 16 March 1812.

which she knew Great Britain could never accept, hoping thereby to foment disunion between her and the United States.[63]

In a second letter of the same date Castlereagh told Foster that, owing to the fact that the internal politics of America had "so much connected the interests of the party in power with the French alliance," he had little hope of inducing them "to assume any authoritative tone towards France," whatever they might feel in their hearts. It was possible, however, that they might awaken to a sense of the desperate folly of seeking either to force or intimidate Great Britain and so seek some opportunity "of receding without disgrace from the precipice of war." It was to the interest of Great Britain to assist their retreat, and to this end he put forward proposals which, though they proved abortive, have a certain interest as throwing a sidelight on the policy underlying the Orders in Council and the license system.

Although licenses to trade with blockaded ports, in relaxation of the Orders of April 1809, had been uniformly granted to neutral as well as to British trade, occasional complaints, he said, had been received that the neutral merchant, and especially the American merchant "from his remote situation," could not profit from such relaxations in the same degree as the British merchant "regulating his transactions on the spot where the licenses are issued." The extent to which this intercourse under licenses had been carried, and the disposition of the French Government to give greater extension to it would, he continued, probably attract the notice of the American Government and lead them to instance the magnitude of this trade as an additional proof of the injustice of the British system, whereas it was really "strongly indicative" of the effectiveness of the British retaliatory measures, since, in spite of the boasts of the French Minister for Foreign Affairs, France had been compelled, in breach of her system, to yield a very extensive direct trade with Great Britain. If the United States Government, instead of impeaching "the fundamental principles of our defensive rights," had protested against "the partial effects of any particular relaxation of those rights," Great Britain would have been disposed to make concessions, even at the cost of "national inconvenience." The Order of April 1809 had been intended in great measure to meet the wishes of America, as well as to consult the interests of Great Britain's

[63] *Ibid.*, D. No. 3. Castlereagh to Foster, 10 April 1812.

allies, by a modification of the Orders in Council within narrower limits and by applying the principle of the blockade, within those limits, without any modification or exception. But when it was found that this was received in America in as hostile a spirit as the Orders in Council, there seemed no reason, since it had failed as a measure of conciliation, why that Order should not be accompanied "with some of the same regulations, relative to trade to and from the blockaded coast and the ports of Great Britain (not only for ourselves but for neutrals) as were without any licences introduced into the original Orders, and formed a material part of the system from which they proceeded."

The effectiveness of this blockade, he continued, had been destroyed by the opposition of the United States, large numbers of American ships having succeeded in evading the blockade, "thus relieving the necessities of the enemy."

Under these circumstances [he argued] America cannot fairly object to our accepting from the enemy such partial and progressive practical relaxations of his own rigorous system, as his necessities, arising out of the pressure of these very measures, may constrain him to yield, nor to our enabling our merchants, by licences, to avail themselves of those reluctant concessions, without being exposed to capture by ships of our own country for engaging in a prohibited trade.

So long as American merchants, with the connivance of their Government, contravened the rule, the United States had no right to resent the exceptions made to it by British license. He concluded by empowering Foster to make the American Government an offer.

If the American Government [he said] are disposed to open the intercourse with us, upon condition that we shall resort to the principle of rigorous blockade against the French dominions, to the exclusion of our own trade, equally with that of neutral nations, an arrangement on this basis you are hereby authorized to conclude. Upon an assurance being received from you, that the American Government had actually determined to reopen the intercourse with Great Britain, from a period to be named, when it might be presumed that such notification had been received here; no fresh licences in defeasance of such blockade will be issued by this Government.[64]

Foster duly presented this proposal to the Secretary of State. But Castlereagh had been over sanguine in supposing that this "new step" would be accepted by the American Government as an excuse for a change of policy. Both Madison and Monroe remarked drily that they had no objection to British merchants trading wherever

[64] *Ibid.*, D. No. 4.

they could find an outlet for their goods; that, though they objected to trading under license, it was not the license system they objected to, but the fact that America, as a neutral nation, was prevented from trading direct with France. In spite of the Duke of Bassano's report, they still maintained that the French decrees had been unconditionally withdrawn, in so far as America was concerned; they adhered to the view that the blockade of May 1806 was a violation of international law; and therefore, since Foster had been forbidden to make the slightest concession in matters of principle, the situation remained unaltered.[65]

THE PRINCE REGENT'S DECLARATION

Meanwhile, on learning the terms of the French Minister's report, the British Government thought it would be well also publicly to define its own attitude, and on 21 April a declaration was issued by the Prince Regent which announced that "if at any time hereafter the Berlin and Milan Decrees shall, by some authentic act of the French Government publicly promulgated, be absolutely and unconditionally repealed, then from thenceforth the Order in Council of 7 January 1807 and the Order in Council of 26 April 1809 shall, without further order, be . . . wholly and absolutely revoked." [66] This was a direct challenge which it was impossible for the French Government to ignore. Joel Barlow, indeed, whom the declaration had taken by surprise, was determined that it should not be ignored. In a note addressed to the Duke of Bassano on 1 May he called attention to these oft repeated assertions that the decrees had never

[65] Foster to Castlereagh, 6 June 1812. *Ibid.*, D. No. 21. On 30 May, Foster, in a letter to Monroe, protested against the view of the American Government that the confiscation of neutral property on shore, on the ground of such property being British produce or manufacture, was a mere municipal regulation, which neutral nations had no right to resent. He denied that this system partook of the character of municipal regulation. "It is a mere war measure, directed with the most hostile spirit against Great Britain, and in order to extend this system on the principle of municipal regulation, all the rights of the independent neutral nations are to be violated, their territories to be seized, without any other cause of war whatever, but that they may be incorporated in the French nation, and thence, becoming subject to her rights of dominion, receive the continental system as a municipal regulation of France. . . . Great Britain cannot believe that America will not feel a just indignation at the full developement of such a system. . . . America must see that the partial relaxations of the decrees were merely an insidious device of Buonaparte to persuade the United States to close their ports against Great Britain."—*Ibid.*, D. Inclosure 1 in No. 22.

[66] Inclosure in Castlereagh to Jonathan Russell, 21 April 1812. *Ibid.*, A. No. 37.

been withdrawn, and said that it was "much to be desired" that the French Government would now publish an authentic act declaring that the Berlin and Milan decrees, as far as regarded the United States, had ceased in November 1810, that they had not since been applied and that they would not be applied in the future. He added that the matter was urgent, and that a fast corvette was waiting at Cherbourg to convey copies of the repealing acts to the American Government in time to serve as an antidote to the declaration of the Prince Regent, which would otherwise be certain to produce a deleterious effect.[67]

In reply to this Maret produced what purported to be a decree signed by Napoleon at Saint-Cloud on 28 April 1811, which declared that, since by the law passed on 2 March 1811 the Congress of the United States had ordered the execution of the provisions of the Nonintercourse Act against Great Britain, and considering that the said Act was an act of resistance to the arbitrary pretensions advanced by the British Orders in Council, the decrees of Berlin and Milan were, as from 1 November 1810, definitively considered as no longer in force as regards American vessels.[68]

This document, which was dated a year back and had hitherto been unknown, was naturally regarded with suspicion in the United States and with still greater suspicion in England. In the British Parliament, however, and in the country at large; the opposition to the Orders in Council had gathered strength; the danger of war with the United States, which everyone was anxious to avoid, was seen to be imminent; and the British Government was therefore inclined to welcome the excuse given by this newly revealed decree to yield in the matter of the Orders in Council.

REVOCATION OF THE ORDERS IN COUNCIL

The decree was communicated to Lord Castlereagh by Jonathan Russell, the American chargé d'affaires in London, on 20 May. Unfortunately, the assassination of Spencer Perceval, the Prime Minister, on the 11th had thrown the administration into confusion; it was a week or two before Lord Liverpool's new Government was in a position to turn its attention to the matter, and it was not till 16 June that Lord Castlereagh was able to announce that it had been

[67] A.S.P., F.R., III, 602.

[68] *Ibid.*, p. 603; *Parl. Papers*, 1813. Corresp. relative to the French Decrees and the Orders in Council. Inclosure 1 in No. 1.

decided to revoke the Orders in Council as from 1 August. On the 18th, in the House of Lords, Earl Bathurst explained the delay and stated the terms of the revocation which had now been decided on.

His Majesty's Government [he said] had taken this subject into consideration as soon as possible, and the result was a determination to revoke the Orders in Council conditionally, on a day to be named (allowing sufficient time for such intended revocation to reach the United States), the conditions being, that the government of the United States should admit British ships of war on the same terms as the ships of war of other belligerents, and also repeal all their restrictive acts upon our commercial intercourse with the United States. These conditions having been complied with, the Orders in Council would cease on the day so to be named. Whether they were to be revived or not depended upon the acts of France and of the United States.

In reply to Earl Grey, who asked why the Government did not revoke the Orders at once, Bathurst said that they were merely following the precedent set by the President of the United States, who, when notified by the French Government that the decrees would cease to operate on 1 November, had fixed this date also for the revival of the Non-intercourse Act against Great Britain. As for the postponement of the date of revocation, Lord Liverpool said that this was the only possible course with a power so distant as America.[69]

The formal revocation, passed on 18 June and published in the *Gazette* on the 23d, after reciting the Order in Council of 21 April 1812, continued as follows:

Whereas the American chargé d'affaires resident at this court did on the 20th day of May last submit to Lord Castlereagh a copy of a certain instrument, then for the first time submitted to this court, purporting to be a Decree passed by the government of France, on the 28th day of April 1811, by which the decrees of Berlin and Milan are declared to be definitively no longer in force, in regard to American vessels,

His Royal Highness the Prince Regent, although he cannot consider the tenour of the said instrument as satisfying the conditions set forth in the said Order of the 21st of April last, in order to restore the intercourse between neutral and belligerent nations upon its accustomed principles, orders and declares that the Order in Council of the 7th of January 1807 and the Order in Council of the 26th of April 1809 shall be revoked, so far as regards American vessels, their cargoes being American property, from the 1st day of August next.

If after due notification the American government shall not revoke the acts interdicting British trade . . . this Order shall be null and of no effect.

---

[69] 23 Hansard, pp. 587 ff.

All American vessels and their cargoes, being American property, captured subsequently to the 20th of May last, for a breach of the aforesaid Orders in Council alone, and not actually condemned before the date of this Order, and all ships with their cargoes captured under the said Orders prior to the 1st day of August next, shall not be proceeded against to condemnation till further orders, but shall in the event of this Order not becoming null and of no effect, in the case aforesaid, be forthwith liberated and restored, subject to such reasonable expenses on the part of the captors, as shall have been justly incurred.

Provided that nothing in this Order, respecting the revocation of the Orders mentioned, shall be taken to revive, in whole or in part, the Orders in Council of the 11th of November 1807, or any other Orders not herein mentioned.[70]

THE UNITED STATES DECLARE WAR ON GREAT BRITAIN

Even if the decision to issue this Order had been reached within a few days of the receipt of the news of the French decree of 28 April 1811, it would have been impossible to communicate it to Foster in Washington in time to prevent the catastrophe of a war between the United States and Great Britain. In America the war fever had been growing apace. Little or nothing was known of the strong influences in England making for concession, and Foster's instructions contained no hint of any change in the policy of the British Government. The Declaration of 21 April was, therefore, taken as the final statement of this policy, and Monroe took it to mean that, as a necessary preliminary to the repeal of the earlier Orders to which objection was taken, "the repeal of the French decrees must be absolute and unconditional, not as to the United States only, but as to all other neutral nations; nor as they affect neutral commerce only, but as they operate internally and affect the trade in British manufactures with the enemies of Great Britain." These were conditions which the United States could not possibly accept, and he informed Foster that he could see no possible basis for further discussion, though the President, in his solicitude to see a happy termination to the differences between the two countries, had charged him to receive whatever further communications or propositions he might be authorized to make.[71] Foster replied in a note, dated 14 June 1812, in which he said that, if the United States could at any time produce a full and unconditional repeal of the French decrees, which

[70] *Ibid.*, p. 716.
[71] A.S.P., F.R., III, 469 f.; *Parl. Papers*, 1813. America. D. Monroe to Foster, 13 June 1812. Inclosure 2 in No. 24.

as a neutral nation they had a right to demand, and if it were dis-engaged from any question concerning British maritime rights, Great Britain would be ready to meet them with a revocation of the Orders in Council. "You well know," he said, "that if these two questions had not been united together, the Orders in Council would have been, in 1810, revoked." [72]

These were but parting shots; for already, on 1 June, President Madison had sent his message to Congress advocating war with Great Britain. The list of grievances by which he justified this ad-vice was a long one. The impressment of American citizens was put in the forefront. Then came the violation of the coasts of the United States by British cruisers, the plunder of American shipping under color of paper blockades, the Orders in Council, and the refusal to repeal them on any reasonable conditions. Then followed the ob-viously absurd charge that the real aim of the British system was to destroy American shipping and secure a monopoly of the carrying trade, and the suggestion—which veiled the expansive ambitions of the "new West"—that the renewed Indian warfare on the frontiers of the United States had been fomented by the British.[73]

Napoleon had every reason to be satisfied with the result of his diplomacy, which had deceived Madison and his advisers into be-lieving that the responsibility for continuing the violation of neutral rights now rested upon Great Britain alone. In Congress, indeed, as in the country at large, feeling against France was exceedingly bit-ter, and it was only the pressure brought to bear by the President during its secret deliberations of Congress that prevented it from declaring war against both Great Britain and France.[74] As it was, on 4 June, the House of Representatives, by a vote of seventy-nine to forty-nine, passed a declaration of war against Great Britain alone. There was more delay in the Senate, where opinion was more evenly divided. Had the electric telegraph existed, indeed, it is all but certain that the most unfortunate, unnecessary and futile of wars would have been avoided, for Castlereagh's announcement of the impending withdrawal of the Orders in Council was made on 16

---

[72] *Parl. Papers,* 1813, Inclosure 3 in No. 24; A.S.P., F.R., III, 470.

[73] For the full text of the message, together with the report of the Foreign Rela-tions Committee of the Senate, see *Parl. Papers,* 1813. America. D. Inclosures 2 and 3 in No. 25.

[74] General Sérurier, French envoy in Washington, to the Duke of Bassano, 23 June 1812. Quoted by R. B. Mowat, *The Diplomatic Relations of Great Britain and the United States,* p. 55.

June, the day before the Senate, in ignorance of what was happening in England, passed the resolution in favor of war by nineteen votes to thirteen, so that a change of only four votes would have reversed the decision.[75] The declaration of war was actually signed by President Madison on the 18th, the very day on which the Orders in Council were revoked in London.

Foster still had hopes that actual war might be avoided, and in taking leave of the President, on the 23d, pressed him to declare an armistice or at least to defer active operations pending the arrival of fresh instructions from England. The President said that his desire was to avoid, as much as possible, pushing matters to extremity, though he did not well see how it could be avoided, as he had no power to modify the terms of an Act of Congress declaring war. Asked if peace would be restored in the event of the Orders in Council being rescinded, he replied that, if the Orders were revoked during the next ten days or a fortnight while Congress was still in session, "they would certainly take some step in consequence." Asked further if there was no danger of any of the American officers undertaking measures which might further commit the two countries, he replied that the only measures taken would be for defense.

Both Mr. Madison and Mr. Monroe [wrote Foster] left the impression with me, that should the Orders in Council be revoked, while Congress was in session, hostilities would be suspended on the part of America. I urged repeatedly, the good policy of at once suspending all hostility by agreement, until further intelligence should be received from Great Britain; the President being only authorized by Congress, but not directed to carry on the war, it would seem that he might, if it so pleased him, have suspended all military and naval operations; and I engaged, on my own responsibility, for Admiral Sawyer's observing the armistice in such case. I could, however, obtain no satisfactory answer to this proposition, although I was assured by Mr. Monroe, in the most decided manner, that the marine league would be as much as possible the limits of the operations of the United States navy.

---

[75] "Three of these would almost certainly have been supplied by Giles, Leib and Samuel Smith, and among the five pro-war Republicans from New York, New Jersey and New England, the fourth vote would almost certainly have been found."—Pratt, *James Monroe*, p. 252. In his letter to Lord Castlereagh, of 20 June, enclosing a copy of the Act of Congress declaring war, Foster wrote: "I have to remark on this extraordinary measure, that it seems to have been unexpected by nearly the whole nation; and to have been carried in opposition to the declared sentiments of many of those who voted for it, in the House of Representatives, as well as in the Senate, in which latter body, there was known to have been at one time, a decided majority against it."—*Parl. Papers*, 1813. America. D. No. 25.

The chief objection of the American Government to enter into such an agreement was, that there did not appear at present any certainty of the Orders in Council being repealed.[76]

It would have been impossible, of course, for the news of the revocation of the Orders to have reached Washington before Congress rose; but, had the war at the outset been restricted as suggested, it might have been in time to stop any serious development of hostilities. Unfortunately, the order from Washington to restrict naval operations within territorial waters arrived in New York too late; for, on learning of the declaration of war, Commodore Rodgers had put to sea with his squadron "from his own impulse," without waiting for specific orders. On the very day that Foster had his farewell audience with President Madison, the 23d of June, the first act of hostility on the part of the United States was committed by an attack on H.M.S. "Belvidere" by one of the American frigates, "the remainder of the American squadron being in sight."

Anthony St. John Baker, who had been left in charge of the British legation pending the settlement of outstanding business connected with the "Chesapeake" affair, suggested to Monroe that the activities of the American navy seemed to show that the views of the United States, as stated by Mr. Foster, had undergone some change. Monroe, in reply, said that he regretted the precipitate action of Commodore Rodgers; that the American Government still retained the same pacific sentiments and would do its best to avoid putting obstacles in the way of restoring peace between the two countries; but that "as war existed, something must be left to the course of events." [77] So events took their course.

No More Neutrals

The Emperor of the French was now at the height of his power. His Empire stretched from the shores of the North Sea to the eastern shores of the Adriatic; the lesser German princes were his vassals, Austria, Prussia, Saxony, Denmark-Norway and Sweden his more or less willing allies; Germans, Poles and Italians marched under his banners—formed, indeed, the larger part of the Grand Army with which he proposed to chastise the Russian Tsar for his unfaithfulness to the pact of Tilsit and the consequent breakdown

[76] *Minute of Conversation. Ibid.,* Inclosure 8 in No. 27.
[77] Baker to Castlereagh, 17 July 1812. *Ibid.,* D. No. 29.

of the Continental System. England, his implacable foe, was showing signs of exhaustion; her best troops were engaged in the war in
the Spanish Peninsula, the issue of which was still undecided; if
the United States could be drawn into the war against her, her commerce would be ruined and her sea power hampered, if not crippled.
All the omens seemed favorable for the great Russian adventure. On
24 June, six days after Madison had signed the declaration of war
against Great Britain, Napoleon gave the order to his troops to cross
the Niemen, the first stage in the fateful march to Moscow. It was
not till later, of course, that he heard of the action of the United
States and could say with truth that in this war there were now no
neutrals.

PART TWO

THE EFFECTS OF THE WARS UPON NEUTRAL COMMERCE AND INDUSTRY

by

ARTHUR H. REEDE

VIII

INTRODUCTION [1]

In the course of his judgment in the case of the *Immanuel,* in the British High Court of Admiralty, Sir William Scott took occasion to comment on the general situation of neutral commerce in time of war. "Some neutrals," he said, "will be unjustly engaged in covering the goods of the enemy, and others will be unjustly suspected of doing it; these inconveniences are more than fully balanced by the enlargement of their commerce; the trade of the belligerents is usually interrupted in a great degree, and falls in some degree in the lap of neutrals." [2] This is the usual thesis of the belligerent power. There are serious objections, however, to the manner in which the issue is raised and met. The question suggested indicates no grasp of the complex nature of the problem. The phrasing of the answer shows no realization of the difficulties to be overcome in analyzing it.

Plainly, the balance between inconveniences suffered and the enlargement of commerce is not the only issue. But even were it so, this dictum would seem overly simple. Should it prove possible to demonstrate that the enlargement of commerce represented a greater value than losses due to inconveniences, many doubtful points would still remain to be cleared up. The enlargement concerned was accomplished only in part by simple expansion, for new enterprises as well are attracted by the brisk demand for transportation and materials. That the balance as between increased trade and damage would be the same for the average firm as for the nation, or for individual firms as for either, may be doubted. So far as simple justice to neutral shippers and owners is concerned, it is the situation of individual firms, or at least of the average firm, that is important. Nor is it easy to decide just how much of the expansion in commerce may rightly be attributed to the state of war. What is particularly lacking in this line of analysis, however, is a considera-

[1] For much of the material, statistical and historical, used in preparing this analysis, the writer is indebted to Professor Phillips.
[2] 2 C. Robinson 198 (1799).

tion of repercussions on the economic life of the neutral nations. The balance between profits and damages is hardly more important than that between wage increases and wage losses (due to impressment or to detention of crews); or between increases in income generally, and in the price level; or between the prosperity conferred on certain industries (shipping, production of naval stores, foodstuffs, etc.), and the discouragement of other industries for lack of capital; or between the sort of prosperity fostered by the artificial demand and the economic crisis that threatened whenever this demand slackened.

But it is not only by failing to discern the ramifications, some of which are mentioned above, that this approach to the problem falls short. The problem is as difficult as it is intricate. Neither of the magnitudes referred to by the learned judge and none of the magnitudes mentioned in the preceding paragraph can be measured with even fair precision. The statistical materials for this period are not only scanty but seldom in a suitable form. No complete and systematized lists of captured merchant vessels seem to exist in either the French or British archives. Nothing approaching an accurate index of profit levels for this period can be constructed. Figures indicating the movements of imports and exports are official and therefore take no account of smuggling. Shipping registry data are misleading because they are unable to allow for the increases in numbers of ships made necessary by seizures and detentions. Wage and price statistics for the period are based on small and not always reliable samples. It is accordingly often necessary to fall back upon indirect or incomplete measures of all these relevant matters. The sort of findings to which such analysis tends may scarcely be couched in the clear and definitive terms of the quoted pronouncement.

Were the data complete and in satisfactory form, however, there would remain the problem of apportioning the changes noted among the causal factors concerned, of which the war was only the most important one. Any attempt at apportionment is complicated by the circumstance that none of the neutral nations, whether in Europe or America, succeeded in preserving its neutrality during the whole period of the war. The United States, though close to war with England in 1794, and virtually at war with France in 1798-1799, enjoyed the longest interval of neutrality, but in June, 1812, they became involved. Sweden remained neutral during the "first war," but after 3 December 1804, when she joined the Coalition, was constantly at war on one side or another. Denmark was neutral until 31 October 1807, when she allied herself with Napoleon. The neutrality of Prussia lasted from 5 April 1795, when she signed the treaty of peace with France at Basel, until 15 February 1806, when she signed the treaty with Napoleon under which, a few days later, she occupied Hanover. The Hanse cities clung to their neutrality until, one by one, they were absorbed into the French Empire. Russia, though nominally neutral until she joined the Coalition in 1798 and effectively so during the first two years of the "second war" (May 1803 to April 1805), was almost continuously engaged in the war on one side or the other. Evidently the effects of eventual belligerency must be taken into account.

It is proposed in this chapter and in the succeeding chapters to examine somewhat more closely than hitherto has been done, the nature of the adverse effects to which neutral commerce and industry were subjected by the belligerents, and the beneficial effects by which Sir William would have us think that these hardships were more than fully balanced. The principal baneful effects of a visible sort were the exercise by the belligerents of the right of search and capture at sea; the losses (even when the captured vessels were ultimately released) incident to the long-drawn-out proceedings of the prize courts; and the extensions of blockades to cover long stretches of coasts, culminating in Napoleon's Continental System and comparable measures under British Orders in Council. It will be useful to attempt to assay the inconveniences caused neutrals by captures of their trading vessels, and by the character and procedure of the British and French prize courts. Some impression of the extent of this may be gathered from partial lists available in published and unpublished sources. The captures seem to have been on a large scale. Thus, in March 1794, it was stated that more than 250 American vessels were awaiting adjudication in West Indian ports; and 307 were enumerated in a list issued by the State Department in the following July.[3] In the eight and a half years ending 29 September 1801, as many as 948 captured vessels, of which 345 belonged to neutrals, had been brought into Plymouth alone.[4] The reports of the British admirals stationed in various parts of the world are also illuminating. The admiral commanding the West

[3] Hammond to Grenville, 5 September 1794. P.R.O. F.O. 5. 1.
[4] *Naval Chronicle*, VII, 276; Mahan, II, 219.

Indian station, for example, reported from Jamaica that as many as 203 vessels had been captured, detained or destroyed between 1 March and 3 August 1800.[5] From the Mediterranean, Lord Keith reported 180 captures during five months of the same year.[6] These are only samples from the numerous similar reports.

In the French archives is preserved a list of 3,575 vessels captured by the warships (*bâtiments de l'Etat*) and privateers (Corsaires) from 1793 to 27 March 1802.[7] The list includes enemy vessels, whether ships of war or traders, but since in each case the flag is specified, it is possible to give the number of trading vessels belonging to each of the principal neutral states. Denmark appears to have been the chief sufferer, her vessels numbering 467. There were 268 American vessels, 218 Swedish, 105 Genoese, and 48, 16 and 2, respectively, from Hamburg, Bremen and Lübeck. In addition to the captures at sea by the French, there were recurrent sequestrations of neutral merchantmen in French harbors. The climax was the seizure, by Napoleon's orders, of some 600 neutral vessels driven by stress of weather into the various Baltic ports in the autumn of 1810.[8]

Taken all together, these captures by France and Great Britain must have constituted a formidable total. It has been contended, of course, that the character of navigation was wholly different from that of the present day, when the destruction of a single freighter weighing several thousand tons represents a serious loss to owners or underwriters. Most of the trading vessels of the Revolutionary period were admittedly small and readily replaceable. The total tonnage of the 728 vessels entering the ports of Great Britain from the United States in 1801, was 159,412—an average of just over 200 tons to the vessel.[9] It must be remembered, however, that firms were smaller as well. The seizure of one small vessel may well have been as serious a loss to the parties concerned as a similar depredation against a much larger vessel in the war of 1914-1918.

[5] *Naval Chronicle*, IV, 150; Mahan, *loc. cit.*

[6] *Naval Chronicle*, IV, 326; Mahan, *loc. cit.*

[7] *Service historique de la marine.* Registre: "Prises 107, Guerre de 1793. Liste de prises faites . . . 1793 à 1801," ff. 1-87, and ff. 88-134; "Liste de prises faites de l'an 8 à la paix d'Amiens," ff. 88-134.

[8] See *supra*, p. 159.

[9] Of 25 American vessels reported by Admiral Lord Hugh Seymour from Jamaica, on 22 February 1801, as captured only four were "ships," all the rest being described as "schooners" or "brigs."

So far as Great Britain was concerned, prizes brought into home ports were adjudicated on in the first instance by the High Court of Admiralty: those taken into colonial ports, by the Vice-Admiralty Courts. From the latter, an appeal lay to the High Court of Admiralty: and from both, to the Lords Commissioners of Appeal in Prize Cases. The High Court of Admiralty was seated in Doctors Commons.[10] The reputation of the court was high: the authority of its judges, of whom Sir William Scott (Lord Stowell) was the most famous, was respected; and its advocates and proctors, who had to pass through a severe training in civil and international law, could be trusted in prize cases adequately to represent the interests of claimants. Opinions might and did differ as to the rules of law applied in this court, but few serious attacks were made on the impartiality of the court in administering these rules. The principal grievance, and it was a very real one, was the great delay of justice due to the procedure of the courts and to the great number of cases coming up for adjudication. Such delays sometimes involved as great a loss as positive injustice.

The measures to be taken by the captor and the neutral claimant on a ship or cargo being brought in as prize were set forth with great clearness in a memorandum drawn up by Sir William Scott and Dr. Nicholl for the instruction of John Jay, on his arrival in London in the autumn of 1794. The captor had first to send, or deliver upon oath, all papers found in the vessel, to the registry of the Court of Admiralty. Then in the course of a few days, the examinations "in preparatory" of the captain and crew were taken, on a set of standing interrogatories, before the commissioner of the port and forwarded to the registry of the Admiralty. This done, the captor extracted a monition and served it upon the Royal Exchange, notifying the capture and calling on all persons interested to appear. After a lapse of twenty days the monition was returned into the registry, with a certificate of its service, and if a claim had meanwhile been given, the case was ready for hearing. It was usual for the neutral master to make a protest, which he either carried to London himself or forwarded to his consul or to the correspondent of his owners in London. Application was then made to a proctor, who prepared the claim. This was supported by the affidavit of the

[10] A "College of Doctors of Law exercent in the Ecclesiastical and Admiralty Courts," which had originated in a society of lawyers practicing in the civil and canon laws and which had been incorporated by royal charter in 1768.

claimant, and the sum of £60 was given as security to cover costs. As soon as the claim was given, the case could proceed.[11]

The delays caused by these preliminary proceedings would alone have been vexatious enough to merchants anxious to realize on their investments. Far more irksome, however, were the much longer delays, due to the glut of business in the High Court of Admiralty and to the leisurely proceedings of the Lords Commissioners of Appeal. Two passages in the diary of Samuel Bayard, the American Commissioner of Claims, bear on these delays. On 12 December 1796, he observes that Sir John Marriott (Sir William Scott's predecessor in the Admiralty Court) was above two hundred cases in arrears, which would take more than two years to finish.[12] At another point, he complains that the Lords Commissioners of Appeal in Prize Cases sat only from 12 to 3 o'clock on one or two days a week during the winter, rarely met at all during the summer, and could not meet during assizes because common law counsel were not then available.[13] In short, two or three years and more might pass between the capture of a neutral vessel at sea and its final condemnation or acquittal by the prize courts in Great Britain.

Whatever grievances neutrals might cherish against these courts were, however, as nothing compared with those created by the arbitrary and sometimes corrupt decisions of the Vice-Admiralty Courts.[14] The most notorious instance was that of the prize court set up by Admiral Sir John Jervis (afterward Lord St. Vincent) and General Sir Charles Grey in Martinique after the capture of the island from the French. The judges of this court were later declared by the British Government to have acted without authority, while their conduct was described by the Master of the Rolls as "shameful and abominable." [15] In these courts, which often had to be improvised, it was not indeed to be expected that the proceedings would be as orderly, or the adjudications as well founded in law, as in the High Court of Admiralty. What neutral masters had a right to expect was integrity; and the most that can be said for

[11] Statement of the general principles of proceedings in prize cases, in British courts of Admiralty, and of the measures proper to be taken when a ship and cargo are brought in as prize within their jurisdiction. *Annual Register*, 1795, pp. 170 ff. See also 4 Moore, pp. 43 ff., and Vol. I of this series, ch. vii.

[12] *Ibid.*, p. 58.

[13] *Ibid.*, p. 40.

[14] See *supra*, p. 46, also Clowes, *The Royal Navy; a History* (1897-1903), p. 8.

[15] 4 Moore, pp. 37 ff. and 47 ff.

the British Government is that it attempted to remedy the injustices of which such courts were guilty and, as the war progressed, to set them in better order.[16]

In France the status of prize courts was complicated by the far-reaching political changes that had taken place. The Revolution had destroyed the old admiralty courts, with their legal traditions, and when the war on neutral commerce broke out, a new machinery had to be devised to deal with prize cases.[17] A decree, passed by the Convention on 14 February 1793, directed that prizes taken were to be adjudicated on by the Commercial Courts (*tribunaux de commerce*) of the ports into which they were brought. If there was no such court, jurisdiction was accorded to the court of the district, from which an appeal was to lie to the district court of the nearest port. The functions of the old admiralty courts were to be provisionally assigned to the justices of the peace (*juges de paix*). They were to conduct the preparatory enquiries and to forward the evidence collected in each case, with as little delay as possible, to the registry of the commercial or district court empowered to adjudicate upon it. The old prize laws were to remain in force provisionally.[18]

Since under the Constitution of 1791 all judges were elected, and since one of the earliest acts of the Convention was to decree that neither they nor the advocates who pleaded before them need be lawyers, it is not difficult to imagine the kind of justice which was dispensed in these prize courts. The *tribunaux de commerce* in the seaports proved to be composed in the main of merchants directly or indirectly interested in the fitting out of privateers.[19] So scandalous did the proceedings and judgments become that the Convention revoked the decree of the 14th of February, and passed that of 8 Brumaire, An II (8 November 1793), which laid down that all questions affecting the validity or invalidity of prizes were to be decided by the Provisional Executive Council as a matter of administration (*par voie d'administration*).[20] Under the Directory the

---

[16] "The judges of the Courts of Admiralty of these English and Dutch islands pretend to derive their sole authority from Mr. Dandas' instructions . . . and some of these gentlemen are so candid as to say, that the Powers combined against France mean to suppress every species of neutral commerce, with the people of that nation, while at war."—Fulwar Skipwith, American consul at St. Eustasia, to the Secretary of State, 1 March 1794. A.S.P., F.R., I, 428.

[17] Cf. *supra*, p. 51.   [18] 5 Martens, p. 379.

[19] A.S.P., F.R., II, 8; Mahan, II, 255.

[20] But, though the ultimate decision was thus placed in the hands of the Executive, the Courts of first instance continued to function.

procedure was established by a law passed on 3 Brumaire, An IV (25 October 1795), which directed that the *juge de paix* was to examine the ship's papers, interrogate the captain and at least three of the crew, make an inventory of the goods on board, etc., and forward his report, together with the evidence, to the registry of the commercial court within twenty-four hours.[21] Another law, passed by the Council of Ancients on 8 Floreal, An IV (27 April 1796), provided that appeals were to lie from the commerce courts to the courts of the department. Cases of interest to neutrals, however, were to be reported within twenty-four hours to the commissary of the Executive Directory. In urgent cases, the latter might refer them at once to the Minister of Justice, who was to consult with the Directory and decide within the decade (week of ten days). Consuls and vice-consuls in foreign ports to which prizes captured by the French might be taken, were to make their chancelleries perform the functions assigned by the law of 3 Brumaire to the *juges de paix*.[22]

These successive decrees illustrate the confusion into which the Revolution had thrown legal procedure in France and the harassing uncertainties which faced any unfortunate neutral skipper caught in the toils. The situation was vividly described by the American consul general in Paris, in a report to James Monroe, dated October 1794. Referring to the indiscriminate capture of American vessels at sea, he complained that they were "stripped of their officers and crews, and taken into port by boys and inexperienced hands," so that they were often seriously damaged and sometimes a total loss. When they arrived in port, the crews were locked up, seals were placed on the cargoes and the ship's papers were sent to the Commission of Marine in Paris, which caused "unwarrantable hardship and delays." "All our vessels," he said, "experience the same difficulties, even those with cargoes on account of the Republic. . . . Months elapse before the captains can get their clearances or papers, many of which are often lost or mislaid." The delays of the Commission of Marine were "incredible."

The captains whose vessels are brought into port . . . cannot withdraw their papers from the hands of the marine agents, but are forced to Paris, to solicit, time after time, of the Commission of Marine to report upon them to the Committee of Public Safety. The report must have the signature of the commissaries, and go through other formalities, and when it receives the

---

[21] 5 Martens, p. 385.   [22] *Ibid.*, p. 387.

sanction of the Committee of Public Safety, has to travel nearly the same road back.[23]

Even after a just verdict had been reached, satisfaction was not certain.[24] An award might be ordered, but paid only after vexatious delay. Corruption seems to have obtained even in high places. Merlin of Douai is pointed to as having made a fortune out of prize cases while holding office as Minister of Justice. If so, it can scarcely be supposed that lesser functionaries passed up their golden opportunities.

There were other less apparent ways in which the incidents of war reacted to the disadvantage of neutral states. Since these repercussions usually differed from nation to nation in character and incidence, however, it is perhaps more proper to consider them separately in the coming chapters. The same may be said for the benefits growing out of the status of neutrality. The principal direct benefit was an increase in volume of foreign trade. This had come about, in the first instance, as a result of the greatly increased demands of the belligerent powers for produce, notably foodstuffs and naval stores. As the struggle developed, the effect was heightened, for all the powers came to see the necessity for relaxing their re-

[23] A.S.P., F.R., I, 749. Compare *ibid.*, II, 8.
Fulwar Skipwith to James Monroe:
The troubles facing the masters of vessels brought into French ports as prizes may, perhaps, be appreciated after a comparison with those which faced them when they had the honest intention of doing business with the French Government, through which all foreign trade was now conducted. To sell to the Commission of Commerce, was a matter of still greater difficulty. "When a bargain is concluded with them [the Commission], an order is issued to the keepers of the public magazines to receive the cargo sold; who often pretend there is no room and keep the captain waiting weeks before their whim or convenience will induce them to receive it. For payment application must now be made to the Commission of Commerce in Paris, who refer the captain to the Board of Agency; they make a report to the *Comptabilité* of the same Commission; from thence it must go to the Committee of Finance, then to the Committee of Public Safety, whence it returns to the *Comptabilité*. This labyrinth of perplexity, of course, throws the captain into the hands of an agent, who preys upon his distress and when these forms are fulfilled the captain cannot always touch the money. The Commission may refuse to buy, and tell him to go away; but the agents of the port will not let him sail . . . In short, after every sort of delay and vexation, should the captain claim an indemnity, he has to wade through double the difficulties heretofore stated, and perhaps, after all, to leave his business incomplete in the hands of an agent."

[24] Discontent was also expressed by the owners of vessels unjustly detained, over the amount of compensation granted by the British Admiralty Courts. The British awards seem, however, to have been always paid promptly.

strictive laws against foreign trade. France, unable to protect her own sea-borne commerce, opened her colonies to neutral vessels.[25] Great Britain, with an eye to the paramount demands of her navy for both men and material, modified her Navigation Laws so as to allow the ships of neutrals at least a limited access to her colonies, and to open her ports to the produce of the colonies even when aboard foreign carriers.

How did these actions affect the economic life of the neutral nations? Did the accessions to trade counterbalance the losses incident to the inconveniences, some of which have been noted above? What happened to the course of prices, wages and production? Were the effects on industry uniform, or did overexpansion take place in some lines? Was a heritage of economic maladjustments left by the war, when the extraordinary demands it had created came to an end with the conclusion of peace? An attempt to answer these and similar inquiries is the purpose of the succeeding chapters.

[25] As in 1756; see Vol. I of this series, pp. 153 ff.

IX

THE UNITED STATES OF AMERICA

At the beginning of the French Revolutionary Wars, the separation of the United States from the British Empire was still recent, and in general, this separation had produced but little change in their exchange relations. Under the old Colonial System the function of a colony was to supply raw materials and foodstuffs to the mother country, which in return supplied it with processed articles. Artificial restrictions on the trade and manufactures of the colony were typically defended by the assertion that upon the mother country fell the whole burden of the colony's protection by sea. In these conditions the acquisition of independence by the American States had made little change, for the nature of their economic life was still influenced by the fact they were a huge country, with unlimited natural resources and a small population. Agriculture, forestry and fisheries were still the chief industries and, though efforts were early made to establish native manufactures, the development of these was hindred by want of capital, the dearness of labor, and the "facility with which the less independent condition of the artisan could be exchanged for the more independent condition of the farmer." [1]

The interchange of materials for manufactures, which long persisted, seems to have been mutually beneficial.[2] The total value of the exports of the United States for the year ending 30 September 1791 is given as $17,571,551, of which $6,953,418 were exports to Great Britain and her dominions. The British were by far the largest consumers of certain commodities, such as wheat, Indian corn, wood of various kinds and tobacco,[3] while they continued to be the main source of supply of the manufactures demanded in

[1] Alexander Hamilton, Report on Manufactures, 5 December 1795. A.S.P. *Finance,* I, 123.

[2] "England's prosperity flows over upon us, as ours upon England." Richard Rush, *Residence at the Court of St. James,* 2d series, I, 295.

[3] A.S.P. *Commerce and Navigation,* I, 103 ff. Report of Alexander Hamilton on exports for the year ending 30 September 1791. Of 101,272 hogsheads of tobacco exported, 67,286 were sent to the British Dominions.

America.[4] The political separation from Great Britain had, to be sure, been bought at a price; the United States were deprived of the privileges which, as colonies, they had enjoyed in the Empire, and their trade and shipping fell under the ban of the English Navigation Acts. The restrictions on their commerce with the British West Indies were especially felt and resented. These disadvantages, however, had less effect upon the economy of the country than might have been expected, and they were presently counteracted by the effects of the European wars and the contemporaneous progress of the Industrial Revolution in England and later in the United States.

The chief effect of the European war on the economy of the United States was to throw into American hands the greater part of the colonial carrying trade of the world and to create a European market for the products of the northern states (foodstuffs, naval stores, etc.). The Industrial Revolution, on the other hand, led to a great demand, especially in Britain, for those raw materials which it was easy for the newer communities to supply, such as the wool and cotton, required in ever increasing quantities for the rapidly developing textile industries.

The increases in the sea-borne commerce of the United States are of fundamental interest. The value of both exports and imports are indicated in Table 1,[5] and the correlative price changes are included. By reference to the latter, we may guard against the error of inferring changes in quantities from changes in value. As appears from Table 1, the value of the foreign trade of the United States experienced an upward movement until 1808. The peak was reached in 1807. During that year, the sum of the exports and imports amounted in value to $247,000,000, a figure that was not again attained until 1835. A marked decline in imports in the early nineties, and recessions of both imports and exports in 1797-1798 and following the Peace of Amiens, were the only interruptions of that trend.

The value of goods exported was more than four times as great in 1799 as in the last year before the war; nearly five times as great in 1801, and nearly six times as great in 1807. Since these increases were accompanied by advances in prices, one must allow for the latter in gauging the physical volume of exports. Even when this is done, exports appear to have more than doubled by 1796, and

---

[4] A.S.P. *Commerce and Navigation*, I, 50 ff. Imports for the year 1790.
[5] Page 226, *infra*.

to have nearly trebled by 1801. The adjusted figure for 1807 is almost four times as great as the corresponding figure for 1791. But although exports declined only three times between 1789 and 1808, the advances were not uniform. After a gradual expansion until 1794, exports rose sharply in 1795 and 1796, probably because of the adjustment of strained relations with Great Britain by the Jay Treaty.[6] The declines in 1797 and 1798 were doubtless occasioned by the consternation in commercial circles over French sequestrations. Following the *de facto* war with France in 1798-1799,[7] exports rose sharply only to fall again in 1800. This decline was in part a reflection of a business recession and in part the result of further belligerent efforts to curb the transit trade.[8] The short-lived truce of 1802-1803 effected considerable declines. From 1804-1807, exports mounted at a rapid rate in spite of the lapse of the Jay Treaty and the restrictive measures of both France and England.

As might be expected, the fluctuations of imports followed a somewhat different course. From a much higher pre-war value, they slumped sharply during the opening years of the war. The decline was a logical outcome of the pressure on prices and production in the belligerent nations, of the extraordinary demands incidental to the conduct of war. A minor factor may have been the mild increases in duties effected by the Tariff of 1792. The revival of imports in 1795 came about largely as a result of the gradual removal of barriers to direct trade with the colonies of France and Great Britain. Although, particularly following the invention of the cotton gin, a brisk demand for British textiles was evidenced, the chief prop to the growing value of imports was the increasing transit trade indicating the extent to which the colonial trade had been absorbed by the American merchant marine.[9]

Of the foreign articles reëxported, by far the greater quantity consisted of colonial goods. Sugar and coffee were the largest items. The quantities of these latter commodities exported from 1791 onward are a surer index than a table of values to the great increase in the transit trade of the United States, which resulted from the war in Europe.[10] In 1791, the United States exported only 74,504 pounds of sugar. From this year until 1799, when the corresponding figure was 78,821,751 pounds, marked and yet consistent gains

[6] Cf. *supra*, pp. 63 ff.　　　　　[7] Cf. *supra*, pp. 72 ff.
[8] Cf. *supra*, p. 112.　　　　　[9] Cf. *supra*, p. 120.
[10] Table No. 11 giving these quantities will be found in Appendix I, *infra*.

TABLE I. FOREIGN TRADE OF THE UNITED STATES a, 1791-1815

Year	Exports (Dollar values, thousands)	General Price Level Index	EXPORT INDICES b		Imports (Dollar values, thousands)	Price Level Index: Imported Products	IMPORT INDICES b	
			Unadjusted	Adjusted for Price Level Fluctuations			Unadjusted	Adjusted for Price Level Fluctuations
1791	19,012	64.6	27.4	43.9	52,200	64.6	66.0	101.9
1792	20,753	68.3	31.0	45.4	31,500	68.3	39.8	58.2
1793	26,110	72.2	39.0	54.0	31,100	72.2	39.3	54.3
1794	33,026	83.9	49.3	58.8	34,600	83.9	43.7	52.0
1795	47,989	95.5	71.6	75.0	69,756	95.5	88.1	92.1
Average	29,378	76.9	43.7	55.4	43,831	76.9	55.4	71.7
1796	67,064	106.2	100.1	94.1	81,436	101.3	102.9	101.4
1797	56,850	101.4	84.8	83.5	75,379	99.1	95.3	95.9
1798	61,527	95.6	91.8	95.9	68,552	102.4	86.6	84.4
1799	78,666	98.0	117.4	119.9	79,068	100.2	99.9	99.5
1800	70,972	98.9	105.9	106.9	91,253	96.9	115.3	118.8
Average	67,016	100.0	100.0	100.0	79,138	100.0	100.0	100.0
1801	94,116	107.7	140.4	130.2	111,364	100.2	140.7	140.2
1802	72,483	92.5	108.2	116.7	76,333	90.4	96.5	106.5
1803	55,800	97.5	83.3	85.4	64,667	95.9	81.7	85.0
1804	77,699	101.5	115.9	114.1	85,000	101.3	107.4	105.8
1805	95,566	104.5	142.6	136.3	120,000	100.2	151.6	151.0
Average	79,133	100.7	118.1	116.5	91,473	97.6	115.6	117.0
1806	101,537	103.3	151.5	146.5	129,000	101.3	163.0	160.6
1807	108,344	100.0	161.7	161.3	138,500	98.0	175.0	178.2
1808	22,431	97.6	33.5	34.2	56,990	107.8	72.0	66.7
1809	52,204	102.7	77.9	75.7	59,400	117.6	75.1	63.7
1810	66,757	102.2	99.6	97.3	85,400	108.9	107.9	98.9
Average	70,255	101.2	104.8	103.0	93,858	106.7	118.6	113.6
1811	61,317	98.2	91.5	93.1	53,400	102.4	67.5	65.8
1812	38,527	98.4	57.5	58.3	77,030	118.7	97.3	81.8
1813	27,856	120.1	41.6	35.8	22,005	140.5	27.8	19.8
1814	6,927	137.8	10.3	7.5	12,965	158.0	16.4	10.3
1815	52,557	122.8	78.4	63.8	113,041	117.6	142.8	121.2
Average	37,437	115.5	55.9	51.7	55,688	127.4	70.4	59.8

a Import figures are from John MacGregor, *Commercial Statistics* (London, 1847), III, 767. Export figures are a summation of data in Table 2, *infra*, except for the first five years. The latter, as well as the later export figures, are from, J. R. McCulloch, *Dictionary of Commerce and Commercial Navigation*, p. 844 (1832 edition). Price level indices are adapted from two sources, one measuring movements of prices at Boston, *1795-1824* (Smith, W. B., "Wholesale Commodity Prices in the United States, 1795-1824," in *Review of Economic Statistics*, IX, 181); the other, movements of prices at Philadelphia, 1791-1840 (*Journal of the American Statistical Association*, XIV, 808, and XV, 844 f.). For Boston, two parallel series were available, one for imported and the other for domestic commodities. The Philadelphia series was not so divided, and accordingly the data are not strictly comparable. Their movements seemed to accord with those of a weighted average of the two Boston series, however. Hence, the error in using them for the period for which the Boston figures were not available, is probably not considerable. The ratio between the two series having been computed, adjusted figures were first obtained in absolute form; then converted to index numbers; base: 1796-1800 = 100.

b Base: 1796-1800 = 100.

were registered. Following the brief interlude of the Peace of Amiens, a similar trend began, and lasted until the "long Embargo." In 1806, the last full year before the embargo, the high-water mark was reached—145,832,320 pounds. The increases are also marked, if less steady, in the case of coffee exports. Beginning with 962,977 pounds in 1791, the latter rose to 62,385,117 pounds in 1796. Though this figure was not again attained, there was no figure lower than 30,000,000 pounds, except in the year of peace, until 1808.

The reëxports of other colonial wares show a similar remarkable increase. While in 1791 only 492 pounds of pepper were exported, the amount rose to 7,559,224 pounds in 1805. The export of cocoa, which in 1791 was 8,322 pounds, was 8,540,524 pounds in 1807. The outbreak of war with Great Britain, in spite of the American successes at sea, put a stop to this lucrative transit trade. In 1814 only 762 pounds of sugar and 220,594 pounds of coffee were exported.[11]

In a summary statement of the exports of articles, the growth, produce or manufacture of the United States, presented to the House of Representatives on 26 February 1805, Albert Gallatin classified these under the headings: agriculture, the sea, the forest, the manufactures. For the fiscal year 1803, he reported, the value of the exports falling under these headings was respectively $32,995,000, $2,635,000, $4,220,000 and $1,355,000.[12] This shows clearly enough the preponderant place held by products of the soil in the economy of the United States at that time. Of these products the most important were cotton and tobacco, grain and flour, wood in various forms and the so-called "naval stores" (pitch, tar, rosin and turpentine). In the case of these and other domestic products it is far more difficult than in the case of the transit trade, to estimate the effect of the war in stimulating or depressing them. Many other factors have to be taken into consideration, such as the yield of the harvests both in Europe and America and the increased demand for raw materials created by the rapid progress of the Industrial Revolution.

This latter factor accounts for the immense increase in the exports of cotton, though the conditions produced by the war also played their part, from 1796 onward, in transferring the principal

[11] In 1816 the amounts were 17,536,416 and 8,948,713, respectively.
[12] Annex A to the report, A.S.P., *Commerce and Navigation*, I, 592.

TABLE 2

EXPORT TRADE OF THE UNITED STATES a

1796-1815

Year	Domestic Exports (Dollar values, thousands)	Price Level Index: Domestic Products	INDICES OF DOMESTIC EXPORTS b		Reëxports (Dollar values, thousands)	Price Level Index: Imported Products	INDICES OF REËXPORTS b	
			Unadjusted	Adjusted for Price Level Fluctuations			Unadjusted	Adjusted for Price Level Fluctuations
1796	40,764	109.9	124.2	113.1	26,300	101.3	77.0	75.9
1797	29,850	104.0	90.9	87.6	27,000	99.1	79.1	79.6
1798	28,527	89.1	86.9	97.7	33,000	102.4	96.6	94.2
1799	33,143	95.0	101.0	106.4	45,323	100.2	132.7	132.2
1800	31,841	102.0	97.0	95.2	39,131	96.9	114.6	118.0
Average	32,825	100.0	100.0	100.0	34,151	100.0	100.0	100.0
1801	47,473	116.8	144.6	124.0	46,643	100.2	136.6	136.1
1802	36,708	95.0	111.8	117.9	35,775	90.4	104.8	115.7
1803	42,206	98.0	128.0	131.4	13,594	95.9	39.8	41.4
1804	41,467	102.0	126.3	124.0	36,232	101.3	106.1	104.6
1805	42,387	110.9	129.1	116.6	53,179	100.2	155.7	155.1
Average	42,048	104.5	128.0	122.8	37,085	97.6	108.6	110.6
1806	41,254	106.9	125.7	117.7	60,283	101.3	176.5	174.0
1807	48,700	103.0	148.4	144.2	59,644	98.0	174.6	177.9
1808	9,434	87.1	28.7	33.0	12,997	107.8	38.1	35.2
1809	31,406	95.0	95.7	100.8	20,798	117.6	60.9	51.7
1810	42,367	99.0	129.1	130.5	24,391	108.9	71.4	65.5
Average	34,632	98.2	105.5	105.2	35,623	106.7	104.3	100.9
1811	45,294	97.0	138.0	142.4	16,023	102.4	47.9	45.7
1812	30,032	94.1	91.1	97.4	8,495	118.7	24.9	20.9
1813	25,008	113.9	76.2	67.0	2,848	140.5	8.3	5.9
1814	6,782	137.6	20.7	15.0	145	158.0	0.4	0.3
1815	45,974	123.8	140.0	113.3	6,583	117.6	19.3	16.4
Average	30,618	113.3	93.2	87.0	6,819	127.4	20.2	17.8

a Trade figures are from J. R. McCulloch, *Dictionary of Commerce and Commercial Navigation*, p. 844. Price level indices are adapted from two parallel series, one measuring prices of domestic, the other of imported, commodities at Boston, from 1795 to 1824. Source: W. B. Smith, "Wholesale Commodity Prices in the United States, 1795-1824," *Review of Economic Statistics*, IX, 181. The two sets of indices were in terms of 1825 as 100. Adjusted figures were first obtained in absolute form, then converted to index numbers; base: 1796-1800 = 100.   b Base: 1796-1800 = 100.

market from Holland and the Hanse cities to Great Britain.[13] Only
189,316 pounds of cotton were exported in 1791, and still less in
the following year. Ten years later, in 1801, the amount exported
was 20,911,201 pounds, and it is significant that, unlike the case of
so many other American exports, the year of peace that followed
showed not a decrease but a further increase to 27,501,075 pounds.
This growth continued during the following years and, in spite of
the Continental System, reached its highest development in 1810,
in which year the export amounted to 93,261,462 pounds.[14] Exports
of the other great staple of the South, tobacco, though they fluctuate
greatly,[15] show no such sensational increase as in the case of cotton.

In the case of grain exports, fluctuations are indicated in Table 3.
Wheat exports fell from a high of 1,450,575 bushels in 1793 to a
low of 10,056 bushels in 1799; then rose again in the early years
of the new century, amounting to 686,797 bushels in 1803, only to
drop off again to 18,041 bushels in 1805. Exports of flour behaved
quite similarly, declining between 1794 and 1799, recovering between
1801 and 1803; slumping again from 1804 to 1806 and after 1807
(which was a good year) because of the embargo. After this latter
slump, a marked increase occurred from 1809 to 1811, during which
year a record export of 1,445,012 barrels was made. In 1793 and
1794, the shortage of foodstuffs in France was undoubtedly a factor
in the sudden activity in grain exports.[16] The great decline subsequent to 1794 may have been partly due to Great Britain's position
that grain was contraband of war. Similarly, the sudden activity in
1807 may have been because of an Order in Council that expressly
stated that grain was no longer to be reckoned as contraband.[17] The
very low level of 1797-1799 perhaps resulted from the virtual state

[13] In 1794, of 7,222 bales of cotton exported, 2,667 went to Holland, 1,614 to
Hamburg and other Hanse cities and 1,164 to Great Britain and Ireland. In 1796,
of the 6,106,729 pounds exported, 5,628,176 went to Great Britain and Ireland,
288,958 pounds to the Hanse cities and 54,025 pounds to Holland.

[14] This increase, as well as that of the export of other colonial goods in this
year (see Table 11, *infra*), is explained by the fact that in the previous year
Napoleon had been too much preoccupied by the Austrian campaign to trouble
about the efficiency of his Continental System, and so a vast smuggling trade had
developed between England and the Continent, Heligoland being the principal
entrepôt; see *supra*, p. 142.

[15] Such growth in foreign demand as took place during the war was for manufactured, rather than unmanufactured, tobacco.

[16] In 1793, e.g., France imported 117,485 bushels of American wheat, more by
117 per cent than in the previous year.

[17] Cf. *supra*, p. 150.

of war with France. The high price of wheat in Great Britain, especially during the first few years of the century, may have spurred the American farmer.[18] Exports of maize rose from 1,713,241 bushels in 1791 to 2,079,608 bushels in 1801 and 2,790,850 bushels in 1811. The steady increase of maize exports resulted largely from increased

TABLE 3

EXPORTS AND PRICES OF WHEAT AND FLOUR[a]

1790-1811

Year	Wheat Exports (Bushels)	Average Price Per Quarter (England)		Flour Exports (Barrels)	Average Price Per Barrel (Philadelphia)
		s.	d.		
1790	1,124,458	53	2	724,623	$ 5.56
1791	1,018,339	47	2	619,681	5.22
1792	853,790	41	9	824,464	5.25
1793	1,450,575	47	10	1,074,639	5.90
1794	698,797	50	8	846,010	6.90
1795	141,273	72	11	687,369	10.60
1796	31,226	76	3	725,194	12.50
1797	15,655	52	2	515,633	8.91
1798	15,021	50	4	567,558	8.20
1799	10,056	66	11	519,265	9.66
1800	26,853	110	5	653,052	9.86
1801	239,929	115	11	1,102,444	10.40
1802	280,281	67	9	1,156,248	6.90
1803	686,415	57	1	1,311,853	6.73
1804	127,024	60	5	810,008	8.23
1805	18,041	87	1	777,513	9.70
1806	86,784	76	9	782,724	7.30
1807	776,814	73	1	1,249,819	7.17
1808	87,333	78	11	263,813	5.69
1809	393,889	94	5	846,247	6.91
1810	325,924	103	3	798,431	9.37
1811	216,833	92	5	1,445,012	9.95

a Source: John MacGregor, Commercial Statistics, I, 591.

[18] On the average, wheat brought £5 19s. 6d. the quarter in 1801. Before the war, the average had been £2 6s. 3d. the quarter. The British consul general in Philadelphia predicted in the early spring of 1801 that exports would probably be larger this year. ". . . immense quantities of grain, and flour . . . (have) . . . been brought to this market from distant parts of the country with which there had been no previous intercourse of this sort."—Bond to Grenville, 11 March 1801. P.R.O. F.O. 5. 33. Tooke attributed the rise in price to a succession of bad seasons after 1791, to the increased cost of production consequent on devaluation of the currency, and to "obstructions to importation at a time when our own supply was inadequate."—Tooke, History of Prices, I, 117. Among these obstructions was the drastic Corn Law of 1804. For the balance of the war, American wheat was admitted duty-free only when the price of home-grown wheat had reached £3 6s. the quarter. See supra, p. 67.

demands in the various West Indian colonies and in the Spanish dominions. It is difficult from these figures to form an exact estimate of the influence of the war and especially of belligerent actions upon the cereal industry of the United States. What seems clear, however, is that there was no steadily mounting demand for grain sufficient to cause such an extension of acreage as took place in Great Britain and Ireland. There was, nevertheless, some migration to the fertile valleys of central New York during the middle and late nineties, particularly from Connecticut and Massachusetts. The high prices of farm produce seem to have attracted these settlers.

A much closer connection obtained between the exigencies of the war and the demand for the products of the forest, "naval stores" and wood. But though a growth in export of all "naval stores" is discernible, marked fluctuations appear from year to year.[19] The broad contraband classification of Great Britain induced concealment of shipments of "naval stores," and so the official figures are often misleading. Another factor tending to produce fluctuations was the competition of the Baltic states, which varied with the fortunes of war and affected the amount of American exports year by year. Thus, the great increase in export in 1811 was probably the result of Napoleon's seizure of some 600 neutral ships in the Baltic ports in the autumn of 1810 [20] which forced Great Britain to draw her supplies mainly from America.[21]

It is unnecessary for the purpose of this study to give in detail the figures for the export of the various kinds of wooden articles, which included everything wooden from lumber and timber to masts, handspikes, hoops, staves and shingles. The increased trade in these articles created by the war is sufficiently illustrated by the figures for the export of boards and planks of oak and pine for which there was an ever-growing demand in the shipyards. In the year before the war, 1791, the amount exported was 38,252,750 feet. In 1793 it was 64,846,024 feet, an amount which was not exceeded until 1801, when 71,629,831 feet were exported. In 1802 the amount was 80,877,657 feet and in 1805 it was 94,939,000 feet, the highest figure reached. A sudden rise from 63,042,000 feet in 1810 to 85,340,000

[19] Table 12 showing these fluctuations will be found in Appendix I, *infra*.
[20] See *supra*, p. 216.
[21] Great Britain had always been the best market for these products of the United States. In 1791, e.g., the year before the outbreak of the European War, the British Empire took 56,166 of the 58,107 barrels of turpentine exported, and 39,039 of the 51,044 barrels of tar.

feet in 1811 may, as in the case of other commodities, be attributed to the collapse of the supply from the Baltic, due to the French captures of neutral ships in the autumn of 1810.

It is clear from this analysis that the increased trade of the United States due to their neutrality was derived far less from any increase in the export of their domestic produce than from the carrying trade, especially the importation and reshipment of those colonial goods the demand for which in Europe the Americans were alone in a position to supply. This conclusion is confirmed by Table 2,[22] from which it may be seen that in six of the twelve years prior to the enactment of the embargo in December 1807, the value of reëxports exceeded the value of domestic exports. In fact, the average value of the reëxports for this twelve-year period is actually greater than the corresponding average for the American produce exported. As might be expected, however, the domestic exports are more stable. The immediate effect of the Treaty of Amiens on both classes of exports was approximately the same. But in 1803, when reëxports suffered a sensational drop of 70 per cent, the value of domestic exports actually increased. Except as a result of the nation's commercial policy, or of loss of neutral status, the domestic exports series shows considerable stability. Even after the embargo was lifted, reëxports did not regain their previous level.

It has been shown that the export trade of the United States increased during the period of their neutrality. It remains to consider in how far this was a result of the neutrality itself. Other factors operating to produce changes in volume of trade have been alluded to in treating the products separately. But were there general factors, affecting the total foreign trade, which might have accounted for a part of the increase noted? So far as the colonial trade is concerned, only relaxations of trade restrictions incidental to the war made the great increases possible. With regard to the domestic export trade, however, the causal significance of the war is not so clear. It appears from the figures themselves that a movement upward was in progress at the time the war broke out. For this trend two factors were chiefly responsible. The ratification of the Federal Constitution and the assumption by the new Government of an authority that had hitherto been lacking, particularly as affecting interstate and international commerce, had established

[22] Page 228, *supra.*

conditions in which trade was encouraged. The second factor was population increase. The first census of the new republic (1790) indicated a population of 3,929,214. By 1807 there were about 6,300,000 inhabitants,[23] an increase of 61 per cent. In the same interval, domestic exports increased 214 per cent,[24] and the domestic price level about 60 per cent.[25] Allowing for increases in prices, then, the increase of domestic exports was hardly greater than the increase in population. When these percentages are considered in their relationship to one another, and the factors other than the war affecting the export of a particular product are taken into account, it becomes a matter for conjecture whether the status of a neutral brought any appreciable increase in the domestic export trade of the United States. It certainly increased the export of certain products, notably forest products, but no marked increase of a general nature attributable to demands of belligerents, is apparent.

The effect of the war was to divert the carrying trade from British ships to those of the United States and other neutrals. This is vividly illustrated by the comparative statement of the tonnage of vessels engaged in foreign trade entering the ports of the United States from the beginning of 1790 to the end of 1796, which was communicated to the House of Representatives on 5 April 1798.[26] During this period the tonnage of American ships thus entering increased from 354,767 a year to 675,046; that of Danish ships from 1,113 to 10,430; and that of Swedish ships from 535 to 5,560. The tonnage of British vessels entering, which was 216,914 in 1790, was only 19,669 in 1796. The proportion of foreign tonnage to the whole amount of tonnage employed in the foreign trade of the United States, which was 41.4 per cent in 1790, was only 6.9 per cent in 1796,[27] and sank as low as 3.4 per cent in 1811.[28] The effect of these

[23] The estimate for the year 1807 is by Pitkin, in *A Statistical View of the Commerce of the United States* (1835), p. 152.

[24] Exports were not classified prior to 1796; but war had not broken out in 1790, and colonial trade was surrounded by a host of restrictions. The proportion of reëxports must accordingly have been so small that the error is but slight in regarding all exports as domestic exports.

[25] For this computation, the 1790 index is not strictly comparable, since it measures the general price level rather than the domestic price level.

[26] A.S.P., *Commerce and Navigation*, I (No. 43), 389.

[27] A.S.P., *Finance*, I, 713. The average for the three years 1790-1792 was 39.4 per cent; that for the six years 1793-1798 was 13.6 per cent. Annex K to the report of Gallatin on the finances, communicated on 18 December 1801. A.S.P., *Finance*, I, 713.

[28] *Ibid.*, II, 582.

changes on the freight earnings of American vessels was considerable. It has been estimated that for the period, an annual average of $32,500,000 was earned.[29]

Naturally this provided a stimulus to the shipping industry. In 1792 the registered tonnage of American ships employed in foreign trade was 411,438, falling in 1793 to 367,734. From this time onward it shows an annual increase, except in 1802 (the year of peace) and in 1808 (the year within the period of the embargo), reaching its highest figure, 984,269, in 1810. Table 4 gives the official figures year by year.

TABLE 4

REGISTERED VESSELS EMPLOYED IN FOREIGN TRADE[a]

(In thousands of tons)

Year	Tonnage	Year	Tonnage	Year	Tonnage
1789	127.3	1796	576.7	1804	672.5
1790	354.8	1797	597.8	1805	749.3
1791	363.1	1798	603.4	1806	808.3
1792	411.4	1799	669.2	1807	848.3
1793	367.7	1800	669.9	1808	769.1
1794	438.9	1801	718.5	1809	910.1
1795	529.5	1802	560.4	1810	984.3
		1803	597.2		

[a] Adapted from a report communicated to the House of Representatives by Albert Gallatin, Secretary of the Treasury, on the 3d of February 1812; A.S.P., *Commerce and Navigation* (No. 171 B), 895. In his covering letter Gallatin says that these figures "correspond with the annual statements made to Congress." There are, however, a few discrepancies. The only important one is that Gallatin gives the tonnage for 1801 as 718,549.60, whereas in the report of the Register, Robert Nourse, of 12 February 1803, it is given as 632,907.08 (*ibid.*, p. 531).

That all of this increase in tonnage was caused by the war, could hardly be maintained after a careful examination of this table. The most spectacular year to year increase in tonnage took place between 1789 and 1790, before the war broke out. This is the case, whether the increase is measured relatively or by absolute amount. It is apparent, in this connection, as in regard to exports, that the new situation created by the establishment of the new government was a factor favorable to an upward trend. But even after making an allowance for this and for increase in population, the war seems quite clearly to have been the principal factor in what Pitkin has described as an increase with "no parallel in the commercial annals of the world." [30]

[29] E. L. Bogart, *Economic History of the United States*, p. 122.

[30] Pitkin, *op. cit.*, p. 425. Measured relatively, the increase appears greater than it is, because the start was made from so low a point.

In these circumstances the expansion of the American shipbuilding industry is easy to understand. The remarkable growth in American tonnage was only the principal reason for this expansion. In the years between 1798 and the outbreak of the war of 1812, our shipbuilding industry sold over two hundred thousand tons to foreigners.[31] Rabbeno has pointed to the influence of these developments on the course of capital investments during these years. "The capital possessed by the country," he observes, "was not very great, and all, or nearly all, the disposable part of it was invested in international commerce, shipbuilding, and in agricultural pursuits which were encouraged by increased prices." [32] Writing in 1819, Seybert complained of this tendency. The advantage, he felt, was necessarily temporary and the effect on industry in general, baneful.[33]

Whatever one may think of this view, it will be well to consider the effect of the war on the growth of the still embryonic manufacturing industries of the United States. Except in the literal sense of the term, manufacture had scarcely existed in the colonial period, because of the restrictive acts of the mother country. Prior to the establishment of the new government in 1789, little opportunity for remedying this state of affairs had been given. But since the Americans had been unable to establish such trade relations with the rest of the world as would have enabled them to pay for imports of manufactured articles with exports of their own produce, household and family manufactures increased in this period. In his report on manufactures in the United States, presented to Congress in 1791, Hamilton stated that in certain districts two-thirds, three-fourths and even four-fifths of the clothing was homemade. It is evident that he hoped that the change in government would foster an expansion of manufacturing industry. The milling of flour and manufacture of tobacco did make progress. Some textile mills were erected during the early 1790's. But with the coming of the war, the demand for American exports and reëxports proved ample to pay for all the imported manufactured articles necessary to meet the home demand. With her improved mechanical processes, more competent and yet less costly labor supply, larger scale of production and more effective methods of business organization, England could manufacture a better and yet cheaper product. Accordingly, it

[31] H. U. Faulkner, *American Economic History* (1890), p. 248.
[32] U. Rabbeno, *The American Commercial Policy* (1895), p. 153.
[33] A. Seybert, *Statistical Annals* (1818), p. 59.

was more profitable for America to import her manufactured goods than to produce them. To this generalization, certain exceptions may be noted: the production of pig and bar iron and the already-mentioned progress of shipbuilding in New England.

As early as 1806, the depredations of the belligerents had so far interfered with the smooth working of this interchange as to lead to an initial expansion of manufacturing in the United States. The proclamation of the long embargo stimulated further expansion in two ways. By cutting off supplies from abroad, it offered a pro-tected market to the American manufacturer; by severely limiting investment opportunities in the commercial field, it released a supply of capital that was swiftly attracted by the favorable prospects now opened to the manufacturing industries. Interesting examples of the shift from the vessel and the countinghouse to the factory are such well-known and widely respected shipping families as the Appletons, the Jacksons and the Lowells. To the profit incentive was added a patriotic motive. The governments of cities and counties and states pressed bounties and premiums on the new concerns or underwrote their security flotations. In a relatively short period of years, whole industries were transformed from the domestic to the factory system.

As early as 1810, Secretary Gallatin could point with pride to the results of this development, quite as remarkable in its own sphere, as had been the earlier boom in shipping and shipbuilding. "A great American capital has been acquired during the last twenty years," he said, "and the injurious violations of the neutral commerce of the United States, by forcing industry and capital into other channels, have broken inveterate habits, and given a general impulse, to which must be ascribed the great increase in manu-factures during the last two years." He proceeded to give a long list of manufactures "which may be considered adequate to the consumption of the United States." Among the "branches firmly established were iron and manufactures of iron, manufactures of cotton, wool, and flax, and several of lead." Many of these manu-factures, notably carding and spinning of wool, were still largely household industries.

The particulars as to the progress of cotton manufacture fur-nished his best case in point. In 1803, there had been but four mills in the United States. New England had fifteen mills with 8,000 spindles in 1808. By the end of 1809, eighty-seven new mills had been erected, of which sixty-two were already operating with 31,000 spindles. Gallatin predicted that by 1811, 80,000 spindles would be operating.

The iron industry, he said, was hampered by the poor quality of the material and the lack of the ordinary supply of Russian iron, which had been felt in some of the slitting and rolling mills. He instanced, however, two new developments in the iron industry which are of interest: the manufacture of cut nails (an American invention) from bar iron flattened by machinery, and the making of steam engines by an iron foundry at Philadelphia. Manufactures of wood now supplied the whole need of the United States. Manufactures of leather also showed a great advance. There were tanneries in every part of the United States, some on a large scale, and the exports of certain leather goods, such as boots and shoes, already exceeded the imports.[34]

Gallatin's forecast of the future of American industry was naturally not entirely borne out by the course of events.[35] Pin-point accuracy in such estimates, however, is hardly to be expected. What matters is that, in the years that followed, manufacturing continued to grow. Patents issued for new inventions, which had averaged 77 annually in the period, 1790-1811, jumped to 237 in 1812. A corporation with $800,000 capital was established in the manufacturing industry, during the same year. Late that year, Niles wrote that "the world has no parallel . . . nor can it furnish any for the increase of our fabrications." In 1814, Massachusetts alone chartered thirty corporations for the manufacture of cotton, wool, glass, wire, and so forth. The New England states, during that year, drew a monthly average of $500,000 from the banks of the South for articles produced in their new mills. Small wonder that Cobbett warned his countrymen that the new developments in America threatened to make them completely independent of the English manufacturer.

Although there is little clear evidence on the point, the effects of the war on the status of the working classes deserve some attention. Wages of sailors, in the period between 1791 and 1807, rose from $8.00 a month to $30.00 a month.[36] During the expansion of manufacturing, salaries in that field appear to have risen. Such

[34] A.S.P., *Finance*, II (No. 325), 425 ff.
[35] He seems not to have foreseen the changes that were bound to accompany the return of peace. For the immediate future, his predictions were, in many cases, surpassed. By the end of 1810, e.g., not 80,000 but 87,000 spindles were operating.
[36] H. U. Faulkner, *American Economic History* (1890), p. 248.

evidence as is available points to some general increase in wage disbursements. What is not clear is whether this was sufficient to compensate for the higher prices that obtained for much of the time after the middle 90's. Demands from abroad brought sharp increases in the prices of wheat, corn and meat. Flour, which from 1785 to 1793 sold for an average of $5.41 a barrel, averaged $9.12 a barrel during the twelve years in which Europe was at war between 1793 and 1807.[37] As indicated in Table 1,[38] the price level was 65 per cent higher in 1796 than in 1791, and through most of the war years, was 50 per cent higher. But whether or not these price increases meant reduced real earnings, there can be no doubt whatever that employment opportunities were greater throughout the war, except for the interval of the embargo. McMaster's estimate that the embargo threw 55,000 sailors and 100,000 mechanics and laborers out of work,[39] may give some inkling as to the amount of employment provided by the expansion of American commerce. This affected the development of the country's resources.

Another interesting indirect check on the extent to which employment opportunities were increased, may be gained from a consideration of the course of westward migration. This movement was noticeably reduced during the 90's. The only considerable movement in the northern states was to central New York, and as has been observed, this was stimulated by the rise in the foreign demand for foodstuffs. The bulk of the migration in the 90's was from the back country of the South, to which the effects of commercial prosperity seemed not to have penetrated. During the brief interval of peace that began in 1802, the amount of migration increased sharply, and large numbers moved westward from every state. With the renewal of hostilities, however, the movement westward once more diminished. The hard times that began late in 1807 gave rise to a greater migration than ever.[40] By this analysis, it is not contended for a moment that the course of the war was the only factor in accelerating or retarding westward migration; but rather that it was an important and an easily recognizable factor.

"I hope the new world will fatten on the follies of the old," Jef-

[37] T. Pitkin, *Statistical View of the Commerce of the United States* (1835), p. 372.

[38] Page 226, *supra*.

[39] J. B. McMaster, *History of the People of the United States*, III (1891), 279-338.

[40] H. J. Carman and S. McKee, *History of the United States*, I (1935), 437 ff.

ferson had written in 1790.[41] His hope had been realized but much of the fat was unhealthy and was destined to melt away with the ending of the conditions which had produced it. That the coming of peace in Europe would show the artificial nature of the war-time prosperity, had been made abundantly evident during the short-lived Peace of Amiens.[42] In his report on the finances of 21 December 1801, Secretary Gallatin revealed his misgivings as to the likely effect of peace in Europe on customs receipts which at that time constituted almost the entire revenue of the United States.[43] This peace was, however, of too brief a duration to have its full effect, and it was not until after the final peace in 1815 that the carrying trade was thrown back into those channels from which it had been violently diverted during the war.

One result was a severe, if only temporary, check to the recovery of American commerce and industry, especially of the shipping industry, which had suffered much during the war with Great Britain. The British Navigation Acts, relaxed during the European war, came once more into force six months after the peace.[44] The ports of the British West Indian colonies and of the British possessions on the continent of North America remained closed to American vessels until, in 1822, they were opened, under certain restrictions and on the basis of reciprocity, by Act of Parliament. The loss thus occasioned was, indeed, partly compensated for by the right secured to United States ships, under the Commercial Convention of 1815, to conduct a direct trade with the British dominions in Europe, and

[41] Ford, ed., *Writings of Jefferson* (1892-1899), V, 197 (to Edward Rutledge, 4 July 1790).

[42] Phineas Bond to Lord Hawkesbury, Philadelphia, 7 December 1801. P.R.O. F.O. 5. 3. "The immense benefits which, for many years past, have resulted to this country in consequence of the deranged state of the commerce and navigation of France, Spain and Holland, must now, upon the restoration of peace, undergo a material reduction: the carrying trade of the colonial produce of these respective Powers will revert to its former and natural channel. It will be occupied to a great degree with their own vessels—while most of those rich staples which, for a long time, have been conveyed through the medium of these States, circuitously, to Europe, will be carried directly thither: and as to the tonnage of Great Britain, it will now again be restored to a participation in the carrying trade of that extensive and increasing supply of our manufactures which the United States required and which, during the late war, has been almost entirely engrossed by American vessels."

[43] A.S.P., *Finance*, I, 701. At best, he said, revenues would be liable to "sudden and considerable fluctuations."

[44] At the time when the Commercial Convention of 3 July 1815 was negotiated American vessels were still admitted to the West Indian free ports.

on terms of complete reciprocity. In this trade the Americans more than held their own.[45] In 1819, however, there was a sudden and very significant drop in the number of United States vessels entering the harbors of Great Britain.

Rush ascribed this "extraordinary falling off" to "the numerous commercial failures and the depression of business generally in the United States."[46] The causes of the crisis of 1819 were various, but among them must be reckoned the sudden change in the conditions which had prevailed during the European war. With the coming of peace, the still infant industries of the United States found it always hard, and sometimes impossible, to compete with those of Great Britain, even in the home market, partly owing to the greater perfection of British mechanical processes, partly to the "dumping" in America, as elsewhere, of the vast quantity of goods accumulated in the warehouses of Great Britain. Thus the economic relations between the United States and Great Britain tended to revert to what they had been in colonial days, the former supplying raw materials, the latter paying for them in manufactured goods.[47]

This formidable competition led American manufacturers to

---

[45] "Our shipping are rapidly eating out the British from almost the whole of the direct trade between the United States and England."—John Quincy Adams, *Memoirs*, IV, 181; under date of 25 November 1818.

[46] Richard Rush, *The Court of London, 1819-1825*. Ed. 1873, p. 184. Instead of the three or four hundred American vessels which had entered the port of Liverpool every year before and after the War of 1812, records Richard Rush, there were only two there in November of that year. The setback of 1819 was clearly only temporary, for on 12 August 1820, Richard Rush wrote to the Secretary of State: "So far as the direct trade between the United States and Britain is concerned, our vessels continue to have the decided preference inwards and outwards. If I were to say in the proportion of ten to one, I do not think I would go beyond the truth."—A.S.P., F.R., V, 84.

[47] The total value of the exports of the United States, in 1817, was $87,671,569; that of exports to Great Britain and her dominions, $43,468,242. In 1818, the figures were $93,281,133 and $46,717,832, respectively. As early as 1815, the value of imported goods from Great Britain was outstanding. Thus, of goods paying duties of 25 per cent ad valorem, the total value was $69,805,243 and that of goods imported from Great Britain and her dominions, $41,512,871. The trade done by the United States with the British dominions, i.e., was equal to, and sometimes exceeded, that done with the rest of the world. Note that, while the transit trade in colonial goods greatly declined (e.g., 31,423,477 pounds of coffee were exported in 1810, and only 6,095,837 pounds in 1818), the export of the great home staples soon regained its high level. Thus, the export of cotton (which had been 93,261,462 pounds in 1810) after a complete collapse in 1815 (257,542 pounds) rose to 92,471,178 pounds in 1818. See the returns under the respective years in A.S.P., *Commerce and Navigation*, II.

clamor for protection, and petitions to this end poured into Congress. Their pleas were answered in 1816 and again in 1824, over the protests of the farmers and the shipping interests. Speaking for this latter group, Daniel Webster addressed himself to the question we are considering.

The depression of prices [he argued] and the stagnation of business have been in truth the necessary result of circumstances. . . . We have enjoyed a day of extraordinary prosperity; we had been neutral while the world was at war, and found a great demand for our products, our navigation and our labor. We had no right to expect that that state of things would continue always. With the return of peace, the foreign nations would struggle for themselves, and enter into competition with us in the great objects of pursuit.[48]

What the speaker was decrying was a political attempt to make permanent an achievement of the preceding years. Unfortunately for our purposes this particular achievement, the growth of manufacturing, could hardly be regarded as one of the benefits of neutrality. Instead, it was an indirect effect of the cessation of neutral benefits. On the general question whether or not the prosperity fostered by a neutral status in war time is capable of projecting itself beyond the period concerned, the American experience does shed some light. It would seem that the gains from the carrying trade, the expansion of shipbuilding, and the extraordinary demands for certain products were necessarily transitory, except in so far as they were capable of building up capital for use in other lines. In any event, whether or not one is able to maintain one's neutrality to the end, the deflection of capital to the type of industries that flourish most in such times, appears bound to leave in its wake, economic maladjustments.

We have seen that the shipping, shipbuilding, lumber and food industries made substantial gains in the period during which the United States remained neutral. In the same period, certain losses were noted. A conservative estimate of the seizures by England of American merchantmen would be two thousand. France can hardly have seized more than half that number. Substantial as these losses were, it is difficult to believe that they can have equalled the profits of successful voyages. The losses in time and money of crews detained appear also to have been overbalanced by the increases in employment and wages in the shipping industry. The less direct

[48] Ironically enough, Webster later became an ardent champion of protectionism.

effects of the belligerent restrictions and war-time demands lend themselves even less readily to analysis. Speculations in commodities and in shipping, shipbuilding and marine insurance seem to have been largely liquidated during the intervals such as during the embargo or after the war. The temporary lull in certain activities does not appear to have involved a permanent injury to the industries or resources affected.

X

THE SCANDINAVIAN STATES

DENMARK-NORWAY

NORWAY

Up to the year 1807 the kingdom of Denmark-Norway was almost alone in standing out of the war in which, one by one, most of the other European states had become involved. Although the two areas which comprized this kingdom were politically one, the differences in their economic life were sufficiently great to justify separate treatment of the effects of the war on their commerce and industry. In some cases, however, quantitative measures refer to the entire kingdom and the proportion attributable to each part is indeterminate.

During the War of American Independence, Norway had had recent experience of the effects of neutrality. While the other northern maritime powers, Great Britain, France and Holland, were engaged in hostilities, her ships were free to sail all the seas, hampered only by "the one-sided control and ever shifting rules which the Ocean's Mighty Mistress imposed on all seafaring peoples."[1] From 1776 to 1781, not only did she obtain high prices for her exports, but, as neutral territory, she became an entrepôt for foreign goods and so gained additional wealth by a lucrative trade.[2] Accordingly, if we credit the glowing reports of the condition of Norway's trade and shipping at the close of the American War, the prospect for Norway seemed particularly bright at the opening of the French Revolutionary Wars.

The main sources of Norway's wealth were her forests, and the North Sea fisheries, her principal exports being timber, fish and fish products. The export of timber was mainly from the southern part of the country; her northern regions had never been well forested and had early been exhausted. The exports from the northern section

---

[1] J. C. Aall, *Erindringer som bidrag til norges historie fra 1800-1815*, 3 vols. (Christiania, 1844, 1845), I, p. 42.
[2] A. M. Schweigaard, *Norges statistik* (1840), p. 130.

were almost entirely fish and fish products, which were shipped mainly through Bergen. In France, Spain and the lands bordering on the Baltic and Mediterranean, these products found their largest and most profitable markets.

As we have seen, the war created a vastly greater demand for timber, especially for masts, spars and planking. This demand Norway was in the best position to supply, not only because of the extent of her forests and the superior quality of the timber they produced, but because her geographical position made her commerce with England less liable to interruption than that of the Baltic countries. Unfortunately, comparable data are not available for the exports of timber from Norway during the period of her neutrality; the extent to which such exports were abnormally large is difficult to gauge because of the absence of comparable prewar data. Some interesting comparisons are afforded, however, with exports for the years of peace that followed the war. The average annual export from 1804 to 1806 was 200,000 *laester*.[3] In 1815 the amount exported was only 98,976 *laester*, and in 1819 there was a further fall to 69,448 *laester*.

The extent of the trade in timber between Norway and Great Britain produced a curious situation when Norway, unwillingly enough, was drawn into the war against her best customer. As a neutral she had enjoyed almost a monopoly of the exports of timber to the British Isles. The wharves of the British and Irish ports were piled high with Norwegian timber which, owing to the rapidity with which it was used up, had continually to be renewed.[4] With the outbreak of war in 1807, these harbors were closed to her, and so they remained until 1810. The paralysis of the Baltic trade in that year, due to the rigorous enforcement of the Continental System, forced Great Britain to turn once more to Norway for her supplies. Licenses were therefore freely issued to Norwegian ships to trade with England, with the result that, although the two countries were at war, an active trade once more sprang up between them. Not until 1812, when Norway was suffering from a food shortage and it was considered advisable for political reasons to put pressure upon her, did the issue of these licenses cease.[5]

---

[3] The *laest* (German, *Last;* English, "last") is a load of 2,000 kilogrammes; 1,000 kilogrammes equal 0.9842 ton. The last is thus roughly the equivalent of two tons.   [4] Aall, *op. cit.,* p. 43.

[5] Licenses were not refused; the fee for them was simply made prohibitive (£4,000 to £5,000). Cf. *supra,* pp. 158 ff.

For the export of fish and fish products, data are more complete if not more satisfactory. The difficulty with these statistics is that they often reflect the vagaries of herrings more accurately than the course of war demands. During the American War, the export of dried and salted fish from Bergen had increased markedly.[6] From one cause or another, however, the increases during the French Revolutionary Wars seemed not to have been as great. "Their fishery made some advance," wrote Oddy in 1805, "yet not so rapid as might have been expected, when we consider that the war in Europe annoys the principal maritime powers, and that Holland was altogether excluded from the fishery, while England neglected it."[7] It is, of course, apparent that the geographical position of Norway, given the British command of the seas, was much less favorable to trade with those nations which had usually provided her best markets for fish and fish products. That England's definition of food as contraband of war interfered with this trade, cannot be doubted. But it is difficult to determine how far the activities of belligerent cruisers were responsible for checking the increase in fish exports, because other causes operated.[8] In spite of these checks, Denmark-Norway encouraged her fisheries and did supply the contending nations with larger amounts of their produce. "The rapid increase from 1799 to 1802," says Oddy, "is sufficient proof that they tasted the fruits of their industry."[9] In 1799, Norway exported 256 cargoes of fish, weighing about 17,900 tons. In 1802, 411 cargoes (26,500 tons) were exported, not counting overland shipments to Sweden.

No direct measure of the import trade of Norway is available, but the figures for the receipts from customs provide an indirect measure. For the years 1785 to 1789 the average annual receipts had been 563,697 *Rigsdalers*. The corresponding average from 1795 to 1799 was 655,146 *Rigsdalers;* and from 1800 to 1802, 782,005 *Rigsdalers*. During the remaining years of neutrality the receipts continued this upward trend, the high point of which was attained in 1806.

[6] Ewald Bosse, *Norwegens Volkswirtschaft vom Ausgang der Hansaperiode bis zur Gegenwart* (Jena, 1916), I. Teil, p. 271.

[7] Oddy, *European Commerce* (London, 1805), p. 377.

[8] Bosse, *op. cit.*, p. 315. At Lister, in 1793, the spring herrings failed to put in an appearance, and at Ryfylke, where the herring fishery had been good from 1700 to 1784, they remained away for twenty-five years.

[9] Oddy, *loc. cit.* Great Britain took 894 tons of this export, which Oddy thought "strange."

In that year the receipts amounted to 1,292,275 *Rigsdalers*.[10] These increases measure changes in imposts and in prices, as well as in imports. The fees for naturalizing foreign ships, imposed by the ordinance of 20 April 1796, brought in 4,800 *Rigsdalers* annually. The duty on freights, under the ordinance of 24 February 1796, produced on an average, from 1797 to 1803, 20,000 *Rigsdalers;* and after its increase by the ordinance of 1 February 1804, yielded an annual average of 50,000 *Rigsdalers*.[11] In so far as these receipts reflected ad valorem charges, they measure changes in prices. The correction for these is indeterminate, for on the one hand there is no way of knowing what proportion of the imposts were specific and what proportion ad valorem; and on the other hand there is no information available on prices of imports in Norway by reference to which one might adjust this proportion, were it known. There is little reason to believe, however, that either of these types of change were so spectacular, as to affect the conclusion from the data given, that imports increased substantially. How far this reflected increase in the transit trade, it is impossible to say. It is known that goods were reëxported by Norway both overland to Sweden and by sea, but no measures of the amount of this traffic are available.

The growth of Norway's trade, chiefly because of her neutrality during the French Revolutionary Wars, is illustrated by the available statistics of her shipping during this period. In 1767, the total tonnage of her merchant fleet had been about 50,700 (25,394 *commerzien-laester*)[12] but by 1792, largely as a result of the American War, her merchant fleet had grown to 860 vessels with a tonnage of about 91,000, not including craft of under twenty tons burden.[13] In 1802, ten years after the outbreak of the Revolutionary War, the merchant fleet consisted of 990 vessels with a total tonnage of 107,506; and in 1807, the year in which Norway became involved in the war, this fleet had increased to 1,514 vessels with a tonnage of 131,168.[14] These latter figures tend to overestimate the increases in both vessels and tonnage. It was a common practice for foreign ships to register themselves as Norwegian in order to secure the advantages of a neutral flag.[15]

[10] Data for preceding years were as follows: 1803—980,917 Rdl.; 1804—1,055,303 Rdl.; 1805—1,110,348 Rdl.

[11] Schweigaard, *op. cit.*, pp. 131 ff.   [12] That is, commercial lasts.

[13] F. Thaarup, *Archiv fur Statistik u.s.w.* (Copenhagen, 1796), p. 274.

[14] This figure includes vessels of less than 20 tons burden.

[15] It is difficult to estimate the extent of this, but it seems not to have been such as to impair seriously the validity of the measure of increase; cf. *supra*, pp. 119 ff.

These figures can be supplemented by those giving the number of vessels from Denmark-Norway entering the ports of Great Britain during the period 1792 to 1806. For the year 1792, when Great Britain was still at peace, the number recorded was 638, the tonnage, 104,253; the number had increased to 801 by 1794, and the tonnage to 124,591. The number of vessels continued to increase until 1800, in which year it was 1,126. Larger ships seem to have been built for the trade, for the tonnage continued to increase until 1806, the last year of Danish-Norwegian neutrality, when 1,075 vessels weighing 291,487 tons, entered.[16] In these lists no distinction is made between Danish and Norwegian ships, and it is possible that some other neutral carriers are included. It may be safely assumed, however, that the great increase in the navigation between Great Britain and Denmark-Norway during these years was mainly in response to the increased demand for timber. Norway, as we have seen, supplied most of this demand.

Norway seems to have suffered rather less than most neutral states from the depredations of belligerent cruisers. She had the advantage that her most important customer was Great Britain. The latter was vitally interested in maintaining her intercourse with Norway as the chief source of her supplies of timber. Norwegian shipping was, therefore, less subject to vexatious interference under British Orders in Council and Instructions than was that of Denmark. The latter's gains as a neutral were regarded as having been largely derived from "the collusive and fraudulent commerce so openly carried on from the ports of the Baltic."[17] The limited amount of inconveniences to which Norwegian shipping was subjected makes such benefits as she derived from her neutral status almost in the nature of a net gain.

Schweigaard considered the period from 1775 to 1807 the golden age of Norwegian trade and navigation. Their flourishing condition during the decade before 1807 led to so widespread a prosperity among the commercial classes that this period was long spoken of as *den gode Tid* (the good time).[18] The effects of this prosperity seem not to have been distributed uniformly. Important industries

---

[16] Cesar Moreau, *Chronological Records of the British Royal and Commercial Navies* (Lithographed, London, 1827). These lists, which are very full, are taken from various official sources.

[17] Grenville to Hammond, 10 May 1794. F.O. 5. 4. No. 12, cf. *supra*, p. 138.

[18] Schweigaard, *op. cit.*, p. 130.

of Norway at this time were agriculture and pasturage, and both suffered deflection of energy and capital to shipping and the export trade. The high prices paid for exportable goods had a depressing effect upon the fortunes of the owners and workers who continued to till and to herd. Only during the interval between the outbreak of war in 1807 and the union with Sweden in 1814, when Norwegian foreign trade was either depressed or irregular, did these industries begin to progress.[19] Most of the benefits that accrued to the trading and shipping interests proved impermanent. Individual fortunes had certainly been made; and these may have contributed to the up-building of Norwegian industry. There had been, however, much rash speculation: excessive purchases of timber and foreign ships, and bidding up of the prices of forests, saw mills, ships and mer-chandise beyond all reason. With the changes accompanying peace, a readjustment of values had been made, and in the liquidation of contracts which had been entered into during "the good time" nu-merous bankruptcies were involved.[20]

DENMARK

The wealth of Denmark lay neither in her forests nor her fish-eries. The *horrida silva* which in Adam of Bremen's day had cov-ered the land had long since disappeared, and a whole series of ordinances, for a hundred years past, had not availed to stay the progress of deforestation.[21] There was, to be sure, still some export of timber, but this trade was of no great importance.[22] The fisheries were a greater source of gain; but the elusive herring being the most important catch, the returns were so uncertain a quantity, that the fisheries played alternately a very great and a rather unimportant part in the country's economy.[23]

The Mercantilists had in Denmark a poor case in point. Those in-dustries artificially created during the eighteenth century were dying out even before, in 1797, the Government abandoned the policy of

[19] *Loc. cit.*, p. 135.

[20] *Loc. cit.*, pp. 135 f. Ewald Bosse, on the other hand, says that, in spite of the numerous captures, the profits of neutrality "come very great," and that the fortunes made in Norway during these times contributed to strengthen the eco-nomic foundations which had been laid at the beginning of the period by the privileges granted to the towns; *Norwegens Volkswirtschaft* (Jena, 1916), I. Teil, p. 428.

[21] Falbe-Hansen og Scharling, *Danmarks statistik*, Copenhagen, 1887, II, 4.

[22] Fred. Thaarup, *Statistik der danischen monarchie* (1795), p. 532.

[23] Falbe-Hansen og Scharling, *op. cit.*, I, 353.

protection. After Denmark became involved in the war, the impossibility of obtaining foreign goods kept certain industries alive, but this life was precarious and ended in the economic depression that followed the peace.[24]

The great source of Denmark's wealth was her trade. Commanding as she did the passage between the North Sea and the Baltic,[25] she was in an admirable position to act as the intermediary between Russia and the other Baltic States and the world beyond the narrows. She was thus able to take full advantage of her neutrality during the succession of wars from 1756 onward. During the first half of the eighteenth century, her trade had been of little importance. From the middle of the century onward, however, it developed with mighty strides, reaching its greatest volume between 1793 and 1799. In spite of the commercial crisis of 1800, the volume continued high until, in 1807, Denmark became involved in the war.

These increases were in large part in the carrying and entrepôt trade. Of the maritime powers engaged in war, Great Britain alone was able to protect her sea-borne commerce, and this protection was by no means always effective. As James Stephen complained, the rates of insurance on cargoes in neutral bottoms were at times actually lower than on those aboard British vessels. The merchants of Great Britain were thus tempted to employ neutrals as carriers of their goods; [26] and in any case, the English merchant service was

[24] Samsoe, Jens, *Die Industrialisierung Danemarks,* in *Probleme der Weltwirtschaft,* XLIV, 59.

[25] Oddy (*European Commerce* (1805), p. 363) remarks that "the whole of the Baltic Trade is tributary to Denmark," since her right to exact dues from all vessels passing the Sound, though often disputed, had long been submitted to; and the only other routes to the Baltic, through the Holstein Canal or overland through Holstein to Lübeck, were equally subject to tolls on goods in transit. The Sound dues, which were collected at Elsinore (Helsingörs) formed "a considerable branch of the revenues of Denmark." The average number of ships passing the Sound each year was 7,752 during the period 1750-1799 and 10,157 during the period 1800-1808. It was stated in September 1800 that the revenue derived from this source, which was principally appropriated to the royal household, amounted to £160,000 sterling annually (*State Papers,* XI, 169, quoted by J. B. Scott, *The Armed Neutralities of 1780 and 1800,* p. 494). In 1808, the year after Denmark declared war, the number of ships passing sank to 121. During the rest of the war merchant ships passed the narrows under British convoy, and of course no dues were paid. See Falbe-Hansen og Scharling, *op. cit.,* III, 425, and Thaarup, *Tabellen til den statistisk udsigt over den danske stat* (1825).

[26] "The rate of insurance works out at less for neutral ships carrying enemy produce than for British ships under convoy. For one per cent Lloyd's gives an honorary guarantee against the perils of capture and discovery."—*War in Disguise,* p. 85. Six years earlier, however, on 17 January 1799, in the course of a debate in

hampered by the drain of seamen required for their royal navy. It was the Danes, in common with the Americans, who benefited most by these conditions.

The Danes had from of old been a seafaring people, and long before the outbreak of the French Revolutionary Wars, their ships were trading in all parts of the world. During the period from 1785 to 1792, a yearly average of 485 Danish ships sailed to the ports of France, Spain, Portugal and Italy; in 1786, as many as 1,204 entered the twelve chief Baltic ports. No full statistics of these voyages are available, nor of those to Great Britain and Holland, but some indication of the extent of the trade is given by the value of imports by Great Britain from Denmark, which in 1791 was £182,040. With the outbreak of the European war, this trade received a great impetus. A lively trade developed with the ports of France, Spain and Portugal, to which Danish ships carried the products of the West Indies, of the Far East and of the Baltic lands. The French harbors especially were much frequented by the Danes and Norwegians. They unloaded their cargoes of butter, cheese, pickled meat, dried fish and all manner of Baltic produce; and they returned laden with wines, brandies, dyes, paper and many articles of silk and wool.[27] Incidentally, they would often load up at one French port with French goods to be discharged at another French port, thus relieving the French of the perils of carrying on their own coasting trade.[28] The actual trade between Denmark and the Mediterranean countries was in itself of no great importance. It consisted in the main of exchanging dried fish for silk and other Italian wares. The Danes had, however, made friendly alliances with the Barbary States; and accordingly they were given preference as carriers by the merchants in the Mediterranean ports.[29] The period from 1793 to 1799 also witnessed a marked increase in the trade between Denmark and the United States, a considerable number of Danish ships being chartered by American merchants for the conveyance of their goods. The Americans brought their wares to Copenhagen, where they either

---

the Conseil des Anciens on the effects of the decree of 18 January 1798, it was stated that English ships were insured at a premium of 5 per cent, while neutrals bound to France had to pay 20 to 30 per cent. *Moniteur,* An VII, p. 564, quoted in Mahan, II, 257. Cf. *supra,* p. 120.

[27] Thaarup, *Statistik der danischen monarchie,* p. 538.

[28] This abuse of the rights of neutrality was the subject of strong protests by the British Government; cf. *supra,* p. 91.

[29] Thaarup, *op. cit.,* p. 539. The alliances were very expensive.

bought Baltic products imported by the Danes, or were provided with letters of credit by the house of Ryberg, with which they voyaged on to Russia.[30]

The development of the entrepôt trade was facilitated by an ordinance, issued early in 1793, allowing goods intended for transshipment to remain in bond without paying duty. At this time the duchies of Slesvig[31] and Holstein were under the Danish crown. They provided a convenient back door through which colonial and other goods could be supplied to France and other countries whose seaports were blockaded by the British. The plan of rationing neutral countries, which was applied during the World War, was not adopted by the British at this time. Indeed, the British Admiralty Court ruled that for a neutral ship to carry goods to a neutral port, to be forwarded by land or by interior canal navigation to a blockaded port, did not constitute a breach of the blockade.[32] There was, therefore, nothing to stop this trade, so long as Denmark remained neutral. It continued even after the enforcement of Napoleon's Continental System, large quantities of colonial and other products, for example, being smuggled into Hamburg by way of Altona. There are, of course, no statistics in existence measuring a trade which was largely illegal; but some idea of the extent of it may be gathered from the statistics of Danish trade with Great Britain. As the war continued, these figures indicated an increasing preponderance of imports from over exports to Great Britain. Evidently Denmark played a stronger and stronger part in the distribution on the Continent of the goods of the world.[33]

In Table 5 are brought together the value of foreign trade with Great Britain and the price and exchange rate data by reference to which some inference regarding changes in quantities of exports and imports may be made. In 1793 and 1794 exports were stimulated by belligerent demands. They rose sharply in 1803, when the blockade of the Elbe forced the wares of central Germany into Danish channels. The changes in imports are quite as pertinent. Following the

---

[30] Nathanson, *Danmarks handel*, I, 206.

[31] See p. 255, *infra*, for alternative spelling of this duchy.

[32] *The Jonge Pieter*, 4 C. Robinson (1801) 79.

[33] Oddy, *op. cit.*, p. 390, ascribed the great increase in imports to the causes "which have driven the trade of the continent to the northern ports of Europe." Cf. *supra*, p. 110. Exports, he added, have admittedly not increased so rapidly, but more so than the figures indicate. He felt that the English customs officials tended to undervalue the Danish products.

TABLE 5

DENMARK'S TRADE WITH GREAT BRITAIN [a]

1791-1803

Year	Exports (Value in pounds sterling, hundreds)	British Exchange on Hamburg (Percentage of par)	British General Price Level Index	EXPORT INDICES [b]		
				Unadjusted	Adjusted for Exchange Rate Fluctuations	Adjusted for Price Level Fluctuations
1791	1,820	102.0	95.5	97.2	99.2	106.9
1792	1,850	98.0	99.8	98.8	96.9	104.0
1793	2,052	104.6	106.2	109.6	114.7	108.4
1794	2,099	100.1	105.2	112.1	112.3	111.9
1795	1,543	93.3	125.5	82.4	77.0	68.9
1797	1,346	102.9	118.0	71.9	74.0	64.0
1800	2,416	87.1	151.3	129.0	112.5	89.6
1801	2,088	88.3	164.2	111.5	98.6	71.3
1802	1,557	93.2	127.7	83.1	77.6	68.4
1803	3,247	95.8	137.3	173.4	166.3	132.6

Year	Imports (Value in pounds sterling, hundreds)	IMPORT INDICES [b]		
		Unadjusted	Adjusted for Exchange Rate Fluctuations	Adjusted for Price Level Fluctuations
1791	3,543	91.0	93.8	101.9
1792	3,127	80.3	79.5	86.0
1793	2,912	74.8	79.0	75.3
1794	4,892	125.7	127.1	127.7
1795	4,985	128.1	120.7	109.1
1797	6,709	172.4	179.1	156.2
1800	5,407	138.9	122.2	98.2
1801	4,165	107.0	95.4	69.7
1802	5,375	138.1	130.0	115.6
1803	20,206	519.2	502.3	406.9

[a] The values in pounds sterling are from Oddy, *op. cit.*, p. 392. Oddy gives the figures for England and Scotland separately; in this table they are added together.

In making the adjustments in this table, British exchange rate figures were adapted from a table in an article by Norman J. Silberling, "British Financial Experience, 1790-1830," in the *Review of Economic Statistics*, I (1919), 287, Unlike the Swedish exchange figures given in the table illustrating the foreign trade of Sweden, they show appreciation and depreciation directly. Accordingly. absolute figures were obtained by simple multiplication; then converted to index numbers (adjusted for exchange rate fluctuations); base: 1791-1795 = 100. British price level indices are adapted from those of W. S. Jevons, *Investigations in Currency and Finance* (London, 1884), pp. 119 ff. Jevons used data gathered by Tooke (*History of British Prices*). The price indices in this table are in terms of 1790-1794 as 100, because 1795 was a year of sensational price advances. Adjusted absolute figures were obtained by simple division; then converted to index numbers; base: 1791-1795 = 100.

[b] Base: 1791-1795 = 100.

conquest of Holland and the blockade of the Texel in 1795, they moved up sharply in 1797. The adjusted figures indicate that imports were approximately 45 per cent higher in 1797 than they were in 1795.[34] Another even more striking increase took place in 1803, the year of the blockade of Hamburg. By this time, the value of the pound was approximately 6 per cent below the 1791 level, and the British price level had moved up nearly 40 per cent. Since the value figures are from British sources, they must accordingly be used with caution. Even the adjusted figures, however, show a tremendous increase. Allowing for price changes, imports in 1803 were more than 250 per cent higher than they were in 1802. The gains in imports represented deflections of transit trade, rather than increases in Danish consumption.

The figures indicating the course of Danish shipping reflect the increases in trade. Nathanson cites an increase in tonnage of Danish-Norwegian vessels, between 1792 and 1798, from 208,000 tons to 268,368 tons.[35] During the same period the Danish-Norwegian shipyards turned out 387 new vessels, weighing a total of 51,222 tons. The number of seamen employed in the overseas trade during these years is estimated to have been 20,000.[36] If Oddy is correct, declines must have taken place after 1798, for he gives the tonnage in 1802 as only 239,864 tons.[37] In interpreting these figures, it must be remembered that various authorities differ. Such differences will be understood if one reflects that many of the ships which flew the Danish flag were actually foreign vessels registered as Danish and perhaps fraudulently transferred to nominal Danish owners for a money payment.

Doubts have been cast on the trustworthiness of figures purporting to show the growth of the Danish carrying trade, but a full list of Danish vessels entering foreign ports in the year 1800 exists. This list, printed by Nathanson, may be compared with that given by Falbe-Hansen and Scharling for the year 1805, "the most prosperous

[34] The figures adjusted for exchange rate fluctuations point to a 48 per cent increase, while those adjusted for price fluctuations indicate a 43 per cent increase.

[35] Nathanson, *Danmarks handel*, I, 202. The 1792 figure includes vessels under 20 tons burden. Oddy, *op. cit.*, p. 386, estimates the tonnage for 1797 as 266,566 tons, and the number of vessels as 2,447. Nathanson's figures for 1797 are 2,438 vessels and 264,054 tons.

[36] Oddy, *op. cit.*, p. 386. The number of vessels is given as 2,268, of which 683 are credited to Denmark, 990 to Norway, 401 to Slesvig, and 194 to Holstein.

[37] Nathanson, *op. cit.*, I, 203. He also estimates the number employed in the coasting trade: 6,000 to 8,000.

year for Danish shipping." [38] The most striking fact revealed by a comparison of these lists, is the immense increase in the number of Danish vessels entering the ports of Russia and Prussia. It was in 1805 that the vessels of Denmark (exclusive of Norway and the duchies) reached their maximum number in this period; [39] it was also a year of increased demand for the timber and grain of which the Russian port of Riga and the Prussian port of Memel were the

TABLE 6

DANISH VESSELS ENTERING FOREIGN PORTS

Country	1800		1805	
	Number	Tons	Number	Tons
England..................	1,651	263,512	1,578	222,950
Holland..................	444	47,646	575	66,388
France..................	587	47,222	555	53,156
Spain....................	550	68,848	425	52,604
Portugal................	148	18,638	193	25,236
Italy....................	127	14,900	225	26,496
Hanse Towns............	558	28,330	564	18,276
Prussia..................	168	14,624	627	34,736
Russia..................	235	25,754	783	55,350
Sweden..................	21	1,050	18	631
North America...........	...	...	15	1,952
East India and China......	...	...	21	6,080
Danish West Indies.......	...	...	87	15,624

chief Baltic centers of supply; and it was also the year following the proclamation of the British blockade of the Channel ports. Perhaps all of these facts had a bearing on this increase. Other outstanding increases are in entries of the ports of Italy, of Portugal and of Holland.

By far the most important Danish trading center was Copenhagen. Unfortunately, statistics recording the number of vessels entering this port exist only for the years 1796 and 1798. Certain of these figures are quite significant. From China and the East Indies came ten ships in 1796 and sixteen in 1798. Of the ships of the privileged West India Company, forty-three entered in 1796, and forty in 1798, bringing coffee from St. Croix and St. Thomas. Twenty-nine ships came from North America in 1796, and thirty-seven in 1798, with cargoes of rice, sugar, coffee, tobacco and rum. The majority

[38] Nathanson, *Danmarks handel*, I, 203; Falbe-Hansen og Scharling, *op. cit.*, III, 421.

[39] 1,020 vessels of over 20 tons burden; Falbe-Hansen og Scharling, *op. cit.*, III, 420.

of this colonial produce was destined for Germany or Russia. If we may judge from the later course of customs receipts, this trade increased.[40]

All the writers on this phase of Danish history comment on the profitableness of the trade. "The great warehouses and rich palace-like mansions of the merchant princes," exclaim Falbe-Hansen and Scharling, "stand to this day as the living memorials of that golden age." [41] Thaarup points to the dividends of the Danish East India Company which rose from 30 *Rigsdalers* per share in 1792 to 90 *Rigsdalers* per share in 1802.[42] Both Nathanson and Oddy advert to the profits made in the entrepôt trade.[43] Produce from the Far East alone sold in Germany and Holland for 18,000,000 *Rigsdalers* annually. This prosperity was accompanied by a rise in prices, largely due to violent fluctuations in the value of paper money. Together these factors contributed to both the feverish speculation of the period, and to the severe liquidation which ensued when the conditions which had supported the prosperity passed. That the prosperity was not widespread is indicated by the periodic shortages of food and low wage rates that characterized the period.[44]

SCHLESWIG-HOLSTEIN

Although, as already pointed out, the duchies of Schleswig (Slesvig) and Holstein shared in the prosperity which the earlier years of the war brought to Denmark as a whole, they were economically more dependent upon their German neighbors. It was through Holstein that the trade of Bremen and Lübeck with Hamburg was conducted; while Holstein's principal port, Altona, was so close a neighbor of the great Hanse city on the Elbe that it shared all the vicissitudes of fortune which befell that city during the wars. Like Hamburg it flourished during the earlier years of the war; and like Hamburg, it suffered severely when, in 1803, the British blockade diverted the traffic which had passed up the Elbe.

[40] In 1796, receipts were 610,650 Rdl.; in 1798, 787,198 Rdl.; in 1810, 810,300 Rdl.; and in 1806, 1,213,018 Rdl.—Nathanson, *Historisk-statistisk fremstilling af Danmarks national og stats-husholdning* (Copenhagen, 1836). Nevertheless, Nathanson states elsewhere that navigation in and out of Copenhagen was not as lively from 1800 to 1805, as in 1796 and 1798; *Danmarks handel*, II, 253.

[41] Falbe-Hansen og Scharling, *op. cit.*, III, 418.

[42] Thaarup, *Tabellen til den statistiske udsigt over den danske stat* (Copenhagen, 1825), Tabel XXV.

[43] Nathanson, *Danmarks handel*, I, 206; Oddy, *op. cit.*, p. 386.

[44] Nathanson, *op. cit.*, p. 795; Falbe-Hansen og Scharling, *op. cit.*, III, 421.

But although the blockade of the Elbe caused suffering in Altona, it brought a period of great prosperity to the duchies as a whole. The great increase in the trade of Tönning, Husum, Flensburg, and Kiel led to the establishment of manufacture in these towns. Under the protection of the Continental System, the manufactures developed rapidly. During the French occupation of Hamburg the trade in smuggled goods, always profitable, flourished especially; in this, Altona shared. Its share, however, hardly compensated for

TABLE 7

VESSELS BELONGING TO ALTONA [a]

Year	Number	Tons
1789	112	15,154
1794	154	20,908
1799	249	36,352
1802	143	22,012
1805	148	15,998
1806	150	20,772
1809	37	4,771
1813	39	5,403

[a] From Heinz Munte, *Das Altonaer Handlungshaus van der Smissen* (Altona, 1932).

the disastrous effects of Napoleon's economic policy. If it was not occupied by the French, its trade was interfered with quite as much as if it had been.[45] The effect of the Continental System on the trade of Altona is illustrated by its shipping statistics. (See Table 7.)

To ports like Tönning on the Eider and the smaller Holstein ports, had come the traffic diverted from Hamburg and Altona. With the conclusion of peace, however, this artificially stimulated prosperity came to a sudden end. Commerce once more took its old course to Hamburg.[46] The new manufacturing industries, deprived

[45] The harbors of Altona and Hamburg, then as now, were separated by no barrier; and their wharves on the banks of the Elbe were continuous. With Denmark allied to France, moreover, Altona could expect nothing less than the strictest enforcement of Napoleon's decrees; cf. *supra*, p. 140.

[46] "Look at Tönning . . . at Husum, Flensburg and Kiel which thought maybe that the Goddess of Commerce would establish a community among them and so opened wide their gates and caused their barns to be enlarged! Because a few dozen clerks from the imperial cities had settled in their midst and taken possession of their warehouses in order to tide over a time of trouble, they believed themselves to be half Hamburg and the whole of Lübeck."—Hedemann-Hesspen, "Westensee," *Zeitschrift der Gesellschaft für schleswig-holsteinische Geschichte*, XLVIII, Band S (1918), 41 ff.

of such protection as had been theirs during the war, proved unable to meet the competition of English products.

SUMMARY

Norway was the first section of the kingdom to prosper as a result of its neutrality. Her fisheries and more especially her forests made her a beneficiary of the war-time demands. By her ready supplies of "naval stores" she was able to extract favorable treatment from the Mistress of the Seas even after nominally at war with her. Agriculture and pasturage suffered because incomes in these fields could not keep pace with the rising prices and also because of the deflection of capital to shipping and shipbuilding. Except for this, Norway's gains from her neutrality appear far to have overbalanced such losses as were occasioned by belligerent activities.

Denmark's prosperity dated from the conquest and blockade of Holland in 1795, which diverted to her ports and particularly to her vessels, some portion of the trade of central Europe. This advantage was accentuated by the occupation of Hanover and the blockade of Hamburg in 1802. Only in the transit trade, and later in the smuggling trade, does Denmark seem to have benefited by her neutrality. The gains were not widely distributed and represented, in part, returns to foreign investors. The losses were considerable, Denmark having been, next to the United States, the chief sufferer at belligerent hands. In proportion to her resources, the losses were perhaps greater. It seems unlikely, however, that they were great enough to equal the profits of the transit trade.

Altona shared the benefits of the transit trade until the blockade of the Elbe in 1803. Her part in the smuggling trade that ensued hardly compensated her for the loss of regular trade. Industry in the duchies in general was stimulated, first by smuggling from the smaller Holstein ports, and later by the protection given manufactures by the Continental System. Although ephemeral, the prosperity of the duchies seems to have been more than enough to compensate for the losses occasioned by belligerent restrictions.

SWEDEN

In his survey of the conditions of trade in Europe, published in 1805, Oddy remarks that Sweden, in spite of her long coast line and numerous harbors, had never been famous for sea power or commerce. The Swedish kings, in pursuit of conquests on land, had wasted the revenues that might have been employed to foster trade and industry. Thus when the Revolutionary Wars broke out, the internal resources of the country remained largely undeveloped, communication between the interior and the coast especially being hampered by the fact that the projected canal system, which was to link up the great lakes and so provide a purely Swedish waterway from the North Sea to the Gulf of Bothnia, remained incomplete.

Other causes contributed to deprive Sweden of the full benefit she might have derived from her neutrality. The overseas trade of Sweden was in a certain measure hampered by old-world restrictions. Foreign commerce (imports and exports) was the exclusive privilege of the staple towns, while the "land towns," which included the ports not having staple rights, were confined to the coasting trade. The old staple towns were twenty-four in number, and there were in addition several new ones. Only two were, however, of first-class importance, namely, Stockholm and Gothenburg (Göteborg).[47] There were also several political factors. The internal dissensions, which culminated in the deposition of King Gustavus IV in March 1809, hardly provided the stability that encourages commercial expansion. Then too, the perpetually strained relations with Russia ultimately led to war and the conquest of Finland by the armies of the Emperor Alexander I. Moreover, with the advance of Napoleon's conquests on the Continent, the possession of Swedish Pomerania became a doubtful blessing.[48]

In general the trade returns tend to show that the commerce of Sweden, during the period of her neutrality, rather diminished than increased. Not until 1807, with the enforcement of Napoleon's Berlin Decree, did she begin to make considerable advances in trade. In that year she became the entrepôt for contraband goods seeking entrance through the Baltic ports to the countries subjected to the Continental System. Hitherto her exports, expressed in *Riksdaler*

[47] The former of which absorbed five-twelfths and the latter four-twelfths of the total foreign trade. Only the remaining fourth was left to be divided among the rest.

[48] Sweden was eventually forced into an alliance with France (November 1810). "Any hostilities against Great Britain," Count Axel von Rosen, governor of Gothenburg, assured Admiral Saumarez at this time, were "merely extorted by the precarious position of Pomerania."—Rosen to Johnson, for transmission to Saumarez. P.R.O. F.O. 7. 2. In No. I Johnson. Gothenburg 20 November 1810. Cf. *supra*, p. 129.

values, had been consistently greater than her imports. Beginning with 1808, however, this relation was reversed, and in each of the remaining intervals imports exceeded exports. The value of exports was somewhat higher in 1794 than in 1792; and in the closing years of the century, and from 1801 to 1803, it rose again above the pre-war level. It is abundantly evident, however, that these increases did not represent a greater volume of exports. As indicated in Table 8, the value of the *Riksdaler* fell sharply by reason of inflation. Ac-

TABLE 8

SWEDEN'S FOREIGN TRADE *a*

1792-1813

				EXPORT INDICES *b*		
Year	Exports (*Riksdaler* value, thousands)	Index of Exchange on Hamburg	General Price Level Index	Unad-justed	Adjusted for Exchange Rate Fluc-tuations	Adjusted for Price Level Fluc-tuations
1792	6,147	91.6	91.3	99.0	107.8	108.1
1793	5,695	104.7	97.0	91.8	87.4	94.3
1794	6,965	109.7	102.7	112.2	102.0	108.7
1795	6,019	94.1	109.0	97.0	102.8	88.7
Average	6,207	100.0	100.0	100.0	100.0	100.0
1796	6,493	93.7	106.5	104.6	111.3	97.9
1797	6,136	102.0	110.3	98.9	96.7	89.3
1798	7,163	117.6	116.8	115.4	97.9	98.5
1799	6,618	134.5	134.2	106.6	79.0	79.2
1800	5,754	125.7	148.1	92.7	73.6	62.4
Average	6,433	114.7	123.2	103.6	91.7	85.5
1801	7,229	134.5	147.9	116.5	86.4	78.5
1802	8,228	135.0	139.4	132.6	97.9	94.8
1803	6,898	136.6	149.7	111.1	81.1	74.0
1804	6,156	137.2	153.5	99.2	72.1	64.4
1805	6,118	136.8	166.6	98.4	71.9	59.9
Average	6,926	136.0	151.4	111.6	81.9	74.1
1806	6,155	138.4	176.9	99.2	71.4	55.9
1807	7,423	143.6	178.8	119.6	83.0	66.7
1808	5,836	144.9	228.8	94.0	64.7	41.0
1809	9,405	166.2	244.6	151.5	90.9	61.7
1810	11,170	207.9	241.6	180.0	86.3	74.2
Average	7,998	160.2	214.1	128.9	79.3	59.9
1811	6,357	288.7	274.5	102.4	35.4	37.2
1812	9,126	244.9	317.9	147.0	59.9	46.1
1813	17,335	248.3	318.8	279.3	112.2	87.3
Average	10,939	260.6	303.7	176.2	69.2	56.9

For notes *a* and *b*, see p. 260.

TABLE 8 *(Continued)*

SWEDEN'S FOREIGN TRADE *a*

1792–1813

Year	Imports (*Riksdaler* value, thousands)	IMPORT INDICES *b*		
		Unadjusted	Adjusted for Exchange Rate Fluctuations	Adjusted for Price Level Fluctuations
1792	3,760	107.1	116.1	116.7
1793	3,214	91.6	86.8	93.9
1794	3,517	101.8	92.1	98.6
1795	3,490	99.5	104.9	90.8
Average	3,509	100.0	100.0	100.0
1796	3,510	100.0	106.0	93.4
1797	3,840	109.4	106.5	98.7
1798	3,592	102.4	86.4	87.2
1799	3,072	87.5	64.6	64.9
1800	2,997	85.4	67.4	57.4
Average	3,402	96.9	86.2	80.3
1801	3,976	113.3	83.6	76.2
1802	3,597	102.5	75.4	73.1
1803	3,355	95.6	69.5	63.5
1804	4,946	140.9	102.0	91.3
1805	4,170	118.8	86.2	71.0
Average	4,009	114.2	83.3	75.0
1806	4,522	128.9	92.4	72.5
1807	4,830	137.6	95.2	76.6
1808	8,131	231.7	158.7	100.8
1809	11,196	319.1	190.6	129.2
1810	15,749	441.1	210.6	181.6
Average	8,832	251.7	149.5	112.1
1811	7,176	204.5	70.3	74.1
1812	12,699	361.9	146.7	113.3
1813	29,265	834.0	333.4	260.2
Average	16,380	466.8	183.7	149.2

a Figures for exchange rates and the price level are adapted from Karl Amark, "En svensk prishistorisk studie," *Ekonomisk tidskrift*, XXIII (1921), 152-153; 166-168. The exchange rate index is so constructed as to indicate the fluctuations in the amounts of Swedish media that exchanged for corresponding Hamburg media. The adjusted figures were first obtained in absolute form, by simple division, then converted to index numbers; base: 1792-1795 = 100.

b Base: 1792-1795 = 100.

cordingly prices advanced sharply, and when allowance is made for these two types of change, exports are seen to have fallen off in volume.

Unfortunately, figures indicating directly the physical quantities of goods exported are not available, except in the case of one or two commodities. The principal exports of Sweden were iron, naval stores and some copper. Swedish iron was plentiful, of high quality and in great demand in England for making steel. There can be no doubt that the export of bar iron was adversely affected by war conditions. The amount exported in 1792, 56,599 tons, was only equaled in 1802, the year of peace, when it was 59,288 tons. The export to England, her best customer, followed the same trend. England took 29,807 tons in 1792 and 30,406 tons in 1802; but in the years of war never took more than 24,767 tons (1794) and in 1811, when Great Britain and Sweden were nominally at war, took as little as 1,615 tons.[49] Exports to other nations also shrank and showed even more violent fluctuations.[50] Two of the more spectacular increases represent effects of the increases in imports during the operation of the Continental System. The export to Holland, for instance, rose from 27 tons in 1809 to 13,669 tons in 1811. In this latter year part of the export may have been destined for England. The export to the West Indies, which in 1792 was 232 tons, increased to 4,034 in 1809 and 14,214 in 1810.[51]

During the early years of the war, the export of naval stores increased, as might be expected. Shipments of tar rose from 113,274 barrels in 1792, to 179,586 barrels in 1800. After 1807 there was a distinct decline, however, and in 1809 only 53,486 barrels were exported. The value of timber exports increased, with occasional lapses, throughout the war; and the increases in general seem to have more than kept pace with the changes in the value of money.[52]

The only other products which seem to have been exported in notably greater amounts are fish and fish products. After remaining stable from 1792 to 1797, the value of their export more than dou-

[49] Before the Declaration of War in November 1810, the export to England had never been less than 16,203 tons.

[50] Exports to France, e.g., which in 1792 had amounted to 4,720 tons, fell off 50 per cent during the next five years; then declined even more sharply to 611 tons in 1800. From 1802 to 1804 they were above the pre-war level, but from 1807 to 1811 slumped badly. In 1812, they rose once more above the 1792 figure.

[51] The connection of this extraordinary increase with the increase in imports is confirmed by the figures for the export from Gothenburg, the chief center for the entrepôt trade. These figures reached their highest point in 1810, viz., 16,143 tons, about ⅝ths of which were exported to America. The corresponding figure for 1800 is only 510 tons.

[52] The value of timber exports in 1792 was 335,882 Rdl.; in 1802, 720,901 Rdl.; in 1808, 1,372,291 Rdl.; and in 1813, 1,192,820 Rdl.; since no data on prices of timber are available, it is impossible to be certain that this increase in value represented some increase in volume.

bled in 1798; and after a slump in 1800, it was more than three times as great in 1801. Until 1807 the values fluctuated through a range just below this point. In the years that followed the closing of the German Baltic ports, however, the export fell to unprecedentedly low levels. In the case of fish as in the case of timber, the increases in value appear to have outdistanced the increases in prices.[53]

Even the value of Swedish imports failed to increase until 1804. Prior to that year only twice had the value of imports in 1792 been equaled or surpassed. The increases in the period from 1804 to 1807, while unquestionably representing an advance over the level of the immediately preceding years, can hardly have indicated a greater volume of imports than obtained in 1792. It is not until 1808 that the increases in the value of imports outdistanced the change in the value of money; and not until 1809 did the rate of increase exceed the rate of increase in prices. In only one year after this, however, was the upward trend of imports reversed. This occurred during the war with England in 1811.

The extraordinary behavior of the import series is emphasized by comparing it with the course of trade with Great Britain. In the opening years of the century, exports to Great Britain were three times as valuable as imports from it. This was the case despite the fact that the League of Armed Neutrality and the bombardment of Copenhagen strained the relations of the two countries almost to the breaking point. In 1808, however, the situation was completely reversed; for when the Continental System became effective, Sweden became the principal entrepôt for British goods seeking an entrance to the continent through the Southern Baltic ports. Other foreign merchants as well made use of Sweden in this way.

A proof that the bulk of this increase in imports was not intended for Swedish consumption will be found upon examining the figures for the goods in bond. In 1792 these had been valued at 51,807 *Riksdalers;* and the highest figure reached before the issue of the Berlin Decree was 158,475 *Riksdalers* (1804). In 1807 their value was 511,197 *Riksdalers,* and a year later it was five times as great. Except for the interval of the war with England, this trend continued until, in 1813, the value of goods in bond was 10,219,283 *Riksdalers.* An analysis of these imports will be pertinent. The principal cate-

[53] This inference is also made from a comparison of the changes in value of exports with the changes in the price level and in exchange rates, because of the absence of information bearing directly on the prices of the particular products.

gories under which they may be listed are colonial goods, textiles, raw materials and liquors.

Imports of tobacco, in 1808, were valued at 165,608 *Riksdalers;* in 1809, at 417,319 *Riksdalers;* and in 1810, at 575,648 *Riksdalers.* The value of imports of sugar was more than twice as great in 1808 as in 1807, and twice again as great in 1810. Textile materials were smuggled into Germany to supply the needs of Saxon, Silesian and other weavers. Sweden imported twice as much silk in 1812 as in 1792; the volume of cotton imports was nearly eight times as great in 1809 as in 1792 and twice again as great in 1810. Imports of hemp reached their high point in 1809, at which time they were two-thirds again as great as in 1792. The value of imports of wine in 1807 had increased 400 per cent over 1792 and after further increases in 1808 and 1809, reached their high point in 1813. In this year their value was more than 900 per cent greater than in 1792. The value of imports of spirituous beverages rose at an even greater rate.[54]

The principal port whence goods "forbidden" under Napoleon's Continental System were smuggled to various points on the Continent, was Gothenburg. Conveniently situated on the North Sea coast, it had become as early as 1650 an important center for the overseas trade of Sweden. It seemed to the Swedish East India Company the logical point for its headquarters, when given a royal charter in 1731. Gothenburg then became a distributing center for imports from the Far East. After 1760 the port developed a West Indian trade, and beginning in 1783, was favored by shippers from the United States.

What led to its importance in the transit trade was the granting in 1794, by King Gustavus IV, of "A general liberty of entrepôt for foreign merchandise." [55] After the Berlin Decree, the port joined with Heligoland in providing a channel through which foreign trade might succeed in circumventing the barriers created by that pronouncement. The growth of this transit trade is most aptly illustrated by the rise in value of goods taken out of bond for reëxport. Goods in bond in 1800 have been valued at 49,207 *Riksdalers,* and in 1805, at 73,434 *Riksdalers.* In 1810, however, the value of reëxports was 2,745,190 *Riksdalers.* Most of these goods were colonial wares. Rice, spices, sugar, coffee, tobacco and cotton were all represented,

[54] Detailed data showing the increases in importation (or value of importation) of all the mentioned commodities will be found in Appendix II, *infra.*

[55] 5 Martens, p. 617.

and they commanded high prices wherever they found a market during the Continental Blockade. The amount of sugar transshipped from Gothenburg in 1810 was fully sixteen times as great as in 1805. In the case of coffee the proportion was as nine to one; and of cotton, as one hundred and seventy-four to one.[56]

These increases in trade were naturally reflected in the shipping statistics. Reporting from Gothenburg in May 1808, Admiral Saumarez called the port "a place of great trade," and stated that at the time at least twelve hundred vessels flying different flags were in the port.[57] From 1791 to 1795, the annual average tonnage of outgoing vessels had been 50,000 tons. Later, declines took place, and in 1805 the figure was only 28,700 tons. For 1810, however, it was 160,000 tons. The growth of Swedish shipping generally must be treated more critically, for it was largely due to the transference of vessels to the Swedish flag. The growth was nevertheless remarkable. Of 9,493 ships passing the Sound in 1790, only 430 were Swedish. For the period 1793-1804, inclusive, an average of 2,160 of the average of 10,002 vessels passing the Sound were Swedish.[58]

The damage to the trade of Sweden caused by her enforced declaration of war on Great Britain, on 17 November 1810, was less serious than might have been expected, owing to the determination of the Swedish Government not to engage in active hostilities and to the tactful way in which Admiral Saumarez dealt with the situation. Merchant ships flying the British ensign had ceased to engage in the Baltic trade since 1807, but large quantities of British goods continued to be exported to the northern countries under neutral flags. This gives a special significance to the royal instructions given to Count Axel von Rosen, the governor of Gothenburg, after the declaration of war. In the case of vessels and cargoes belonging to Swedish subjects and flying the American or any other acceptable flag, he was not to recur to "extremities of diligence"; but, on the contrary, to "suppress facts and facilitate traffic," so far as he could do so without compromising his position.[59] The result of this accom-

---

[56] For absolute figures reflecting these increases see Appendix II, *infra*, Table 15.

[57] Ross, ed., *Memoirs and Correspondence of Admiral Lord de Saumarez*, II, 105. In September 1810, Count Rosen, governor of Gothenburg, described the roadstead as presenting an appearance such as had never been seen since the Creation. Nineteen British men-of-war and eleven hundred twenty-four merchantmen lay at anchor; quoted by Heckscher, *The Continental System*, p. 236.

[58] Oddy, *op. cit.*, p. 369.

[59] Heckscher, *The Continental System*, p. 236.

modating spirit on both sides was that, though there was a very sharp fall in the quantity and value of imports and exports in 1811, they still considerably exceeded those of any previous year up to and including 1807.[60]

After the breakdown of the Continental System, Swedish trade rebounded from the 1811 levels, and 1813 was a year of unexampled prosperity. Peace was soon to come, however, and the world's trade to flow back into the old channels. The prosperity of Sweden during the wars had been due to the transit trade gained after 1807 rather than to growth of domestic exports during the period of her neutrality. Such prosperity was necessarily impermanent, for with the gains, no attempts had been made to build up industry. All of Sweden suffered in the period of depression that followed. The inflation proved the only lasting heritage of the Napoleonic era. The vaunted trade volume of 1810 and 1813 was not again equaled until 1830.

Unlike the neutral states thus far treated, Sweden did not benefit greatly from the war while still neutral. Hampered by traditional commercial restrictions and political instability, she was unable to avail herself of the opportunities for expanding her export trade. Her geographical position was not such as to make her an important factor in the transit trade until the Berlin Decree drove the trade of the Continent to the northernmost routes. Then her import trade expanded enormously and reflected on Swedish shipping, shipbuilding and such of the peasantry as entered upon smuggling, a temporary prosperity. But by this time, Sweden had been involved in the war on both sides. The country had not enjoyed the fruits of neutrality and as a beneficiary of the smuggling trade had been subjected to relatively little inconvenience even while a belligerent. Her gains were consumed, not principally by belligerent activities, but by speculation in commodities and in shipping. Even the persistence of inflation far beyond the war period could not prevent the liquidations brought about by the diversion of trade into the old channels.

[60] *Memoirs . . . of Admiral Lord de Saumarez, op. cit.,* II, 245. "I knew nothing of politics," wrote the Swedish Admiral Krusenstjerna to Lieutenant (afterwards Sir John) Ross, "but I find our situation very singular. Our *friends* the French and Danes express their friendship to us with unremitted zeal in capturing and robbing from us our merchant vessels, whilst our *enemies* the English let them pass unmolested from one port to another. We did not suffer by one hundred times as much from these two nations, the time we were at war against them, as we do now when they call themselves our friends and allies!"

XI

GERMANY

At the time of the outbreak of the Revolutionary Wars, Germany was far from either political or economic unity. It was a loose confederation of several hundred virtually sovereign states, some large, some small, and bound together only by the shadowy overlordship of the Holy Roman Emperor. The violation by the French Constituent Assembly of the rights of the German princes in Alsace produced a temporary unity in 1792, and the Empire as a whole became involved in the war which France had declared on "the King of Hungary and Bohemia." This unity was, however, of brief duration. It was symbolic that separate treaties should have ended the association.[1] Henceforth Germany, as a political entity, bore no definite relation to the conflict, the several states remaining neutral or taking part in the war on one side or the other as their interests or their fears dictated. Germany became a mere geographical expression when, in 1806, Napoleon established the Confederation of the Rhine, and the faded symbol of the old ideal of political unity, the Holy Roman Empire, came to an end.

As a geographical expression, however, Germany must be considered in any attempt to estimate the economic effects of the French Revolutionary and Napoleonic Wars upon such states as succeeded in maintaining an attitude of neutrality during considerable periods of the war. The most important of these states was Prussia, which remained neutral from 1795 to 1806. The Hanse Towns, though nominally engaged in the war as members of the Empire, succeeded in maintaining a *de facto* neutrality until they were absorbed into Napoleon's system. To understand the economic effect on these states of the commercial war waged by the belligerents, the economic conditions in Germany as a whole, before the war and as affected by the war, must be taken into account; for it was into Germany, and through Germany to other countries, that the great trade from the neutral states passed.

[1] Prussia made a separate peace in April 1795, an example which was followed by the Electorate of Hesse in August of the same year.

In 1790, Germany was predominately an agricultural country. With half a dozen exceptions the cities were small, and had the character of country towns. Industry was undeveloped. Raw materials were processed by hand, either by craftsmen in their own homes or in small establishments. Mines were ill-equipped and incapable of producing for export. Foreign trade was carried on chiefly through Hamburg, Bremen, Lübeck and Stettin. Grain and other agricultural produce, wood and goods in transit (principally from Russia) were the chief exports. Among the outstanding imports were colonial wares, textiles, manufactured and luxury articles, tallow, leather and, at times, wheat and rye from Russia.

Internal trade was little developed, being hampered by the bad state of most of the roads and by the tariff walls by which the numerous small states sought to protect their economic self-sufficiency. All trade was handicapped, moreover, by the variety of the currencies, which differed so greatly in value as to make the marketing of any except local products very difficult. In northern Germany commerce was also hampered by the political power of the great landowners, which made the agrarian interest supreme. These conditions may explain why up to this time there had been in general but little of the spirit of commercial enterprise. It was otherwise, however, with the great German seaports, whose shipping and overseas trade actually profited by the backward condition of the commercial and industrial life of the German hinterland.

The exigencies of the commercial struggle between France and England determined the nature of the benefits to Germany and shifted the favored regions from time to time. From 1795 to 1803, the war gave a marked impetus to the trade of Hamburg. The blockade by the British of the Texel had closed the old trade route from England to western Europe by way of Holland. The stream of goods which had used this route was diverted to Hamburg and up the Elbe, which was linked by a system of canals with the Oder and the Vistula. From Hamburg, British goods might go by water, not only to the heart of Germany, but also to its northern and eastern extremities; to Austria in the south and to Prussia in the north whence they could be forwarded to Russia by way of the Niemen, the Oginsky Canal and the Pripet and so down the Dnieper to the Black Sea.[2] So beneficial did the route through Hamburg prove, to the

---

[2] Oddy, *op. cit.*, pp. 412 ff.

countries of central Europe as well as to England, that it promised permanently to replace the alternative route through Holland. In 1803, however, the French occupied Hanover, and the British felt compelled to blockade the Elbe. This action shattered the new network of communications which had developed and diverted most of the trade of Hamburg to Denmark and Prussia. Stettin, Magdeburg [3] and the hitherto obscure port of Emden in East Friesland profited by this shift.

The export trade in general was not so clearly benefited as the reëxport trade. Because of the war and more especially because of the Continental System, the trade in domestic exports often suffered. Like other subject states, those of Germany were not allowed to export their processed wares to France but were obliged to admit French products free of duty. To some extent, this depressing effect was offset by the stimulation of the internal commerce. The removal of many customs barriers, as the progress of Napoleon absorbed small states into larger units,[4] provided one stimulus. Another was imparted by the very presence of Napoleon's forces and the sums poured into the country from abroad for their upkeep.[5]

Centers which remained consistently Francophile were sometimes rewarded by grants of privileges. Examples of this favoritism were Leipzig and Frankfurt, the capital of the Confederation of the Rhine. Not only because of their French sympathies, but also because the great fairs, held twice a year in these cities, were regarded as channels through which French wares might pass to the other German states, Napoleon had confirmed their privileges. To the extent that the Continental System shut out British goods, German merchants benefited during these fairs, for they were usually able to undersell their French competitors. That the Continental System was not completely effective is illustrated by the trade in colonial goods at Frankfurt in 1810. These goods had come in through the North Sea and Baltic ports and were distributed as far south as Italy and southern France and to the west across the border in France and in Holland.[6]

---

[3] Which became an entrepôt for colonial wares.

[4] Such as, e.g., the Kingdom of Westphalia.

[5] This was a doubtful benefit from the standpoint of the states, because of the drain on their finances.

[6] That autumn, however, General Friant occupied the city, carried out orders to destroy all British manufactures and subjected colonial goods to the Trianon Tariff.

Leipzig, as well as Frankfurt, became a distributing center for smuggled goods. The demands of the textile industries of Germany and Switzerland had been satisfied with increasing difficulty as the blockade of the North Sea ports became more effective. Then Königsberg and other towns on the southern coast of the Baltic began to smuggle in American cotton. Leipzig became the distributing point for this and for colonial goods. At the Michaelmas Fair in 1810, the value of the colonial goods in the city was estimated to be 65,500,000 francs; and after five-sixths of the wares had been distributed, the cellars, vaults and storehouses were still full to overflowing.[7] The war on commerce, then, had encouraged the trade of some German cities and ruined that of others. By cutting off supplies of certain needed articles, it led to the development of some industries and, in certain cases, protected them from foreign competition. With the inauguration of the Continental System, even agriculture profited by the restriction of the imports of such products as dyestuffs, sugar and chicory. It was at this time that the cloth factories of Aachen and Euppen had their origin. The silk manufactures of Krefeld also developed rapidly, so much so, indeed, that the population of the town doubled. The cotton industry likewise began to flourish, particularly in Saxony, owing to the measure of protection given against British competition. The number of spindles in Saxony, which had been between 140,000 to 150,000 in 1800, rose to 276,625 in 1814. Of these, 104,289 were in the Vogtland, and this latter district thus represented a twentyfold increase.[8] Cotton weaving showed a similar increase. On the other hand, the linen industries of Silesia and Lusatia,[9] whose main export was by

[7] Chiefly with cotton, but also with coffee, sugar and indigo. Heckscher, *op. cit.*, p. 185. See also A. Konig, *Die sachsische Baumwollenindustrie am Ende des vorigen Jahrhunderts und wahrend der Kontinentalsperre* (in "Leipziger Studien aus dem Gebiete der Geschichte," V. c. Leipzig, 1899), pp. 241 f.

[8] For the immense growth of cotton spinning in Saxony and Switzerland see Tarle, *op. cit.*, p. 192. He quotes a report to the French Minister of the Interior (Arch. nat. A.F. IV. 1061. September-October 1810) which says: "C'est là une veritable guerre qui menace d'une grande décadence le commerce anglais parce qu'elle assurera son exclusion absolue du continent, lors même que les mesures prohibitives auraient cessé."

[9] The export of linen to Cadiz and thence to South America, was stopped by the Spanish declaration of war against Great Britain in 1795. Agents were then sent to the United States to barter German goods for Latin American products. This "hazardous speculation" was stopped by the financial crisis of 1799 in Hamburg. Commerce through Cadiz was renewed after the Peace of Amiens, but was

way of Hamburg to Spain and America, were ruined by the closure of the Elbe and by British competition.

At the close of 1813, a new era of prosperity for German trade and industry seemed to be opening for German goods followed in the wake of the Allied armies, which destroyed Napoleon's customs barriers as they advanced. A certain amount of machinery had been introduced into Germany, and the processes of manufacture had been otherwise improved. As peace drew near, however, these improvements were still insufficient to enable German manufacturers to meet the lower prices of English goods, or to produce a product of as high quality. To a more detailed examination of these developments, region by region, we now turn.

THE HANSE CITIES

HAMBURG

It was the French conquest of Holland in 1795 that opened for Hamburg a brief period of prosperity. Dutch trade, which had been increased by the new commerce opened up with the United States of America, was now interrupted by the British blockade of the Texel. Since most of western Europe was now closed to Holland, the stream of goods in search of a market on the Continent had to find new channels through Germany. The most obvious channel was that by way of Hamburg and the Elbe. The great Hanseatic city had for centuries carried on a flourishing trade with England, the Scandinavian countries, the Baltic generally and Russia. It now obtained a practical monopoly of the commerce for which it had hitherto been competing with Holland, namely, the trade in colonial goods and that with southwestern Germany and Switzerland.[10]

The effect on the imports of Hamburg was immediate and sustained. Imports of sugar, which had declined since the opening of the war from nearly 53 million pounds to about 35 million pounds, increased to nearly 87 million pounds in 1795; and in 1799 and 1801 exceeded 100 million pounds. Imports of coffee, which had been 21½ million pounds in 1791, were 42 million pounds in 1795

---

again stopped in 1803 with the cessation of exports from Hamburg and Altona. "And now," wrote Oddy, "an opening is made for the Irish merchants and manufacturers to introduce theirs."—*European Commerce*, p. 219.

[10] Ernst Baasch, *Hamburg und Holland im 17ten und 18ten Jahrhundert* (reprinted separately from the *Hansische Geschichtsblätter*).

and nearly 46 million pounds in 1798. In 1794, Hamburg had imported 8½ thousand tons of rice; the following year imports increased to nearly 13½ thousand tons and in 1797 reached a figure of
more than 30 thousand tons. Hamburg had imported 70,411 hides in
1791, but in 1795 imported three times that many. In 1797, imports
of hides reached their high point of 269,862, and in three of the
next five years exceeded the 1795 figure. Imports of cotton rose
from a pre-war figure of 3,685 bales to 10,143 bales in 1795 and
12,668 bales in 1800. Hamburg had imported as high as 5,606 sacks
of pepper in 1793, but in 1795 this rose to 5,723 sacks and in 1799
to 10,944 sacks.[11] Imports and exports of grain showed an even
more remarkable increase. The annual average for the decade 1793
to 1802 was two-thirds again as great as for the preceding ten
years in the case of imports, and twice as great in the case of exports.[12]

Some of the import figures began to exhibit an upward trend as
early as 1793. This was due to the operation of a second factor.
During the period from 1793 to 1802, England supplied a great part
of the Continent with West Indian produce, and the chief entrepôt
for this trade was Hamburg. The value of British goods exported to
Germany had never exceeded two million pounds before 1792. Under
the impetus of these two kinds of transit trade, however, it rose during the next decade, as high as eight million pounds.[13] Before the
war, France had supplied a considerable portion of the demand of
the Continental countries for this produce. By the middle of the
last decade of the eighteenth century, she was importing her own
supplies from these countries, especially from Germany.

Direct trade with France was greatly curtailed by the activity of
British cruisers and privateers, but it was never wholly interrupted.
This decline was more than compensated by the new trade now
opened up. A new direct trade with the West Indies and Latin
America developed, and that with the United States made rapid
strides. Increased trade with Russia also played an important part
in furthering the prosperity of Hamburg. Russian exports of tallow

[11] Detailed data on the effect of the French conquest on the course of imports
by Hamburg of colonial and American produce will be found in Appendix III,
Table 16, *infra.*

[12] Complete figures for the import and export of grain by Hamburg for the
period 1793 to 1804 will be found in Appendix III, Table 17, *infra.*

[13] Even allowing for the depreciation of the pound, this represents an increase
of 250 per cent.

and cereals increased immensely when commerce with Holland was interrupted, and these were diverted to the northern seaports of Germany.

The mercantile marine of the city, however, in spite of the attractions of the neutral flag, was small compared with the great volume of its trade. In 1782 the number of vessels sailing under the city's flag had been 159, and by 1798 it had risen to 248, a number never again equaled until 1840. The bulk of Hamburg's trade, in short, was carried in foreign bottoms. As to the exact number of ships entering or leaving the port there is some uncertainty, as no trustworthy and systematic statistics have been published. It has to be remembered, too, that organized smuggling played a large part, and of this naturally no record remains. The figures available, however, sufficiently prove the great increase of traffic through the port. The number of ships entering the port from 1791 until 1802, the year before the blockade, is given in Table 9.[14]

TABLE 9

THE NUMBER OF SHIPS WHICH ENTERED THE PORT
OF HAMBURG

1791-1802

Year	Number	Year	Number
1791	1,504	1797	1,869
1792	1,700	1798	1,901 [a]
1793	1,455	1800	1,895
1794	1,820	1801	2,177
1795	2,107	1802	2,108
1796	1,919		

[a] Oddy's figure for 1798 is 2,005. He estimates that in the year of the blockade (proclaimed June 1803) 1,615 vessels entered; and that in 1804 no vessels entered.

[14] The figures for the shipping and trade of Hamburg are taken, unless otherwise stated, from the following works: T. F. Ehrmann, *Allgemeines, historisches, statistisches, geographisches Handlungs-, Post- und Zeitungslexikon* (Erfurt, 1804-1824); Ernst Baasch, "Hamburgs Handel und Schiffahrt am Ende des 18. Jahrhunderts," in *Hamburg um die Jahrhundertwende*, Hamburg, 1900; Baasch, "Beiträge zur Geschichte der Handelsbeziehungen zwischen Hamburg und Amerika," in the *Festschrift der Hamburger Amerikafeier*, 1892; and Baasch, *Quellen zur Geschichte von Hamburgs Handel und Schiffahrt im 17. 18. und 19. Jahrhundert* (Hamburg, 1910). Statistical material is very imperfect owing to the great fire which in 1842 destroyed the business quarter of the city. For this reason the figures given by Oddy in his *European Commerce,* published in 1805, may have a special value. They do not always agree with those given by the above authorities; but it is impossible to check them, nor is it necessary to do so for the purposes of this work, since they point to the same general conclusions.

The increase from 1793 to 1794 was apparently in response to the English trade in colonial wares. The sharp increase in 1795 obviously reflects the diversion of the Dutch traffic. The peak year was 1801. These figures, be it noted, refer only to large seagoing ships. A considerable quantity of goods was also brought to the city by smaller craft, plying down the Elbe or along the coast. In 1795, for instance, 2,596 such vessels entered the port.

A comparison of the numbers of the ships of various nationalities entering the port reveals the extent of the change brought about by the French occupation of Holland. The Dutch ships entering in 1793 numbered 342, and in 1794, 533; in 1795 the number sank to 55. There was, however, more than an equivalent increase in the number of vessels of other nationalities. The number of British ships entering rose from 245 in 1793 to 323 in 1795. The most remarkable increases were those of the Danish and American vessels. The number of Danish ships entering, which had been 218 in 1793 and 303 in 1794, rose to 664 in 1795, while that of vessels under the American flag in port, which in 1793 had been only 52, rose in 1794 to 208, and to 236 and 239 in 1795 and 1796, respectively.[15]

The importance of all this new trade was realized in Hamburg. When in 1801, Russia laid an embargo on Hamburg ships, the representatives of the traders of the Free City, in order to facilitate negotiations, laid before the senate a statement of Russia's interest in Hamburg. Material portions of this statement follow:

The extent of the direct trade of Russia with Hamburg, which has increased in such an exceptional manner since the ruin of Dutch commerce, is too well known to require anything further to be said about it . . . Hamburg imports from Russia many more goods than it exports to that country on its own account . . . In Hamburg the importation or exportation of no single product or manufacture is forbidden . . . The whole trade of Russia with the Mediterranean goes through Hamburg. The Portuguese, Spaniards and others would not be able to buy such large quantities of Russian produce, if the Hamburger did not in return buy their sugar, or at least give them a sufficient advance on the security of it. The North Americans, too, during the winter months when the Baltic is no longer navigable, obtain Russian

---

[15] American vessels entering the port from the United States numbered 33 in 1793, 91 in 1794, 77 in 1795 and 110 in 1796. Some doubt is thrown on the number of American ships entering Hamburg, as it is possible that other nationals used the cover of the American flag. But it is possible to check the figures from American sources, and these show a remarkable increase in trade between Hamburg and the United States. Baasch, *op. cit.*, refers to Seybert, *Statistical Annals* (Philadelphia, 1818).

hemp, flax, tar, iron, sail-cloth etc. in Hamburg, where in consequence a very considerable store of such articles has always to be kept . . . For a mere commission the Hamburg merchant takes charge of Russian goods in transit, takes all risks, and collects the payments for the exports in the more distant countries, even those which are at war with Russia . . . So long as the Hamburg Bank remains as it is at present, Russia will not be exposed to the great stoppages and obstructions which it experienced in Holland and England.[16]

These arguments seem to have carried weight. At any rate, as a result of the negotiations, the Emperor Alexander I revoked all measures which had been calculated to damage the trade of Hamburg and expressed his deep sense of Russia's great and abiding interest in the prosperity of the city.

Quite as important as the increases in trade was the pivotal position that the Hamburg Bank came during these years to occupy in European financial circles. The transference of the bullion market from Amsterdam to Hamburg had begun before the war. It is surprising to find from the few figures that survive that it was precisely in 1789, when the notes of the Amsterdam Bank began to be at a discount, that the hitherto modest establishment in Hamburg began to assume larger responsibilities. It was, however, during the period 1792 to 1797, which a contemporary Hamburger described as "full of blessing" (*segensrich*), that the significance of the institution developed beyond all expectations. As soon as war threatened, goods and money from countries in peril poured into Hamburg as into a city of refuge.[17] The business of the bank developed enormously during and largely because of the war itself. Its deposits, which in 1772 had been only 3½ million marks, rose to 38½ million marks in 1799 and to over 41 million marks in 1800, the highest point reached before 1813. Its turnover, which in 1774 had been 230 million marks, grew to over 1,500 million marks in 1799.[18]

The bank was the focus of the immense commercial boom during this period. In the closing months of 1799, a severe financial crisis occurred. A series of bankruptcies took place, the total sum for which the firms involved failed being more than 36 million marks.

---

[16] This entire statement will be found in Appendix IV, *infra*.

[17] I. G. Büsch, *Geschichtliche Beurtheilung der in der Handlung Hamburgs im Nachjahr 1799 entstandenen grossen Verwirrung* (Hamburg, 1799). In 1792, "four-and-twenty richly laden vessels came in on a single tide."

[18] A. Soetbeer, *Beiträge und Materialien zur Beurtheilung von Geld und Bankfragen* (Hamburg, 1855). Data are not available for all years, and so the increases noted are not strictly comparable.

Accompanying this flood of commercial failures was a sudden and disastrous collapse of prices. The price of sugar, which had been rising steadily since 1793 (from 11$^{15}/_{16}$ *groschen* per pound to 21⅝ *groschen* per pound) fell as low as 6$^{7}/_{16}$ *groschen* at the end of the year. The price of coffee, which had risen from 10 schillings *banco* in 1793 to 20½ schillings, now sank to 12½ schillings. The price of Virginia tobacco, which had been 2 schillings per pound in 1793 and 9$^{3}/_{16}$ schillings during the first half of 1799, was 4$^{3}/_{16}$ schillings at the end of 1799. These drops in price seem to reflect a rapid decline in the demand for goods in all countries. Warehouses were over-stuffed. There seemed to be a lack of money. Sound exchanges were hard to procure. The causes of this crisis were numerous and various. In the severe winter of 1798 and 1799, ice had closed the Elbe to navigation for five months. On 9 October 1799, the French Directory laid an embargo on all ships flying the Hamburg flag in the harbors of the French Republic.[19] Perhaps more to the point were the evidences of want of foresight and of rash speculation.[20] A mushroom growth of insurance firms had so far increased the competition in this field as to bring the premium rates to a level lower than the perils of the times warranted.[21] Losses on unsound exchanges had precipitated the crisis. When the collapse began, the speculation in commodities had rendered many concerns vulnerable.

The recovery from the crisis was rapid. A discount house was established, relieving the credit stringency. Loans were floated on the security of goods as well as of silver. With the coming of spring, the needs of the military campaigns and the shortages incidental to commercial warfare revived the slackened demands. The year 1800 proved to be one of flourishing trade.

As has been indicated in other connections, Hamburg suffered some losses as a result of the exercise of belligerent rights. Although the great commerce with France which she had carried on before the war was not entirely destroyed, it was nearly so. In the conduct of their blockade, the British sometimes greatly excited public

---

[19] *Moniteur*, An 8, numero 27. This was in retaliation for the extradition of the Irish rebel Napper Tandy and three other British subjects who had been naturalized as Frenchmen. The French had denounced the extradition as a breach of neutrality.

[20] *Hamburg und Altona; eine Zeitschrift zur Geschichte der Zeit, der Sitten und des Geschmacks* (Hamburg, 1801-1806).

[21] Grasmeyer, *Geschichtliche Wahrnehmungen bei der See-Assecuranz* (Hamburg, 1824).

opinion in Hamburg.[22] Changes in the British instructions as regards search and detention were often irritating. Moreover, heavy subsidies had to be paid through much of the period, in the first instance to the Prussian Army of Observation and to the Empire, and later to France. If we may judge from what information we have available on captures, claims and cases, however, these losses were less important than in the case of most of the neutrals. Until 1803, Hamburg, in spite of such repressive measures, seems to have benefited considerably by her neutrality.

The British blockade of the Elbe and Weser, proclaimed in June 1803 as a counterstroke to the French occupation of Hanover and the district of Ritzebüttel, interrupted all access to these rivers for a whole year. It was not till the end of July 1804 that the blockade was so far relaxed as to allow the coasting trade between the Eider, Elbe, Weser and Jade to be carried on in neutral vessels. The oversea trade of the city still had to depend on the transport of goods by land, for the most part to and from Tönning, Kiel and Lübeck by way of Holstein. Owing to the costs of transshipment, the loss of time and the risks involved in transport by land, the expense of importation and exportation was greatly increased. Those who had been accustomed to draw their supplies, especially of colonial goods, from Hamburg turned to places not affected by the blockade.[23] There is some evidence, indeed, that Great Britain was willing to spare the city, so far as the exigencies of the war permitted. In June 1805, for instance, when the rise in the price of cereals inflicted great hardships on the poorer classes, fourteen ships were allowed to sail to Archangel and return with cargoes of grain. Greenland whalers were likewise permitted to sail, and the importation of coal was allowed. Some British goods continued to be imported, principally through Tönning, but also through Emden, Lübeck and Stettin.

Some of the wealthier citizens in Hamburg were not so seriously affected by the blockade, for it was precisely at this time that the city's importance as a financial center increased. There were, more-

[22] One of the ships seized for attempting to run the blockade was the "Merkurius," a Hamburg vessel laden with American goods from Baltimore to Amsterdam. The ship was condemned in December 1798, but the cargo was restored in August 1799 on proof that the owner could not have known of the blockade; 1 C. Robinson 80-85.

[23] Report of the Prussian Minister, quoted from A. Wohlwill, *Neuere Geschichte der freien und Hansestadt Hamburg* (Gotha, 1914).

over, numerous foreign immigrants (of whom there were from eight
to ten thousand in Hamburg and four thousand in Altona), who
engaged in the smuggling trade with Great Britain. But though some
individual traders profited by the blockade, it was exceedingly harm-
ful to the State, which was deprived of the dues levied on the regular
trade of the city. Its effect on the small tradesmen and craftsmen
was disastrous. Numbers of people were thrown out of work, and in
1804 as many as 15,400 were in receipt of poor relief, an increase of
3,000 over the previous year. Many of the middle-class people, also,
lost their regular incomes and their savings and could find no work.

At the end of September 1805, the French evacuated Ritzebüttel,
and on 17 October the British raised the blockade. In May of the
following year, however, a new blockade was proclaimed, which
lasted till the following October. Then, in November, the French
occupied Hamburg, which made any commerce between the city and
England still more difficult. Many English merchants became loathe
to send goods to Hamburg unless the price, or a substantial part of
it, was paid in advance. Hamburg merchants, fearful of French
surveillance, tried to send the English goods in their possession into
Holstein or some place in the interior of the Continent; or, failing
this, back to England.

The Berlin Decree, issued on 21 November 1806, caused a cessation of British exports to the Continent during the next three
months,[24] and there was a rise in marine insurance premiums. When,
however, it was found that the French made no effort to enforce the
decree at sea, the trade revived. The revival was stimulated by an
Order in Council of 18 February 1807 by which the commanders of
British warships and privateers were instructed to allow free passage to the vessels of the Hanse Towns and other ports of North
Germany occupied by the French. Up to the middle of 1807, it was
possible for the merchants of Hamburg to circumvent the Berlin
Decree by importing British goods by way of Tönning, and, in spite
of the increased cost of land transport, to do this profitably owing
to the rise in the prices of colonial produce. Direct navigation did
not wholly cease. Hamburg shipping, it is true, could no longer ply
directly between the Elbe and England, but it found other employment; for instance in the trade between Great Britain and Portugal.
Moreover, under the lax and corrupt administration of Marshal

[24] Heckscher, *The Continental System*, p. 164, cf. *supra*, p. 133.

Brune, the French governor of the city, a considerable trade was carried on up the Elbe previous to the strict enforcement of the Decree ordered on 6 August. During the five and a half preceding months there had arrived in Hamburg 1,475 vessels, laden in large part with English goods. The city, according to a report presented to Napoleon, was full of such goods, which were sold as openly as in London, and not a single seizure had occurred.[25]

Then, in the first days of September 1807, came the destruction of the Danish fleet by the British, which made Denmark a party to the war on the side of France,[26] and so rendered the trade route by way of Tönning more difficult. The Danish Prince Regent, resentful of the British action, showed particular zeal in applying Napoleon's System. The route was, however, by no means closed, for the fishermen and peasants of Holstein had developed into expert smugglers and were little inclined to forego the opportunities the war offered them. In order to facilitate the traffic, the British on 5 September seized Heligoland, a Danish possession. As time went on, this became a distribution point for British goods, which were carried to Tönning or to Husum by British ships flying the American flag, and thence by land through Altona to Hamburg.[27]

The loss consequent on the confiscation of British goods, under Articles 3 and 4 of the Berlin Decree, fell with greater weight on the Hamburg merchants than on the British. The value of such goods confiscated in Hamburg was 17,000,000 francs. Since, however, the property of Hamburg merchants in England and on the high seas was valued at 24,000,000 francs, they preferred to pay the owners of the property confiscated rather than risk reprisals on the part of the British. Another action courting English favor was the purchase by the Senate of Hamburg, at this time, of the Merchant Adventurers' Court, in order to save it for the English. They presented it to its members, who became Hamburg citizens.[28] The members of the "Court," though in later years the importance of the

---

[25] According to his own account, Bourienne, Napoleon's envoy in Hamburg, obtained cloth and leather from England in order to be able to supply Napoleon's army with the uniform coats, boots, etc., which he had to procure; *ibid.*, p. 166.

[26] Cf. *supra*, p. 141.

[27] The trade of Hamburg was also helped by the venality of the French customs officials, and by the licence system, by which means France and Great Britain, in their own interests, tempered the severity of their measures against trade. Cf. *supra*, pp. 158 ff.

[28] Heckscher, *op. cit.*, p. 164.

"Court" had much diminished, had enjoyed certain privileges, among them that of paying smaller customs duties than the Hamburgers themselves. The abolition of these privileges seems to have been the only advantage gained by Hamburg from the Continental System.

The balance of loss and gain to Hamburg, resulting from the war as a whole, is hard to determine. Even after the blockade, profits must have been made by the smuggling trade. Some commerce was carried on especially in shallow-draft boats (*Wattenfahrer*) which navigated the intricate channels between the sandbanks that fringe the North German coast and so avoided the attentions of belligerent cruisers. Thus, even during these later and more difficult years, there were individuals who continued to prosper. The French authorities sometimes connived for a share in these profits. It was far otherwise, however, with the majority of the citizens. Their condition became worse as time went on. Dock laborers, stevedores and craftsmen were for years out of work. Owing to the shortage of coal, two-thirds of the 2,000 workpeople engaged in the sugar refineries had to be dismissed. In these circumstances, the violent fluctuations of prices, and their general upward trend, must have fallen with crushing weight on the poor.

The great difference in prices inside and outside the French customs frontier made all trade in Hamburg highly speculative, but the risk was taken owing to the considerable profits of successful sales. How far this trade was affected by the exercise of belligerent rights it is impossible to estimate with any exactness. The fluctuations in prices can only be understood in detail by citing in each case the political or other circumstances that caused them. Prices, for instance, were naturally raised by the blockade of the Elbe, but less than might have been expected, owing to the trade carried on through Tönning. According to contemporary accounts, prices were actually affected by every rumor from the seat of war, by reports of diplomatic negotiations, by news of battles lost or won, and by exaggerated alarms or hopes deliberately propagated by would-be profiteers. The Hamburg market, in short, was in a nervous state; and, dependent as it was on trade with most of the belligerent powers—Prussia, Russia, Denmark, England, France, and Holland—was kept by the shifting fortunes of the war in a state of constant unrest.

The city was freed from foreign domination on 25 May 1814, and efforts at once began to be made to revive its economic life in which the war had, in fact, made no permanent change. With the coming of peace, the trade that had formerly passed through Hamburg was regained. Ports such as Tönning on the Eider and Glückstadt on the Elbe, which had blossomed into sudden prosperity during the war and seemed likely to become permanent rivals to Hamburg, relapsed into their old insignificance. As soon as access to Hamburg was easy, the British, French and Dutch took advantage of the long credits given to ship their goods there as before. Accordingly the city rapidly recovered its trade and its prosperity.[29]

BREMEN

A considerable transit trade passed through the Free City of Bremen,[30] not only to various parts of Germany, but to Switzerland, Italy and other countries. By way of the Weser and its tributaries,

[29] In addition to the works cited, the following books, and so forth, on Hamburg have been consulted: *Freyer Handel Immerda! Sämtlichen Europäischen Mächten, Vorzüglich England und den Hansestädten zur Beherzigung vorgelegt* (Hamburg, 1806) ; Gustav von Gülich, *Geschichtliche Darstellung des Handels, der Gewerbe und des Ackerbaues der bedeutendsten handeltreibenden Staaten unserer Zeit* (Jena, 1830) ; Heinrich Sieveking, *Das Handlungshaus Voght und Sieveking* (in *Zeitschrift des Vereins für hamburgische Geschichte*, XVII, 123 ff.) ; Robert Hoeniger, "Die Kontinentalsperre und ihre Einwirkung auf Deutschland," in *Volkswirtschaftliche Zeitfragen*, Jahrgang 27, Heft 3, Berlin, 1905; Ernst Baasch, *Die Handelskammer in Hamburg 1665 bis 1915*, 2 vols. (Hamburg, 1915) ; Adolph Soetbeer, *Ueber Hamburgs Handel* (Hamburg, 1840) ; Erwin Wiskemann, *Hamburg und die Weltpolitik von den Anfängen bis zur Gegenwart* (Hamburg, 1929) ; Friedrich Johann Jacobsen, *Handbuch über das practische Seerecht der Engländer und Franzosen in Hinsicht auf das von ihnen in Kriegszeiten angehaltene neutrale Eigentum, mit Rücksicht auf die englischen Assekurancegrundsätze über diesen Gegenstand*, 2 vols. (Hamburg, 1803) ; Heinrich Hitzigrath, *Hamburg und die Kontinentalsperre* (Schulprogramm des Realgymnasiums des Johanneums zu Hamburg, 1900) ; Ludolf Holst, *Ueber die bisherige allgemeine Sperre des Hamburgischen Handels; inwiefern sie für das wahre Staats-Interesse Dänemarks berechnet worden ist* (Hamburg, 1801) ; also the collection of records in the Hamburg Weltwirtschaftsarchiv and Commerzbibliothek; R. Ehrenberg, "Das Haus Parish in Hamburg," in *Grosse Vermögen*, Vol. II (Jena, 1905).

[30] Bremen is situated on the Weser, 46 miles from the North Sea, and 60 miles, as the crow flies, from Hamburg. During the period of the Revolutionary and Napoleonic Wars, the chief port for the unloading of vessels bound for the city was Braake, some thirty miles below Bremen on the Weser. Here vessels of from 200 to 250 tons burden could discharge their cargoes into lighters and lie up "with tolerable safety." Larger ships had to do this some ten or fifteen miles below Braake, near a small village named Bremer Lehe (now Bremerhaven) in the dominions of Hanover. All lighters passing up the Weser to Bremen had to call at Elsfleth, where an account of the cargoes had to be given and a small duty paid to the Duke of Oldenburg.

notably the Werra and the Fulda, Bremen imported from Saxony, Hesse and Hanover certain manufactured goods (especially linen), a little wood, some grain and seeds. For them Bremen exchanged the produce of Portugal, Spain and the East and West Indies. Bremen also carried on a very considerable forwarding trade in British produce and manufactures to and from the interior of the Continent, but more particularly to southwestern Germany.[31] One convenience of Bremen for purposes of trade was that goods could be carried to it by water and then, being already a considerable way into Germany, be carted a shorter distance to their destinations by land. Until the blockade of the Weser in 1803, the city escaped all the inconveniences—such as the Danish occupation—to which Hamburg had been exposed. Traffic on the Weser was accordingly not subject to interruptions such as those suffered on the Elbe.

It was these "inconveniences" which led to the rapid growth of Bremen's prosperity from 1800 onward. True, the blockade of the Elbe, which interfered so disastrously with Hamburg's trade, was extended to the Weser a month later; but the Jade remained open, and this provided an excellent port of entrance through which an increased traffic reached Bremen.[32] During the three years following the blockade of the Elbe, Bremen shared with Lübeck, Stettin and Copenhagen the temporary boom in trade caused by the embarrassments of Hamburg. The city took advantage of the sudden development of the port of Emden in East Friesland, through which a large part of its trade was now carried on. Judging from the receipts from the tonnage dues levied, 1802 was the year of the most active import trade before 1814. After the blockade of the Weser some falling off occurred, but in 1805-1806 the figures rose to the earlier level. Beginning with 1807, a sharp decline took place until the trade revival that began in December 1813. This great setback in the trade of the city was the result of three factors, operating successively. The first was the strict enforcement of the Berlin Decree. There followed the American Embargo and Non-intercourse Acts, and the annexation

---

[31] "This city," wrote Oddy, "partakes so much of the trade of Hamburg, that the description of the commerce of that city becomes applicable to that of Bremen." He adds, however, that the trade of Bremen is far more limited, being chiefly confined to the Circle of Westphalia. Nevertheless, the share of the trade of Germany which it enjoyed was "by no means contemptible."—Oddy, *European Commerce* (London, 1805), pp. 441 ff.

[32] Oddy seems to have been unaware of this, for he remarks that in 1804 no ships entered, as at "Hamburg, on account of the blockade."—*Op. cit.*, p. 443.

to France in December 1810. The last, of course, stopped all direct trade with England.[33]

In the case of Bremen as well as of other neutral states, however, the official statistics give a very imperfect idea of the trade actually carried on during the war. All the evidence tends to show that, from 1806 onward, smuggling was of more importance than regular trade in the whole area of which Bremen was the distributing center. The smuggling was facilitated by the sandbanks and shallows (*Watten*) bordering the seacoast and by the large drainage canals intersecting the country. The whole population eagerly engaged in this illicit trade, and when the French authorities took severe measures in the attempt to suppress it, the peasants rose *en masse* on both sides of the Weser, in Budjadingen and Wursten. They marched through the villages to the sound of the tocsin and stormed the batteries at Blexen and Geestendorf. This was the only instance of a spontaneous rising of the peasantry, and it made a correspondingly deep impression.

Evidence also exists that Bremen carried on an extensive smuggling trade with England through the grand duchy of Oldenburg. For the purpose of organizing this trade, agents of commercial houses established themselves in several towns. One of these, Varel, was described in a report of the French customs authorities as "the centre of the intercourse between Heligoland and the Continent." As in the case of Hamburg, Heligoland was the *point d'appui* of this trade in smuggled goods from London. The trade seems to have been largely carried on in the smallest of sailing craft, which managed to run the gauntlet of the cruisers and to convey considerable amounts of goods. What amounts cannot, of course, be determined; but some idea of the extent of the trade may be gained from the fact that in 1810, British smuggled goods to the value of 1,653,000 francs were discovered in the neighborhood of Bremen.

In general, the statistics of ships entering confirm the indirect measures of import trade. The number increased until 1802, declined with the blockade, recovered from 1804 to 1806, and then fell sharply until 1813. The high point was reached in 1805, when 1,796

---

[33] A table giving the receipts from tonnage dues levied at Bremen from 1801-1814 will be found in Appendix III, Table 19, *infra*. The rate of the levy was ⅔ per cent of the value of the cargo. The receipts accordingly measure values rather than volumes. Unfortunately no data are available with which to adjust for price fluctuations.

entries were noted.[34] The development of Heligoland into an entrepôt for the trade of Bremen in the later period, is illustrated by the fact that of 163 ships entering Bremen in December 1813 as many as 159 were from Heligoland.[35]

With the revival in December 1813 of the overseas commerce of Bremen, English goods poured into the city in exchange for agricultural produce. Though peace had been restored in several countries in 1814, Hamburg, Magdeburg and other fortresses were still in the hands of the French. This was extremely favorable to Bremen, which attracted much of the trade which had formerly passed through Hamburg, the process being facilitated by the fact that a vast quantity of English goods had long been waiting for the opening of a German port. In these circumstances the commerce of Bremen flourished for a while as hardly ever before, and continued to do so even after Hamburg was once more open to English shipping. The profit, however, was not always commensurate with the volume of trade, since the market became glutted. In time, too, the superior advantages of Hamburg as a distributing center began to tell, and the number of English ships entering Bremen fell off.[36] The ultimate recovery of the city was slow and was due in the main to the increase in its purely Hanseatic trade.[37]

LÜBECK

Celebrated of old as the founder and head of the Hanseatic League, Lübeck [38] had little territory of its own. Entirely hemmed in by Holstein, Hanover and Mecklenburg, its prosperity depended upon its transit trade. For this purpose, however, it was very advantageously situated, being a convenient entrepôt for the trade be-

[34] Complete figures for shipping at Bremen from 1800-1815 will be found in Appendix III, Table 18, *infra*.

[35] In 1814, 70 ships entered from Heligoland. After that year, the island ceased to be used as an entrepôt.

[36] Of the vessels entering in 1796 one in every seven had been English, and in 1799 one in every nine; in the years 1818 to 1820, the proportion was only one in every fifteen.

[37] Max Schäfer, "Bremen und die Kontinentalsperre" in *Hansische Geschichtsblätter*, XX (1914), 413 ff.

[38] The city is situated on a ridge between the rivers Trave and Wakenitz, 10 miles southwest of the mouth of the river. Here, at Travemünde, was the roadstead where ships drawing more than from nine to ten feet of water unloaded their cargoes into lighters for conveyance to the city, while vessels of shallower draft could proceed up to the "commodious basin" which formed the harbor of Lübeck.

tween the Baltic countries and northwestern Germany and with southern Europe as well. In addition to its Baltic trade it had a share in that of the Elbe, for the Stecknitz Canal ran direct from its harbor to the Elbe at Lauenburg. By the Holstein Canal it was connected directly with the North Sea.[39]

During the first few years of the Revolutionary Wars the commerce of Lübeck grew considerably. In spite of conflicts with Russia, shortly before the death of the Emperor Paul, and later with Great Britain, this development continued until it was suddenly checked by Napoleon's Continental System. Through Lübeck considerable quantities of British produce and manufactures, as well as British colonial goods, were distributed to the various Baltic ports. The city also carried on a flourishing trade with Hamburg, partly by sea, partly through the Elbe-Trave Canal (by which heavy goods were conveyed) and partly by road. Road transport, however, was expensive; for although the distance by road to Hamburg was only some forty miles and the country was flat, the surfacing was in such bad condition that the heavy wagons needed from eight to twelve horses to draw them. Even then they sometimes foundered in the mud.[40] There was, before 1803, no great increase in exports to Hamburg.[41]

The earlier increases in trade are reflected in the shipping statistics. Ships entering the port rose from 802 in 1792, to 1,109 in 1795 and increased further to 1,194 in 1798. In 1801 and again in 1802 this high point was approached. Ships leaving followed a similar trend but reached their high point, 1,216, in 1801.[42] Subsequent fluctuations in trade were reflected in the numbers of entries and clearances.

The British blockade of the Elbe and Weser in 1803 considerably increased the commerce of Lübeck, for the city provided a convenient back door by which goods could be forwarded to Altona and Hamburg. By 1805, the number of ships entering the port had risen to 1,572. Then came Napoleon's Berlin Decree, threatening the city with utter ruin. In 1807, all trade was at a standstill; the

[39] Oddy, *European Commerce*, p. 291.

[40] "The road, if it can be so called, betwixt Hamburg and Lübeck, is perhaps the worst which is passable in Europe, although there are heavy tolls to keep it in repair, as well as tolls on merchandise."—Oddy, *op. cit.*, p. 293.

[41] With the exception of hemp, of which 2,865 bales were exported in 1794 and 6,080 in 1798.

[42] Table 21 in Appendix III gives the figures for 1792-1802.

inhabitants began to leave, and many houses stood empty. In 1808, only 51 vessels entered the port; in 1809, 86; and in 1810, 78. Of these, many were only small Danish coasting craft.

Thus matters remained until 1813. After the peace, however, the recovery of Lübeck was rapid. In 1818 the number of ships entering was 957, and leaving, 975. This represented a considerable advance on the figures for 1792. Perhaps the diversion of trade to Lübeck under war conditions had produced some permanent effect.[43]

PRUSSIA

Prussia escaped the depressing effects of the belligerent restrictions for a longer time than did the Hanseatic cities. She had made peace with France in April 1795, and on 5 August 1796 signed a treaty with her by which she recognized the annexation to France of the German territories on the left bank of the Rhine, in return for the recognition of the neutrality of northern Germany and the acquisition of certain bishoprics and abbeys on the right bank.[44] From this time until her rash declaration of war on Napoleon in 1806, Prussia enjoyed the advantages of neutrality; and was in a position to profit even from the misfortunes of her German neighbors. The trade diverted from Hamburg and Bremen by the blockade of the Elbe and the Weser, for instance, passed largely into Prussian ports.

With the exception of Emden in East Friesland, all of these ports were on the Baltic coast. Especially favorable to the smuggling trade was the succession of landlocked lagoons (*Haffen*) by which that coast is lined. The principal ports, from east to west, were Memel on the Kurisches Haff; Königsberg and Elbing on the Frisches Haff; Danzig at the mouth of the Vistula; Kolberg on the coast of Pomerania; and Stettin on the Oder, which empties into the Grosses Haff. Internal waterways for trade were provided by the rivers and the canals by which these were connected. Thus, the Frisches Haff was connected by a branch of the Vistula with Danzig, and by this channel a regular trade was carried on between Elbing, Königsberg and Danzig.

The produce exported from Prussia consisted of hemp, flax, a little tallow, ashes, bristles, fir and oak timber, planks and staves

---

[43] Voeltzer, *Lübecks Wirtschaftslage unter dem Druck der Kontinentalsperre* (Hamburger Dissertation).

[44] Cf. *supra*, p. 67.

and also grain, of which large quantities were shipped from Danzig more particularly. Prussian manufactures [45] were heavily protected at this time. In spite of protective tariffs, however, they were unable to compete with English goods, as much because of the superior quality of the British product as because of difference in price. Of the manufactures exported, by far the most important was linen, that of Silesia in particular having "gained a great reputation in the world for its durability and excellence in general." [46] In normal times, this linen was carried for export by way of Upper Saxony and Luneburg to Hamburg, whence it was shipped to Spain, Portugal, Great Britain and the United States. When the Elbe was blockaded, however, it was carried down the Oder and shipped from Stettin. A fine quality of linen was also manufactured at Bielefeld and in Ermeland.

No complete data for the course of the foreign trade of Prussia as a whole during this period is available. The imports from England, however, may be derived from English sources. It will be seen from the figures in Table 10 that the years 1801-1805 witnessed a phenomenal growth of Prussian import trade. The especially marked increases in the years 1803-1805 reflect the blockade of the Elbe and the Weser. The decline beginning in 1806 was due to the troubled state of Anglo-Prussian relations, the war with France and the enunciation of the Berlin Decree. The 1809-1810 boom may be traced to a lapse in the enforcement of the Continental System, and to the brisk export trade in grain and lumber in those years.

The benefits derived by Prussia from her neutrality, up to and including the year 1805, are suggested by the great increase of her shipping, in spite of the obstacles to trade presented by the fact that the Prussian territories possessed sixty different tariff systems. The increase was, indeed, largely due to the transference of Dutch, French and Spanish ships to the protection of the neutral flag of Prussia. The most convenient, and therefore the most usual, place

[45] Among the principal manufactures were linen, blue cloth and woolens in general, velvet, Manchester goods, silk stockings, ribands, chintz and cotton goods, fancy articles, carpets, leather, hardware, refined sugar, gunpowder and porcelain.

[46] Oddy says that the chemical process of bleaching introduced into Ireland had been "wisely done away with" there, and that in Silesia the "gentle process" had always been in use, the cloth being generally three or four months in bleaching "and the lyes made very mild and moderately used." It was this that gave Silesian linen its reputation. He adds, however, that "Irish linen manufacture must soon command a preference to any other."—*Op. cit.*, pp. 215 ff.

for arranging such fraudulent transferences was the port of Emden.[47]

The Anglo-Prussian difficulties in 1806 dated from the treaty between France and Prussia, signed on 15 February, which was followed by the Prussian occupation of Hanover and the closing of

TABLE 10

PRUSSIA: IMPORTS FROM GREAT BRITAIN [a]

1801-1812

Year	Imports (Value in pounds sterling, hundreds)	British Exchange on Hamburg (Percentage of par)	British General Price Level Index	IMPORT INDICES [b]		
				Unadjusted	Adjusted for Exchange Rate Fluctuations	Adjusted for Price Level Fluctuations
1801	5,320	88.3	164.2	22.4	20.6	19.0
1802	8,180	93.2	127.7	34.5	33.4	37.5
1803	15,440	95.8	137.3	65.1	64.9	65.9
1804	39,410	99.4	131.0	166.3	171.8	175.9
1805	50,170	95.1	145.9	211.7	209.3	201.6
1806	468	95.0	142.7	2.0	2.0	1.9
1807	700	96.6	141.6	3.0	3.0	3.5
1808	700	91.4	159.9	3.0	2.8	2.6
1809	5,940	80.5	172.7	25.1	21.0	21.6
1810	25,970	82.0	176.0	109.6	93.4	86.5
1811	570	69.1	157.7	2.4	1.7	2.1
1812	840	76.4	158.8	3.5	2.8	3.1

[a] British exchange rate figures were adapted from a table in an article by Norman J. Silberling, "British Financial Experience, 1790-1830," in the *Review of Economic Statistics*, I (1919), 287. Since they show appreciation and depreciation directly, adjusted figures were first obtained in absolute form, by simple multiplication; and then converted to index numbers; base: 1801-1805 = 100. British price level indices are adapted from those of W. S. Jevons, *Investigations in Currency and Finance* (London, 1884), pp. 119 f. Jevons used data gathered by Tooke, *History of British Prices*. The above price indices are in terms of 1790-1794 as 100. Adjusted figures were obtained in absolute form by simple division and then converted to index numbers; base: 1801-1805 = 100.

[b] Base: 1801-1805 = 100.

Prussian ports to British shipping (1 April). On 8 April, by way of retaliation, Great Britain laid an embargo on 400 Prussian ships in British harbors [48] and at the same time proclaimed a blockade of the German coast from the Ems to the Elbe. On the 21st she de-

[47] It was asserted in 1806 that 3,000 sail (Dutch, French and Spanish) were navigating under the Prussian flag. British cruisers were therefore apt to send in valuable Prussian ships on the chance of their being disguised enemy vessels.— Mahan, *op. cit.*, II, 309 f. Cf. Vol. I of this series, p. 175.

[48] A considerable number of Prussian ships which had taken refuge in French harbors were also lost.

clared war on Prussia. The blockade was relaxed in May, in favor
of neutral vessels carrying British goods, and was raised on 25 September, when Prussia was on the eve of declaring war on France.
Then, on 14 October, came Napoleon's crushing victory at Jena,
the effect of which was to reduce Prussia to the position of one of
his vassal States. On 21 November, the conqueror issued from Berlin
the famous decree barring the Continent to British trade, and
Prussia had no choice but to fall into line with the other States affected by this action.[49]

As already stated, the protection given by this system encouraged
certain industries, notably cotton manufactures. In general, however,
the effect upon Prussian trade was depressing, and would have
proved more so but for the elaborate organization of smuggling,
which enabled the artificial barriers erected to be broken through
in various directions and at various times. Thus the importation
of British manufactures and colonial goods into the Baltic ports
of Prussia was not so carefully guarded as in the case of the North
Sea ports, until 1810. In that year, however, trade with Britain was
made more difficult by the rigorous enforcement of the "self-
blockade." For a time colonial wares continued to enter by way of
the Oder, to be sold at prices eight to ten times what they fetched
in London. The execution of the Fontainebleau Decree of October
1810, however, which ordered the destruction of all goods of British
origin, tightened the web.[50] "All the ports of this once powerful
kingdom," wrote a contemporary, "are filled with French soldiers,
who seize and burn every article which can possibly have passed
through British hands. Prussia is described as in a deplorable state,
almost disorganized and no employment for industry." [51] The description was, on the whole, accurate. But it was not only from
internal repression that Prussia suffered.

The depredations of the belligerents on the high seas also caused
distress. There were bitter complaints of the continued captures of
Prussian merchantmen at sea by the British and the Swedes and
later (in 1807 and 1808) by the Danes. They continued, nevertheless, even during the armistice of 1813. These belligerent operations
were, to be sure, not all on one side. The French cruiser "Le Tilsit"

[49] Cf. *supra*, pp. 131 ff.
[50] A royal patent of 10 October 1810 ordered all colonial goods to be considered
as British. Cf. *supra*, p. 164.
[51] *Monthly Magazine* XXXI (February 1811), 67.

in 1808, brought into Danzig six British merchantmen bearing over six hundred thousand pounds of coffee and nearly three hundred thousand pounds of sugar; and in 1811 the Prussian Government handed over to France, British goods to the value of 36 million *Talers*, in part payment of Prussia's enforced subsidy. The State, in fact, profited to a certain degree both by the obligation laid upon it to enforce the Continental System and by the possibility of evading it. Thus between August 1810 and the beginning of 1813, the Prussian Government gained twelve million *Talers* by fictitious confiscations and other devices. This was no inconsiderable sum for those days, and it was to prove useful in financing the War of Liberation.[52]

EMDEN

Of all the Prussian ports, Emden benefited in the most unexpected degree from the war. Although, before the war it had had a share in transit trade, the main source of its modest wealth had been the fisheries. Its position, however, made it a natural center of the entrepôt trade between England, Holland, Germany and the Baltic, and as has been pointed out, a vast impetus was given to this trade when the French overran Holland and the British proclaimed a blockade of the Texel. Since Emden had been declared a free port by the King of Prussia as early as 1751, the duties on vessels entering were very light, and they could take their clearance without unloading and at small expense. As Oddy remarks, this enabled the Dutch to carry on their commerce with great security in time of war.

The facilities for communication with the interior of the Continent which Emden possessed, gave it a special importance in war time. By means of the East Frisian canal system it could carry on trade with the Low Countries, and even with France. Through this channel, the Dutch, the Flemings and the French were enabled to trade with the Baltic, either by way of the Holstein Canal or along the coast.[53] As a waterway, the Ems could not be compared with the Elbe, but goods could be shipped up it as far as Münster, when there was enough water. From there they could be forwarded by

[52] In addition to the works cited, the following have been consulted: M. Peters, *Die Entwicklung der deutschen Reederei seit Beginn dieses Jahrhunderts* (Jena, 1899) and I. D. A. Höck, *Statistische Darstellung des deutschen Fabrik und Handelswesens nach seinem ehemaliger und jetzigen Zustand* (Schmalkalden, 1823).

[53] Oddy, *op. cit.*, pp. 447 ff.

land to various parts of the Continent. It was by this route that the
French obtained the indigo with which to dye the blue cloth for
their army.[54]

The situation of the port on the very border of Holland made
it easy for its merchants to secure Dutch ships, either by purchase
or by fraudulent transfer, which they could navigate safely under
the neutral flag of Prussia. Emden was, indeed, the chief *point
d'appui* of that "war in disguise" which James Stephen denounced
in his famous brochure.[55] Information on the number of ships entering and leaving the port is available only for the years 1784 and
1799. In 1784 the number entering was 482, and clearing, 568. In
1799, the numbers were 3,402, in, and 2,151, out. This tremendous
increase antedated the blockade of the Elbe and Weser. The only
available evidence of growth in traffic after that event, is Oddy's
quotation of a statement, made in 1804, "till the French interrupted
trade, the harbor could not hold the ships seeking entrance." [56]

It appears that the stoppage of French and Dutch trade brought
the period of great prosperity to Emden. The port also profited,
for a short time, by the blockade of the Weser, since Bremen exported some goods through this channel. But this ceased, when
Bremen arranged to take the cheaper and more convenient route
through Oldenburg. All of these accessions of trade proved transitory. With the coming of peace, Emden relapsed into its old insignificance.

MEMEL

Memel stands at the extreme northern end of the Kurisches Haff,
close to its opening into the Baltic and on the river Memel (or
Niemen). By means of this river and its principal tributary, the
Szczara, connected with the Dnieper by the Oginsky Canal, the city
had access to the Black Sea. Its principal article of export was
timber. Great Britain took a considerable portion of this export
because the timber was better squared than elsewhere, there were
large supplies at reasonable rates, always available, and the port was
convenient. The chief supply was derived from the forests belonging
to Prince Radziwill, but a certain amount was floated down the
rivers from as far off as eight hundred to one thousand miles,
Volhynia being one of the sources of supply. The number of ships
loaded with timber clearing from this port averaged seven hundred

---

[54] Oddy, *op. cit.*, pp. 446 ff.   [55] Cf. *supra*, p. 127.
[56] Oddy, *op. cit.*, p. 447.

yearly, and the value of the timber averaged £350,000. Other principal exports were flax and grain.[57]

Most of the trade figures for Memel point to 1803 as the outstanding year. Exports of wood reached their high point in that year, with 993,418 balks, 1,863 masts, 1,916 spars and 565 bowsprits as the peaks of their respective series. In the same year, 159,046 stones of flax were exported, a record figure. Exports of grain, on the other hand, were for the most part higher in 1801 and 1804. Only rye and pease were exported in greatest quantities, in 1803. Wheat attained its highest volume of export in 1804, as did oats; while barley exports were largest in 1801. The highs for grain, however, were more a function of weather and crops than of demand. The import trade also reached its highest recorded point in 1803. Coffee was imported in larger amount in 1804, as was French wine. With these exceptions, 1803 was the most active year.[58]

Memel was one of the chief centers of the smuggling trade on the Continent after the Berlin Decree, and this contributed considerably to its prosperity. British manufactures and colonial wares were brought to the Russian Baltic ports in British ships, carted thence by land to Memel and from there sent by water into various parts of Prussia and into the countries beyond. Of the amount of this trade, of course, no statistics exist. Naturally it did not continue beyond the period of the war.

KÖNIGSBERG

Königsberg [59] had "a safe and complete interior navigation, even to the Black Sea, through the Oginsky Canal." This route was used by small vessels (100-120 tons burden) which made two voyages annually into the interior. They carried up imported goods in the spring, returned in the late summer with produce, and having un-

[57] Oddy, op. cit., pp. 220 ff.

[58] Tables indicating the course of trade at Memel for the years 1797-1804 will be found in Appendix III, Tables 22, 23, infra.

[59] The capital of East Prussia is situated on the River Pregel, which reaches the Frisches Haff a short distance below the city. The river itself was of little use for the purposes of internal navigation, but was joined by a series of canals with the left arm of the Memel (Niemen) just before it empties into the Kurisches Haff. The port of Königsberg was Pillau, situated at the opening of the Haff into the Baltic, 30 miles from Königsberg. Bars in the Haff prevented vessels not adapted to such navigation from proceeding to Königsberg itself. Those of large draft discharged their cargoes into lighters in the "large and safe harbour" of Pillau. The port was icebound in winter.

loaded, went back once more. The produce, largely from Poland, consisted of wheat, rye, linseed, hemp, flax, timber and so forth. "By their capital and the convenience of this canal . . . (the merchants of Königsberg) . . . monopolized, as it were, from the merchants of Memel, the use of the river of that name." [60]

The export trade of Königsberg was subject to marked fluctuations. In part, this reflected the character of the produce: the dependence of yield on the whims of the weather, or (as in the case of timber) on the extent of exhaustion in particular localities. In part, it was the result of the disorganization of certain industries. Finally, it was in part due to the successive diversions of traffic as the strength of belligerent interference was felt, now in one area, now in another. Shipments of wheat amounted to 14,484 tons in 1796, and approached that figure later only in 1800, when 13,686 tons were shipped. Exports of rye fluctuated violently, rising from 260 tons in 1795, to 22,400 tons in 1796 and 36,190 tons in 1798. The sensational decline in the export of hemp is difficult to account for. Fir balks which were exported in only mildly fluctuating amounts until 1802, felt an increase in demand of more than 100 per cent in 1803, and were still being shipped in large amounts in 1804. This may have resulted from the blockade of the Elbe. The movements of linen seem to have been affected by this same factor, although it is probable that the industry in general was depressed by the difficulties the war created, particularly in the matter of procuring a dependable supply of raw materials. One notable characteristic of the export figures is the tendency they reflect for Great Britain to take a high proportion of certain commodities, particularly wheat, linen and fir balks.[61]

The chief imports consisted of colonial produce. Importations of coffee moved up nearly 264 thousand pounds between 1795 and 1798, but did not reach their high point until 1804. In that year, after an increase of 91 per cent over the preceding year, they amounted to 844,693 pounds. Large increases in the same year affected imports of ginger and indigo. The blockade of the Elbe appears to have been the principal factor in these increases.[62]

[60] Oddy, *op. cit.*, pp. 228-236.
[61] Detailed data of the principal exports of Königsberg appear in Appendix III, Table 24, *infra*.
[62] Detailed data of the principal imports of Königsberg appear in Appendix III, Table 25, *infra*.

The shipping statistics also indicate an upward trend with highs in 1798 and 1802-1803.[63] The trade of Königsberg then appears to have been increasingly flourishing during the period of Prussia's neutrality, notwithstanding marked fluctuations. In particular, it seems to have benefited from the distress of Hamburg after 1803. With the fateful year, 1806, however, its prosperity ceased. Captures at sea during the years that followed cost the merchants and shipowners of the city over five hundred thousand *Talers*. The interruption of the trade of the city, especially with Great Britain, led to numerous failures and much unemployment. The shipping industry of Königsberg never recovered from the blow dealt it at this time.

ELBING

The situation of Elbing [64] as regards facilities for commerce, was much the same as that of Königsberg. Accordingly its trade followed much the same lines during the war, though in general on a smaller scale. Its exports of certain articles, however, and notably of wheat and yarn, were considerably larger than those of the other city. At its height, in 1797, the wheat exports of Elbing were 38,356 tons. In 1800, the city exported 37,184 shocks of Ermeland yarn, a figure not again attained. The bulk of the wheat, and nearly all the yarn were exported to Great Britain. While Elbing had a share in the transit trade to Austria and Russia, its exportation to France and Spain was "but of trifling moment." [65] Some trade with France went on, however, as appears from the figures for imports of wine. Much of this trade was indirect. Colonial wares were imported and re-exported in considerable quantities. The most remarkable increase in this trade was in the case of refined sugar, the export of which rose from 196,374 pounds in 1797 to 581,687 pounds in 1804. The increase seems to have represented a diversion from Hamburg.

[63] Entries and clearances of vessels at Pillau from 1795-1804 are indicated in Appendix III, Table 26, *infra*.

[64] Elbing is situated on the river of the same name which flows into the Frisches Haff at its southern end. Only vessels of shallow draft could come up to the warehouses of the city itself, larger ships having to discharge their cargoes into lighters at Pillau, fifty miles away at the other end of the Haff. A short canal connecting the Elbing with the Nogat (the name given to the southern arm of the Vistula flowing into the Kurisches Haff) provided Elbing with the opportunity for an extensive trade in the interior of the Continent, similar to that which has been described under Königsberg.

[65] Oddy, *op. cit.*, p. 240.

DANZIG

From 1795 to 1806, Danzig [66] enjoyed all the advantages of Prussian neutrality, since its principal trade was precisely in those commodities (grain, timber, etc.) which were most in demand during the war. The blockade of the Texel, more especially of the Elbe and Weser, diverted to Danzig a large part of the imports of colonial goods which had normally entered by those rivers. The constitution of the port, moreover, ensured that the lion's share of the proceeds should remain in the hands of its citizens. Danzig was a staple town, and no pure transit trade was allowed. All goods had to be sold to burghers of the city, from whom alone foreign merchants were allowed to buy them. It is not surprising, in these circumstances, that during the earlier years of the war, the wealth of the citizens increased by leaps and bounds. The heavy transit dues imposed by Prussia on traffic passing down the river, indeed, led the Poles in course of time to divert their exports from the Baltic, to which the Vistula was their only route, to the Black Sea (by way of the Dnieper, Bug and Dniester); but Danzig continued to prosper until, in 1806, it was involved in the ruin of Prussia.

The principal grain export had been that of rye; but during the war this was greatly restricted owing to home consumption and to

[66] Danzig, founded by the Order of Teutonic Knights, developed into a Free City in the 15th century. Subsequently it prospered greatly under the protection of Poland until, in 1793, it was incorporated in Prussia, as a result of the second partition of Poland. Its situation at the mouth of the Vistula, which with its tributaries provided waterways into vast stretches of central and eastern Europe, had early made it one of the most important entrepôts of the trade of these inland countries with the outside world. Especially was this true as regards Poland, whose cereals, wood, linen and other products were carried to Danzig and thence shipped to the countries of Western and Southern Europe. The Donajec, which rises in the Carpathians and flows into the Vistula, brought down wood rafts only, which carried to Danzig oak planks, staves and Bukovina ashes. The San, which flows into the Vistula at Zawichost in Sandomierz, carried down from Galicia grain, ashes, hempen linen and yarn, timber, planks and staves. The Wieprz, which joins the Vistula at Ivangorod, also brought timber, planks and staves, together with small Polish vessels laden with grain. The Bug, which rises near Lemberg (Lwów), is navigable in wet seasons as far as Ustilug or Dubienka. It enters the Vistula at Zakroczym. Down this to Danzig came all the products of the Ukraine and a superior quality of rye from Podlachia. The Narew, which has its sources in East Prussia and Lithuania and enters the Vistula at Zakroczym about twelve miles below Warsaw, carried to Danzig the better sorts of balks, timber and masts and the heavier qualities of wheat. Finally, at Bromberg the Vistula was connected by a canal with the Netze, a tributary of the Warthe (Warta), which latter stream flows into the Oder at Küstrin.

the requisitions of pumpernickel for soldiers. Barley was exported in considerable quantities in some years. The export of wheat increased greatly even before the war, mainly owing to the demand in Great Britain, who had opened the trade by the Corn Law of 1770 and had herself ceased to be an exporting country. The largest importations of grain were from Poland and Galicia. The fluctuations in the quantities imported and exported are, it seems, no certain index to the effects of the operations of war upon commerce, for they were affected by other causes. The amount imported from Poland, for instance, depended on the depth of water in the rivers in summer and on the prices ruling in Danzig.[67] The primitive methods of agriculture employed in Poland and Lithuania, moreover, led to frequent failures of the harvest. There was also enormous wastage in transit, the grain being brought down in open boats, unprotected from the weather so that it often sprouted. The birds likewise took a heavy toll of it. Tarpaulins there were none, though hemp and tar were cheap.

The movement of exports of grain was upward, with few minor interruptions. Shipments of all grains, which in 1791 had amounted to 54,688 tons, averaged 85,118 tons for the period 1796-1799; and the average for the five years following was 131,596 tons. In the case of wheat, exports rose from 30,828 tons, in 1793, to an average of 51,118 tons for the four years ending in 1799; they averaged 82,728 tons for the years 1800-1804. As suggested above, the trend for rye was not the same. Shipments declined from 24,218 tons in 1793 to a four-year average of 20,384 tons, 1796-1799. But after touching bottom in 1800 they rose so sharply that the average from 1800 to 1804 was 29,810 tons.[68]

The figures for shipments of timber reflect the same tendency. Balks, of which 23,811 pieces were shipped in 1793, were exported in a slightly smaller amount in the years 1795-1799: 23,062 pieces. The average for the next five years, however, was 50,778 pieces. Exports of oak planks rose from 380 shocks, in 1793, to a five-year average of 562 shocks, 1795-1799; and it increased further to an average of 683 shocks for the period 1800-1804. Of fir planks 420 shocks were shipped in 1793. For the five years 1795-1799, the

[67] The Poles refused to sell rye for less than ten ducats per ton or wheat for less than 17½ per ton.

[68] Appendix III, Table 28, indicates in detail exports of grain from Danzig for the period 1793-1806.

average shipment was 510 shocks. There was a further rise to an average of 673 shocks from 1800 to 1804. The best market for this and other timber exports, was England.[69]

In return for these exports, the principal imports were colonial wares. These fluctuated in amount from year to year but exhibited the same general tendency to rise. The movements of coffee and sugar imports will illustrate this tendency. Receipts of coffee, which in 1793 were 1,324 thousand pounds fell to an average of 1,085 thousand pounds for the period 1795-1799; then rose to an average of 1,726 thousand pounds for the next half decade. Imports of sugar had been 324 thousand pounds in 1793. They averaged 595 thousand pounds from 1795 to 1799. The continuance of this trend carried the average to 942 thousand pounds for the years 1800-1804.[70] There are also significant increases, particularly in the opening years of the nineteenth century, in imports of both French wine and English beer.

The great growth of the overseas trade of the City was reflected in the number of ships entering and clearing from port. The number of entries rose from 810 in 1793, to 1,079 in 1798, and after a brief decline continued the trend until 1803, attaining the figure of 1,088 vessels. There had been 783 clearances in 1783. There were 1,043 in 1798, and 1,916 in 1802.[71] The magnitude of the disaster that fell upon the City after the collapse of Prussia, in 1806, may be inferred from the fact that in 1808, only 32 vessels entered the port. Although in 1810 this number increased to 310, as many as 258 of them were in ballast.

The evidence so far given tends to indicate that Danzig prospered during the Revolutionary Wars, so long as Prussia remained neutral. The zenith of this prosperity was attained in 1802 and 1803. After 1806, it shared the misfortunes that befell Prussia following the defeat at Jena. The smuggling trade, by resort to which many of the other Prussian ports mitigated their hardships in some measure, could not be carried on at Danzig. Under the crushing weight of French occupation and strict enforcement of the Berlin Decree, the economic life of the city was paralyzed, its business

---

[69] Table 29 indicating these exports of timber and others, in detail, has been included in Appendix III, *infra*.

[70] Appendix III, Table 30, *infra*, contains detailed data bearing on imports by Danzig of colonial produce for the period 1793-1804.

[71] Statistics of ships entering and clearing the port of Danzig are given in Appendix III, Table 27, *infra*.

rendered bankrupt, its wharves left to decay and its populace given over to unemployment. Naturally the hinterland of the port shared its sufferings. The suicidal character of the Continental System was demonstrated by the developments that followed. The agencies for producing, purchasing and storing produce were disorganized. As prices dwindled, acreage under cultivation followed suit. By the irony of fate, the armies of the instigator of the System were eventually made to feel the shortage which their shortsighted policies had tended to create. Although, after the terrible retreat from Moscow, the promise of an end to the distress seemed given, Danzig's troubles were not over. Russia and Prussia laid siege to the "Free City" in 1813, and this investment seems to have been quite as trying as the earlier experiences. In no region was the passing of an ephemeral prosperity followed by so contrasting a period as in Danzig.[72]

STETTIN

The inland trade of Stettin [73] extended as far as Poland, Silesia and Austria. Exports by the Baltic consisted chiefly of oak timber for shipbuilding, staves, fir timber, glass, salt, potash, hemp seed, oil and tallow, linseed, flax and yarn. Imports from the Baltic consisted of colonial goods, French wines and so forth.

Figures for exports and imports are only available for the years 1798 to 1804.[74] The value of timber exported in 1798 was 30,259 *Reichstalers*, and in 1803 was 66,237 *Reichstalers;* 4,107 planks were exported in 1798 and 14,105 in 1803. Except in the case of wood, exports show no well-defined trend. Imports behaved in general in a similar fashion. In the case of tobacco and wine, substantial increases were registered in 1802 and 1803.

The blockade of the Elbe in 1803 brought an increase of trade to Stettin, especially in the export of linen goods. Goods hitherto sent from Silesia, Austria and Bohemia through Berlin and Magdeburg were now diverted down the Oder. The city gained, however, only what Magdeburg and Berlin lost, and the gain was very temporary. In 1806, Stettin was involved in the general collapse of Prussia.

[72] Fuller details of the plight of Danzig after Jena, are contained in a contribution by Professor Hans von Eckardt that is included in Appendix V.

[73] Stettin, the capital of Prussian Pomerania, is situated on the western bank of the Oder, 17 miles above its entrance into the Stettiner Haff and 46 miles from Swinemünde, the city's port on the Baltic. Stettin itself was a port for ships able to cross the bar; those of deeper draft having to unload at Swinemünde.

[74] See Appendix III, Table 32, *infra,* for detailed figures on imports.

During the period 1806-1815 but few vessels entered and cleared from the port. Of the actual numbers no trustworthy records remain. The confiscation of ships and goods belonging to the city by the British, after the Prussian occupation of Hanover, cost the citizens 745,704 *Talers*. The seizure and plundering of their ships at sea and on the rivers by the French and the loss of ships caught in French harbors cost another 498,017 and 421,688 *Talers*, respectively. The Danes, too, took their toll of the city's vessels and wares to the amount of 188,476 *Talers*. The French Government, under the Trianon Tariff, forced the Stettin merchants to hand over 278,421 *Talers* as duty on the wares which the Prussian Government had confiscated and sold to them. Like Danzig, the city suffered siege in 1813; and this was followed by a disastrous fire in the same year. The losses of the city, after 1806, from these and other causes, have been estimated to be 3,986,311 *Talers*.[75]

SUMMARY

The prosperity of the German ports was created by belligerent restrictions elsewhere and arrested by similar restrictions in the ports themselves. It became therefore a function of shifting belligerent expedients. Whether the benefits of the period of artificial prosperity were sufficient to counterbalance the damage resulting from these restrictions, depended on the extent to which they were enforced. The British Blockade of the Elbe and the Weser was so lightened as to spare the Hanseatic ports in some measure. The corruption of the authorities charged with the enforcement of the Continental System enabled some of the citizenry to replace the regular transit trade with an irregular smuggling trade. Neither of these factors was sufficient to alleviate completely the distress, particularly among the working classes. In Hamburg and Bremen, however, they seem to have turned the balance in favor of the gains during the period of neutrality. In the case of Lübeck, the ruin brought by the Continental System appears to have outweighed the earlier prosperity. The balance as regards the Hanse cities as a whole is left in some doubt.

For the Prussian ports, the situation was even more equivocal. Emden and Memel became important centers for the smuggling trade. The Continental System seems to have ended the prosperity

[75] Theodor Schmidt, *Zur Geschichte des Handels und der Schiffahrt Stettins von 1785-1840* (Stettin, 1875).

of Königsberg and Elbing. The dead hand of strict and blind enforcement was ruinous at Danzig and at Stettin. Their earlier prosperity can hardly be regarded as even approximately compensating
them for the economic derangement and paralysis of the years
1807-1814.

XII

SOME CONCLUSIONS

One effect of the war was to open the ports of the West Indies to neutral, chiefly American, vessels. Simultaneously the bulk of American export trade was diverted to American bottoms. Principally by reason of the accession of the transit trade, but also because of an expanding trade in certain domestic exports, the United States prospered during most of the years 1793-1811. Another early effect of the war was the diversion of the channels of trade with central Europe northward. A contemporary writer compared this diversion to "a great river changing its bed." Holland was the first to profit by this phenomenon but in 1795 she was overrun by the French and her trade snuffed out by a cordon of British vessels. The stream of traffic moved northward to the Elbe, Hamburg now becoming the principal entrepôt for the commerce of the outside world with the European Continent and replacing Amsterdam as the great financial center. In spite of the financial crisis of 1799, of the Prussian occupation of Cuxhaven in November 1800, and of the Danish occupation of the city itself a few months later, it continued prosperous until, in June 1803, the French occupation of Hanover was answered by the British blockade of the Elbe. Once more the channels of commerce shifted to the north. Denmark, owing to her favorable situation commanding the entrance to the Baltic and the facilities for land transport through Slesvig and Holstein, provided for a while the principal routes by which colonial goods and British manufactures found their way into the interior of the Continent. But if Copenhagen thus profited by the embarrassments of Hamburg, so too did the Hanse cities, Bremen and Lübeck. Prussia, also, benefited greatly, for now it was that the insignificant Prussian port of Emden, in East Friesland, suddenly developed an important entrepôt trade, while on the southern shores of the Baltic, the ports of Elbing, Stettin, Königsberg, Memel and, above all, Danzig, entered on a brief period of unexampled prosperity. The year 1807 witnessed yet another shifting of the channels of trade. Denmark-Norway was now at war in alliance with Napoleon, Prussia lay crushed under his heel and he was taking measures to perfect the Continental System by means of which he hoped to bring Great Britain to her knees. His plan was countered by the organization on a vast scale of the smuggling trade. Heligoland, hitherto a Danish possession, was occupied by the British and became the entrepôt for this trade on the coast of the North Sea. The Swedish port of Göteborg (Gothenburg), conveniently situated at the entrance to the Cattegat, became the principal entrepôt for the Baltic trade. Of what nature was the prosperity thus brought to these several areas?

At the close of Chapter I certain questions were raised with regard to the commerce and industry of the neutral regions. The material presented in the preceding three chapters has put us in position to answer those questions, at least in part.

Did the accessions to trade counterbalance the losses incident to the inconvenience? In all the neutral areas, with the exception of Sweden, the period of neutrality witnessed considerable increases in trade. In many cases these increases amounted to several hundred per cent. For the most part they reflected rather increases in the transit trade than increased exports of domestic produce. The only increase in the latter class of exports were in shipments of staple foodstuffs and of naval stores. Such evidence as has come down to us from contemporary sources indicates that the industries affected (shipping, shipbuilding, grain cultivation and distribution, lumbering and its correlative industries) experienced notable increases in profits. This evidence must be discounted for two factors: the nature of evidence on which contemporary writers rely and the prevalent ignorance at the time of sound accounting practice. It is certain that these writers did not have access to the books of any considerable number of firms. Often enough, no doubt, they relied upon the wild phrases circulating in speculative circles. What is more important, however, is that many enterprises counted their profits injudiciously. When arriving at the figure to be subtracted from the gross earnings, it is necessary not only to count accurately past expenditures but to estimate carefully future prospects. In view of the number of bankruptcies that took place, some within the period of neutrality, it may be doubted whether, in all cases, all the costs were counted or the prospects conservatively estimated. We may perhaps safely conclude, even after these reservations, that the rate of profit was notably higher in these fields, and particularly in shipping and shipbuilding. It may be doubted, however, that it was much in excess of the amount properly attributable to the far greater risks incurred. On the one hand, war necessities frequently compel customers to pay any price; on the other hand, the industries concerned were highly competitive, as is emphasized by the amount of diversion of capital to them in this period, and this tended to keep profit rates from becoming extortionate. The probabilities are that they were sufficiently high in most cases to offset, and perhaps to overbalance, losses due to the exercise of belligerent rights. To balance the account with exactness is, of course, impossible, for neither of the magnitudes is known or can be determined.

What happened to the course of prices, wages and production? Statistical materials measuring these phenomena are both inadequate and unsuited to the task. Such as they are, they indicate an upward trend in each case. Prices seem to have advanced sharply, for the most part and to have been subject to violent fluctuations. Wage advances, outside the favored industries mentioned above, appear not to have been sharp. Production seems to have felt a general upward impulse, but marked increases were confined to foodstuffs, naval stores and shipbuilding. Some effects of a hardly beneficial nature seem to have issued from these unequal changes. Income in general, while it advanced, hardly kept pace with prices. The violent fluctuations in prices led inevitably to widespread speculation.

Were the effects on industry uniform, or did overexpansion take place in some lines? It is certain that not all industries felt the impetus in the same degree. The opportunities were greatest in the shipping and shipbuilding industries, and accordingly much capital was diverted to them which in other years would have been attracted to other lines. Instances have been cited in which industries already well established actually suffered because of the diversion of energy and capital to other lines. The development of manufacturing in the United States appears to have been retarded, so long as the nation maintained its neutrality and to have been accelerated, as soon as the prosperity arising from neutrality had passed.

Was a heritage of economic maladjustment left by the period, when the extraordinary wartime demands came to an end? It is difficult to decide whether the straitened circumstances, in which all of the neutral states found themselves after the ephemeral prosperity had vanished, was due to such maladjustment or to the exigencies of the war in which they all eventually became involved as belligerents. Even if we can not draw hard and fast lines between the operations of these factors, however, it is difficult to believe that the extraordinary demands for the service of transportation, and for supplies, did not have disrupting effects on the economic life of the neutral communities. Overexpansion certainly occurred in the shipbuilding, shipping and marine insurance industries. Some liquidation would have been necessary here, even had the neutral states remained neutral. It is not probable, however, that the impairment of certain established industries resulting from the diversion to these activities was permanent.

How far-reaching were these effects? It is difficult to discern much lasting change in economic conditions and relationships. The capital accumulated in American countinghouses between 1793 and 1807 probably helped establish the manufacturing industries of the country. Bosse thinks a similar development took place in Norway. But for the most part, the economic situation of the several neutral states in 1825 was pretty much what one would have anticipated, had one projected the trends from 1750 to 1790. The wartime changes in direction and character of the transit trade could not perpetuate themselves. The demands created by military and naval movements were necessarily transitory. Only as the earnings from these temporary factors were used to lay the foundations of new industries or to alter economic relationships, could they prove a lasting benefit. More often, they raised false hopes, encouraged rash speculation and issued in recurrent liquidations.

BIBLIOGRAPHY

UNPUBLISHED SOURCE MATERIAL

Records preserved in the Public Record Office, London:
Admiralty Records
Foreign Office Records
Privy Council Register

PUBLISHED SOURCE MATERIAL

Ballagh, J. C., Letters of Richard Henry Lee (1911).
Bourrienne, Louis A. F. de, Mémoires sur Napoleon, 10 vols. (1830).
Great Britain
Annual Register, A Review of Public Events at Home and Abroad, London (1758-   ).
Cobbett, Parliamentary History (to 1803).
Fortescue, J. B., Manuscripts, Preserved at Dropmore (Dropmore Papers). Historical Manuscripts Commission Report XIII, Appendix iii.
Hansard, Parliamentary Debates (1803-   ).
London Gazette.
Naval Chronicle.
Papers presented to Parliament.
Statutes at Large (1870-1875).
Martens, Georg Friedrich von, Recueil de traités servant à la connaissance des relations étrangères des puissances et états de l'europe depuis 1761 (2ᵐᵉ ed.), 8 vols. (1817-1842).
Piggott, Sir Francis, and Omond, George, Documentary History of the Armed Neutralities, 1780 and 1800 (1919).
Robinson, Christopher, Reports of Cases in the High Court of Admiralty, 6 vols. (1802-1808).
Scott, James Brown, The Armed Neutralities of 1780 and 1800: a collection of official documents preceded by the views of representative publicists (1918).
Stephens, Henry Morse, The Principal Speeches of the Statesmen and Orators of the French Revolution, 2 vols. (1892).
United States
American State Papers
Commerce and Navigation, 2 vols. (1789-1823).
Finance, 1789-1828, 5 vols. (1832-1859).
Foreign Relations, 1792-1815, 6 vols. (1789-1828).
Annals of the Congress of the United States, 1789-1824, 42 vols. (1834-1856).

Miller, Hunter, Treaties and Other International Acts of the United States, 3 vols. (1931-   ).

Richardson, James Daniel, A Compilation of the Messages and Papers of the Presidents, 1789-1897, 9 vols. (1903-1909).

Statutes at Large.

CONTEMPORARY WORKS

Büsch, I. G., Geschichtliche Beurtheilung der in der Handlung Hamburgs im Nachjahr 1799 entstandenen grossen Verwirrung (1799).

Hamburg und Altona, Eine Zeitschrift zur Geschichte der Zeit, der Sitten und des Geschmacks (1801-1806).

Holst, Ludolf, Ueber die bisherige allgemeine Sperre des hamburgischen Handels inwiefern sie für das wahre Staatsinteresse Dänemarks berechnet worden ist (1801).

Jacobsen, Friedrich, Handbuch über das praktische Seerecht der Engländer und Franzosen in Hinsicht auf das von ihren in Kriegszeiten angehaltene neutrale Eigenthum, mit Rücksicht auf die englischen Assekurancegrundsätze über diesen Gegenstand, 2 vols. (1803).

Macpherson, David, Annals of Commerce (1805).

Oddy, J. Jepson (William Playfair), European Commerce (1805).

Quarterly Review.

Stephen, James, War in Disguise: or, the Frauds of the Neutral Flags (2d ed., 1805).

Thaarup, F., Statistik der dänischen Monarchie (1795).

GENERAL WORKS

Adams, Henry, History of the United States during the Administrations of Jefferson and Madison, Vols. I-IV (1889-1891).

Alison, Sir Archibald, History of Europe, 10 vols. (1833-1842).

Atkinson, C. T., A History of Germany, 1715-1815 (1909).

Bemis, Samuel Flagg, Jay's Treaty; a Study in Commerce and Diplomacy (1923).

Bogart, Ernest L., Economic History of the American People (1935).

Brenton, Edward Pelham, The Naval History of Great Britain, 1783-1836 (1836).

Bülau, Friedrich, Geschichte Deutschlands von 1806-1830 (1842).

Callender, Guy Stevens, Selections from the Economic History of the United States, 1760-1860 (1909).

Cambridge Modern History: Vol. VII, The United States; Vol. VIII, The French Revolution; Vol. IX, Napoleon.

Channing, Edward, History of the United States, Vol. IV (1925).

Clowes, Sir William Laird, The Royal Navy; a History, 7 vols. (1897-1903).

Conan, Katharine, The Industrial History of the United States (2d ed., 1910).

Dalgren, Lars Ejnar, Sverige och Pommern, 1792-1806 (1914).

Day, Clive, A History of Commerce (1907).

Drachmann, Povl, The Industrial Development and Commercial Policies of the Three Scandinavian Countries (1915).

Faulkner, Harold U., American Economic History (1931).

Fryxxel, Anders, The History of Sweden, 2 vols. (1844).

Gjerset, Knut, History of the Norwegian People, 2 vols. (1915).

Haüsser, Ludwig, Deutsche Geschichte vom Tode Friedrichs des Grossen bis zur Gründung des deutschen Bundes, 4 vols. (1854-1857).

Heckscher, Eli F., The Continental System; an Economic Interpretation (1922).

Hildebrand, E., Sveriges historia intill tjugonde seklet (1910).

Hirst, Francis W., Life and Letters of Thomas Jefferson (1926).

James, William, Naval History of Great Britain, 1793-1820, 6 vols. (1886).

Knight, Melvin M., Barnes, Harry E., and Flugel, Felix, Economic History of Europe in Modern Times (1928).

McMaster, John Bach, History of the People of the United States, Vols. I-IV (1931).

Mahan, Alfred Thayer, The Influence of Sea Power upon the French Revolution and Empire, 2 vols. (1892).

———— Sea Power in Its Relation to the War of 1812, 2 vols. (1895).

Mathiez, Albert, La Révolution française (1922). English translation by Catherine Alison Phillips (1928).

Menzel, Wolfgang, History of Germany, Vol. III (1872).

Moore, John Bassett, International Adjudications, Vol. IV (1931), Vol. V (1933).

Mowat, Robert Balmain, The Diplomatic Relations of Great Britain and the United States (1925).

Ogg, Frederick A., Economic Development of Modern Europe (1921).

Rabbeno, Ugo, The American Commercial Policy (1895).

Rand, Benjamin, Selections Illustrating Economic History since the Seven Years' War (1911).

Roloff, Gustav, Von Jena bis zum Wiener Kongress (1914).

Rose, John Holland, Life of Napoleon I, 2 vols. (1922).

Ross, Sir John, Memoirs and Correspondence of Admiral Lord de Saumarez, 2 vols. (1838).

Sears, Louis Martin, A History of American Foreign Relations (1928).

Sorel, Albert, L'Europe et la Révolution française, 8 vols. (1885-1911).

Stomberg, Andrew A., A History of Sweden (1931).

Tarle, Deutsch-französische Wirtschaftsbeziehungen zur napoleonischen Zeit, Schmoller, "Jahrbuch für Gesetzgebung," Vol. XXXVIII (1914).

Tooke, Thomas, A History of Prices and of the State of the Circulation from 1793-1837, 6 vols. (1838-1857).

Webster, W. C., A General History of Commerce (1903).

Willson, Beckles, America's Ambassadors to France (1928).

ADDITIONAL ECONOMIC AND STATISTICAL WORKS AND MATERIALS

Aall, J. C., Erindringer som bidrag til Norges historie fra 1800-1815, 3 vols. (1844).

Baasch, Ernst, Beiträge zur Geschichte der Handelsbeziehungen zwischen Hamburg und Amerika, "Festschrift der Hamburger Amerikafeier" (1892).

———— Die Handelskammer in Hamburg 1665 bis 1915, 2 vols. (1915).

———— Hamburg und Holland im 17ten und 18ten Jahrhundert, reprint from "Hansische Geschichtsblätter," Vol. XVI, pp. 45-102.

———— Hamburgs Handel und Schiffahrt am Ende des 18. Jahrhunderts, "Hamburg um die Jahrhundertwende" (1900).

———— Quellen zur Geschichte von Hamburgs Handel und Schiffahrt im 17ten, 18ten, und 19ten Jahrhundert (1910).

Bishop, James Leander, History of American Manufactures, Vols. I-II (1868).

Bosse, Ewald, Norwegens Volkswirtschaft vom Ausgang der Hansaperiode bis zur Gegenwart mit besonderer Berücksichtigung der internationalen Handelsbeziehungen, 2 vols. (1916).

Ehrenberg, R., Das Haus Parish in Hamburg, "Grosse Vermögen," Vol. II (1905).

Ehrmann, T. F., Allgemeines, historisches, statistisches, geographisches Handlungs-, Post- und Zeitungslexikon.

Falbe-Hansen og Scharling v., Danmarks statistik, 2 vols. (1887).

Grasmeyer, Geschichtliche wahrnehmungen bei der See-Assekuranz (1824).

Gülich, Gustave v., Geschichtliche Darstellung des Handels, der Gewerbe und des Ackerbaues der bedeutendsten handeltreibenden Staaten unserer Zeit (1830).

Hitzigrath, Heinrich, Hamburg und die Kontinentalsperre, "Schulprogramm des Realgymnasiums des Johanneums zu Hamburg" (1900).

Hock, I. D. A., Statistische Darstellung des deutschen Fabrik und Handelswesens nach seinem ehemaligen und jetzigen Zustand (1823).

Hoeniger, Robert, Die Kontinentalsperre und ihre Einwirkung auf Deutschland, "Volkswirtschaftliche Zeitfragen," Jahrgang 27, Heft 2 (1905).

König, Albin, Die sächsische Baumwollenindustrie am Ende des vorigen jahrhunderts und während der Kontinentalsperre, "Leipziger Studien aus den Gebiete der Geschichte" (1899).

McCulloch, J. R., Dictionary of Commerce and Commercial Navigation (1832).

MacGregor, John, Commercial Statistics, 3 vols. (1847).

Marvin, W. L., The American Merchant Marine (1902).

Moreau, Cesar, Chronological Records of the British Royal and Commercial Navies (1827).

Munte, Heinz, Das Altonaer Handlungshaus van der Smissen (1932).

Nathanson, Mendel Levin, Danmarks Handel, Skibsfart, Penge-og Finantsvaesen fra 1730 til 1830, 3 vols. (1832).

———— Historisk-statistisk fremstilling af Danmarks National og Stats Huusholdning fra Frederik den Fjerdes Tid indtil Nutiden (1836).

Peters, Max, Die Entwicklung der deutschen Reederei seit Beginn des 19. jahrhunderts (1899).

Pitkin, Timothy, A Statistical Survey of the Commerce of the United States; Its Connection with Agriculture and Manufactures (1835).

Samsoe, Jens, Die industrialisierung Dänemarks, "Probleme der Weltwirtschaft," Vol. 44.

Schäfer, Max, Bremen und die Kontinentalsperre, "Hansische Geschichtsblätter," Vol. XX (1914).

Schmidt, Theodor, Zur Geschichte des Handels und der Schiffahrt Stettins von 1785-1840 (1875).

Schweigaard, A. M., Norges statistik (1840).

Seybert, Adam, Statistical Annals, Embracing Views of Population, Commerce, Navigation, . . . of the United States of America (1818).

Sieveking, Heinrich, Das Handlungshaus Voght und Sieveking, "Zeitschrift des Vereins für Hamburgische Geschichte," Vol. XVII.

Soetbeer, Adolph, Beiträge und Materialien zur Beurtheilung von Geld- und Bankfragen (1855).

Thaarup, F., Tabelen til den statistiks Udsight over den danske Stat (1826).

Voeltzer, Lübecks Wirtschaftslage unter dem Druck der Kontinentalsperre.

Wiskemann, Erwin, Hamburg und die Weltpolitik von den Anfängen bis zur Gegenwart (1929).

Wohlwill, A., Neuere Geschichte der freien und Hansestadt Hamburg (1914).

Wright, Carrol D., Comparative Wages Prices and Cost of Living (1899).

APPENDIX I

TABLE 11

SELECTED EXPORTS OF THE UNITED STATES [a]

1791-1816

Years	Sugar (Pounds)	Coffee (Pounds)	Pepper (Pounds)	Cocoa (Pounds)
1791	74,504	962,977	492	8,322
1792	1,176,156	2,134,742	5,046	6,000
1793	4,539,809	17,580,049	14,361	234,875
1794	20,721,761	33,720,983	23,884	1,188,302
1795	21,377,747	47,443,179	301,692	525,432
1796	34,848,644	62,385,117	491,330	928,107
1797	38,366,262	44,521,887	1,901,130	875,334
1798	51,703,963	49,580,927	501,982	3,146,445
1799	78,821,751	31,987,088	441,312	5,970,590
1800	56,432,516	38,597,479	635,849	4,925,518
1801	97,565,732	45,106,494	3,153,139	7,012,155
1802	61,061,820	36,501,998	5,422,144	3,878,526
1803	23,223,849	10,294,693	2,991,430	367,177
1804	74,964,366	48,312,713	5,703,646	695,135
1805	123,031,272	46,760,294	7,559,224	2,425,680
1806	145,832,320	47,001,662	4,111,082	6,846,758
1807	143,136,905	42,122,573	4,207,166	8,540,524
1808	28,974,927	7,325,448	1,709,978	1,896,990
1809	45,248,128	24,364,099	4,722,098	2,029,336
1810	47,038,125	31,423,477	5,946,336	1,286,010
1811	18,381,673	10,261,442	3,057,456	2,221,462
1812	13,927,277	10,073,722	2,521,003	752,148
1813	7,347,038	6,568,527	99,660	108,188
1814	762	220,594	...	27,386
1815	3,193,908	7,501,384	746,349	1,065,582
1816	17,536,416	8,948,713	769,329	531,571

[a] Source: Pitkin, *A Statistical View of the Commerce of the United States of America* (1835), p. 147.

TABLE 12

EXPORTS OF NAVAL STORES BY THE UNITED STATES

1791-1814

Fiscal Year	Pitch (Barrels)	Tar (Barrels)	Rosin (Barrels)	Turpentine (Barrels)	Spirits of Turpentine (Gallons)
1791	3,818	51,044	228	58,107	1,172
1793	8,338	67,961	1,715	36,957	...
1796	...	64,600	...	41,490	28,628
1797	...	47,397	7,015	53,291	54,151
1799	2,592	58,254	16,396	40,382	33,899
1802	3,091	37,497	3,189	38,764	8,990
1803	4,808	78,989	5,861	61,178	11,336
1805	13,977	72,745	9,057	95,640	26,247
1809	5,433	128,090	8,998	77,398	7,923
1811	11,375	149,796	13,412	100,242	43,133
1812	9,615	87,937	8,564	57,266	21,960
1813	3,270	10,065	2,097	16,123	3,589
1814	511	5,222	465	3,507	404

APPENDIX II

TABLE 13

SWEDISH IMPORTS OF TEXTILE MATERIALS [a]
1792-1813

Year	Silk (Marker) [b]	Cotton (Marker)	Linen Yarn (Marker)	Cotton Yarn (Marker)	Hemp (Lispund) [c]
1792	34,490	269,569	32,398	35,281	180,273
1796	40,191	396,483	15,317	31,512	238,714
1808	24,020	37,770	...	621	198,548
1809	39,027	1,976,707	...	9,166	308,250
1810	45,935	4,161,060	...	4,306	242,160
1811	41,297	850,949	...	3,770	201,323
1812	69,612	210,179	...	17,063	264,926
1813	20,654	239,706	...	20,654	215,031

[a] Source: Materials made available by Professor Heckscher.
[b] Marker = 0.36 kg.
[c] Lispund = 6.8 kgs.

TABLE 14

SWEDISH IMPORTS OF TOBACCO AND SUGAR [a]
1791-1813

(Value in Riksdalers)

Year	Tobacco	Sugar	Year	Tobacco	Sugar
1791	141,084	252,791	1810	575,648	2,071,125
1804	186,402	404,524	1811	329,269	682,462
1807	131,469	449,612	1812	186,992	589,285
1808	155,608	1,063,784	1813	256,608	2,530,443
1809	417,319	1,388,945			

[a] Source: Materials made available by Professor Heckscher.

TABLE 15

IMPORTS BY GOTHENBURG OF COLONIAL AND AMERICAN PRODUCE [a]
1790-1810

Year	Sugar	Coffee	Tobacco	Cotton
(Quantity in Lispund)				
1790	25,462	7,041	15,602	1,130
1805	32,362	16,831	17,032	591
1810	521,888	144,378	199,728	102,957
(Value in Riksdaler)				
1790	22,675	35,763	25,343	8,794
1805	37,721	124,067	33,655	3,420
1810	747,526	1,595,307	394,838	346,975

[a] Source: Materials made available by Professor Heckscher.

APPENDIX III[a]

TABLE 16

IMPORTS BY HAMBURG OF COLONIAL AND AMERICAN PRODUCE[b]
1791-1802

Year	Sugar (In 1000 pounds)	Coffee (In million pounds)	Rice[c] (In tons)	Hides (Single)	Cotton (In bales)	Pepper (Sacks and bales)
1791	52,928	21½	20,098	70,411	3,685	864
1792	48,335	21	17,426	53,012	3,086	1,594
1793	35,289	26	11,865	43,188	2,452	5,606
1794	66,476	38	8,541	153,315	7,967	3,139
1795	86,809	42	13,477	215,385	10,143	5,723
1796	78,254	39⅙	23,399	179,659	7,657	5,709
1797	75,083	39⅞	30,254	269,862	11,017	6,222
1798	79,849	45⅘	24,866	81,036	7,667	5,709
1799	104,963	45½	16,017	242,805	5,132	10,944
1800	70,955	39⅞	6,085	122,709	12,668	8,175
1801	104,115	28	6,019	256,135	9,397	8,335
1802	84,841	24	13,319	226,472	6,793	6,060

[a] For many of the statistics in this section and for much of their elucidation, the writer is indebted to Professor Hans von Eckardt of Heidelberg. Figures have been occasionally added from other sources, to which references are made.

[b] Source: H. von Eckardt, *Handel und Schiffahrt Norddeutschlands*, 1792-1805, p. 18.

[c] In addition from 1795 onward 34,406 sacks of rice were imported, the figures showing extraordinary fluctuations from year to year, varying from 11,569 in 1796, and 19,219 in 1802, to 150 in 1799.

TABLE 17

TRADE IN GRAIN AT HAMBURG[a]
1793-1804

Year	Imports (Quarter)	Exports (Quarter)	Year	Imports (Quarter)	Exports (Quarter)
1793	365,741	263,755	1799	360,631	231,429
1794	424,616	332,819	1800	467,037	330,841
1795	414,179	382,066	1801	430,907	289,702
1796	407,155	255,596	1802	380,202	739,304
1797	391,426	203,434	1803	188,622	109,430
1798	367,214	204,024	1804	216,886	94,300

[a] Source: Oddy, *European Commerce*, p. 425.

TABLE 18

VESSELS ENTERING BREMEN [a]
1800-1814

Year	Number	Year	Number
1800	575	1808	662
1801	645	1809	326
1802	1,148	1810	...
1803	906	1811	291
1804	1,515	1812	421
1805	1,796	1813	1,435
1806	1,392	1814	1,138
1807	665		

[a] Source: von Eckardt, *op. cit.*, p. 46.

TABLE 19

RECEIPTS FROM TONNAGE DUES AT BREMEN [a]
1801-1814

Year	Talers	Grote	Year	Talers	Grote
1801	20,034	20	1807	15,084	39
1802	21,174	62	1808	4,511	9
1803	15,652	37	1809	2,624	38
1804	12,771	8	1810	2,023	17
1805	17,205	69	1811-1813	No figures	No figures
1806	20,066	28	1814	35,905	...

[a] Source: von Eckardt, *op. cit.*, p. 47.

TABLE 20

COMMODITY PRICES AT BREMEN [a]
(Pfennige)

Year	Rye Bread	Sugar	Coffee
1806 (per ⅓ Kg.)	14.2	67.2	136.5
1807 (per ⅓ Kg.)	11.3	79.8	142.8
1808 (per ⅓ Kg.)	9.2	96.6	176.4
1809 (per ⅓ Kg.)	7.9	147.0	201.6
1810 (per ⅓ Kg.)	7.1	201.0	201.6
1811 (per ⅓ Kg.)	6.3	222.6	226.8
1812 (per ⅓ Kg.)	8.4	267.2	352.8
1813 (per ⅓ Kg.)	8.8	302.4	327.6
1814 (per ⅓ Kg.)	7.9	176.6	128.1
1815 (per ⅓ Kg.)	8.4	126.0	84.0

[a] Source: von Eckardt, *op. cit.*, p. 50.

TABLE 21

SHIPS ENTERING AND CLEARING FROM LÜBECK [a]

1792-1802

Year	Entering	Leaving	Year	Entering	Leaving
1792	802	783	1798	1,194	1,115
1793	848	835	1799	1,035	1,007
1794	927	918	1800	990	1,010
1795	1,109	1,091	1801	1,184	1,216
1796	981	1,011	1802	1,188	1,209
1797	990	985			

[a] Source: Oddy, *op. cit.*, p. 294.

TABLE 22

TRADE OF MEMEL IN SELECTED ARTICLES [a]

1797-1804

Exports	1797	1799	1801	1803	1804
Wood as Balks, Fir......	334,905	157,886	98,700	993,418	170,968
Masts.................	14	1,303	44	1,863	90
Spars.................	81	1,136	59	1,916	998
Bowsprits.............	9	245	11	565	224
Wheat (tons)...........	1,024	1,088	2,524	1,500	5,088
Rye (tons).............	6,064	5,728	3,860	6,722	4,144
Barley (tons)...........	440	48	2,908	1,042	2,298
Oats (tons).............	140	100	1,766	1,356	2,538
Pease (tons)...........	40	30	64	130	96
Flax (stones)...........	114,257	804	30,552	159,046	158,095

Imports	1797	1799	1801	1803	1804
Coffee (pounds).........	27,424	15,230	47,836	54,957	60,590
Indigo (pounds).........	458	154	671	2,156	1,359
Lemons, etc.............	58,430	50,400	9,200	68,990	15,180
Raw Sugar (centner).....	318	227	342	502	626
French Wine (hogsheads).	489	67	90	67	191

[a] Source: Oddy, *op. cit.*, pp. 226, 227, where full lists of exports and imports will be found for the five years.

TABLE 23

SHIPS ENTERING AND CLEARING FROM MEMEL [a]
1762-1810

Year	Entering	Leaving	Year	Entering	Leaving
1762	133	...	1802	908	918
1783	784	...	1803	890	890
1796	774	768	1804	831	...
1797	608	605	1806	155	...
1798	767	766	1807	...	1,404
1799	542	543	1808	...	75
1800	567	542	1809-10	...	300
1801	560	567			

[a] Sources: Oddy, *op. cit.*, pp. 223 f.; data after 1804 furnished by Professor von Eckardt.

TABLE 24

EXPORTS FROM KÖNIGSBERG [a]
1795-1804

Year		Wheat (Tons)	Rye (Tons)	Hemp (Tons)	Fir Balks (Shocks)	Yarn Linen (Shocks)
1795	Total to all...	8,626	260	289,660	3,689	77,791
	To Britain....	3,724	...	...	2,092	16,921
1796	Total........	14,484	22,400	3,712	3,152	14,289
	To Britain....	7,502	1,490	...	1,009	14,289
1797	Total........	8,730	21,028	2,466	2,150	9,956
	To Britain....	2,888	120	...	399	9,604
1798	Total........	7,828	36,190	3,966	108	19,729
	To Britain....	2,686	...	...	70	19,729
1799	Total........	11,226	22,984	3,794	3,988	23,198
	To Britain....	6,524	302	58	1,630	21,861
1800	Total........	13,686	572	4,882	851	16,898
	To Britain....	12,038	...	512	237	15,226
1801	Total........	5,204	11,178	4,230	5,336	12,359
	To Britain....	3,080	14	542	1,422	9,855
1802	Total........	8,192	31,730	4,968	6,409	6,449
	To Britain....	1,322	186	746	146	5,840
1803	Total........	5,734	25,528	6,494	14,855	12,921
	To Britain....	246	40	1,428	2,468	12,787
1804	Total........	7,942	11,364	1,758	8,849	23,593
	To Britain....	4,590	...	224	7,717	23,331

[a] Source: Oddy, *op. cit.*, pp. 234, 236.

TABLE 25

IMPORTS BY KÖNIGSBERG OF COLONIAL PRODUCE [a]

1795-1804

Year	Coffee (Pounds)	Lemons, etc.	Ginger (Pounds)	Indigo (Pounds)	Rice (Pounds)	Tobacco (Pounds)
1795	532,797	296,886	18,855	16,917	128,604	1,368,119
1796	676,726	384,955	26,960	33,783	329,325	91,284
1797	547,079	375,369	19,425	27,584	261,696	405,302
1798	796,226	406,351	19,405	20,944	315,847	771,560
1799	370,032	332,204	10,198	20,206	225,207	1,418,005
1800	677,065	186,391	17,675	30,636	190,224	1,156,795
1801	384,991	309,053	6,427	14,447	41,624	621,932
1802	566,906	317,315	6,088	32,499	214,946	1,672,967
1803	441,482	491,763	4,564	31,030	230,826	691,152
1804	844,693	325,749	11,996	38,334	196,284	633,837

[a] Source: Oddy, *op. cit.*, pp. 235 ff.

TABLE 26

SHIPS ENTERING AND LEAVING PILLAU [a]

1795-1804

Year	Entering	Leaving	Year	Entering	Leaving
1795	537	566	1800	664	684
1796	997	995	1801	921	920
1797	1,002	1,017	1802	1,412	1,398
1798	1,281	1,295	1803	1,371	. . .
1799	1,054	1,085	1804	942	. . .

[a] Source: Oddy, *op. cit.*, pp. 234 ff.

TABLE 27

SHIPS ENTERING AND CLEARING FROM DANZIG [a]

1793-1804

Year	Entering	Leaving	Year	Entering	Leaving
1793	810	783	1799	1,021	974
1794	898	828	1800	966	949
1795	494	537	1801	1,217	1,207
1796	851	829	1802	1,874	1,916
1797	765	751	1803	1,888	1,907
1798	1,079	1,043	1804	1,430	1,424

[a] Source: Oddy, *op. cit.*, p. 259.

TABLE 28

EXPORTS OF GRAIN FROM DANZIG [a]

1793-1806

Year		Wheat (Tons)	Rye (Tons)	Total of All Sorts (Tons)
1793	Total...................	30,828	24,218	48,136
	To Great Britain...........	18,902	5,164	
1794	Total...................	37,546	22,990	74,404
	To Great Britain...........	12,488	2,790	
1795	Total...................	27,548	358	42,080
	To Great Britain...........	8,566	...	
1796	Total...................	53,762	17,344	77,372
	To Great Britain...........	40,814	7,416	
1797	Total...................	47,978	15,364	80,724
	To Great Britain...........	35,992	1,606	
1798	Total...................	52,696	23,520	79,672
	To Great Britain...........	36,714	670	
1799	Total...................	50,048	25,306	102,702
	To Great Britain...........	33,426	2,506	
1800	Total...................	41,726	4,428	99,184
	To Great Britain...........	74,404	3,480	
1801	Total...................	75,206	19,184	117,572
	To Great Britain...........	67,496	4,342	
1802	Total...................	104,832	47,244	170,366
	To Great Britain...........	54,056	2,804	
1803	Total...................	68,298	57,742	136,564
	To Great Britain...........	23,450	1,066	
1804	Total...................	83,574	18,648	133,794
	To Great Britain...........	47,494	426	
1805	Total...................	...	...	104,824
1806	Total...................	...	...	29,780

[a] Sources: 1793-1804, Oddy, *op. cit.*, p. 252; 1805-1806, data furnished by Professor von Eckardt.

TABLE 29

PRINCIPAL TIMBER EXPORTS FROM DANZIG [a]

1793-1804

Year	Balks (Pieces)	Oak Planks (Shock)	Fir Planks (Shock)	Oak Deals (Shock)	Fir Deals (Shock)	Ash Slips (Shock)
1793 Total.............	23,811	380	420	64	1,415	197
To Great Britain...	21,913	335	323	53	813	197
1794 Total.............	15,907	409	526	81	1,711	256
To Great Britain...	12,491	408	453	58	927	256
1795 Total.............	23,738	427	530	.119	1,590	153
To Great Britain...	22,476	402	488	70	1,088	153
1796 Total.............	20,819	513	582	191	1,305	198
To Great Britain...	18,904	473	480	108	833	190
1797 Total.............	21,561	618	405	213	1,800	123
To Great Britain...	18,218	520	335	130	782	123
1798 Total.............	19,665	591	474	367	1,780	155
To Great Britain...	15,269	520	379	255	646	154
1799 Total.............	29,527	663	557	171	1,456	301
To Great Britain...	25,756	620	516	120	1,000	225
1800 Total.............	38,710	682	542	220	1,908	293
To Great Britain...	34,458	627	502	155	1,300	293
1801 Total.............	32,114	602	558	198	1,819	295
To Great Britain...	30,343	595	538	192	1,211	257
1802 Total.............	49,233	541	685	278	2,583	154
To Great Britain...	38,522	445	539	186	831	150
1803 Total.............	70,532	792	739	154	1,877	49
To Great Britain...	68,830	766	684	130	1,312	49
1804 Total.............	63,300	798	863	218	1,962	254
To Great Britain...	60,546	765	783	143	1,088	253

[a] Source: Oddy, *op. cit.*, pp. 263, 265.

TABLE 30

IMPORTS OF COLONIAL WARES BY DANZIG [a]

1793-1804

Year	Coffee (Pounds)	Rice (Barrels)	Sugar (Pounds)	Tobacco (Smoking) (Pounds)	Snuff (Pounds)	Tobacco (Leaf) (Pounds)
1793	1,323,699	111,462	324,290	318,542	256,696	...
1794	1,024,312	281,996	348,984	1,200,000	79,896	...
1795	1,402,102	98,492	704,069	282,024	140,867	297,093
1796	1,045,037	345,182	673,609	321,189	111,557	339,848
1797	1,087,970	288,043	596,184	272,322	95,474	115,492
1798	1,134,467	390,555	500,301	184,113	91,505	380,976
1799	758,402	239,981	501,291	142,245	95,142	156,488
1800	2,130,000	169,616	725,121	145,431	285,759	190,519
1801	1,374,382	45,203	951,261	128,974	149,524	162,716
1802	1,907,153	398,240	1,396,793	244,692	145,692	176,493
1803	1,444,606	447,599	964,879	328,060	140,594	122,485
1804	1,775,763	358,866	671,355	132,019	122,544	188,663

[a] Source: Oddy, *op. cit.*, pp. 264, 266.

TABLE 31

IMPORTS OF WINE AND BEER BY DANZIG [a]

1793-1804

Year	Champagne and Burgundy (Bottles)	French Wines (Hogsheads)	English Beer (Barrels)
1793	28,008	4,567	1,037
1794	5,601	1,665	1,306
1795	10,592	5,765	1,053
1796	26,822	6,132	2,504
1797	20,109	3,621	2,849
1798	7,350	2,378	2,789
1799	7,182	6,476	2,663
1800	20,614	4,939	2,893
1801	12,166	5,832	4,882
1802	24,650	6,583	6,199
1803	37,387	10,812	10,781
1804	54,904	8,027	16,362

[a] Source: Oddy, *op. cit.*, pp. 264, 266.

TABLE 32

PRINCIPAL IMPORTS OF STETTIN [a]

1798-1803

Year	Coffee (Centner)	Tobacco (Centner)	Sugar (Hogsheads)	French Wine (Hogsheads)	Champagne and Burgundy (Reichstaler)
1798	18,537	4,140	4,586	13,002	4,271
1799	9,712	3,606	2,384	23,280	2,278
1800	24,900	3,701	3,634	13,689	4,985
1801	10,434	3,702	1,562	18,682	6,229
1802	13,819	8,630	3,610	18,800	12,232
1803	16,943	7,203	5,521	29,810	9,940

[a] Source: Oddy, *op. cit.*, p. 275.

APPENDIX IV

A MEMORANDUM OF HAMBURG TRADERS IN 1801 ON RUSSIAN TRADE [1]

"The extent of the direct trade of Russia with Hamburg, which has increased in such an exceptional manner since the ruin of Dutch commerce, is too well known to require anything further to be said about it. The balance of trade is wholly in Russia's favor. Hamburg imports from Russia many more goods than it exports to that country on its own account. . . . Russian exports are in part sent here on Hamburg account. Hamburg, for instance, imports as many mats from Archangel as England does, and more than Holland did even in time of peace. The largest export of Russian candles is to Hamburg. England and other nations do not allow the importation of Russian fish oil, cordage and candles. In Hamburg the importation or exportation of no single product or manufacture is forbidden.

"Of yet greater importance is the Baltic trade of Hamburg in Russian products, which in part do not even come to Hamburg. Thus every year a very considerable number of ships laden with flax, hemp, wheat, timber, iron, Russia leather and other articles on Hamburg account sail from St. Petersburg, Liebau, Riga, Pernau and other ports direct to Portugal, Spain and Italy. The Hamburg merchant contracts for or buys these products for hard cash. In time of war such deliveries of goods are extended to English and French ports.

"Imports consist more especially of sugar, dyestuffs, oil, etc. . . . No less important is the business transacted by Russia through Hamburg direct with other countries. Apart from England, this place is to a certain extent the entrepôt for all wares in transit to and from Russia. . . . Thus a great quantity of Russian produce goes, on Russian account, through Hamburg to Portugal, Spain, France and Italy. The whole trade of Russia with the Mediterranean goes through Hamburg. The Portuguese, Spaniards and others would not be able to buy such large quantities of Russian produce if the Hamburger did not in return buy their sugar, or at least give them a

[1] Translated by W. Alison Phillips.

sufficient advance on the security of it. The North Americans, too, during the winter months when the Baltic is no longer navigable, obtain Russian hemp, flax, tar, iron, sail-cloth, etc., in Hamburg, where in consequence a very considerable store of such articles has always to be kept. It is particularly as a place of payment that Hamburg is of quite exceptional importance to Russia.

"When during the present war the business of exchange on Holland and England stopped, Hamburg was for a considerable time the only place of payment for Russia . . . it was through our Bank that the English subsidies to Russia as well as the Russian interest due to Holland were paid.

"The establishment ten years ago of a direct rate of exchange of Russia on Hamburg is alone sufficient to show the importance of Hamburg in this connection. Remittances on Holland and England are subject to great fluctuations; the bank money, on the other hand, which the Russian obtains from Hamburg for his bills of exchange never varies.

"On account of this obvious advantage, the Russian merchant, even in the case of goods sent to England, bargains for at least part payment on Hamburg. Or he draws a bill of exchange direct on Hamburg and lets the Englishman remit the money there. He knows that in Hamburg silver or bank money is always to be had in exchange for English paper. The same is the case with the other States which do direct business with Russia.

"Now that Russia is involved in the war, neutral Hamburg continues to carry her produce to market and to supply her wants. If Russian trade is no longer secure in the North Sea, it passes from the Baltic by way of Hamburg. For a mere commission the Hamburg merchant takes charge of Russian goods in transit, takes all risks and collects the payments for the exports in the more distant countries, even those which are at war with Russia. Moreover, the Russian who has debts owing to him in a hostile country can obtain advances on them in Hamburg, so that the effects of a possible embargo would be less detrimental to him than would otherwise be the case. . . . So long as the Hamburg Bank remains as it is at present, Russia will not be exposed to the great stoppages and obstructions which it experienced in Holland and England." [2]

[2] Ernst Baasch, *Quellen zur Geschichte von Hamburgs Handel.*

APPENDIX V

DANZIG, 1806-1815

by

PROFESSOR HANS VON ECKARDT [1]

The figures given show clearly enough that Danzig, as a Prussian city, profited greatly from the Revolutionary Wars so long as Prussia remained neutral. It reached the peak of its prosperity in the years 1802 and 1803. In 1806, however, it shared in all the misfortunes that fell upon Prussia after the battle of Jena. In 1807, it was occupied by the French; and though in the same year Napoleon once more proclaimed it a Free City, it remained in fact wholly under French domination. As already pointed out, the shipping industry perished at a blow, only a few coasting vessels, and many even of these only in ballast, being able to enter the port. The smuggling trade, which it was possible to carry on during all the years of the Continental System in Riga, Königsberg, Lübeck and Bremen, could not be carried on in Danzig. The French authorities stood in the way of any possibility of preserving the economic life of the city. The transport of Polish grain ceased; and though this meant that grain became very cheap in the city, it meant also the stopping of business, numerous bankruptcies, unemployment, and the decay of the city's ships laid up in the harbor.

In the following years the population suffered intensely. The French garrison was constantly being enlarged, and the cost of this and of the new works of fortification was laid upon the unfortunate burghers. This cost was reckoned at 1,400,000 francs per annum, in addition to which the city had to find 1,500,000 francs per annum as a contribution to France. Nor was this all; the total payments exacted by the French amounted to 4,500,000 francs each year. The city already had a deficit of 2,500,000 francs, and it was to be a very long time before it recovered from the tribulations of these years. As in the case of Königsberg, loans contracted at this time by Danzig were not discharged until 1814.

[1] Translated by W. Alison Phillips.

"Owing to the stoppage of trade," says a contemporary writer,[2] "wheat which in 1810 fetched 75 ducats the last fetched only 35 in 1811, while the price of rye fell from 25 to from 10 to 12 ducats. Other wares fell in the same proportion. Several merchants, who had stored from 1,200 to 1,800 lasts of grain in their warehouses in anticipation of future demand, have lost 60,000 ducats or 720,000 francs, and others have lost in proportion. And since, for lack of ready money, the wares have usually been bought for bills of exchange the Poles have been involved in the ruin of Danzig."

This last fact was to have important political consequences, which Napoleon had certainly not foreseen when he struck at the prosperity of Danzig. Economically the Poles were but little developed, and they needed the inflow of money which their export trade brought them. The cessation of this trade deprived the magnates and great landowners of their financial basis. The creation of the grand duchy of Warsaw, in the circumstance, brought the Poles nothing but economic loss and so hindered their patriotic revival. Lithuania, more especially, with its wealth in forests and corn lands, could not be persuaded that, faced as it was with economic ruin, it was in a "better" position than it had been when its political oppressors, Prussia and Russia, had brought it economic prosperity. It was at this point that the Continental System defeated Napoleon's political objects and produced results the opposite of what he had intended. This was due, above all, to the length of time during which his measures were in force. A very primitive system of cultivation which for six years is deprived of any market for its produce must in the end be completely robbed of all its resources. Thus in Poland-Lithuania, agriculture suffered a severe setback; less grain was sown and the area of cultivated land so decreased that Napoleon's Grand Army was unable to secure from the great Polish landowners the provisions which they had been relied on to supply. The excellent organization for producing, purchasing and storing grain, which had once existed, existed no longer.

What this meant for Poland can only be understood by taking into account the antiquity of the export of Polish grain through Danzig. Evidence of this survives from the thirteenth century, and exact data are available from 1608: in the record year 1618 Poland thus exported 116,000 lasts of grain. This may give the measure of

[2] A. F. Blech, *Geschichte der 7 jährigen Leiden Danzigs von 1807-1814* (Danzig, 1815).

the dependence of the great Polish landlords on Danzig as a free market for their produce. The complete and, as was assumed at the time, the permanent stoppage of this outlet brought ruin to precisely those Polish noblemen to whom Napoleon made his appeal in 1812. Added to this was the fact that the smuggling trade brought much money to the anti-French elements in Prussia and the Baltic provinces of Russia, and that of this Danzig, which was Poland's supply base, could have no share. So that even this advantage was denied to the country to which Napoleon had promised everything. Thus for Poland, as for Russia and Prussia, the year 1812 gave promise of the end of the hated System and the return of earlier prosperity.

In 1813 Danzig, which had suffered far more severely than either Hamburg or Bremen, had to stand a siege by the allied Prussians and Russians, and it is hard to say whether the effects of this investment or those of the French exactions were the more disastrous. Everywhere in Germany the French garrisons confiscated, expropriated and levied heavy contributions, but nowhere, it seems, with such utter ruthlessness as in Danzig. The plight of the city can be seen from the enormous rise in prices. During the last months of 1813 a *Scheffel* [3] of wheat cost 45 *Reichstaler;* a *Scheffel* of rye, 40 *Reichstaler;* a pound of coffee, 7½ *Reichstaler;* and a cow, 364 *Reichstaler.* [4]

[3] That is, rather more than a bushel. 1 Scheffel = 54.96 liters; 1 bushel = 36.35 liters.

[4] For Danzig see G. Löschin, *Geschichte Danzigs von der ältesten bis zur neuesten Zeit.* 2 vols. (Danzig, 1828); *Kleine Chronik der Stadt und Festung Danzig* (Berlin, 1807); F. K. G. von Duisburg, *Geschichte der Belagerungen und Blokaden Danzigs* (Danzig, 1808).

INDEX

Economic war—Contd.

embargoes, *see* Embargoes

purposes of, 16, 35, 51, 68, 76, 129, 153, 155, 162

relaxation of, through license system, *see* Licenses, system of

sequestration of neutral vessels, *see* War losses, neutral

smuggling, *see* Smuggling

tariff war, 126, 128, 156, 162, 163, 166, 170, 190

Ehrenswärd, Baron d', 105

Eldon, Lord Chancellor, 11, 12, 168

Elizabeth, Queen of England, 13, 14

Embargoes: Denmark, 106; England, 28, 90, 104, 105, 107, 230, 287; France, 27, 51, 54, 86, 87, 164, 275; Russia, 101, 107, 167, 273; Spain, 10; Sweden, 106, 107; United States, 57, 58, 160, 167, 176-86, 227, 229, 232, 236, 287

Employment, effect of war on, *see* under names of countries

Enemy character (*see also* Economic war): denationalization of neutral vessels, 84, 132, 133, 154, 163, 198; enemy association, as evidence of, 80, 83, 87, 132, 133, 135

Enemy coasting trade, *see* War profits, neutral

Enemy destination, *see* Contraband, continuous voyage, doctrine of

Enemy origin of goods as basis for condemnation, 29, 77, 84, 85, 128, 134, 150. *See also* Blockade

Enemy goods, enemy ships, *see* Enemy property

Enemy property: coloring, *see* Fraudulent practices; enemy goods, enemy ships, rule of, 46; enemy ships, enemy goods, rule of, 88; free ships, free goods, rule of, 12, 32, 33, 34, 61, 65, 75, 88, 89, 92, 96; in neutral ships, 12, 32, 33, 65, 66, 73, 80, 88, 168; penalty for carriage, 46; retaliatory practices, 132

Enemy ships, enemy goods, *see* Enemy property

England (*see also* Legislation, belligerent, affecting neutral rights, England)

advocates broad belligerent rights, 12, 16

balance of power, views on, 8, 9

carrying trade of, 115, 119, 120, 233

contraband, views on, 12, 13, 15, 29, 30, 32, 33, 37, 39-41, 63, 92, 108, 114, 245

controversy with the United States over neutral rights: colonial trade, 31, 33, 45-47, 84, 185; contraband, 33, 39, 40, 41, 42, 65, 67, 68, 88, 114; paper blockades, 114, 182, 196, 206; privateers, *see* Privateers; prize courts, complaints against, 46, 59, 64, 115; visit and search, 22, 23, 88, 171

embargoes, *see* Embargoes

enemy goods, enemy ships, views on, 46

free ships, free goods, views on, 12, 32, 33, 92

impressment of seamen, controversy with United States over, 21, 22, 23, 24, 56, 115, 116, 117, 170, 171, 172, 173, 174, 206

naturalization, views on, 22

naval supremacy of, 16, 18, 19, 25, 128, 134, 155, 199

navigation acts of, *see* Legislation, belligerent, affecting neutral rights

prize courts, *see* Prize courts

relations with: Denmark-Norway, 91, 92, 98-100, 103, 104, 106, 107, 137-39, 141, 142, 278, 301; France, 6, 7, 8, 27, 126; Hansa Towns, 14; Netherlands, 4, 6, 7, 67; Prussia, 10, 30, 101, 102, 105, 129, 139, 286, 287, 288; Russia, 9, 10, 29, 100, 101, 102, 107, 108, 109; Spain, 10, 14, 30; Sweden, 91, 92, 105, 106, 107, 129, 157, 162, 264; United States, 39-42, 43, 45-49, 56, 57, 59, 64, 66, 72, 90, 91, 114-17, 170-87, 188, 190, 225

revolutionary principles, views on, 7, 8

English prize courts, *see* Prize courts, England

Entrepôt trade, *see* Transit trade

Erskine, David, British Minister to the United States, 171, 179, 180, 183-86

Essex, Orne, The, 72, 111, 123, 124, 159, 170

Europe: balance of power of, 6, 8, 9; public law of, 3, 4, 6, 7, 10

COLUMBIA UNIVERSITY PRESS

COLUMBIA UNIVERSITY

NEW YORK

———————

FOREIGN AGENT

OXFORD UNIVERSITY PRESS

HUMPHREY MILFORD

AMEN HOUSE, LONDON, E.C. 4

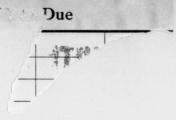

Due